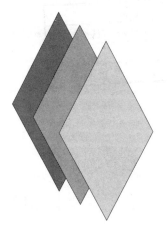

The Principles and Future of AACR

Proceedings of the
International Conference
on the Principles
and Future Development
of AACR

Toronto, Ontario, Canada
October 23–25, 1997

JEAN WEIHS
Editor

CANADIAN LIBRARY ASSOCIATION / Ottawa
LIBRARY ASSOCIATION PUBLISHING / London
AMERICAN LIBRARY ASSOCIATION / Chicago

1998

Published by

AMERICAN LIBRARY ASSOCIATION
50 East Huron Street, Chicago, Illinois 60611

CANADIAN LIBRARY ASSOCIATION
200 Elgin Street, Ottawa, Ontario K2P 1L5

LIBRARY ASSOCIATION PUBLISHING
7 Ridgmount Street, London WC1E 7AE

Library Association Publishing is wholly owned
by The Library Association

Library of Congress Cataloging-in-Publication Data
International Conference on the Principles and Future Development of
  AACR (1997 : Toronto, Ontario, Canada)
    The principles and future of AACR / Jean Weihs, editor.
        p.   cm.
    "Proceedings of the International Conference on the Principles and
Future Development of AACR, Toronto, Ontario, October 23-25, 1997,
American Library Association, Chicago and London, 1999."
    Includes bibliographical references (p.   ) and index.
    ISBN 0-8389-3493-5
    1. Anglo-American cataloguing rules—Congresses. 2. Descriptive
cataloging—United States—Rules—Congresses. 3. Descriptive
cataloging—Great Britain—Rules—Congresses. 4. Descriptive
cataloging—Canada—Rules—Congresses. 5. Descriptive cataloging—
Australia—Rules—Congresses. I. Weihs, Jean Riddle. II. Title.
III. Title: Principles and future of Anglo-American cataloguing rules.
Z694.15.A5I55   1997
025.3'2—dc21   98-34562

Canadian Cataloguing in Publication Data
International Conference on the Principles and Future Development of
  AACR (1997 : Toronto, Ont.)
    The principles and future of AACR : proceedings of the International
Conference on the Principles and Future Development of AACR,
Toronto, Ontario, Canada, October 23-25, 1997
    Co-published by American Library Association and Library Association.
    Includes bibliographical references.
    ISBN 0-88802-287-5
    1. Anglo-American cataloguing rules—Congresses. 2. Descriptive
cataloging—United States—Rules—Congresses. 3. Descriptive
cataloging—Great Britain—Rules—Congresses. 4. Descriptive
cataloging—Canada—Rules—Congresses. 5. Descriptive cataloging—
Australia—Rules—Congresses. I. Weihs, Jean, 1930-   II. American
Library Association. III. Library Association. IV. Title. V. Title:
Principles and future of Anglo-American cataloguing rules.
Z694.15.A5I58   1997   025.3'2   C98-901015-5

British Library Cataloguing-in-Publication Data
A catalogue record for this book is available from the British Library.
    ISBN 1-85604-303-7

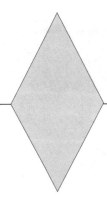

Contents

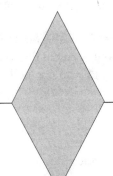

Preface

The papers in this book were developed over several months, during which time they were refereed, suggestions offered, and modifications made. At the end of this process the papers were mounted in the conference web site and comments on their contents invited. Calls for responses were also sent to thirty-two professional journals, five listserves, and four library associations, which published the "call" in various ways.

Most of the responses came from the Anglo-American community (Australia, Canada, United Kingdom, United States). International interest in the *Anglo-American Cataloguing Rules* was reflected in the attendance at the conference by participants from Denmark, Germany, Iran, Russia, South Africa, and Sweden. In addition, comments on the papers or the theme of the conference were received from Costa Rica, Greece, Israel, Italy, Jordan, New Zealand, Norway, and Romania.

Sixty-four invited participants attended the conference, at which the authors summarized the main points of the papers and their recommendations, and responded to comments made about their papers on the conference listserve. A question-and-answer period and/or a general discussion of the topic followed each presentation or, in one case, two presentations (because of time constraints).

The authors were asked to submit their papers for this book after they had considered the discussions about their work, both on the conference listserve and at the conference. Many of the papers have been revised to a greater or lesser extent as a result of this consideration.

The conference listserve commentators covered a wide range of topics and offered many useful suggestions. The authors of some of the papers debated points raised by the commentators on the listserve prior to the conference. Not all of the points raised on the listserve were considered by the authors and conference participants because some issues dealt with particular aspects of the *Anglo-American Cataloguing Rules, Second Edition, 1988 Revision* rather than its principles. One principle that was a hot topic on the listserve—the issue of main entry—caused little discussion at the conference because those participants who had been studying the concept of bibliographic relationships, super records, and/or hierarchical structures agreed that, if the work authority record concept is adopted, the main entry will function as the unifying point.

I wish to thank those people who have contributed to the production of this book: Robert Allison, who converted content from disks received from many sources including files that had defied some authors' efforts at electronic file amalgamation and who reconciled various design layouts, saving me hours, if not days, of time; Cameron Riddle, who solved computer problems promptly and pleasantly; Ronald Hagler, who organized the conference listserve comments in a meaningful order, a time-consuming task; Ralph Manning and Margaret Stewart, who answered my questions quickly; and the authors of the conference papers and the panelists, who also responded to my e-mail queries promptly. It was a pleasure to work with all of you.

JEAN WEIHS

Welcoming Remarks

It is a great pleasure for me to be here today to welcome you to Canada and particularly to Toronto. I know from the very ambitious programme and from the calibre of the speakers and participants who have been invited to this Conference that we will have a provocative and productive three days. I do hope, however, that you will find time during your stay here to take advantage of the many activities and sights that this exciting city has to offer.

Canada, and the National Library in particular, have always been strong supporters in the development of bibliographic standards, and we believe very much in their importance. I understand that the Canadian Committee on Cataloguing was a strong and vocal advocate for convening this conference of cataloguing experts as a means of ensuring broad and open discussion on the future direction of the rules. The fact that the Discussion List established for this meeting has over six hundred subscribers illustrates the significant interest that this conference has generated worldwide.

The last time we had a similar opportunity to reflect on cataloguing principles was in 1961. The Paris Principles have served us well. In recent years, we have moved away from the traditional card catalogue environment to online catalogues. However, the fundamental functions of the catalogue—to identify and locate bibliographic items—are still relevant today. On the other hand, the bibliographic universe is changing rapidly and will continue to do so. Is *AACR2* flexible enough to respond to the challenges—or should I say opportunities—presented by the emergence of new information and database technologies? Let us take this occasion to evaluate the principles that are with us today, keeping in mind what Andrew Osborn said in 1941—"We know and respect what was good in the past. We honor the traditions in which to greater or less extent we participated. And for such reasons our leadership in charting new courses should and can be much the wiser."

I look forward to a stimulating and productive three days.

MARIANNE SCOTT
National Librarian
National Library of Canada

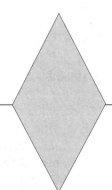

Introduction

RALPH MANNING

Cataloguing rules must respond to changing needs. In recognition of this fact, a formal agreement was established in 1989 between the American Library Association, The British Library, the Canadian Library Association, The Library Association (of the United Kingdom), and the Library of Congress in order to clarify the responsibilities and relationship of the various bodies charged with the production and publication of the *Anglo-American Cataloguing Rules*. In 1991 the National Library of Canada also became a party to the agreement. These six organizations became known as the Principals of AACR and form the Committee of Principals. One of the key functions of the Committee of Principals is reviewing developments and progress in the work of the Joint Steering Committee for Revision of AACR (JSC) which has responsibility for the ongoing process of rule revision.

JSC is a committee made up of representatives from the American Library Association, the Australian Committee on Cataloguing, The British Library, the Canadian Committee on Cataloguing, The Library Association (of the United Kingdom), and the Library of Congress. It meets approximately once per year and deals with proposals for rule revisions which come to it formally from any of the constituent bodies or from the chair. In considering proposals for rule revision, JSC has been very conscious of the cost of change while at the same time keeping in mind the need for flexibility and responsiveness to continuing developments.

A number of continuing issues affecting implementation of *AACR* have been compounded in recent years by the fast-moving pace of technological development with its concomitant impact on publishing patterns. Some of the issues date from the beginning days of implementation of *AACR*, such as the early decision by the Library of Congress not to implement chapter 11 for microform reproductions. In the years since then we have witnessed the creation of a considerable opus of specialized manuals which were developed to enhance or improve *AACR* for certain types of material. More recently we have seen the publication of cataloguing interpretations outside the structure of *AACR2*, such as the American Library Association's *Guidelines for Bibliographic Description of*

Interactive Multimedia[1] and *Guidelines for Bibliographic Description of Reproductions.*[2] Such issues led to the need for an in-depth consultation and review of *AACR2.*

The idea of holding an invitational meeting of cataloguing experts to deal with issues facing the *Anglo-American Cataloguing Rules* was first discussed by the Joint Steering Committee for Revision of AACR at its meeting in Boulder in March 1994. Interest in such a meeting continued to increase, particularly as momentum grew. In the United States many of the issues surrounding *AACR* were the subject of an ALCTS preconference of the American Library Association held in Chicago on June 22, 1995, with the title *The Future of the Descriptive Cataloging Rules.*[3] In Canada the development of the *Rules for Archival Description,*[4] which were strongly based on *AACR2,* gave rise to an expressed need for clear direction for the cataloguing rules. The Canadian Committee on Cataloguing, a member of JSC, therefore prepared a formal proposal for a meeting of experts, which was discussed at the May 1995 meeting of JSC in Leeds. This resulted in the development of an initial framework for a conference which was enhanced by the Committee of Principals; the final proposal was approved and detailed planning began in the summer of 1996.

Because only a limited number of participants could attend the conference, a web site was established to publicize the conference and to make the conference papers available to anyone who was interested. From January 1997 to November 1997 the site received over 7,000 visits. In addition, a preconference discussion list was established with the objective of stimulating discussion on the issues presented in the conference papers in order to bring out different points of view. The list was established in early July and had approximately 650 subscribers at its peak with about 500 posted messages.

The International Conference on the Principles and Future Development of AACR has helped JSC to develop a plan of action which will test the applicability of *AACR* in the current and future environments and balance the need for a sound and workable cataloguing code with the cost of cataloguing and the cost of change. One of the most important projects is the application of a data modeling methodology to the cataloguing code. It is expected that this model will provide a solid tool for ensuring that future rule revision will be consistent and responsive to user need.

A conference such as this cannot be organized without the dedicated contribution of many people and organizations. I would like to give particular thanks to Ross Shimmon, Chair of the Committee of Principals for AACR; to the members of the Joint Steering Committee, who served while the conference was being organized (Susan Brown, Nick Eden, Ann Huthwaite, Brian Schottlaender, Sally Strutt, and Barbara Tillett); to the JSC Secretary, Margaret Stewart, and her staff (Mary DiSipio and Denise Lim), without whose tireless record-keeping all would have collapsed; to Gisèle Herman and the National Library of Canada for working so hard to ensure that speakers were able to travel to Toronto; to Lynne Howarth and the Faculty of Information Studies at the University of Toronto, whose local arrangements ensured a successful conference; and finally to Jean Weihs, whose dedication and commitment shepherded us through the myriad tasks necessary to make this a success.

Of course the greatest thanks are due to the speakers, panelists, and participants without whose thoughtful preparation and input the conference could not have accomplished its goals.

Notes

1. Association for Library Collections & Technical Services, Interactive Multimedia Guidelines Review Task Force, *Guidelines for Bibliographic Description of Interactive Multimedia* (Chicago: American Library Association, 1994).

2. Association for Library Collections & Technical Services, Committee on Cataloging: Description and Access, *Guidelines for Bibliographic Description of Reproductions* (Chicago: American Library Association, 1995).

3. Brian E. C. Schottlaender, ed., *The Future of the Descriptive Cataloging Rules: Papers from the ALCTS Preconference, AACR2000, American Library Association Annual Conference, Chicago, June 22, 1995,* ALCTS Papers on Library Technical Services and Collections, no. 6 (Chicago: American Library Association, 1998).

4. *Rules for Archival Description* (Ottawa: Bureau of Canadian Archivists, 1990-).

Modeling the
Logic of *AACR*

TOM DELSEY

In the twenty years that have elapsed since the publication of the second edition of the *Anglo-American Cataloguing Rules* in 1978, the environment within which the rules function has changed significantly. As a result of technological innovation we have seen the emergence of a number of new media used as information carriers, new forms of publication, and new modes of dissemination and access. The development of the Internet has significantly changed our view of the library "collection." Advances in information and database technologies have also begun to change the way we store and process bibliographic data. In addition, budgetary constraints and concerns about the cost effectiveness of the cataloguing process have had an increasingly significant influence on policies relating to the application of the rules and have prompted practitioners in the field to search for more efficient means of generating and managing bibliographic information.

Paralleling these changes there has been increasing recognition of the opportunities that the new technologies offer for improving the way we create, process, and display bibliographic data, and the potential inherent in the technology for realizing efficiencies and cost savings as well as increased effectiveness. On a theoretical as well as a practical level, a number of commentators and researchers have speculated on the desirability of reconceptualizing the structures we use to record and store bibliographic data with a view to exploiting more effectively the technologies that are currently available for managing bibliographic information.

Several of those who have advocated a reexamination of conventional data structures have endeavoured to illustrate and test the value of reconceptualizing the bibliographic record by sketching out (and in a few cases, developing in considerable detail) conceptual models for the restructuring of bibliographic records and databases. Not long after the publication of the second edition of *AACR,* Michael Gorman posited a new schema for the logical restructuring of bibliographic data into a number of "linked packages" of information for use in what he envisioned as the "developed" catalogue.[1] More recently, that same notion has been further developed by Michael Heaney, who has "deconstructed" the MARC record using the techniques applied in object-oriented analysis,[2] and by Rebecca Green, who has used an entity-relationship analysis technique for the same purpose.[3] Building on work done by Barbara Tillett on the representation of relationships in bibliographic databases,[4] Gregory Leazer and Richard Smiraglia have developed a conceptual schema for modeling derivative relationships within "bibliographic families" of works.[5] And in what is in some respects the most comprehensive undertaking of this kind to date, the IFLA Study Group on the Functional Requirements for Bibliographic Records has used the entity-relationship analysis technique to develop a model designed to serve as a framework for relating bibliographic data to user needs.[6]

As we embark on a reexamination of the fundamental principles underlying *AACR* and endeavour to set directions for its future development, it is worth considering whether the approach to logical analysis that has formed the basis for those studies and the models that have been developed as a result could be used to clarify our understanding not just of record and database structures but of the assumptions, principles, structures, and conventions that underlie the cataloguing code itself. Taking that as a starting point, what I propose to do in this paper is to illustrate how a systematic analysis of the logic of *AACR* might help us to understand more clearly how some of the structural elements of the rules relate to the key underlying principles of the code. I will also try to illustrate how modeling the logic of the code might help us as we chart the future development of the code to respond to emerging issues associated with the evolution of digital technologies and a networked environment.

The Application of Modeling Techniques to an Analysis of *AACR*

Modeling techniques such as entity-relationship analysis and object-oriented analysis are commonly used in systems development projects as a means of understanding in clearly defined terms the entities or objects about which an organization needs to keep information and the logical relationships between those entities or objects. The modeling approach is used to clarify understanding of the data-related business rules that apply within that organization prior to establishing a schema for storing in a database the information that is needed to operate the business. Such techniques assist both the database designers and the users of the data in understanding from a logical perspective the nature of the data, the relationships that exist between the entities or objects on which the data are centred, and the rules that constrain those relationships.

In proposing that we apply a technique of that kind to *AACR*, I am in effect suggesting that we view the cataloguing process as our business and the code itself as the set of business rules that apply to the entities or objects that we catalogue. In developing our model we would attempt to analyze the underlying logical structure of the code, to identify in clearly defined terms the entities or objects that are at the centre of that structure, and to express in a systematic way the operative rules that govern the relationships between those entities or objects. The model emerging from the analysis would serve as a formalized schema, a kind of anatomical representation of the logic that gives the code its shape. If we were to apply such an approach to the analysis of *AACR* we would not be modeling in the abstract the information universe or the universe of recorded knowledge, but in more precise terms we would be modeling how that universe is reflected in the logic of the code *per se*.

The principal value to be gained from modeling the logical structure of *AACR* is that it would assist us in shifting our focus from the process of cataloguing to the entities or objects that we are endeavouring to represent in our catalogues, from the specifics of individual rules to the operative assumptions and principles that inform the rules, and from the formal structure of the catalogue record to the logical structure underlying the data in the record. The discipline of the modeling exercise itself would oblige us to clarify our thinking with regard to the concepts that are integral to the logical design of the code. It would also serve to highlight anomalies within the rules and inconsistencies in the application of basic principles. Perhaps most important of all, the development of a model would provide us with a clear framework to be used in determining how to develop and extend the code to reflect newly emerging phenomena in the universe of information objects.

To illustrate how modeling the logical structure of *AACR* could assist us in reexamining the fundamental principles underlying the code and in setting directions for its future development, I will focus on a number of issues that are of particular relevance to the tasks that lie ahead as we endeavour to revise and extend the code to accommodate the products of an evolving digital environment.

Intellectual Content versus Physical Form

Because the cataloguing process, for obvious practical reasons, tends to focus on the physical object that the cataloguer has in hand, and because the description that is produced is normally structured in the form of a single record, there is a natural inclination for us to view the bibliographic record as a description of a single object. However, on closer examination of the process involved and the data that are recorded as a result of that process, it is evident that the record does more than just describe a physical object. The records we create describe intellectual or artistic content as well as physical form. They not only describe the individual objects housed in a library's collection, but they describe those objects as publications, recordings, etc., copies of which normally may be obtained from other sources as well. They also describe the works and particular versions of works that those objects contain.

The multifaceted, multilayered nature of the cataloguing process and of the descriptions that result from that process is reflected in *AACR,* both in the overall structure of the code and in the key concepts and terms that recur throughout its instructions. The division of the code into two parts is linked directly to the two-stage sequence of the cataloguing process, the first part dealing with the description of the object being catalogued, the second dealing with the determination and establishment of headings under which the description will be presented in the catalogue. The rules in part 1 are centred primarily on the "item"; those in part 2 focus on the "work."

It is important to recognize, however, that even though the division of *AACR* into two parts roughly parallels the logical division that exists between entities or objects that are "physical" in nature and those that are associated with "intellectual or artistic content," the data elements and rules embodied in the two parts of the code do not necessarily divide themselves neatly along those lines. The most obvious examples are the data recorded in notes pertaining to the nature, scope, or artistic form of the contents, notes on language, medium of performance, etc., notes on intended audience, and notes providing a summary of the content. Although the rules pertaining to these notes are interspersed with other rules in part 1 that pertain to the physical aspects of the item, these particular notes are clearly associated with the intellectual or artistic content of the work represented in the item. Other data elements that might be less obvious but in fact are associated more closely with intellectual or artistic content than with physical form surface in various elements such as the material specific area (especially the data elements associated with cartographic materials and music) and to some extent even in the so-called physical description area. By the same token, even though the introduction to part 2 emphasizes that the rules contained therein "apply to works and not to physical manifestations of those works," it is instructive to note, for example, just how many of the rules in chapter 21 give directions for choice of entry that are based entirely on information derived from the item in hand, relying on the wording or layout of the chief source of information of the item being catalogued as the sole determinant for choice of entry.

Given the complexity of the relationships that exist between the physical nature of the object being catalogued and the intellectual nature of its content, and the interweaving of aspects of both elements across the two parts of the code, it is perhaps not surprising that there has been continuing debate around the "content versus carrier" issue. I would suggest, however, that we might gain some new insight into the issue by constructing a logical model for *AACR*. By defining key concepts such as "item" and "work" in more precise terms, and mapping individual attributes to the specific entities or objects to which they pertain, we should be able to separate the threads that run through the code and see more clearly how intellectual content and physical form are each reflected in the catalogue record, and how they each influence the selection of data that is recorded.

To illustrate how a logical model could be used to assist us in understanding the workings of the code with respect to the "content versus carrier" issue, we might examine the key statements of principle that underlie parts 1 and 2 respectively, and look at how those principles play themselves out in relation to the key entities or objects that would be defined in a logical model, the item and the work.

Describing the "Item"

The so-called cardinal principle for the application of the rules in part 1 is that "the starting point for description is the physical form of the item in hand, not the original or any previous form in which the work has been published." In practical terms that means that the subset of rules to be applied in describing an item is determined by the "class of materials" to which the item belongs: a sound disc is to be described according to the rules set out for the class of materials defined as sound recordings, a microfiche is to be described according to the rules for the class of materials defined as microforms, etc. On the surface, at least, it would appear that the physical form of the carrier is the principal criterion for determining the class of materials to which an item belongs and hence the specific set of rules that is to be used to supplement the general rules in chapter 1 when describing the item.

However, if we look more closely at how part 1 is structured and how each "class of materials" is defined, it is apparent that "physical form" is not in all cases the principal criterion for determining the scope of application for a given subset of rules. Figure 1 illustrates that in fact there are several criteria at play in defining the scope of the individual chapters in part 1. The physical form of the carrier for the item is one of the defining criteria, but the type of work contained in the item, the form of intellectual expression of the content, and the mode in which the content is recorded in the item also serve as key criteria for defining the scope of individual classes.

If we examine the matrix presented in table 1, we see that the physical form of the carrier actually serves as the defining criterion for only four of the classes: sound recordings,

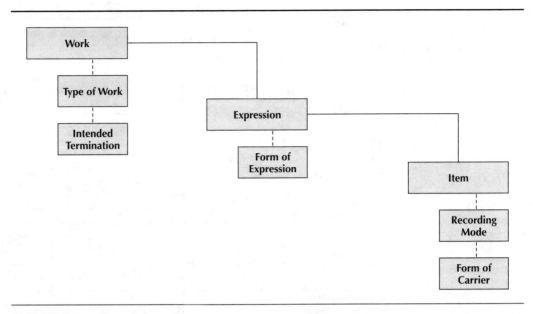

FIGURE 1
Criteria for determining class of materials

motion pictures and videorecordings, computer files, and microforms as indicated in the shaded areas in table 1. Each of those classes encompasses a defined set of physical carriers (e.g., sound cassettes, sound discs, etc.; film and videocassettes, videodiscs, etc.) that are exclusive to that class and are in fact the basis for the definition of the class.

By contrast, the classes defined as cartographic materials, graphic materials, and three-dimensional artefacts and realia each centre on a group of materials that derives its definition not from the physical form of the carrier, but primarily from the intellectual content of the item. In fact there is a significant overlap between the carriers that fall within these three classes (e.g., slides, transparencies, photographs, etc., are common to both cartographic materials and graphic materials; models are common to both cartographic materials and three-dimensional artefacts). The defining criterion for each of these classes is actually the type of work contained in the item, not the physical form of the carrier.

Music provides us with yet another way of defining a class of materials. In this instance the class is defined exclusively with reference to the intellectual form in which the content of the item is expressed; the class is restricted to materials whose content is expressed in the form of musical notation. The physical form of the carrier is not the defining criterion. Nor is the type of work contained in the item. Unlike cartographic materials, graphic materials, and three-dimensional artefacts and realia, music as a class does not encompass all materials containing a particular type of work. In this case musical works expressed in the form of musical notation are included, but those expressed in the form of recorded sound are not.

What this analysis serves to point up is that the concept of "class of materials" that provides the underlying structure for the rules in part 1 is more complex than it might appear on the surface, and contrary to what might be inferred from the statement of the principle in rule 0.24, determining the class of materials to which an item belongs is not synonymous with determining the "physical form" of the item. In fact the class to which a particular item belongs may be determined on the basis of attributes that are associated with "intellectual or artistic content" (i.e., with the work) or with the particular intellectual form in

TABLE 1 Defined scope for classes of materials

Class of Materials	Type of Work								Form of Expression						Recording Mode							Form of Carrier																															
	text	music	graphic	cartographic	cinemagraphic	artefact/object	data	software	alpha-numeric	music notation	sound	still image	moving image	three-dimensional	manuscript	print	tactile	analog	magnetic	digital	structural	book/pamphlet	sheet	score/part	sound cartridge	sound cassette	sound disc	sound tape reel	sound track film	roll	film/video cartridge	film/video cassette	video disc	film/video reel	filmstrip/slip cartridge	filmstrip/slip reel	slide/transparency	photo/negative	chart/flipchart	card, flash card, etc.	computer cartridge	computer cassette	computer disc	computer reel	globe	model/diorama	microscope slide	game, object, etc.	aperture card	microfiche	microfilm	microopaque
Books, pamphlets, and printed sheets	■	×	■	×					■			■				■	■					■	■																										×	×	×	×
Cartographic materials				■								■			■	■	■				■	■	■												■	■	■	■	■	■					■	■						
Manuscripts	■	■		■					■	■					■		■					■	■	■																									×	×	×	×
Music		■								■	×				■	■	■					■	■	■																									×	×	×	×
Sound recordings		■									■							■	■	■					■	■	■	■	■	■																						
Motion pictures and videorecordings			■		■	×						■	■					■	■	■											■	■	■	■																		
Graphic materials			■	×	×	×						■			■								■												■	■	■	■	■	■									×	×	×	×
Computer files							■	■	■					■						■																					■	■	■	■								
Three-dimensional artefacts and realia						■								■							■																									■	■	■				
Microforms	■	■	■	■					■	■		■				■																																	■	■	■	■
Serials	■	■	■	■	■	■	■	■	■	■	■	■	■	■	■	■	■	■	■	■	■	■	■	■	■	■	■	■	■	■	■	■	■	■	■	■	■	■	■	■	■	■	■	■	■	■	■	■	■	■	■	■

■ Inclusions   × Exclusions

which the work is expressed, as distinct from attributes that are associated with the physical object *per se.*

The complexity of the concept of "class of materials" as it is reflected in the code raises a number of significant questions that need to be taken into consideration as we review the rules for consistency and as we attempt to expand them to accommodate new media and new forms of intellectual and artistic expression. We might ask, for example, whether the classes that group materials on the basis of the form of the physical carrier (sound recordings, motion pictures and videorecordings, computer files, and microforms) are conceived in sufficiently precise terms to enable us to determine without question in which class a new form of carrier would fall. As digital technologies evolve, will we continue to be able to distinguish unequivocally between a sound disc and a computer disc? We might also ask whether the rules set out for each class of materials are sufficiently comprehensive to accommodate the various types of work and forms of intellectual expression that might be recorded on the carriers included in that class. Do the rules for computer files adequately cover digital forms of text, musical notation, sound, and video? If certain classes are defined on the basis of the form of the physical carrier and others are defined on the basis of the intellectual form in which the content is expressed, how do we determine which criterion takes precedence in classing new forms of material? Will we class digitally encoded musical notation that can be "played back" in the form of sound as music or as a sound recording? If an item falls within more than one class, how do we determine an order of precedence for applying specific rules that differ for each of the relevant classes?

Given the complexity of the interrelationships between the physical form and intellectual or artistic content of an item, and the problematic nature of accommodating newly emerging forms of information resources within the classes of materials currently defined in the code, it is essential that we understand clearly the association of various attributes of the materials being described with the specific entities or objects that are the centre of focus for the description. To do that I would suggest that we need first to deconstruct the class of materials concept. Examining the rules (both general and specific) in relation to the particular entities or objects and the associated attributes to which they pertain would serve to give us a new perspective from which to assess the appropriateness and consistency of the current rules. Perhaps more importantly, though, it would provide us with a more clearly articulated framework for determining how the rules might be extended to accommodate new materials, particularly those produced and disseminated using digital technologies.

Identifying the "Work"

The introduction to part 2 of the code states that the rules for choice and form of entry "apply to works and not to physical manifestations of those works, though the characteristics of an individual item are taken into account in some instances." The logic behind that statement is that because information relating to intellectual or artistic content as represented in the item in hand may differ in detail from comparable information that could be derived from objects representing other publications, recordings, etc. that contain the same intellectual or artistic content, the cataloguer should not rely exclusively on information derived from the item in hand or on the way the information is presented on that item, but should endeavour to establish the identity of the work on the basis of information derived from a range of sources that may reflect more accurately the work *per se.*

However, a closer examination of the rules in part 2 that pertain to the choice of access points reveals that many of the rules—especially those dealing with works of shared and mixed responsibility—give directions that are based entirely on information derived from the item in hand, relying in fact on the wording or layout of the chief source of information of the item being catalogued as the sole determinant for choice of entry. The question that arises is whether the apparent anomaly in those cases is simply the result of inconsistency in following through on the principle or whether it is indicative of a more fundamental difficulty in operationalizing the concept of the work as an entity independent of the physical entity or entities in which the work is reflected.

The rules in part 2 for determining the choice of access points under which the bibliographic description for an item is to be entered are structured around various categories of works. Figure 2 sets out in schematic form the factors that come into play in categorizing the work contained in an item when the work is one of personal authorship. As can be seen from the diagram, categorizing the work requires the cataloguer to determine the number of persons responsible for the work; the type of responsibility assumed by each if more than one person is involved; the number of works contained in the item; the type of work; whether the work has an antecedent and, if so, the nature of the relationship between the work and its antecedent; the number of persons responsible for the antecedent (if there is one) and the type of responsibility assumed by each if more than one person is involved; as well as (in the case of an item containing more than one work) the presence or absence of a title for the collection of works as a whole.

Figure 3 expands upon the basic schematic to show the range of possibilities associated with each of the factors that must be taken into account in categorizing the work, and gives an indication of the number of candidate entities that may have to be considered as the basis for either the main entry or an added entry. The number of persons responsible for the work may be one, two, three, or more. Responsibility may be attributed to a single person, it may be shared by two or more persons, it may be of a mixed nature, or different persons may be

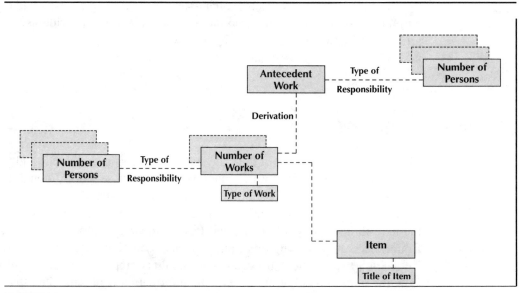

FIGURE 2
Criteria for determining category of work (works of personal authorship)

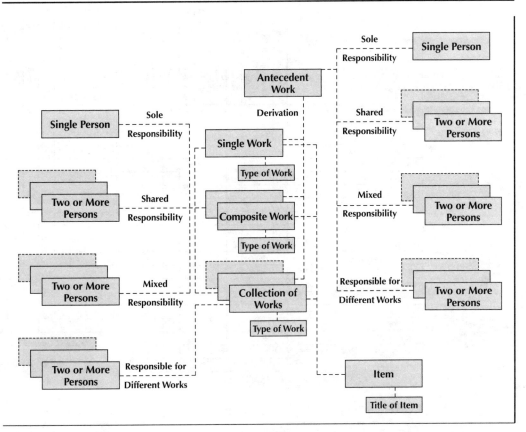

FIGURE 3
Choice of access points (works of personal authorship)

responsible for the individual works within a collection. The item may contain a single work, a composite work combining components of different types (text, music, art, etc.), or it may contain a collection of works. The work or works contained in the item may be derived from an antecedent work (by way of translation, revision, adaptation, etc.). Responsibility for the antecedent work may be attributed to a single person, it may be shared by two or more persons, it may be of a mixed nature, or different persons may be responsible for individual works within a collection. Finally the item itself may bear a collective title or it may lack such a title.

What should be clear from the schematic is that the categorizations that are used to structure the rules for choice of entry are as complex in their make-up as the classes of materials around which the rules in part 1 are organized. Although the work itself is purportedly the entity or object around which decisions on choice of entry are to be made, it is clear that the relationships between the work or works contained in the item and other entities or objects connected with the work(s) (namely the person(s) responsible for the work(s), any antecedent work(s), and the containing item itself), as well as the specific nature of those relationships, all have a direct bearing on the choice of entry.

In tables 2, 3, 4, and 5 the key criteria used in categorizing works of personal authorship (the type of responsibility for the work, the configuration of works within the item, the nature of derivation for works that have an antecedent, and the type of work) are mapped onto

TABLE 2 Choice of main entry for item containing a work(s) for which a single person is responsible

Main Entry Heading	Responsibility				Configuration			Derivation										Type of Work						
	Single person responsible	Shared responsibility	Different persons responsible	Mixed responsibility	Single work	Collection of works / extracts	Composite work	New work	Art reproduction	Translation	Arrangement / transcription	Accompaniment / part added	Revision	Illustrated text	Commentary [etc.] added	Adaptation	Performance	Text	Art work	Musical work	Text / art work	Text / musical work	Cartographic work	Cinemagraphic work
Author / probable author	□				■	■	■	■	■	■	■	■	■	■	■	■	■	■	■	■	■	■	■	■
Principal author																								
First named principal author																								
First named author																								
Reviser																								
Principal reviser																								
First named reviser																								
Adapter																								
Principal adapter																								
First named adapter																								
Performer																								
Principal performer																								
First named principal performer																								
Artist																								
Writer																								
Text																								
Composer																								
Work emphasized																								
First named work / contribution																								
Title	■				■	■	■	■	■	■	■	■	■	■	■	■	■	■	■	■	■	■	■	■

□ Specified by rule   ■ Logical inference

TABLE 3 Choice of main entry for item containing a work(s) of shared responsibility

Main Entry Heading	Responsibility				Configuration			Derivation										Type of Work						
	Single person responsible	Shared responsibility	Different persons responsible	Mixed responsibility	Single work	Collection of works / extracts	Composite work	New work	Art reproduction	Translation	Arrangement / transcription	Accompaniment / part added	Revision	Illustrated text	Commentary [etc.] added	Adaptation	Performance	Text	Art work	Musical work	Text / art work	Text / musical work	Cartographic work	Cinemagraphic work
Author / probable author																								
Principal author		□			■	■	■	■	■	■	■	■	■	■	■	■	■	■	■	■	■	■	■	■
First named principal author		□			■	■	■	■	■	■	■	■	■	■	■	■	■	■	■	■	■	■	■	■
First named author		□			■	■	■	■	■	■	■	■	■	■	■	■	■	■	■	■	■	■	■	■
Reviser																								
Principal reviser																								
First named reviser																								
Adapter																								
Principal adapter																								
First named adapter																								
Performer																								
Principal performer																								
First named principal performer																								
Artist																								
Writer																								
Text																								
Composer																								
Work emphasized																								
First named work / contribution																								
Title		■			■	■	■	■	■	■	■	■	■	■	■	■	■	■	■	■	■	■	■	■

□ Specified by rule   ■ Logical inference

TABLE 4 Choice of main entry for item containing collection of works by different authors

Main Entry Heading	Responsibility				Configuration			Derivation										Type of Work						
	Single person responsible	Shared responsibility	Different persons responsible	Mixed responsibility	Single work	Collection of works / extracts	Composite work	New work	Art reproduction	Translation	Arrangement / transcription	Accompaniment / part added	Revision	Illustrated text	Commentary [etc.] added	Adaptation	Performance	Text	Art work	Musical work	Text / art work	Text / musical work	Cartographic work	Cinemagraphic work
Author / probable author																								
Principal author																								
First named principal author																								
First named author																								
Reviser																								
Principal reviser																								
First named reviser																								
Adapter																								
Principal adapter																								
First named adapter																								
Performer			■			■												■	■	■		■		■
Principal performer			■			■												■	■	■		■		■
First named principal performer			■			■												■	■	■		■		■
Artist																								
Writer																								
Text																								
Composer																								
Work emphasized																								
First named work / contribution			■			■		■	■	■	■	■	■	■	■	■	■	■	■	■	■	■	■	■
Title			■			■		■	■	■	■	■	■	■	■	■	■	■	■	■	■	■	■	■

□ Specified by rule   ■ Logical inference

TABLE 5 Choice of main entry for item containing a work(s) of mixed responsibility

Main Entry Heading	Responsibility				Configuration			Derivation										Type of Work						
	Single person responsible	Shared responsibility	Different persons responsible	Mixed responsibility	Single work	Collection of works / extracts	Composite work	New work	Art reproduction	Translation	Arrangement / transcription	Accompaniment / part added	Revision	Illustrated text	Commentary [etc.] added	Adaptation	Performance	Text	Art work	Musical work	Text / art work	Text / musical work	Cartographic work	Cinemagraphic work
Author / probable author				■	■	■		■		■	■	■	■					■	■	■	■		■	■
Principal author				■	■	■		■		■	■	■	■					■	■	■	■		■	■
First named principal author				■	■	■		■		■	■	■	■					■	■	■	■		■	■
First named author				■	■	■		■		■	■	■	■					■	■	■	■		■	■
Reviser				■	■	■	■			■			■					■	■					
Principal reviser				■	■	■	■			■			■					■	■					
First named reviser				■	■	■	■			■			■					■	■					
Adapter				■	■	■	■				■		■			■		■	■	■	■	■	■	■
Principal adapter				■	■	■	■				■		■			■		■	■	■	■	■	■	■
First named adapter				■	■	■	■				■		■			■		■	■	■	■	■	■	■
Performer				■													■	■	■	■				
Principal performer				■													■	■	■	■				
First named principal performer				■														■	■	■				
Artist				■	■	■	■		■												■			
Writer				■	■	■	■						■								■			
Text				■	■	■	■							■	■						■			
Composer				■	■					■	■	■	■									■		
Work emphasized				■	■						■		■		■					■				
First named work / contribution				■		■					■		■					■	■	■	■		■	
Title				■	■	■	■	■	■	■	■	■	■					■	■	■	■	■	■	■

□ Specified by rule   ■ Logical inference

a matrix similar to the one used to analyze the class of materials concept in part 1. In the left-hand column of the matrix are listed the various entities on which the main entry heading may be based (author, principal author, etc.).

As can be seen from table 2, the rules offer only two basic options for the main entry heading when a single person is responsible for the work(s) contained in the item being catalogued: the author or probable author (if known), or the title of the work (if the author or probable author is unknown). The table also indicates that the rules specify main entry either under author/probable author or title both for items that contain a single work and for those that contain a collection of works or extracts of works for which a single person is responsible. Although there is no specific reference in the rules to composite works for which a single person is responsible (e.g., text and drawings by the same person), the table indicates that a logical inference could be made that the basic rules would still apply. Similarly a logical inference could be made that the basic rules would apply in all cases where the work contained in the item being catalogued is derived from an antecedent work by the same person (e.g., a composer's transcription of his/her own original composition), and that they would apply irrespective of the type of work (i.e., they would apply equally to text, art, music, etc.).

However, as we progress through tables 3, 4, and 5 it is evident that the application of basic rules across the spectrum of variables that are possible for a given category of works becomes increasingly attenuated. The number of entities on which the main entry heading may be based increases to four in the case of works of shared authorship, to five in the case of collections of works by different persons, and to twenty in the case of works of mixed responsibility. The choice of main entry heading becomes increasingly linked to the configuration of works within the item, to the specific nature of the relationship between the work and its antecedent, and to the particular type of work involved. The logical inferences that can be made about the applicability of a basic rule to a particular subcategory become progressively more difficult to extrapolate and less likely to extend across subcategories.

It is also apparent from the range of entities on which the main entry heading may be based that determining the choice of entry where works of shared and mixed responsibility are involved is in a significant number of instances linked directly to either the wording or the layout of the chief source of information for the particular item being catalogued. Hence the proliferation of choices linked to "first named" author, reviser, adapter or performer, and to the "work emphasised." In contrast with the rules for entry of a work for which a single person is responsible, where sources within the item as well as sources external to it are used to determine the authorship of the work, the rules for entry of works of shared and mixed responsibility in many instances base the determination of who is responsible for the work and whether or not the work is a new work entirely on what is in effect "product labeling" information derived from the item in hand.

Analyzing the categorization of works that forms the basis for determining choice of entry in a systematic way, as illustrated in the figures and tables presented here, raises a number of questions that need to be taken into consideration, especially as we attempt to determine the applicability of basic principles for the identification of works to an increasingly broad array of intellectual and artistic productions that involve more than one person and that are "multimedia" in nature. We might ask, for example, whether the line of demarcation between shared responsibility and mixed responsibility is sufficiently clear. If works produced through collaboration or exchange between two or more persons can fall under either category, depending on whether the individuals make the same kind of intellectual or artistic contribution or perform different kinds of roles, do we have a clear enough notion of what constitutes a distinct intellectual or artistic role to enable us to make the appropriate categorization in the absence of a specific rule? We might also ask whether the code needs to be extended to cover additional forms of composite works. Can we extrapolate principles from existing rules for works that combine music and text and those that combine art and text that would be applicable to works that combine music, art, and text into a single production? We might ask further to what extent rules that are specific to a particular type of work are justified. If we have rules that pertain specifically to textual works, to musical works, and to art works, is there a reason why we have no rules that are specific to cartographic or cinemagraphic works?

Given the range of factors that come into play in determining the access points to be used in identifying a work, and the complexity of the categorizations around which the rules are structured, it is essential that we understand clearly the basic underlying principles that determine who is credited with responsibility for a work and where the line is drawn between one work and another. To do that we need to examine in detail each of the factors that have a bearing on choice of entry and the interplay between those factors. With a clearer understanding of the logic underlying the rules for choice of entry as they function currently, we will be in a better position to assess where those rules might require amending or extension as we deal with both residual and newly emerging questions relating to choice of entry for works resulting from collaboration between two or more persons and for derivative works of various kinds.

Reflecting Change in Content and Form over Time

The review and adaptation of *AACR* to accommodate technical innovation in a digital environment will undoubtedly prove to be a more complex matter than has been the case with other media and technologies. The key difference in this instance is that the introduction of digital technologies has effectively undercut many of the *a priori* assumptions we have made about the relationship between the physical form and the intellectual content of the objects that we catalogue. Traditionally we have dealt with media in which the intellectual or artistic content has been permanently fixed within the physical object, and the content has, for all intents and purposes, been considered immutable. The cataloguing rules have taken that relationship as a given. To ensure uniformity of description, it has for the most part been necessary simply to focus the rules on the selection of sources of information, on criteria for determining precedence where information pertaining to a given data element might appear in more than one form within the specified source of information, and on detailing the conventions to be followed in transcribing or recording a particular data element. Implicit in the rules is the assumption that both the source from which the data are derived and the form in which the information is represented in that source will be the same from one copy of a publication or recording to another. In fact the assumption has been made that in general any difference detected in the formalized elements of the descriptions for two items is a signal that the items represent different physical manifestations. With digital media those assumptions may not necessarily hold.

The implications of this undercutting of *a priori* assumptions become particularly problematic when we deal with digitally encoded documents that are stored on a host computer and are accessible only online. In such circumstances the very notion of the physical object becomes somewhat attenuated. The "item in hand" that the rules indicate is the starting point for the description becomes more of a "virtual" than a "physical" object, linked in some ways more with the dimension of time than with physical dimension. This attenuation of the physical object has several implications both for our logical constructs and for the way those constructs are reflected in cataloguing rules.

Consider first the group of attributes associated with the carrier of what has conventionally been regarded as a "physical manifestation." In an online environment the digitally encoded document will normally be stored as a file or set of files on a disk or some other peripheral device along with numerous other documents. In effect there is no carrier associated with the document *per se*. As a consequence, the attributes normally associated with the carrier for the manifestation (form, extent, dimensions, physical medium, etc.) effectively have no relevance.

Secondly, while the document may contain the kind of "product" information (e.g., title, statement of responsibility, publisher/distributor) that is associated with more traditional "physical forms," it cannot be assumed that the information will remain constant from one display of the document to the next. By the same token it cannot be assumed that the intellectual or artistic content within the document will remain constant, or that a change in the content would be signaled by some parallel change in the "product" information. Furthermore, the technology available to the user at the desktop and the functional capabilities of the applications software used to display the document may mean that the copy of the document displayed on the user's screen will differ from the copy stored on the host computer. The differences may only affect incidentals such as character fonts, resolution of images, layout, etc., but they may also extend to characteristics that affect the intelligibility of the document. There is the potential, therefore, to change not only the "physical form" of the document but also its "intellectual or artistic content" each and every time the document is displayed.

In some ways, of course, the problems posed by digital materials are analogous to those associated with conventional materials whose form and/or content is subject to change over time (e.g., serials, loose-leaf updates, and multipart items issued at intervals). In such cases rules have been devised and conventions have been established to address the possibility that as segments of the publication are issued over time the "product" information contained on the chief source of information may change, the physical form may be altered, and the content may be extended or revised. In general the solution has been to record a snapshot of the publication at a given point in its history, to leave certain details open-ended, to record significant variations by means of notes, and to simply ignore others. Basically, however, none of those techniques permit multiple values for a single data element within the record. Either a new record is created (as in the case of successive entry for serials) or the data pertaining to the affected data element are revised (as in the case of changes in responsibility for a multipart monograph). Data that are displaced as a result of such changes are normally reincorporated into the description by means of edition and history notes (including notes linking successive entries for a serial), by the addition of an added entry, by notes explaining variations in physical details, or sometimes simply through a note such as "title varies slightly."

It would be more difficult, however, to apply this snapshot technique to digital materials. Because the changes that occur in digital documents are not necessarily linked to the release of a new issue, a set of updates, or an additional part, there is less probability that the cataloguer would reexamine the document at the point in time when the change is made. Further, there is less likelihood of there being available to the cataloguer an archival record of the document's content at each interval in the process of revision or extension as there is with conventional materials. Thus there is little guarantee that the snapshot descriptions compiled by different cataloguers would coincide. A cataloguer describing the document at any given point in time may have no means of reconstructing and recording the details that pertained to the document prior to that point. And there is little likelihood that subsequent changes will be reflected consistently from one record to another.

If we were to examine this problem in the context of a model in which logical attributes are defined and mapped to the entity or object with which they are associated, we would recognize that the problem is not one that requires the definition of additional attributes, but rather one that requires the model to allow for the possibility that a given instance of an entity or object type may have an attribute that is subject to change over time. The problem then is to determine how the multiple values for that attribute can be reflected in the data, and whether or not it is necessary to recognize a new instance of the entity or object each time the value for that attribute changes. While the model itself would not necessarily provide us with a means of resolving the problem, it would serve as a frame of reference both for analyzing the problem and for assessing the feasibility of options that might be considered as possible solutions. It would also help us to ensure that the logic of the chosen option is reflected consistently through the rules.

Conclusion

The pace of innovation in the information technology field is not likely to diminish in the foreseeable future. We will continue to see the development of new formats for information storage and dissemination. New technologies will continue to spawn innovation among creators and producers and to generate new forms of intellectual and artistic expression. Networks will continue to expand and evolve. Advances in database management systems will continue to have an impact on the way we design bibliographic systems and require us to rethink the way we structure bibliographic data. On the economic front the pressures that have obliged us to seek more cost-effective means of providing bibliographic control of our library collections are not likely to dissipate.

The challenge of responding to continuing change in the environment within which *AACR* operates requires that we revisit first principles and that we understand clearly the logic underlying the code. As we adapt the code to accommodate the products of the new technology and to exploit the benefits of database technology, we have to be able to articulate clearly the logical structures that are embedded within the code in order to ensure coherency in its future development. Systematic, logical analysis of the principles and structures that underlie the code is a necessary first step in that process. The way in which the analysis is conducted, and the techniques that are used to model the logic of the code can be debated. But I believe there can be little argument about the need or the value of a disciplined, comprehensive approach to analyzing the code.

A comprehensive analysis of the logic of the code will be essential in order to satisfy ourselves that its theoretical underpinnings are sound, that it is capable of accommodating change, that it can continue to be responsive to user needs, that it can interface effectively with other systems for bibliographic control, and that it is cost effective. Ultimately the value of modeling the logic of *AACR* will be assessed in terms of the insights it provides us into the way the code functions and the framework it provides for evaluating the end product of its application against the criteria of accuracy, flexibility, user-friendliness, compatibility, and efficiency.

Notes

1. Michael Gorman, "Cataloguing and the New Technologies," in *The Nature and Future of the Catalog,* ed. Maurice J. Freedman and S. Michael Malinconico (Phoenix, Ariz.: Oryx, 1979), 127-36.

2. Michael Heaney, "Object-Oriented Cataloging," *Information Technology and Libraries* 14, no. 3 (September 1995): 135-53.

3. Rebecca Green, "The Design of a Relational Database for Large-Scale Bibliographic Retrieval," *Information Technology and Libraries* 15, no. 4 (December 1996): 207-21.

4. Barbara B. Tillett, "A Taxonomy of Bibliographic Relationships," *Library Resources & Technical Services* 35, no. 2 (April 1991): 150-58.

5. Gregory H. Leazer and Richard P. Smiraglia, "Toward the Bibliographic Control of Works: Derivative Bibliographic Relationships in an Online Union Catalog," in *Proceedings of the ACM International Conference on Digital Libraries* (Bethesda, Md.: Association for Computing Machinery, 1996), 36-43.

6. IFLA Study Group on the Functional Requirements for Bibliographic Records, *Functional Requirements for Bibliographic Records: Final Report* (München: K. G. Saur, 1998).

DISCUSSION

Tom Delsey's paper received general approval from both conference participants and electronic discussion list commentators.

In answer to a question about how *AACR2* could be reorganized to eliminate the way part 1 now classes materials into eleven chapters, Delsey proposed that each chapter deal with a specific area of description, e.g., chapter 1 for the title and statement of responsibility area. Each chapter would have general rules and then specific rules for particular attributes.

A JSC member inquired about the need for a statement of principles in *AACR2*. Delsey noted that *AACR1* accepted the Paris Principles and, perhaps by inference, so does *AACR2*. However, these principles are not always followed, e.g., the rule of three prevents the identification and collocation of all of a person's works when that person is listed as the fourth author on any of his/her works. He believes a statement of principles is desirable.

Delsey agreed with a participant that the meaning of "work" in his paper differs from the meaning of "work" in *AACR2,* and that the *AACR2* "work" may no longer be appropriate.

He declined to give a definite answer to a question about the need for an illustrated *AACR2*.

AACR2 and Catalogue Production Technology

Relevance of Cataloguing Principles to the Online Environment

RAHMATOLLAH FATTAHI

1. Introduction

More than thirty-five years have passed since the International Conference on Cataloguing Principles in Paris (ICCP), and cataloguers have witnessed profound changes in many aspects of catalogue production technology and also in bibliographic control and access during this period of time. In comparison to the past, cataloguers are less involved in the design and production of catalogues and bibliographic databases particularly in terms of the interfaces, the types of indexes, and the ways in which records and retrieval results are displayed. In these areas, changes and developments have presented cataloguers with some basic questions about the fundamental principles of record creation and catalogue construction.

Furthermore, although present online catalogues are benefiting from more advanced hardware and software, there are still considerable, serious problems in searching, retrieval, and display of bibliographic information in present systems, which influence their functions and usefulness. This, as has been highlighted in the literature, may be because some of the present cataloguing principles and rules are inadequate, less relevant, or irrelevant to the new electronic environment.[1] It is often claimed that *AACR2*'s rules are based on concepts and principles from the premachine period and that they do not serve us well in giving guidance in the construction of electronic catalogues.

1.1 The aim, scope, and approach of this paper

In this paper some of the basic principles of *AACR2* which have been highlighted in the literature as those most likely to be influenced by the new technology will be reexamined in the light of both the present and the potential characteristics and capabilities of the online environment. The approach used in this paper is to match individual capabilities of online catalogues with the basic principles of *AACR2R*. A major focus will be the basic concepts of the code's principles, the logic of their application and the relationship of these principles to the logic of the online catalogue, as well as an examination of the types of principles and rules that are likely to change when moving from a manual catalogue to an online catalogue. These principles are:

- The objectives and functions of the catalogue which influence all other principles
- The basis for description and its implications for other principles
- Structure of the catalogue and the concept of multiple entries
- Uniform headings for works (i.e., uniform titles)
- Uniform headings for authors
- The form of personal name headings and corporate name headings
- Presentation of bibliographic information.

2. A Reexamination of *AACR2* Principles in the Online Environment

2.1 Objectives and functions of the catalogue in an online environment

The objectives of the catalogue are not clearly stated in *AACR2*. Nevertheless, it can be inferred that the code has the same underlying principles and objectives as stated in its predecessors, mainly Lubetzky's *Code of Cataloging Rules*[2] and *AACR1*. In fact, the code is based on the Paris Principle's statement of functions of the catalogue and, historically, it follows Cutter's two objectives, the locational and collocational functions of the catalogue. The locational (i.e., the finding) function is predominant in the code, and this is apparent from the treatment of rules for description. The optionality of uniform titles is another indication of this approach.

With respect to the different capabilities of the online catalogue, there are a number of questions regarding the objectives and functions of the catalogue in the new environment. A general question raised is whether the objectives and functions of the catalogue as set forth in the Paris Principles and adopted in *AACR2* are still valid in the online environment. Another question which needs to be addressed in this regard is whether the catalogue in the online network environment should still maintain the same functions formulated for a premachine environment or should widen its scope to include new functions.

While the current objectives and functions of the catalogue continue to be valid in the new environment, the new technology may help fulfil them more comprehensively and accurately. Nevertheless, these objectives and functions are surely inadequate for the new environment. In addition to the finding and collocating functions, the online catalogue helps to better identify and characterise entities in terms of their nature, scope, and orientation through different data fields such as intellectual level, document type, genre, language code, geographic area code, and additional notes. Similarly, a fuller description of the item helps the online catalogue to be used as a selecting aid for different users to choose one item over similar items. The locating of items is another function of the catalogue and, in this respect, online catalogues are far more capable of showing the location and status of the item(s) being sought.

In the following section, the functions of the catalogue will be analysed with regard to the impact of some of the major characteristics of the catalogue production technology and the online environment. These are: (1) the integration of library operations, (2) developments in networking and in global access to catalogues, (3) access to the virtual copy, (4) access to other types of bibliographic databases, and (5) online search/retrieval/display capabilities. The future *AACR* should consider all these factors.

2.1.1 Integration of different library operations

The integrated online library system has made it possible for different library modules to use the same bibliographic records within the same database management system. Acquisitions librarians, cataloguers, circulation librarians, document delivery librarians, serial librarians, and reference librarians all have access to the same database and use it for different purposes. Also in an integrated system, the end user may have access to parts of acquisition status, circulation, and holdings information. In an integrated system it is, therefore, necessary for the catalogue record to fulfil the various bibliographic needs of different operations, from housekeeping functions to reference services. In this context, not only should the catalogue function as a finding tool as well as a collocating tool, but it should also help in the choice between one work and others.

The combination of approaches to an integrated online library system not only makes it necessary for *AACR* to expand the current objectives but also to put more emphasis on principles for the choice and form of access points as well as for description, i.e., data elements beyond author/title information. In other words, description, access points, and additional housekeeping elements should satisfy the needs of different users. For example, a reference librarian may need to find a specific item and at the same time identify different editions and manifestations related to that item to provide more help to the user.

2.1.2 Networking and global access to catalogues

The fact that the resources and bibliographic information of hundreds of libraries participating in national and international networks are now accessible to any remote user calls for a reconsideration of the functions and objectives of the catalogue. The question arises as to whether a catalogue should serve in the first place its local users, that is, to identify the holdings of a particular library, or to enable any user to access the collections of other libraries available through the network. In such an environment, consideration should always be given to the fact that the item in hand for cataloguing may be an expression or manifestation of another work known under a different title being held in another collection.

With respect to the network environment, there is some support for the precedence of the collocating function of the catalogue over its finding function. In a conceptual approach to a catalogue's functions as presented by Lubetzky to the Paris Principles, Wilson proposes that, with regard to the availability of different catalogues in an online network and with respect to the significance of "work" over "publication," priority should be given to the collocating objective.[3] Dempsey points out that a lack of sufficient attention to the collocating objective of the catalogue has resulted in two problems in large shared databases: difficulty in authority control and an increase in duplicate records.[4] Ayres supports a similar concept.[5]

On the other hand, while in a large shared database the potential number of expressions and manifestations of a work increases, it is more likely that access to a very specific bibliographic manifestation of a work, for example, a particular version, would be a common need for some end users and librarians (e.g., reference librarians, document delivery librarians). It is evident that in a shared system or network of catalogues there will be a good chance for the user to select those that suit his/her needs best among different representations of a work. Copy cataloguing through bibliographic utilities, which is usually a known-item search, is another example of such a user approach.

With the availability of catalogues to different remote users, it is hard to give absolute priority to either of the two traditional functions of the catalogue. While catalogues should serve their local patrons well, they should also be useful to remote users.

2.1.3 Access to the virtual copy

With increasing developments in information technology it has become possible, in many online catalogues, to link directly to the work (original or digital reproduction). In other words, online catalogues can also show virtual copies of an item. Access to full texts or digital reproductions through linking tags, such as USMARC field 856, has implications for the functions of the catalogue. In this case, through a useful description, the catalogue should help identify the characteristics of both the actual and virtual objects.

With respect to the volatility of electronic documents and the possible changes in the content of some of the fields, it is important to take a consistent approach in description and the basis for description. In terms of their contents, size of the file, date of updating, layout, links to other sources, and even the title, electronic documents may change over time without any indication. These changes have implications for the different functions of the catalogue. They also make the bibliographic control of such documents very difficult. The contents (i.e., data elements) in some fields need to be updated in order to describe and identify the document properly.

Another problem is how to help the searcher to differentiate between virtual copies of works (such as various copies of *Hamlet* available on WWW), which may differ from one another just as printed editions differ.

2.1.4 Availability of different types of bibliographic databases

With respect to the accessibility of different types of online and/or on-disk bibliographic databases (e.g., library catalogues, book trade bibliographic databases, national bibliographies, and A&I databases) to various users, a combination of approaches in terms of the functions of the catalogue should be considered.

With access to book trade databases, the catalogue goes beyond providing holdings information and becomes a gateway to explore what is newly published, what is to be published, and what is in print. In such an environment, emphasis is also put on functions such as the crucial choice of one item over another. This requires that, for further identification of the item, more descriptive elements, such as physical description, table of contents, and summary, should be provided in the bibliographic record. From a different point of view, the functions of the bibliographic database in the library world and book trade world are similar in many respects, such as the finding function, the selecting function, and housekeeping function. Even the bringing together of works by a particular author and also collocation of series are functions wanted by the two communities. A major difference is in the collocation of different editions and manifestations of a work, which libraries appear to consider important enough to control by rules of entry. All these similarities and differences in the functions have implications for other principles such as the basis for description, content of the bibliographic record, and the choice and form of access points. These will be discussed in the later sections.

2.1.5 Search/retrieval/display capabilities and functions of the catalogue

Through its extensive capabilities the online catalogue can fulfil different functions more effectively than the card catalogue. For example, keyword searching on name of authors, coauthors, editors, titles, series, etc., not only facilitates the finding function but it can also help in the choice of one item over another. Boolean searching can, to some extent, facilitate both the finding function (e.g., ANDing the author's name with date of publication) and the collocating function (e.g., ANDing the author heading with the uniform title to assemble different editions of a work). Hypertext searching on any term or a combination of terms—as offered in the University of Toronto catalogue, the University of California catalogue (MELVYL), the Library and Information Services of Western Australia (LISWA), Hyper-Lynx, GoPAC (from DataTrek, Australia), OhioLink Central catalogue, and the Prototype Catalogue of Super Records—can extend a known-item search to other items which may be unknown to the searcher but may have some kind of relationship with the item first found.

AACR2 does not address the problems that resulted in response to queries for voluminous authors and works. For example, one of the major problems of the present online catalogues is that, in response to a search for voluminous authors and works, the searcher is presented with too many records to conveniently scan. This problem is exacerbated with keyword searching, in that too many records including less relevant and irrelevant data are retrieved. A search in large catalogues under "Hamlet" may retrieve too many records, for different editions and manifestations, for works about Hamlet, as well as works with the title *Hamlet* written by other writers.[6] The problem becomes more serious when the user searches in a large shared catalogue, such as a national union catalogue, in which there will be a greater number of editions and translations or manifestations of a work held by different libraries (see "Demonstration of OPAC Designs" at: http://wilma.silas.unsw.edu.au/students/rfattahi/demo.htm). It can be said that the present approach in *AACR2* toward the collocation of voluminous authors and works is not consistent with the search/retrieval/display capabilities of online catalogues.

2.1.6 Conclusion

The catalogue in the global online environment is used by a wide spectrum of local and remote users and, therefore, is supposed to satisfy different approaches. It can be concluded that the functions of the online catalogue go beyond the present objectives (i.e., locational and collocational functions) laid down in the Paris Principles. It is, therefore, necessary that *AACR2*'s principles should address all these different functions and should also take into consideration the implications of each function for other principles. In making the code relevant to the online environment, the principles and rules should be reformulated with respect to both the functions addressed in the IFLA's study of the *Functional Requirements for Bibliographic Records* and the catalogue's search/retrieval/display capabilities.[7] Although IFLA has not taken the relating function into account as much as it should, *AACR* should consider it because of the nature of some collections such as music, law, literature, and religions which require more control and display of the relationships between related entities.

2.2 The basis for description in the online environment and its implications for *AACR*

The shift in different codes of descriptive cataloguing from "work" to "item" (and vice-versa) as the basis of description is, in fact, an indication of the relative importance of these two different approaches. In the networked, online environment the issue now requires a new look. Where more than one catalogue is involved (e.g., in the case of shared cataloguing systems and union catalogues) and also where catalogues are increasingly becoming a part of the global online environment there must, as a first principle, be consensus regarding the basis for the description of bibliographic entities, that is, what entity should be regarded as the basis for bibliographic description in an online environment.

The basic unit of description (the cataloguing unit) in *AACR2R* is the physical item in hand (rule 0.24). This is also apparent throughout the statements of the rules in part 1 (the title page or its equivalent is chosen as the chief source of cataloguing data for description). To consider providing access to the "work," however, *AACR2R* maintains concepts such as main entries and uniform titles. *AACR2R* prescribes that, although the characteristics of individual items are taken into account, the rules for choice and form of access points should apply to works and not generally to physical manifestations of those works.[8] The following factors indicate the significance of both "works" and "items" and justify the need in *AACR* to maintain a hybrid approach when describing bibliographic entities:

a) Users' needs vary a great deal. While some users may find any edition of a work useful, others may require a specific edition with a particular feature. There are also users who look in the catalogue for a particular manifestation of a work or a work in a particular format.

b) Many users do not know that a work may have several different editions and/or manifestations; the catalogue may contain more than the user may be expecting and it is an objective of the catalogue to display other works or items related to the sought item.

c) Based on the users' familiarity with or knowledge of books as known or seen by them, the item and the cataloguing data on the chief source of information (e.g., the title page) are usually more appropriate as the basic unit of description for most types of publication. However, the basis for the description of reproductions, e.g., equivalent and near-equivalent entities, is a different case; reproductions, particularly in microform, can be described as notes on the records created for the original item.[9] This approach would make access to both works and their reproductions more consistent.

d) For acquisitions, current awareness services, circulation, placing reservations on books and ILL (interlibrary loan), and for the purpose of importing and exporting records (for example, for cataloguing) that usually deal with specific manifestations, the work cannot be a good means of bibliographic data exchange. For this reason, libraries and bibliographic utilities catalogue the item representing the edition rather than the work.

e) For national bibliographies and trade lists, which focus on newly published items, the description based on the item is considered more important.

Choosing the piece in hand as the only basic unit of description, however, does not apply to all types of publication. For example, a single issue of a serial does not provide sufficient cataloguing data for the description and also bibliographic relationships of the whole serial. Crystal Graham criticises *AACR2* for its approach toward describing serials and states that there are structural, philosophical, and practical problems with that approach.[10]

Patrick Wilson proposes a redefinition of "work" to be taken as the basic unit of cataloguing.[11] However, to base description on "work" has strong implications for AACR, in that it influences the choice and form of main entries and uniform titles, structure of the catalogue, and the ways in which the relationship of different entities related to a work should be treated and displayed on the catalogue record. As has been demonstrated in the Prototype Catalogue of Super Records, it is possible to have a hybrid approach towards the basis for description in the online environment. While describing the item in hand can fulfil the finding, selecting, and locating functions, a multilevel, super record for the description of and access to "work" and its different expressions and manifestations would fulfil the identifying and collocating functions in a more meaningful way.

2.3 Structure of the catalogue and the concept of multiple entries

The structure of the catalogue has an important role in the fulfilment of its functions. The principles underlying the structure of the catalogue and choice of entries in *AACR2* include rules concerning the determination and construction of necessary entries for a linear, alphabetical catalogue of main entries, added entries, and references. An online catalogue based on such a linear approach has many problems in searching, retrieval, and display of bibliographic sources.

To overcome some existing search/retrieval/display problems, the future *AACR* should take a new approach to the structure of the catalogue and the bibliographic record.

2.3.1 New approaches to the structure for the catalogue and the bibliographic record

In place of the single, unique, and self-contained main entry record, research (for example, by Heaney; Ridley, Ayres, Nielsen, and Torsun; and Fattahi) has recently attempted to propose a new structure for the catalogue and catalogue record. Such new approaches imply that the existing cataloguing principles do not adequately address the retrieval and display problems of works that appear in many editions and manifestations. Reanalysing the nature of works and their publications, Heaney states that the major access to information is through the "abstract work" and that cataloguing rules and MARC formats should incorporate radical changes, mainly in the content of the MARC tags, to address access problems of "works" and their manifestations.[12]

The experimental prototype OPAC (i.e., the Bradford OPAC) uses a manifestation concept to group together sets of items that are manifestations of the same work.[13] In terms of display, the Bradford OPAC avoids repetition of the author heading and title. What the user sees is an economical display of manifestations which makes clear their differences. However, the catalogue is more concerned with the general concept of manifestations and does not distinguish between different subcategories within each manifestation.

In the Prototype Catalogue of Super Records, Fattahi proposes a multilevel record structure which is more relevant to the online environment.[14] Super records would provide a uniform access to different instances of a work. The super record for a work would contain the uniform title of the work and the author heading, if applicable, along with a categorisation for different expressions and manifestations being linked to actual records for items and copies available in the collection. This approach would result in a better syndetic structure. At its first level, the super record for a work expresses the abstract work only; it is not directly linked to any actual record for items or copies. This helps the searcher to identify and select the category to which an item may belong. With super records in place, online catalogues would be better able to reflect special subarrangements than are current catalogue structures.

Catalogue users will search and retrieve super records through name authority files and/or uniform titles authority files first, so that they can scan the record and decide on the type of edition or manifestation for which they are looking.[15] The reverse is also possible: once a record for an item has been retrieved in response to a specific query, the searcher can move from that record to the relevant super record through an assigned link. This bidirectional approach makes the navigation of the bibliographic universe easier and more understandable. In those cases where an item belongs to more than one category (for example, a translation from an adaptation of *Hamlet*), the linkage can be created between the item and the two categories to which the item belongs. Other advantages with a multilevel record structure such as that of a super record are discussed elsewhere.[16]

A major requirement of a multilevel record is to incorporate links between different records for different expressions and manifestations of a work. A hypertext technique is feasible in the online environment and could provide such links.

2.3.2 New ways to link records in online catalogues

In online catalogues it is also possible to provide different mechanisms for the retrieval and display of different types of relationships. This depends, to a large extent, on both the structure of machine-readable records and the software to allow strings of fields and/or subfields to be organised so that the computer can retrieve and display all related records in a user-oriented manner. It is possible to link two or more fields or subfields in machine-readable records in such a way as to better identify relationships between entities.

Online catalogues and future computerised systems may provide new and more effective linking devices to help the searcher to navigate a catalogue. Using hypertext techniques for linking related records is a promising method in bibliographic databases for the enhancement of retrieval and access. This technique is developed through precoordination, in that the cataloguer consciously creates links between related records in user-oriented ways in order to maintain different kinds of relationships. Connecting related entities directly, hypertext links remove the burden of a further search (i.e., having to return to an index and entering a new query) which may still fail to yield the desired results. Examples of such applications are: the University of Toronto catalogue, the University of California catalogue (MELVYL), the Library and Information Services of Western Australia (LISWA), HyperLynx, GoPAC (from DataTrek, Australia), OhioLink, and the Prototype Catalogue of Super Records.

As demonstrated in the Catalogue of Super Records, data elements in bibliographic records can provide links to a variety of sources, such as related records (for other works by the same author, other expressions, editions, manifestations, versions of the same work, other works about the same subject, other publications by the same publisher, etc.), name authority records (information about other forms of the author's name, author's affiliation, and field of expertise), subject authority records (related terms, broader terms, narrower terms, etc.), holdings and status information, reviews in electronic format, and full text and/or virtual copies available. For example, a link can be provided from the name of the author to the authority record for that author, to his/her other works, or to his/her homepage available on the World Wide Web. Another example: a link from the name of the publisher in the imprint area can be provided to the publisher's homepage, which provides information about other publications by that publisher. In a hypertext bibliographic record, notes will have a more important role in providing access to related documents, such as other versions, editions, or manifestations of a work. In a hypertext catalogue record added entries can act as additional linking devices.

AACR should take into consideration the complex structure of the multilevel bibliographic record and the various implications which new linking mechanisms, such as hypertext linking, have for cataloguing principles and rules.

In the following sections some of the basic principles of *AACR2* which relate to the structure of the catalogue will be reexamined in terms of their relevance to the online environment.

2.4 The concept of main entry

Like its predecessors, *AACR2* distinguishes between main and added entries. However, with the advent of computerised catalogues, the value of the main entry concept, which developed in the context of book and card catalogues, has been questioned, but no satisfactory and practical solution has emerged as to how its functions can be otherwise fulfilled.[17]

As is stated, a major justification for the concept often lies in its collocating function, in bringing together both different editions of a work and the works of an author. As a collocating device, the concept of main entry has been retained not only in multiple-entry card catalogues but also with the same justification in automated catalogues. In terms of collocation, main entry has two specific functions: (1) assembling and displaying works by an author, and (2) assembling and displaying different editions of a work. The following section is an analysis of the main entry concept in terms of its functions in an online environment to see what influences the different capabilities may have on this principle. The focus of this section is only on main entries for personal names.

2.4.1 Online search/retrieval/display and the concept of main entry

Keyword searching

Keyword searching on names will retrieve only those records that match the term(s) keyed in by the searcher, whether the term appears in main entries, added entries, or any other significant word indexed from the text of the record. Keyword searching capability cannot replace the main entry in terms of its collocating function. It can, however, facilitate the collocating function: once access to one or more specific items has been provided through keywords, the searcher can extend the search by keying the exact form of the author heading or the uniform title found on the retrieved record(s) to search for related editions with the same terms only. With hypertext links, as demonstrated in the University of Toronto catalogue, the University of California catalogue (MELVYL), the Library and Information Services of Western Australia (LISWA), HyperLynx, GoPAC (from DataTrek, Australia), OhioLink, and the Prototype Catalogue of Super Records), any keyword in the bibliographic record can potentially be a link to related records which have similar information.

Boolean searching

Boolean search is another capability for bringing together different editions of a work. This can be done by keying in two or more data elements, such as the author heading and the title proper or the uniform title, and by using the "AND" operator. Since the titles proper of different editions of a work may vary, titles proper in conjunction with author heading cannot be a useful element for the collocating function. The "author/title" search key, which many systems provide, is an implicit Boolean search which has the same limitation. Instead, a Boolean search on the author uniform heading and the uniform title, including relevant qualifiers, can achieve the collocating function more effectively. As will be discussed later, this approach is another justification for the main entry concept in a new form and structure.

Index browsing

In browsing, for example, the author index will display together all the works by an author irrespective of his/her type of contribution (e.g., primary author, joint author, editor, compiler). It can be seen that, even with browsing capability, a useful collocation of different expressions and manifestations of a work is not possible with the present structure of entries. Browsable indexes can help solve the collocation problem if the author and the title indexes are precoordinated for meaningful arrangement and display of related entities. Also, for the uniform citation and display of entries in the browsable author index, we need to identify the primary author. To link works, however, the primary author's name should be in a uniform heading. This is again another justification for the concept of main entry in an online environment.

Online display and the concept of main entry

The display format in online catalogues is independent of the storage format. Therefore, when a number of records are displayed (particularly in brief displays) in response to a query, the retrieved titles need to be displayed in conjunction with a second primary identifier such as the author heading. Otherwise, not only is the identification of the retrieved items not complete, but different works by an author are also not distinguished and assembled. This primary element is necessary in online displays of related works. Online displays, for instance default listings in brief displays,[18] require that, in addition to titles proper, another principal element must be displayed. The following example may help to make this idea clearer:

As the convention now exists in many OPACs, when a work is entered under title or under a corporate heading with an added entry for editor or compiler, this person's name would still need to be displayed in conjunction with the title proper in the brief display to uniquely identify the work and to differentiate between works with identical titles. From another perspective, that of the catalogue user who does not understand what main entry is, an editor or a compiler may seem to be the primary identifier or access point which should be displayed in conjunction with the title in brief displays and in single entry listings.

2.4.2 Networks, access to other catalogues, and the concept of main entry

In shared cataloguing systems and networked environments it is important that the same entity be catalogued under the same uniform entry. This is essential for different operations such as searching, checking duplicate records, copy cataloguing, adding new holdings, etc. A work and also different editions and manifestations of a given work should be presented under the same entry. Otherwise, different problems may arise for different users: inconsistencies between catalogues and difficulties in the identification of the relationship of different instances of a work, all leading to confusion for the cataloguer, reference librarian, and the end user. A uniform main entry heading, with variants appropriately linked, avoids such problems in networked environments.

2.4.3 Conclusion

As a concept, the main entry relates rather to the nature of relationships between entities (authors to their works or works to their expressions and manifestations) than to the physical medium through which those entities are to be described. Many works, particularly in the fields of literature, philosophy, religions, law, and music, require such a uniform construct for identification and collocation. Even if technology provides catalogues with sophisticated devices, such as hypertext facility, to link two or more related entities to one another, it does not help the user if catalogues do not show him/her the nature of these relationships. Without such a concept the catalogue, whether manual or computerised, loses its integrity and usefulness. It can be concluded that online catalogues still need a construct to carry out some specific functions which cannot be fulfilled thoroughly through other devices. Of great concern is the fact that the main entry concept is not meant to be a single function element but rather a concept that is essential to fulfil several functions. If the concept is to be retained in the future *AACR,* it is therefore in need of a redefinition that will focus on its rationale and multiple functions: main entry is a uniform construct for the naming and identifying of works and also for the useful collocation and arrangement/display of the different expressions and manifestations of a work.

In addition to the identification of the primary author, the concept of a uniform mode of identification, citation, and collocation, as defined above, is dependent on two key identifying elements which are emphasised in *AACR2:* uniform titles for works and uniform headings for authors.

2.5 Uniform headings for titles

Any work can potentially be produced in different expressions (e.g., editions, translations) and/or in a variety of physical formats. This concept is intrinsic to the bibliographic universe and its control has been an essential principle for catalogues. In this context, the name of the work, i.e., the "uniform title," has been devised in descriptive cataloguing to collocate different editions and manifestations of a work. *AACR2R* has devoted a full chapter to this concept; however, the use of uniform titles is optional in this code.

The functions of uniform titles are: (1) to standardise the original title of a work, (2) to standardise the form of the main entry heading for anonymous works, (3) to group together all editions and manifestations of a work under one particular title, and (4) to identify the relationships between an edition and a work. Smiraglia[19] and Vellucci[20] consider an additional function, i.e., a differentiating role, for uniform titles. In the 1993 amendments to *AACR2R,* a new provision for uniform titles has been added to the functions of the uniform title: "for differentiating between two or more works published under identical titles proper" (rule 25.1A). The rationale for the principle of uniform titles, however, rests mainly with two functions: (1) the uniform identification of a work and (2) the assembling of entities derived from or related to the same work. From a different point of view, uniform titles support at least four types of bibliographic relationship: equivalence, derivative, whole-part, and sequential relationships.[21]

In the following section, the rationale and the functions of uniform titles will be examined in the context of the online environment. The aim is to see whether the structure and content of uniform titles, as formulated in *AACR2,* are appropriate for the catalogue's functions and are compatible with the different capabilities of online catalogues.

2.5.1 Online search/retrieval/display and the concept of uniform titles

A major problem in searching online catalogues is that in response to a query through the name of works, such as *Hamlet,* Bible, or an anonymous classic like the *Arabian Nights,* the searcher is presented with too many records to conveniently scan. This is an indication that in their present state uniform titles are not suitable for useful retrieval and display. In other words, uniform titles as access points or collocating elements are not useful for the effective retrieval and collocation of different expressions and manifestations of a work, and they should be reformulated for such functions in accordance with the capabilities of online catalogues. Without the uniform title associated with the main entry heading, one can see that different editions of the same work are scattered among the retrieved records for other works by the same author. This problem is highlighted in online catalogues: they may need a number of screens to list all retrieved items and the searcher may have to spend considerable time to identify the relationship of a sought item to a work and find what he/she is searching for.

While the occurrence of editions of the same work with different titles and different works with similar titles increases in large catalogues and union databases, the concept of uniform titles can help control this problem. With regard to the catalogue's collocating function, uniform titles can play a more important role in the online catalogue. While uniform titles alone increase the search results (i.e., recall), the addition of other data elements (i.e., qualifiers), such as version (i.e., the physical format), language, date, and part of the work, to the uniform title will narrow down the search results and will increase precision. *AACR2* can prescribe additional qualifiers which would be functional in the meaningful retrieval and collocation of related entities.

In an electronic environment with hypertext facility, uniform titles are needed to provide links between different occurrences of a work and to collocate and display, in a meaningful order, all the available expressions and manifestations of a given work, as has been demonstrated in the Prototype Catalogue of Super Records. Through the uniform title approach in super records, separate records for different versions of a work are grouped and linked to one another. As can be seen, since a uniform title approach is used as a uniform identifier and a collocating device wherever a work has more than one edition and/or manifestation in the catalogue, the concept of multilevel records, in general, reinforces the principle of uniform titles.[22] In hypertext catalogues, a browsable uniform-title index or uniform titles authority file with the name of the author(s) of each work could provide easy access to works.

2.5.2 Conclusion

For the same reasons that a concept equivalent to the main entry will be needed in an online catalogue, the concept of uniform titles will remain a valid principle in the new environment. Even with the different search/retrieval/display capabilities of the online catalogue, there is still a need for a standardised form of the title of a work serving to identify, collocate, and display different expressions and manifestations of that work. These capabilities can also help to simplify and make the application of the concept in online catalogues more understandable. With hypertext linking in place, uniform titles in bibliographic records for items can directly point to the "work" level in which links are provided to categories of expressions and manifestations. Nevertheless, to be useful for searching, retrieval, and display in online catalogues, a restructuring of the content and structure of uniform titles is essential. Another essential component of online catalogues would be a uniform-title index or uniform titles authority file, whether in the MARC format or a hypertext environment. A possible solution is to establish a uniform title authority file linked to bibliographic records. Also, a uniform-title index is useful for easy access to different expressions and manifestations of a work available in a catalogue. This is what *AACR2* should address as a part of its provisions for the structure of the catalogue.

2.6 Uniform headings for persons

Another principle that is essential to the fulfilment of the collocating function and for the integrity of the catalogue is a uniform heading for each person.[23] As will be discussed in the following paragraphs, an examination of this principle in light of different capabilities of online catalogues reveals that the concept is still valid in the online environment but that the new technology may influence the content and form of name headings, as well as the scope and extent to which it would be possible to achieve collaboration in their standardisation.

2.6.1 Online search/retrieval/display and the principle of uniform headings

Keyword searching

Keyword searching facilitates the finding function of the catalogue through the form of an author's name that appears on the title page or in information sources, i.e., the form which is usually familiar to both the book world and the searcher. However, with keyword searching it is only possible to search names under the form in which they have been recorded in the bibliographic record. Keywords, not being subject to authority control, naturally do not always collocate all the works by or about an author if there are variant forms of name. However, keyword searching facilitates the collocation of an author's works: once access is made to a record through any form of the name, it is possible to assemble works by or about a particular author through a further search on the uniform author heading.

Truncation

With right-hand truncation, the online catalogue is able to retrieve those names which begin with the characters defined by the searcher. In other words, names must be entered uniformly, at least for the few beginning characters, to retrieve all the works by a given author. Obviously, however, truncation also allows the searcher to retrieve records which are not relevant to his/her needs. Therefore, the more complete the input heading is, the more chance there will be for retrieval precision. The closer we can get to "natural" forms of names, the more efficiently successful will our catalogue searches be.

Authority control systems

In an online catalogue utilising name authority files, access to the works of a given author by variant forms of the name can be as effective as access by the uniform or preferred heading. The distinction between the established form of a name and any cross-reference to it is invisible to the searcher. This apparent ease of consultation may render catalogue users (and library administrators) unaware of the professional effort which goes into collocating the various works by and about an author. In fact, more emphasis must be placed on this in the online environment than with previous forms of catalogue.

Adherence to the principle of uniform heading is a means of maintaining the one-to-many relationship (i.e., one name to many works) in bibliographic databases and, thus, to achieve the collocation of all works available by a given author in the catalogue. Even in authority control systems there is still a need to establish one form of a person's name as the uniform heading and others as references. In fact, uniform headings are still considered to be an important principle in authority work.

Index browsing

In systems allowing the browsing of name indexes, it is necessary, in general, that any name be presented in a uniform manner in the list to avoid confusion. It is also necessary that works by an author be retrieved through and assembled under a single form of name in browsable author-title indexes. More effective display could result from uniform indexing in browsable indexes. In systems (such as the Bradford OPAC) which do not repeat the main heading on every line in brief displays, uniform headings are essential. The browsing capability thus reinforces the need for the principle of uniform headings.

Online displays and the principle of uniform headings

With regard to differences in the physical forms of the manual catalogue and the online catalogue, the very rigid ideal in the card catalogue of assembling *in one place* all the works a library has by a given author has shifted, in the online catalogue, to the ideal of the system's ability to retrieve all the works of an author through any searched form of his/her name and to display them together under one uniform heading for the author. Under whatever form of name the works by a given author have been searched, the default listing of those works, particularly in brief displays, requires that the name of the author be presented in a uniform manner. Similarly, in catalogues with a hypertext interface, links can be provided from any form of a name to the records, but the name should appear under a uniform heading when records are displayed; otherwise, the catalogue may lose its integrity (consistency?) and the searcher may think that the works displayed are by different authors.

2.6.2 Networks, global access to catalogues, and the concept of uniform headings

The communication of bibliographic records for cataloguing purposes, reference services, interlibrary loan, and document delivery services depends to a large extent on the uniformity of headings. An important factor concerning the value of uniform headings is the ever-increasing use of bibliographic utilities, such as OCLC and RLIN, and national bibliographic agencies, such as Library of Congress. Most libraries attempt to be consistent with the Library of Congress for headings and contribute to the Name Authority Cooperative Project (NACO) initiated by that library.

In searching the different catalogues accessible in a network, the patron, the technical services librarian, and the reference librarian usually expect to find the works of a given author under one form of heading. Except for differences in user interfaces, a first requirement is to conform to the concept of uniform headings at the national level. Links to national online name authority files, such as the Library of Congress Name Authority File (LCNAF), would be a most desirable answer to differences in authors' names and can provide consistent access to catalogues and other bibliographic lists.

2.6.3 Availability of different types of bibliographic databases

A major problem in the online environment is that there are many different types of bibliographic databases and a wide variety of users. A difficulty in searching different databases is that, while there is a uniform approach in library cataloguing in relation to uniform headings, other communities such as the book trade and A&I services are less concerned with this principle, so that in many bibliographic databases the same person may have been entered under a variety of unlinked names.

2.6.4 Conclusion

It can be said that, although the very rigid ideal of uniform headings in Anglo-American cataloguing codes has undergone gradual modification, the principle is still valid and its maintenance can secure the integrity of catalogues particularly in shared cataloguing systems, union databases, and network environments at the national level. Although name authority systems have made it possible to retrieve all the works of a given author through a one-step search in the catalogue, the necessity for collocation and particularly for display of an author's works together requires that one form of name be chosen as the uniform heading.

In summary, while it seems that there may be no solution to the problem of cultural differences giving rise to divergent forms of name heading between different communities, conformity with national name authority files should gradually bring about more standardisation of catalogue headings. This process will naturally be greatly assisted when the national name authorities are available online. This would bring more uniformity in the different environments and would make searching and retrieval of works by a given author easier in various files in the online environment. It would be desirable if the future *AACR*, therefore, provides rules for the construction of name headings for national name authority files extending beyond the library community to other bibliographical communities.

2.7 Content and form of name headings in an online environment

As emphasised in the Paris Principles, the content and form of names in headings, as well as the principle of uniform headings, should be agreed upon nationally and, to some extent, internationally. Over the last one hundred years the Anglo-American cataloguing codes have formulated necessary rules concerning the form of personal and corporate headings.

In the following sections the content and form of personal and corporate headings will be reexamined in light of the searching/retrieval/display capabilities of computerised catalogues and with respect to searchers' expectations of an integrated online environment.

2.7.1 Content and form of personal name headings

According to the general rule (rule 22.1), the name by which a person is commonly known should be chosen as the basis for the heading for that person.

The form of a name is an important factor in searching and retrieval, particularly in online systems in which the searcher has to key in the name as a search string. Research has shown that users often enter personal names in a form and sequence different from those prescribed for *AACR2*.[24] A rather different approach from that adopted in a manual environment is possible, in that searches under the names of authors no longer need to be phrased in the exact form and order of the author's name headings in online catalogues, such as Okapi (Online Keyboard Access to Public Information, developed at the Polytechnic of Central London), MIRLYN (Michigan Research Library's Network, the University of Michigan's Online Public Catalog), and SULIRS (Syracuse University Libraries Information Retrieval System). Cross-references and/or keyword access offer the possibility of entering the search names in any order. Keyword searching also reduces the need for complete "surname+initials+(full forenames)+dates" headings as in *AACR2R*.[25] Wajenberg claims that, with keyword searching, the inversion of surnames and rules for the choice of entry element in compound surnames and names with prefixes become unnecessary.[26] He points out that the most useful form of name is the fullest form. The German code (RAK), which is being revised for online catalogues, takes a similar approach and strongly rejects any substantial reduction in personal name entries.[27]

As will be noted later in this section, there are other factors, such as the need for default listings of the works of an author and the needs of the book world, citation traditions, and international exchange of bibliographic data, which require the standard order of "surname, forename" in full form for personal headings. There is at present no consensus on the content and form of headings among the different creators of bibliographic records. There are, however, to some extent similarities between library cataloguing and the book world: both tend to use the best-known form of name with library cataloguing more inclined to use the complete form.

Truncation of headings, especially automatic right-hand truncation, can help retrieve works by authors whose complete heading (i.e., surname, forename, or initials) is not familiar to the searcher. Variations in the fullness of forenames seem unimportant in systems with a truncation capability. Using "Price, H. H." and "Grossman, Allen R." as examples, Arlene Taylor proposes that an online catalogue with keyword searching of headings and automatic right-hand truncation needs rather different rules for the formulation of headings and references.[28] It should be noted, however, that searching names through truncation may retrieve too many records to scan easily.

Another problem with personal name headings is that initials often cause searching and retrieval problems in online catalogues. According to Drabenstott and Weller, the middle names or initials users include in their queries for personal names are sometimes counterproductive in helping them find the heading used in the catalogue.[29]

2.7.1.1 Differentiation between identical names

Differentiation between identical names is an important requirement, particularly for large files and shared databases in which the frequency of such headings increases as files grow or merge.

The use of dates of birth and death, as in *AACR,* may not always be particularly useful to searchers, who might have no idea of when a particular author was born. Differentiation of author by discipline can be a more useful approach. The field of expertise at least lets the searchers guess which author they want to look at.

Another element which can help in the consistent association of a person with a given work is his/her role in the creation/production of the work. This approach, i.e., using descriptors, has been practiced by a number of A&I services for a relatively long time. It would help users if such differentiation were to become a principle associated with assigning name entries. *AACR* should address this issue in association with the principle of authorship.

2.7.2 Content and form of headings for corporate bodies

The issue of corporate headings was one of the problems on which there was considerable debate at the Paris Conference. Decisions made have not all proved to be entirely workable. Even today different national codes have different approaches toward the form of corporate headings. In terms of names of jurisdictions forming the entry word of some government headings, *AACR2R* uses the English language form, while in the RAK a name in the official language of the country is preferred.[30]

Searching, retrieval, and display of corporate names in online systems are often frustrating to the user. Many of the problems concerning the searching of corporate bodies' publications relate to the content and form of headings for these bodies.[31] *AACR2* prescribes that, in general, corporate bodies should be entered under the name by which they are commonly identified, except when other rules provide for entering them under the name of a higher or related body or under the name of a government (rule 24.1). Some of the problems concerning the searching, retrieval, and display of corporate headings in online systems are:

1) It is particularly difficult to search under the exact form of corporate headings in online catalogues because the user has to key in the search string. How much of the heading should be keyed in by the searcher to initiate the search, since corporate names are usually long, often similar to one another, and appear in different forms, such as acronyms, initials, and subordinations (e.g., World Health Organization, WHO or W.H.O.)?

2) In some cases, headings for subordinate bodies associated with the same parent body do not follow a uniform approach. While the "World Health Organization" appears as the heading for this body, a number of subordinate bodies incorporating the acronym "WHO" are treated as headings in the catalogue; for example, "WHO Collaborating Centre on Environmental Pollution Control," "WHO Commission on Health and Environment," "WHO Expert Group on Pesticide Residues." The same problem exists with the "Food and Agriculture Organization of the United Nations" and some of its subordinate bodies beginning with "FAO."

3) Entering corporate bodies under the name of the higher body would often cause inconvenience for the searcher, especially in large catalogues and shared systems. The use of indirect corporate headings can sometimes appear meaningless to catalogue users. Names "can be considerably distorted because of rearrangement of the elements of the name and, in many codes, by translating the name of the jurisdiction."[32]

4) The addition of a geographic name to the beginning of headings for corporate bodies often does not make sense in the online environment. Exact searching and truncation on headings beginning with the name of a jurisdiction or geographic name often result in too many hits. Headings like "Australia. Australian Parliamentary Observer Group," "Canada. Canadian High Commission," and "Canada. Canadian Armed Forces," which are problematic for searching, could be more straightforward if "Australia" and "Canada" were omitted from the heading.

5) In most cases truncation on corporate headings does not make sense because of the similarity in the first few words at the beginning of such names, particularly when corporate

bodies are entered under a higher or government body or heading beginning with geographic names. Also in brief displays, because of screen limitation, the name of the parent body alone may fill the allotted space. A possible approach, which depends on the software used, is to avoid repeating the name of parent body but to display the name of subordinate bodies for better differentiation.

6) Clustering of all the publications of different departments and divisions of a corporate body is not usually sought by searchers. Also, it does not make sense in brief displays where, because of screen limitation, only the first few elements of the heading are displayed, thus obscuring the name of the actual issuing body. Consider, for example, how frustrating the retrieval of publications of different subordinate bodies of the United Nations would be in an online catalogue.

2.7.3 Conclusion

It can be concluded that direct headings, i.e., subordinate bodies under their own heading, would lessen these problems, provided that the heading for the subordinate body is self-sufficient. There are a number of factors that also justify this:

- direct headings form a shorter string and are more suitable for online displays, especially for brief displays;
- most searchers are usually looking for the publications of a given subordinate body and are not interested in the parent body;[33]
- truncation on direct headings (name of subordinate bodies) is more useful than on indirect headings (name of parent bodies);
- alternative approaches could be provided by means of authority control. As with advanced name authority files linked to the bibliographic file, it is possible to search names in different forms; considerations should also be given to any form which may be looked under by catalogue searchers;
- the addition of geographic names or a general designation to corporate headings for their further identification or differentiation should be re-examined with regard to the difficulties of searching such names. The present approach in *AACR2* rule 24.4, in that a general designation or a geographic name is added in parenthesis to the corporate heading for further identification or differentiation, should be followed in other cases.

In general, while a fuller form of personal names seems more useful in the online environment, corporate names need a simpler approach in that, for example, direct headings for subordinate bodies are more responsive to the search/retrieval/display capabilities of online catalogues. Nevertheless, the problems of corporate headings in online catalogues such as the form and structure (e.g., official name versus name most frequently used; most frequently used versus conventional or modified name; language; transliteration; punctuation and display problems) require further research.[34]

2.8 Principles for online display of bibliographic information

Since cataloguing codes basically deal with providing description of and access to bibliographic entities, it is reasonable that they should also give guidance for data representation and identification, i.e., record displays and arrangement. Description and access are most effective if the information on the catalogue record is clear, useful, and adequate for different users. This is in line with the objectives of the catalogue, in that the catalogue should help in the better identification of works/items.[35] While one of the major differences of online catalogues from card catalogues is their extensive ability for displaying bibliographic information in a variety of formats, *AACR2* does not provide any guidelines for online displays, and many problems in online display stem from the treatment of its rules. Also, many problems in online display could be attributed to lengthy headings prescribed in the code.

2.8.1 Problems in online displays

The ways in which bibliographic information is displayed online have often been criticised by cataloguers. One of the difficulties faced by the user of online catalogues lies in the wide variations in possible format. This is largely due to the fact that, unlike card catalogues which had a fixed storage/display format and usually presented the same level of information, online catalogues differ from one another both in display formats and in the levels of information displayed. These variations may often confuse the user, particularly when moving from one catalogue to another, for example in searching different remote catalogues through the Internet.

A common problem in online displays is related to the brief display, where the information is often the one-line record, which is inadequate or confusing for identifying items. For example, in response to a query for a voluminous work by a given author (e.g., *Hamlet* by Shakespeare), the brief display may show the author heading and the title repeated on every line, the only element being the date of publication. This sort of brief display does not make sense to the user. To increase clarity and save space, it is desirable to include the author statement (main entry heading) once only, where it applies to multiple retrieved records. The display of long corporate bodies also has implications for online catalogues, especially for brief displays: not only may the heading displayed not be distinct enough to identify the body conclusively, but also the title probably cannot be displayed completely.

Library materials are different in terms of their nature and the data elements necessary for their description and access. The case of serials is a notable one: the author/title/publication/date approach generally useful for monographs is not applicable to serials; they are rarely entered under author, and the date of first publication can often be more confusing than helpful.[36]

2.8.2 Conclusion

For the useful display of bibliographic information at national and international levels, *AACR2* should develop guidelines for the minimum requirements for bibliographic displays at different levels, similar to those already provided for levels of cataloguing, but in greater detail. A more international approach toward online displays would be useful, since catalogues from many countries with different languages and scripts are increasingly accessible through the Internet. Online display of bibliographic information should take into account the potential retrieval of records by a variety of remote users. The ISBD, if reexamined thoroughly with regard to the above-mentioned problems, could offer a solution to some of the questions of bibliographic displays in an online network environment. The identification of appropriate headings and other data elements for online displays needs to be considered with respect to the capabilities as well as to the limitations of the online catalogue. In this respect, access points or headings need to be complete and, if necessary, provided with qualifiers. It is essential that the user should be able to interpret the information on retrieved records; for example, the relationship of any data element to the record should be displayed in a clear way that will be useful to the searcher.

In order to identify what data elements are needed for display, consideration should be given to the different functions of the catalogue. A major question in this respect is: which functions are to be considered important for each display level? For example, should the brief display fulfil the identifying as well as the collocating function, and how far? Further, the nature of the relationship between two elements, e.g., authors and titles, should be clear at each display level.

The principles and rules for display should determine for each level what data elements need to be displayed and which functions are expected to be fulfilled. For example, at the first level when more than one record is retrieved in response to a query, the name of the principal author, truncated title, and the date of publication do not provide enough information to users to enable them to determine the relevance of the item. Cataloguing principles, and particularly cataloguing codes, should indicate other useful information such as the edition statement, the name of at least another joint author or contributor, and the format of the item. In summary, all the above-mentioned considerations emphasise the need for a formulation of relevant principles for online display, a concept that is essential to the integrity and usefulness of online catalogues.

3. Summary and Conclusions

This paper is aimed at reexamining the principles of *AACR2* in light of the different characteristics of the catalogue production technology. The matching of some of the basic *AACR2* principles against individual search/retrieval/display capabilities of the online catalogue revealed that, while a number of fundamental principles, such as the main entry, uniform titles, and uniform headings, remain valid in the online environment, current principles are not entirely adequate for online search/retrieval/display requirements. There is a need for additional principles so as to secure more effectiveness in the searching, retrieval, and display of bibliographic data, e.g., concerning the basic unit of description, bibliographic relationships, and online display of bibliographic data.

The following conclusions are derived from the examination of a number of *AACR2* principles carried out in the light of the various capabilities of the online environment.

3.1 Functions of the catalogue

Conceptually, the objectives and functions of the catalogue are independent of its physical form and arrangement. Technology can, however, influence the way in which these functions are carried out: the more developments there are in the technology of catalogue construction and in the online environment, the more possibilities there are of achieving those objectives and functions.

Due to the wide and varied use of bibliographic records in the online environment, the scope of catalogue functions should be expanded in *AACR* to encompass additional functions. The two basic functions (i.e., the finding function and the collocating function) remain valid, but the catalogue also can serve to further identify entities, to choose one item over similar items, to locate items and copies of items, and to maintain databases in terms of record updating. The relating (i.e., collocating) function is of particular importance in the online environment with hypertext facility.

3.2 The basis for description and the structure of the catalogue

In terms of the basis for description, *AACR* should consider all the different functions of the catalogue and should take a hybrid approach, in that both the work and the physical item should be taken into account. The multilevel record structure, as demonstrated in the Prototype Catalogue of Super Records, can incorporate this hybrid approach without the need for radical changes to the MARC bibliographic format. To avoid online retrieval problems for works appearing in different editions and manifestations, as well as for a more useful collocation and display of such works, the concept of super records for works could be applied, particularly in those catalogues which consider the collocating function as being equally important to other functions. To achieve this, principles are needed concerning the structure of super records, categorisation of entities in the bibliographic hierarchy, the data elements associated with the entity at each level, particularly for uniform titles, and also principles for establishing and maintaining bibliographic relationships.

AACR should provide guidelines for the construction of different files (e.g., bibliographic, authority, and holdings and also the links between them) and also for the indexing of different fields and subfields concerning access to required elements in the record. The principles should also suit the structure of a hybrid system including both MARC records for access to items and super records for providing a multilevel approach to works, their expressions, and manifestations. In such a catalogue, different indexes are needed for both string searching and browsing. A possible approach would be to provide guidelines for the construction of (hypertext) browsable indexes for names (personal and corporate) and titles (titles proper, uniform titles, and series). It is also useful to provide name authority files (like those offered by SIRSI and PALS systems[37]) and a uniform-title authority file for searching and browsing.

3.3 The concept of main entry

Rather than being the locus of complete information for the bibliographic record or the primary access point, main entry is an important concept that maintains some basic functions of the catalogue—that of identifying and collocating, in a uniform way, different expressions and manifestations of a work. In other words, if a major function of the catalogue is to identify and collocate works as well as their editions and manifestations, there is a need for a concept such as main entry. Main entry is particularly needed in the online environment for the useful retrieval, display, and arrangement of search results. Unless we devise new mechanisms for the uniform identification and collocation of the different manifestations and editions of a work, it would be unwise to abandon the concept of main entry.

Nevertheless, in order to delineate the concept more clearly and to avoid confusion as to its functions, main entry is in need of redefinition. The new functional definition should address the validity of the concept in terms of its various functions, irrespective of the catalogue's physical environment.

3.4 The concept of uniform titles

Similar to the concept of main entry, uniform titles are needed in online catalogues to perform some basic functions, such as providing links between different expressions and manifestations of a work and to distinguish among works with identical titles proper. Because of present problems in the online retrieval of the various expressions and manifestations of works, a concept such as a standardised form of the title of a work can serve to identify and collocate them. In online catalogues (particularly with hypertext facility) the content and structure of uniform titles need to be simplified in order to avoid online retrieval problems. *AACR* should prescribe more natural qualifiers which would be functional in the useful retrieval and collocation of related entities.

3.5 The principle of uniform headings

It is difficult to maintain the integrity of the catalogue and to fulfil its collocating function without maintaining the principle of uniform headings. Uniformity of headings for authors is especially important in network environments, where different catalogues and other bibliographic databases are accessible to the user through the same terminal. The principle is also of particular significance in shared cataloguing systems and union databases. Library cataloguing, book trade bibliographic databases, and A&I services should at least be consistent or compatible in certain areas such as uniform headings. In effect, standardisation or compatibility in the form of headings, which has long been recognised as a highly desirable requirement for universal bibliographical control (UBC), becomes more critical in the global online environment.

3.6 Content and form of name headings

In terms of the form of personal and corporate name headings for effective searching, retrieval, and display, online catalogues need a simpler approach. The form of headings needs to be reconsidered in terms of its suitability for different searching patterns (exact as well as keyword searching) and for display. But searching under single letters, such as initials, is still a technical problem for many library systems. For corporate bodies, direct headings are usually more responsive to online search/retrieval/displays.

A new comprehensive study like the one carried out by Verona in 1975 is needed to address problems of corporate headings, this time, however, with regard to the different capabilities and limitations of the online environment, especially when remote access is available to a variety of collections in different languages.

Cataloguing concepts are derived mainly from elements that represent the nature of bibliographic entities. In general, it can be concluded that there is not such a close relationship between the conceptual foundations of *AACR* and the technology of catalogue construction. Nevertheless, just as the physical limitations of paper or card technologies imposed some practices, such as the "rule of three" limiting the number of access points, the search/retrieval/display capabilities of online catalogues require that some principles and rules should be modified to take advantage of the new technology whereby computers are able to manipulate, modify, and organise or reorganise bibliographic data far more effectively than was possible in the manual environment.

Notes

1. For a full review of the literature on *AACR2* and the online environment see Rahmatollah Fattahi, "Anglo-American Cataloguing Rules: A Literature Review," *Cataloging & Classification Quarterly* 20, no. 2 (1995): 25-50. Also the relevance of cataloguing principles and rules to the online environment has been addressed elsewhere; see Rahmatalloh Fattahi, "The Relevance of Cataloguing Principles to the Online Environment: An Historical and Analytical Study" (Ph.D. diss., University of New South Wales, Sydney, 1996), also available online at: http://wilma.silas.unsw.edu.au/students/rfattahi/thes1.htm.

2. Seymour Lubetzky, *Code of Cataloging Rules: Author and Title Entry: An Unfinished Draft* (Chicago: American Library Association, 1960).

3. Patrick Wilson, "The Second Objective," in *The Conceptual Foundations of Descriptive Cataloging,* ed. Elaine Svenonius (New York: Academic Press, 1989), 5-16.

4. Lorcan Dempsey, "Users' Requirements of Bibliographic Records: Publishers, Booksellers, Librarians," *ASLIB Proceedings* 42, no. 2 (1990): 61-69.

5. F. H. Ayres, "Duplicates and Other Manifestations: A New Approach to the Presentation of Bibliographic Information," *Journal of Librarianship* 22, no. 4 (July 1990): 236-51.

6. A search in the University of New South Wales OPAC (dated 21/3/1996) under the exact title "Hamlet" retrieved 108 records of which 10 records had no relationship to Shakespeare's *Hamlet* (see below). Another search under "Shakespeare" and "Hamlet" in cross-index keyword resulted in 148 records. A further search under the title keyword "Hamlet" retrieved 170 records of which many records had no relationship to Shakespeare's *Hamlet*. Finally, a subject search under "Shakespeare, William. Hamlet" resulted in a large number of records. A search under "Hamlet" in the uniform title index in University of California's MELVYL resulted in 282 records:

Type of search	*Number of matches*
Exact title search	108
Cross index keyword search	148
Title keyword search	170
Subject search	100

   (Visit also *Demonstration of OPAC Designs* (http://wilma.silas.unsw.edu.au/students/rfattahi/demo.htm) for the results of the same search in different online catalogues.

7. IFLA Study Group on the Functional Requirements of Bibliographic Records, *Functional Requirements for Bibliographic Records: Draft Report for World-Wide Review* (Frankfurt am Main: IFLA Universal Bibliographic Control and International MARC Programme, 1996).

8. *Anglo-American Cataloguing Rules, Second Edition, 1988 Revision,* prepared under the direction of the Joint Steering Committee for the Revision of AACR, ed. Michael Gorman and Paul W. Winkler (Ottawa: Canadian Library Association; London: Library Association Publishing; Chicago: American Library Association, 1988), 305.

9. It should be noted that LC has virtually repealed the force of *AACR2R* 1.11 as well parts of chapter 11 dealing with microform reproductions.

10. Crystal Graham, "What's Wrong with *AACR2:* A Serial Perspective" (1995), available at: http://tpot.ucsd.edu/cataloging.Crystal/Crystal.html.

11. Patrick Wilson, "The Second Objective."

12. Michael Heaney, "Object-Oriented Cataloging," *Information Technology and Libraries* 14, no. 3 (September 1995): 135-53.

13. F. H. Ayres, L. P. S. Nielsen, and M. J. Ridley, "Bibliographic Management: A New Approach Using the Manifestation Concept and the Bradford OPAC," *Cataloging & Classification Quarterly* 22, no. 1 (1996): 3-28.

14. Rahmatollah Fattahi, "Super Records: An Approach Towards the Description of Works Appearing in Various Manifestations," *Library Review* 45, no. 4 (1996): 19-29.

15. This depends on the ability of the system to point to the relevant index for authors or titles first (e.g., browsable name indexes).

16. Fattahi, "Super Records."

17. Fattahi, "Anglo-American Cataloguing Rules."

18. Default listing is the predefined display of data elements in that a value is automatically assigned by the system if no other value has been specified.

19. Richard P. Smiraglia, *Music Cataloging: The Bibliographic Control of Printed and Recorded Music in Libraries* (Englewood, Colo.: Libraries Unlimited, 1989).

20. Sherry L. Vellucci, "Uniform Titles as Linking Devices," *Cataloging & Classification Quarterly* 12, no. 1 (1990): 35-62.

21. Barbara B. Tillett, "Bibliographic Relationships: Toward a Conceptual Structure of Bibliographic Information Used in Cataloging" (Ph.D. diss., University of California, Los Angeles, 1987), microform.

22. Fattahi, "Super Records."

23. As an example, Chan points to an author (Lauran Paine) whose name has been represented by sixty-five different headings in a catalogue! See Lois Mai Chan, "The Principle of Uniform Headings in Descriptive Cataloging: Ideals and Reality," *Cataloging & Classification Quarterly* 3, no. 4 (1983): 19-35. A search by this researcher in the catalogue of Universiteitbibliotheek Utrecht, Netherlands (accessible at http://pablo.ubu.ruu.nl) revealed that the name of the Persian epic poet, Ferdowsi, has been represented by 13 different headings; thus the catalogue is unable to display together all his works.

24. Karen Markey Drabenstott and Marjorie S. Weller, "Improving Personal-Name Searching in Online Catalogs," *Information Technology and Libraries* 15, no. 3 (September 1996): 137.

25. This treatment is not common to bibliographic databases outside the library environment. For example, the heading: Lawrence, D. H. is more common in the book trade than the heading: Lawrence, David Herbert; whilst the form Lawrence, D. H. (David Herbert) is probably unique to *AACR*.

26. Arnold Wajenberg, "Cataloging for the Third Millennium," in *Origins, Content, and Future of AACR2 Revised,* ed. Richard P. Smiraglia (Chicago: American Library Association, 1992), 105.

27. Monika Münnich, "RAK für Online-Kataloge: ein Sachstandsbericht und ein Ausblick," *Bibliotheksdienst* 29, no. 8 (1995): 1276.

28. Arlene G. Taylor, "Authority Files in Online Catalogs: An Investigation of Their Value," *Cataloging & Classification Quarterly* 4, no. 1 (1984): 11, 13.

29. Drabenstott and Weller, "Improving Personal-Name Searching in Online Catalogs," 136.

30. Gisela Sule, "Bibliographic Standards," in *Bibliographic Access in Europe: First International Conference: The Proceedings of a Conference Organised by the Centre for Bibliographic Management and Held at the University of Bath, 14-17 September 1989,* ed. Lorcan Dempsey (Aldershot: Gower, 1990), 250-51.

31. Little has been written on the form of corporate headings in an online environment. Some of the complications of searching corporate names in online systems have been briefly addressed by Arlene Taylor (Taylor, "Authority Files in Online Catalogs"), Brunt (Rodney M. Brunt, "The Code and the Catalogue: A Return to Compatibility," *Library Review* 41, no. 3 (1992): 21-32),

and more fully by Greig (Eugenie Greig, "Corporate Headings Online: Back to the Future?" in *Il Linguaggio della Biblioteca: Scritti in Onore di Diego Maltese,* ed. Mauro Guerrini (Firenze: Regione Toscana Giunta Regionale, 1995), 385-93). The result of a study by Henty (Margaret Henty, "The User at the Online Catalogue: A Record of Unsuccessful Keyword Searches," *LASIE: Library Automated System and Information Exchange* 17, no. 2 (1986): 47-52) concerning unsuccessful keyword searching indicates that the reasons for the users' search failures are, to some extent, due to the implications of variant forms of corporate names.

32. Greig, "Corporate Headings Online: Back to the Future?" 387.

33. According to Lubetzky, it is reasonable to expect that entry under the subordinate body will facilitate the location of its publications, since they are most frequently cited and looked for directly under the subordinate body's own name; and it will also prevent the congestion of entries under the name of the parent body. He proposes that if the subdivision has a proper and self-sufficient name of its own, it should be entered directly. See Seymour Lubetzky, *Cataloging Rules and Principles: A Critique of ALA Rules for Entry and a Proposed Design for Their Revision* (Washington, D.C.: Library of Congress Processing Department, 1953), 52. Greig points out that indirect headings can often be considerably distorted to users and can be a source of confusion to them. See Greig, "Corporate Headings Online: Back to the Future?" 387-88.

34. It should be noted that the question of record displays and arrangement was in Cutter's rules. In a sense, we would be returning to his broader view.

35. As an example of perversities in online display of bibliographic data, some online catalogues do not display authors' name-only titles under subject headings.

36. Graham, "What's Wrong with *AACR2.*"

37. A demonstration of SIRSI is available at: http://www.sirsi.com/webcattoc.html. A demonstration of PALS is available at: http://bingen.cs.csbsju.edu/pals/hyperpals.html.

Additional References

Aroksaar, Richard. "Online Catalogs: A View from the Works." *Cataloging & Classification Quarterly* 7, no. 1 (1986): 45-54.

Attig, John C. "Descriptive Cataloging Rules and Machine-Readable Record Structure: Some Directions for Parallel Development." In *The Conceptual Foundations of Descriptive Cataloging,* edited by Elaine Svenonius, 135-48. San Diego: Academic Press, 1989.

Ayres, F. H. "The Code, the Catalogue and the Computer: An Assessment of *AACR2.*" *Vine* 32 (February 1980): 3-13.

———. "In Place of *AACR2.*" *Technicalities* 1, no. 9 (April 1981): 3-4.

———. "Main Entry: Lynch Pin or Dodo." *Journal of Librarianship* 10, no. 3 (July 1978): 170-81.

Ayres, F. H., L. P. S. Nielsen, M. J. Ridley, and I. S. Torsun. *The Bradford OPAC: A New Concept in Bibliographic Control.* London: British Library Research and Development Department, 1995.

Bierbaum, Esther G. "A Modest Proposal: No More Main Entry." *American Libraries* 25, no. 1 (January 1994): 81-84.

Brooks, Terrence A., and Esther G. Bierbaum. "Database Management Systems: New Homes for Migrating Bibliographic Records." *Library and Information Science Research* 9, no. 4 (October-December 1987): 327-39.

Carpenter, Michael. "Main Entry." In *The Conceptual Foundations of Descriptive Cataloging,* edited by Elaine Svenonius, 73-96. New York: Academic Press, 1989.

———. "The Narrow, Rugged, Uninteresting Path Finally Becomes Interesting: A Review of Work in Descriptive Cataloging in 1991 with Trail Marks for Further Research." *Library Resources & Technical Services* 36, no. 3 (July 1992): 291-315.

Coral, Lenore. "Indexing and Retrieving Special Materials in Online Catalogues." *International Cataloguing and Bibliographic Control* 21, no. 2 (1992): 29-31.

Dickson, Jean. Letter to the editor. *Journal of the American Society for Information Science* 47, no. 2 (February 1996): 182.

Elrod, J. McRee. "Cataloguer's Role in Catalogue Construction: A Modest Proposal." (e-mail article posted to Autocat<listserv@uvbm.cc.buffalo.edu>, 16 January 1996).

Gorman, Michael. "*AACR2:* Main Themes." In *The Making of a Code: Issues Underlying AACR2,* edited by Doris Hargrett Clack, 41-50. Chicago: American Library Association, 1980.

————. "After *AACR2R:* The Future of the Anglo-American Cataloguing Rules." In *Origins, Content, and Future of AACR2 Revised,* edited by Richard P. Smiraglia, 89-94. Chicago: American Library Association, 1992.

————. "Bibliographic Standardization and Machine Records." In *The Interchange of Bibliographic Information in Machine-Readable Forms,* 86-92. London: The British Library; Library Association, 1975.

————. "Cataloging and the New Technologies." In *The Nature and Future of the Catalog,* edited by Maurice J. Freedman and S. Michael Malinconico, 127-52. Phoenix, Ariz.: Oryx Press, 1979.

Graham, Crystal. "Definition and Scope of Multiple Versions." *Cataloging & Classification Quarterly* 11, no. 2 (1990): 5-32.

Hagler, Ronald. "The Consequences of Integration." In *The Conceptual Foundations of Descriptive Cataloging,* edited by Elaine Svenonius, 197-218. New York: Academic Press, 1989.

International Conference on Cataloguing Principles. *Report of the International Conference on Cataloguing Principles, Paris, 9-18 October 1961.* Edited by A. H. Chaplin and Dorothy Anderson. London: Organising Committee of the ICCP, 1963.

Intner, Sheila. "Taking Another Look at Minimum Level Cataloging." *Technicalities* 14, no. 1 (January 1994): 3-5, 11.

Jeffreys, Alan. "AACR after 1978." In *AACR, DDC, MARC and Friends: The Role of CIG in Bibliographic Control,* edited by J. Byford, Keith V. Trickey, and Susi Woodhouse, 49-60. London: Library Association, 1993.

Jolley, Leonard J. "The Function of the Main Entry in the Alphabetical Catalogue: A Study of the Views Put Forward by Lubetzky and Verona." In *International Conference on Cataloguing Principles, Paris, 9-18th October, 1961; Report,* edited by A. H. Chaplin and Dorothy Anderson, 159-64. London: Organising Committee of the ICCP, 1963.

Kilgour, Frederick G. "Cataloging for a Specific Miniature Catalog." *Journal of the American Society for Information Science* 46, no. 9 (October 1995): 704-06.

————. "Effectiveness of Surname-Title-Word Searches by Scholars." *Journal of the American Society for Information Science* 46, no. 2 (March 1995): 146-51.

Lubetzsky, Seymour. "The Function of the Main Entry in the Alphabetical Catalogue—One Approach." In *International Conference on Cataloguing Principles, Paris, 9-18th October, 1961; Report,* edited by A. H. Chaplin and Dorothy Anderson, 139-44. London: Organising Committee of the ICCP, 1963.

Malinconico, S. Michael. "*AACR2* and Automation." In *The Making of a Code: Issues Underlying AACR2,* edited by Doris Hargrett Clack, 25-40. Chicago: American Library Association, 1980.

Martin, Giles. "The Argument for: A Defense of Main Entry in the OPAC," *Cataloguing Australia* 22, no. 1/2 (March-June 1996): 21-25.

Nelson, David, and Jonathan Marner. "The Concept of Inadequacy in Uniform Titles." *Library Resources & Technical Services* 39, no. 3 (July 1995): 238-46.

Shoham, Sunnith, and Susan Lazinger. "The No-Main Entry Principle and the Automated Catalog." *Cataloging & Classification Quarterly* 12, no. 3/4 (1991): 51-67.

Svenonius, Elaine, ed. *The Conceptual Foundations of Descriptive Cataloging.* San Diego: Academic Press, 1989.

Tillett, Barbara B. "Bibliographic Structures: The Evolution of Catalog Entries, References, and Tracings." In *The Conceptual Foundations of Descriptive Cataloging,* edited by Elaine Svenonius, 149-66. New York: Academic Press, 1989.

———. "Cataloguing Rules and Conceptual Models for the Electronic Environment; [paper presented at the 11th National Cataloguing Conference, October 19 & 20, 1995, Sydney]." *Cataloguing Australia* 21, no. 3/4 (September-December 1995): 67-103.

———. "Future of Cataloging Rules and Catalog Records." In *Origins, Content, and Future of AACR2 Revised,* edited by Richard P. Smiraglia, 110-18. Chicago: American Library Association, 1992.

Verona, Eva. *Corporate Headings: Their Use in Library Catalogues and National Bibliographies: A Comparative and Critical Study.* London: IFLA Committee on Cataloguing, 1975.

———. "The Function of the Main Entry in the Alphabetical Catalogue: A Second Approach." In *International Conference on Cataloguing Principles, Paris, 9-18th October, 1961; Report,* edited by A. H. Chaplin and Dorothy Anderson, 145-57. London: Organising Committee of the ICCP, 1963.

Panel Response by Vendors

CANDY BOGAR
Data Research Associates, Inc.

I am here today, a cataloger by nature as well as by training, to talk about the *AACR* from the automated systems point of view. I'd like to approach this by asking several rather simple questions:

- Where are we?
- Why are we here?
- What can automated systems offer?
- Why is *AACR?*
- What do automated systems do with *AACR?*
- What rules should we change?

1. Where Are We?

We are not in card-catalog land. The conference papers and multitudinous postings to the list show that there is strong consensus on two points: *AACR* was strongly influenced by the dominant technology of the time, the card catalog; and those card-based rules are currently inadequate in several respects.

We are in automated-systems land. We currently live in a time in which automated library systems are common. These systems vary, much as card catalogs varied, in appearance, in completeness, and in consistency. There are some problems unique to the automated system, such as overwhelmingly large result sets. There are some problems still with us from earlier days, such as changes in serial titles.

2. Why Are We Here?

The tasks to address basically remain the same. It can be comforting or depressing, depending on your mood, to realize that the problems that the automated system must solve in the online catalog are the same as those that needed to be solved in the card catalog. We continue to need the catalog as an inventory of resources, as a finding aid for those seeking particular resources, and as a source of information in its own right.

The problems we need to address include logical and consistent presentation of information, ease of retrieval of requested information, organization and filing of information, character sets with which to faithfully represent information, and limited space in which to store the information.

3. What Can Automated Systems Offer?

What can we as automated-systems vendors do in this context? We hope to be able to solve old and new problems alike, using new tools available in the automated systems. To understand how we can do that, we need to look at what automated systems allow and what they require.

Automated systems allow a distinction between storage format, transmission format, and display format. This is a crucial point. Transmission format is specified in Z39.2 and in the USMARC communications format. This is unarguable and works extremely well. It is also machine-oriented and not at all easy for a human to understand. Storage format is how the vendor in question chose to store the USMARC data once the records were loaded internally. Display format is what the user gets to see on the public access station screen.

In the days of the card catalog all three were the same. It was possible to specify rules that directly influenced the display of the captured information. Once the information was recorded on the card, it did not change and could not be displayed in any manner other than that in which it was captured. In the current environment the rules govern the capture of information and the formatting of that information in a particular version of the eye-readable record. All other automated uses of the information and other displays are issues separate from the way the information was captured.

The MARC record is at the core of the entire automated system. More than public access needs are addressed by the automated library system. We can confine our remarks to the public access considerations, but the separation of transmission and display formats from storage format frees the library system vendor to do efficient things with the data in many different circumstances. It also allows imaginative display algorithms to meet the needs of the local end-user. A children's room catalog may well have very different display needs from those of a law library.

Automated systems allow for a variety of indexing schemes. Automated systems can generally create a number of indexes on various portions of the catalog record. This allows one to address data combinations not possible in the card catalog, where there was one arrangement—alphabetical, left-justified, on whatever text line was the top line on the card. One could certainly make as many cards with different top lines as one wanted, but the basic arrangement was set and economics usually limited the number of different cards made.

In the automated system we commonly can index the same field in both a keyword and a phrase mode. We can usually truncate the expression. We can often index the same field in different access points (a title both as a title access point and as part of an author/title access point, for example). These are common assumptions underlying the automated system index. In fact, the technology allows for more sophisticated indexing of portions of fields and even of related "words." Soundex indexing is certainly feasible as an alternate representation of the access point phrases.

Automated systems allow for a variety of normalization and collation algorithms. Indexing and sorting algorithms in the automated system can be quite sophisticated, nearing the powers of the well-trained filer. Diacritics can be ignored or normalized. Special sort routines for call numbers of different types can be enabled. Different indexes on the same database sorted by different collations are possible. Use of "filters" is possible. Filters are ways to select records from a result set based on information (usually nonindexed information) in the record itself. This allows not only for precision in result set, but also allows the user to pursue combinations of data elements not formerly accessible other than through curious attention to detail.

Automated systems allow for manipulation of result sets (combining, resorting, merging, etc.). A card catalog has one sort order only. Automated systems allow for many sort options and are very quick in resorting result sets. The ability to essentially fill a shopping basket with records of interest plucked from various searches finds no equal in the card catalog other than the piece of paper on which the user writes call numbers of interest from various searches. Some systems allow merging and deduping of result sets from multiple searches. This ability helps the user see a more manageable result set quickly.

Automated systems allow for exploring resources outside the library collection. This is a truly new capability, opening restricted collections to remote inquiry, allowing the user to visit catalogs of distant resources, and enhancing the climate for resource sharing. It also subtly changes the audience for whom the cataloger catalogs. If the catalog is no longer primarily a description of locally available resources, does this affect time spent in various parts of the task? If the catalog is being used as an information source remotely, does the amount of time spent in description and relationship information, as well as in holdings, get increased?

Automated systems require relative stability and absolute consistency of information definition (tagging, subfielding, naming). To the extent that contextual or explicit clues are provided in the data which make up the records in the catalog, automated systems can optimize validation, verification, display, and indexing routines. What is possible is based on what is available in the data.

Automated systems require consistency in rules. Automated systems work best when rules are consistent. A human may be able to cope with a rule that is true except for certain situations in which another rule takes precedence, but automated systems have trouble with special cases that require a weighted judgement-type decision. For instance, any trained card filer will file by what was clearly intended even if the card itself says something different (Untied States instead of United States, for instance). The machine will always be literal.

Automated systems require complete instructions. Punting is not usual behavior for an automated system. If a system finds itself unable to make a decision, it will usually cause unpleasant results for the user.

Automated systems require standard interfaces in order to communicate with other automated systems. The automated system is more than an index. It needs to communicate with other systems outside the library, such as the financial office or the Internet. Communication between systems is confined to rules and protocols that both systems agree to use. Z39.50 is such a protocol. There are many others. As it becomes essential to communicate with other libraries, and as libraries tend to have systems from different vendors, standards are the only hope for true resource sharing.

Automated systems can affect the rules:

Main entry

As has been eloquently argued on the list, automated systems allow multitudinous access points per record. Collocation on the shelf or in a result set remains a concern for the purpose of serendipity (browsing the shelves) or efficiency (more relevant results in fewer searches). With the demise of the unit card, and the rise of sophisticated filtering, layering, and linking abilities in automated systems, main entry tasks can be performed with different mechanisms.

Record relationship or linking

Links between entries can be expressed. There are at least three common layers of links:

1. links between types of records (classification, authority, bibliographic, holdings, community information, proprietary data);
2. links to associated text or other representations of the resource itself (hyperlinks); and
3. links to other records of the same type representing whole and part relationships or other relationships (editions, versions, etc.)

The linking of works and manifestations, as has been discussed on the list, is another important concept. It can be expressed to a large extent in existing record formats, such as the holdings format.

4. What Is *AACR*?

Let's look at the expressed audience. These are cataloging rules. They are addressed to catalogers to aid them in their tasks of describing and arranging resources. There are two major types of rules:

Specific detailed instructions

These are the mazes of instruction, example, and exception which get my cataloger's brain humming with the sheer joy of the chase. They are indeed useful in their scope, which is to explicate required behavior in particular situations. These are good as far as they go in the current *AACR,* but they do not adequately address new formats or serials because they are constrained by the very detail which drives their existence.

Principled guidelines

These are the general principles, the overriding architecture, the base premises on which the rules are based. It is here that one can explain the purpose and worldview of the rules. These need better and fuller articulation so that one can draw from them in devising rules for the new types of materials that will surely face us in the future.

5. What Do Automated Systems Do with *AACR*?

Access data

Automated systems use the rules and the USMARC formats to identify and exploit the implicit and explicit data element identification within the catalog record.

Transform data

Automated systems use the rules to perform verification routines against new records. The rules are also used to create automated help and templates.

Store data

Automated systems often use the rules to generate certain portions of the records before or upon storage.

6. What Rules Should We Change?

As someone who entered the profession before the adoption of USMARC, I have enjoyed being part of the continuous change we have seen. Change will always be with us. If anything, it will simply increase its pace. I would caution us not to try to freeze any new version of the *AACR* based on the common physical implementations of the catalog at this point in time. Such a freeze would surely be outdated quickly and would unnecessarily constrain further development of automated systems.

Instead, I believe effort should be put into expressions of principles and formulation of guidelines rather than in explicit rules of detail. In a rapidly changing environment, basic guidelines will be more useful to the systems developer and cataloger alike. Let's focus on the basic problems (serials management, logical layers of works, uncontrolled editions in digital resources, for instance) and leave issues like display, filing, character sets, result set management, and indexing to the automated systems developers in concert with their user communities. Those who cannot create pleasing solutions will not prosper.

One further reality for the automated-system vendor cannot go unmentioned. Legacy systems will not easily be able to adopt rules that would invalidate their current databases. Backward compatibility is always an issue, given the large number of systems already automated. Costs of conversion are always something to bear in mind. So drastic architectural changes would be more of a problem than drastic changes in description rules, for instance. Anything that mandated a conversion of all existing data would have a negative impact on resource sharing until that conversion rippled through all the databases. And experience shows that such a ripple is very hard to control in a reasonable time frame.

That said, the imaginative automated system will find a way to cope—perhaps with another form of display layer logic or new indexing.

JOHN ESPLEY
VTLS Inc.

John Espley elected not to submit a paper for this book. The following is a summary of his remarks taken from conference tapes.

One question a company must answer when allocating its resources for development is: will anybody pay me for this if it is developed? There are some things a vendor will do without a clear profit motive, but they are few and far between. Vendors want and need a fairly broad consensus about exactly what is desired.

One of the papers commented that *AACR2* does not provide any guidelines for online displays and suggested that they should. I am not certain that I agree. The look of an online catalogue is one of the principal ways by which one system is distinguished from another. I am not saying we should not have standards—standards are important for vendors—but I am not sure we should have standards for displays. VTLS struggled for years to get labels and display prompts that everyone could accept. No one could agree. If we used "uniform title," someone would object. If we changed "uniform title" to "filing title," someone would object to that. You may think this is a good reason why the cataloguing rules should prescribe labels and display. A better solution has been found by VTLS. We allow each library or system to determine what labels and display prompts it wants to use, and default values permit change if the original selection is unsatisfactory. The same principle applies to actual screen displays. The degree of customization should be one of the determining or distinguishing factors in choosing one system over another.

Before leaving the display issue, I have one more comment, perhaps a heretical one. Suppose *AACR2* prescribes some display constants, such as ISBD punctuation. I was not privileged to participate in the original discussions about ISBD punctuation twenty-odd years ago, and I freely admit my ignorance about their rationale. However, I still remember my bewilderment as a relatively new cataloguer how a space-slash-space conveys to the ordinary user of a library that what follows is an author statement. We are constantly being asked at VTLS why we do not provide the prescribed punctuation with our system. The system does not define the punctuation; the individual library has to do that. Do we really need all that punctuation, especially in a machine catalogue where all the displays can be customized?

The topic of uniform titles has been of special interest in the conference papers. The proper display or listing of titles is very important in any catalogue, and I believe uniform titles to be a necessary evil. They are necessary given the variety of titles proper for the same work, but they are evil in the sense that they are confusing to anybody who is not a cataloguer. One of the most difficult tasks in training those who are not professional cataloguers is to convey the concept of uniform titles. Imagine how difficult it is to explain them to the general public, and it would be a mistake to prescribe uniform titles for every bibliographic record. Uniform titles, as we define and use them now, are not needed on the vast majority of records. Where they are needed, they should be supplied and displayed, and the records associated with them should be retrievable by searching on that uniform title.

At VTLS, MARC is the life and breath of an automated system. MARC has given the library community thirty years of automation experience, greater than many other industries. The movement to consolidate the three primary MARC formats—USMARC, CANMARC, and UKMARC—is something every vendor should cheer about, even though the initial cost is tremendous. The U.S. and Canadian consolidation is completed, and I hope that progress is proceeding with the UKMARC format.

Is not the discussion about "work," "expression," "manifestation," "item," and "super records" a continuation of the dialogue about multiple versions? This is really a topic that has been hanging around for a long while. Isn't it time that we as a library community do something about reaching a consensus? As a local systems vendor, we would adjust to whatever you tell us—two-tier, three-tier, four-tier, multiple versions model. It is often difficult to get a clear answer that everyone agrees to. The reason I am here is to get those answers.

ED GLAZIER
Research Libraries Group

In a posting on the *AACR2* conference listserve on August 7, 1997, John Attig of Penn State University Libraries wrote:

> The current rules are strong on creating single bibliographic descriptions, but are not equally strong on creating a catalogue.

This is a fundamental truth about *AACR2*. Many of the comments on the *AACR2* Conference e-list implicitly or explicitly identified this not only as a truth but as a weakness. Before the days of library automation, for many catalogs, the format of the unit card was an accepted standard that was laid out in the cataloging rules.

Automated bibliographic records, standardized in the various MARC formats, provided opportunities for new kinds of catalogs. While the USMARC format initially automated the standard unit catalog card, it also provided the potential for data elements that were not part of the *Anglo-American Cataloguing Rules,* most particularly, coded values for certain physical characteristics and elements of contents, as well as some forms of automated linkages to other bibliographic records. The Library of Congress, through the USMARC format, was a leader in determining the contents of these machine-readable records, continuing the bibliographic leadership it had provided through the sale of its catalog cards.

When automated catalogs began to make use of the machine-readable records to create replacements for the card and printed book catalogs, each catalog designer had to make decisions about the components of an automated catalog: what the displays would look like, what indexes would be available, and what data would be included in each index. Since each element of a bibliographic description was now "machine-readable," additional access could be provided by indexing such things as standard and other numbers appearing on the item; chronological and geographical data; and links to other bibliographic items.

For the most part, the catalog rules have remained silent, both on the inclusion of such additional points of access and description, and thus, also on the form such access points and descriptive elements should take, though in some cases, some of these data elements were already included in textual form, sometimes in bibliographic notes on catalog cards. In many cases, the USMARC format or Library of Congress rule interpretations have guided the creation and format of these additional catalog record components, rather than the cataloging rules. Since many of these access points and descriptive elements are now standard parts of a MARC catalog record, it seems appropriate that rules for their inclusion and their form should be incorporated in the cataloging rules themselves. These would include rules for those areas that Tom Delsey refers to as "forms of expression" and "forms of carrier." Although USMARC format integration allowed any MARC data element to be used in any MARC record, there is still a requirement to declare a primary material type. The declaration of the primary material type is tantamount to choosing which chapter of *AACR2* to use for the description, thus invoking the cardinal principle in *AACR2* rule 0.24. The decision on how to treat items in digitized format is thus a content vs. carrier issue and belongs more appropriately to the catalog code than to the USMARC Format.

Bernhard Eversberg pointed out in his listserve posting of September 9, 1997:

Presently, there are no rules telling system designers:

- which fields and subfields to index;
- what indexes there should be;
- how to index these fields and subfields (what to do with punctuation, special characters, multiple subfields); or,
- how to arrange short title result set listings (what elements to include, on which of these to sort, and how; and what alternative sorting arrangements the user should be able to choose).

In addition to these omissions, there are no rules for how to display records. Displays in some online systems may be based on catalog card layouts. Many of us still remember what catalog cards looked like, but there are current catalogers who have never used catalog cards, let alone created them. There are also other types of full-record displays and partial record displays, in addition to short title result set listings. Some of these displays include labels for the parts of catalog records so that a user can tell what he is looking at. Many catalogers think that they are looking at a MARC record when they view a system's tagged display format, though this is not strictly true. Think in particular about how the fixed fields are displayed in the utilities and local systems. All of these decisions are really made by catalog designers and are not dictated by the cataloging rules or even by the US-MARC format.

The USMARC Format

I feel a need to defend the USMARC format, which has been attacked a number of times within some of the commentaries. Although the USMARC format was originally used to automate catalog card production, it has served us well as we have built automated catalogs up to this point. Remember that the USMARC format is a communications format and, except for suggested display constants, in itself it does not dictate or control displays. It is a vessel that should be able to convey the information specified by cataloging rules. As we know, it also carries information that is not specified by the cataloging rules. The USMARC format is not without flaws, but it has enabled us to share cataloging data to a hitherto unprecedented degree. This has resulted in a good deal of reduction in the redundancies of catalog record creation, and hopefully, will continue to do so for some years to come.

Many of the supposed weaknesses of the cataloging rules and the USMARC format are, as many contributors to the listserve have indicated, really deficiencies in how their own automated catalogs have been implemented. Unless we choose at this juncture to attempt to standardize display and access in OPACs, we have to keep clear what the differences are between cataloging principles and catalog display and indexing rules.

MARC-formatted records can clearly be used to create a variety of catalogs and displays. One thing that some institutions learned only by hindsight is that a full MARC bibliographic record provides more potential than an abbreviated MARC record. In the early days of OPACs, some institutions or systems saved computer storage space by eliminating from full bibliographic records some data elements, including portions of content-designation, that they did not need for their current OPAC displays, only to discover later that stripping data from these records sometimes severely limited the use of the same bibliographic records in a later-generation OPAC. Even now, some institutions and systems are stripping non-Roman scripts from their records because they currently cannot display them.

Catalog Users and Catalog Design

We have heard much about catalog users, both in the conference papers and in the comments, but users often seem to be regarded as a monolithic, homogeneous group. As we know, there are many categories of catalog users, and in the best of all possible worlds, designers of a catalog take the needs of the specific community of users into consideration when designing displays and indexes of a catalog. This is more likely to happen when the catalog is home-grown than when an external vendor must be contracted to supply a catalog to a number of different institutions.

Here are a couple of generalities about some catalogs and their users:

- They mostly do not know and probably don't care about ISBD.
- They are not likely to read long sets of instructions about how to use a particular catalog.

We know at least from anecdotal evidence that various groups of users have different behaviors and expectations when using library catalogs. Can the needs of various user groups be met by a single set of catalog design principles? Do we really have much hard evidence to describe actual use? Shouldn't we be somewhat wary of major (and expensive) changes in catalog design based on a priori assumptions about what users need?

OPACS and Bibliographic Utilities

Working as I do at an institution which provides as one of its services a bibliographic utility with a multimillion record database, I have read the papers for this conference with interest and perhaps some scepticism. While I can appreciate the intellectual and philosophical underpinnings for the design of such things as super records and work authority records, my practical side says that a catalog designed on such principles might be different but not necessarily better or easier to use than current catalogs. Considering the propensity for users not to read catalog use instructions, and the increasing amount of remote use of library catalogs away from centers of bibliographic instruction, who would be able to understand the reasons and applications of these new principles besides trained librarians, and then, perhaps, only trained catalogers, not necessarily reference and other public service librarians, some of whom do not understand our current catalogs because of insufficient education in cataloging practice and theory?

Because of differences in holdings at different institutions, it is difficult to conceive of a type of super record that would not be confusing or misleading in any catalog that did not contain all the manifestations and related works referenced. Would staff at each institution be required to edit those super records to link and relate only the locally available items? Wouldn't the users of an OPAC be better served by a catalog that consolidated the holdings for serial titles in a single place, rather than under each of several successive titles? The needs of an individual institution's OPAC are not identical with the needs of a large union database. A union database used as a source for cataloging copy and resource sharing may contain individual holdings records and its own internal links that would not be meaningful in a catalog that contained only some of the linked items. If the size of a result set in an individual OPAC has the potential to cause user problems, think of the impact of the size of a result set in a union database that represents the contents of multiple OPACs.

I have not yet come to sympathize with those writers and contributors who feel that the time has come to do away with main entry, understood to be "primary access point." I stand with those who feel that the concept of principal responsibility is still one of the best organizing principles for bibliographic data. In an environment where we have come to value standards in part because of the economies they engender, retaining the principle and the rules for main entry, but making the application optional strikes me as, shall we say, impractical at best. However, I do agree with those who suggest the the rules and LC rule interpretations might benefit considerably from review and streamlining in this area.

Very little has been said in the papers about the millions of existing MARC records often referred to as "legacy data." Since most of the relationships described for different manifestations and related works are intellectually understood but not explicitly recorded or coded in existing catalog records, I am puzzled by those who suggest that creating necessary linkages to support interrelated relationship displays could easily be automated. In purely practical terms, with the trends today toward downsizing catalog departments and the outsourcing of cataloging, who would do this work, even if it were doable? The amount of new material to catalog does not seem to be decreasing. How could one justify revisiting already cataloged works to create automated linkages at the expense of providing access to items not yet cataloged? For example, the RLIN and CitaDel databases consist of copies of millions of records from various parts of the world. Not all of these records were constructed using *AACR* and not all of them came to us in the USMARC format, though that format is the *lingua franca* we use to standardize indexing and retrieval. I suspect it would be impossible, even if desirable, to create new linkages in old records that are created and maintained elsewhere. Instead of directing our efforts toward redoing our existing catalog structures, we might better spend our efforts in integrating those structures with information about things not traditionally included in library catalogs, such as finding aids for archival collections encoded using EAD (Encoded Archival Description) and important web-based information.

In my opinion, one of the greatest challenges before us is embodied in Mr. Fattahi's recommendation for wider application of the principles. Large quantities of material desired by all classes of users is described only in databases not traditionally created in our catalog departments or according to our cataloging rules. It is not realistic to believe that we can persuade the creators of A&I databases or book trade databases or World Wide Web search engines to conform to national name authority files, when we ourselves acknowledge that the creation of authority records may consume at least 30 percent of our cataloging time and costs. Yet somehow, we must find a way to integrate such databases with our own catalogs, since these are among the materials certain classes of users are primarily interested in locating.

MAUREEN KILLEEN
A-G Canada Ltd.

A-G Canada is Canada's bibliographic utility. We started our existence as the University of Toronto Library Automation System (UTLAS) in 1973. Our database consists of over 50 million bibliographic and authority records representing the holdings of over 2,000 libraries in North America and the Far East. Our Catalogue Support System (CATSS) represents our core business. We are currently in transition, migrating the database to a web-based interface on a new hardware platform before the end of this year.

Mr. Fattahi's paper contains a number of suggestions for the construction of electronic catalogues. I believe that the purpose of having vendors respond to this paper is to provide conference attendees with some idea of how difficult it might be for systems to implement some of the suggestions. The focus of my discussion, therefore, is a verbal response to a Request for Information (RFI) on future functions of the catalogue. I shall concentrate on three of Mr. Fattahi's suggestions, following the never-forgotten rule of three from my years spent in cataloguing. These are:

- Multilevel record structure
- Uniform headings for titles
- Principles for online display

To reiterate Mr. Fattahi's thesis, the find and collocate functions of the catalogue will be enhanced by the ability to choose one item over similar items, locate items and copies of items, and maintain databases in terms of record updating. Some of the methods used to realize these additional functions are the use of multilevel records, uniform titles, and standardized labels for online displays.

Multilevel Records

The use of super records for works will provide a multilevel approach to works, their expressions, and manifestations. Super records are useful for collocating, according to Mr. Fattahi's paper. The use of software linkages is a critical component of super records.

Our experience at A-G Canada in maintaining software linkages originates with the way we implemented online authority control in CATSS: we maintained links between authority records and bibliographic records. These links were MARC-based. What we discovered was that the maintenance of software linkages is complicated and expensive.

A recent project of ours relates quite well to this discussion. We recently completed a project for one of our clients in Japan where we concatenated multilevel records (nine levels to be exact) to a single-level MARC record. This client found their database of multilevel records too expensive to maintain. They are reducing nine levels to three for their internal database structure.

Concept of Uniform Titles

The concept of uniform titles is useful for providing links between different expressions and manifestations of a work. These titles enable a user to distinguish among works with identical titles proper.

In CATSS, we have established a uniform title index and again, we maintain MARC-based links between the authority record and the bibliographic record. The bibliographic headings in the 100, 110, or 111 fields plus the heading in field 240 are linked to the authority headings 100, 110, or 111 subfields a and t. The bibliographic headings in the 700, 710, or 711 fields subfields a and t are linked to the authority headings 100, 110, or 111 subfields a and t.

Principles for Online Display

Another way to enhance the function of the catalogue, according to Mr. Fattahi's paper, would be to standardize the way records are displayed. In particular, the *Anglo-American Cataloguing Rules* should prescribe not only the terms to be used in online display labels, but also the order of fields and subfields. We feel that this would be straightforward to implement.

Business Case (or Real Life)

A-G Canada is a for-profit company. As such, we have to make business decisions regarding any software development we do. We ask ourselves:

- Can we provide what our users need?
- What will it cost?
- What is the potential revenue?

We have to balance needs and costs. This is real life.

In real life we developed the ability to produce PRECIS (Preserved Context Index System), a sophisticated method for providing subject access. This development of ours cost hundreds of thousands of dollars. At its height of popularity we had three customers using this product. At present we produce this type of listing for one customer. Clearly, we will never recoup the development costs for this product.

Conclusion

By addressing the impact of implementing some of Mr. Fattahi's ideas in a large existing database of MARC-based records, I hope that I have been able to provide you with some insight into what system developers do.

I thank the Joint Steering Committee for inviting A-G Canada to participate in this important conference. We are delighted to be here and, notwithstanding the reality of our business, we look forward to the future and all its changes.

GLENN PATTON
OCLC, Inc.

Introduction

There are six topics about which I would like to comment briefly from OCLC's perspective as well as from my own perspective as a cataloger who has been around long enough to remember when uniform titles were called "conventional titles" and as a manager who has spent more time in the past two years with resource sharing issues.

Catalog Cards

From the perspective of OCLC member institutions, cards aren't dead . . . but they're not the hot commodity that they once were. In the first year that OCLC printed cards (fiscal year 1975), we printed and shipped about 17 million cards. That increased rapidly as membership increased in the early 1980s to a peak, in fiscal years 1984 and 1985, of 131 million cards per year. In the past decade, the numbers have fallen very sharply as libraries have shifted from full sets of cards to shelflist only to no cards at all.

In fiscal year 1997 (the fiscal year ended this past June), we printed only 18.6 million cards and, for the current fiscal year, we forecast that we will print about 15.4 million cards (or about 1.2 million cards a month) and, thus far, that looks about right. That is still a lot of cards (a ton a month) but, by contrast, in last fiscal year, we distributed 43.3 million bibliographic and authority records in some electronic form (export, FTP, or tape).

Understandable and Teachable

Turning to the rules themselves: if catalogers who create records using the cataloging rules are to be most efficient, they need to be able to understand the logic of how the rules function and to have confidence in that understanding. Over and over, in working via the telephone with OCLC member institutions (in the same kind of advisory, consultative role that a principal cataloger might have in a larger library), I've listened to catalogers explain in detail how they analyzed what rules to apply, how they've worked through the process, even how they've used their judgement to "extend" the rules. In the vast majority of cases, they've done everything correctly but they aren't confident enough of that to leave that item and go on to the next.

I don't mean to suggest that any cataloging code bears the full responsibility for instilling greater confidence—library educators, cataloging managers, and senior staff who assist in the training of others share in that responsibility. However, all things being equal, an understandable, teachable code ought to increase efficiency and reduce needless dithering and tinkering.

Rules That Are "Extensible"

New media formats appear far too frequently! Not all of them catch on in the marketplace and even fewer, perhaps, become part of library collections. Nonetheless, my OCLC colleagues and I have spent a lot of time helping catalogers extend the rules to fit new materials.

Sometimes that has required only a slight "stretch" to achieve a satisfactory result. In other cases (like microcomputer software), a complete restructuring of one chapter of the rules was required. In yet other cases (for example, Internet resources), it appeared that major revisions might be needed but, in the end, only minor adjustments were necessary.

Rules that allow for easy extensibility will certainly serve us better in the long term, and that should be part of our thinking as we examine possible changes.

Structures That Are Compatible with Other Cataloging Rules

One of OCLC's major emphases over the past few years reflects the increasingly global nature of information. More than ten years ago, as we began our international expansion, we were confronted by cataloging rules and practices from outside the world of *AACR2*. We were fortunate in that first confrontation when a group of French academic libraries agreed to adopt *AACR2* (in the French translation) as the basis for their OCLC cataloging activity.

Subsequently, we've often been able, as in two current projects involving German and Russian libraries, to rely on the ISBDs to provide a common foundation for descriptive practice. Global sharing of bibliographic data will, in our view, continue to require that kind of common foundation and we need to keep that in mind as we consider structural changes.

Structures That Are Compatible with Other Bibliographic Information

I want to reinforce one of Mr. Fattahi's points about integrated access to different types of bibliographic information. Libraries, in pursuit of the goal of providing their patrons with the information resources that they need when they need them, are increasingly incorporating more information, such as tables of contents, into bibliographic records (or linking that information to the bibliographic record). Institutions are incorporating archival materials (including finding aids and associated images) into their catalogs and are using bibliographic records as springboards to the full text of the item. Many databases now incorporate bibliographic data provided by publishers or jobbers. We are teetering on the brink of HTML editors that may prompt the author to describe or "catalog" his or her own work in a structure that is not unlike traditional bibliographic data.

One of the hot topics these days is broadcast or multicast searches, a process that facilitates searching across multiple databases. That frequently produces a "clash of cultures" when our carefully crafted *AACR2* entries are integrated into a search result that might include items from several abstracting and indexing databases, *Books in Print,* and the *Encyclopaedia Britannica.*

Bibliographic records in large shared databases like OCLC's are also used for an ever-increasing number of purposes, from initial collection development and selection purposes through acquisitions and cataloging to resource sharing to collection management decisions that lead to weeding. Some of these uses (collection development, for example) would be better served by removing some of the current restrictions on the number of authors that are recorded or the information like institutional affiliation that is recorded.

We must also keep these trends in mind as we evaluate potential changes to bibliographic structures.

Relationships and Links

Finally, I must offer a cautionary note about linkages between and among records. Whether the link is a character string (in the form of the text of a heading or a control number), an object ID, or some other method, there is system and human overhead associated with creating and maintaining those links within a single system. Linking across systems is even more problematic. Linking across systems also raises the question of packaging up sets of records to be communicated between systems, whether that communication is at the point of pre-order searching, at the time of cataloging, or in response to a Z39.50-based search to identify an item for interlibrary loan.

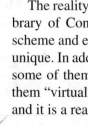

The reality in the United States is that there are at least four "national" databases (the Library of Congress, RLIN, WLN, and OCLC)—each of which has its own ID number scheme and each of which partly duplicates the content of the other databases and is partly unique. In addition, there is a growing number of local, regional, and statewide databases—some of them "real," physical databases (like Melvyl or ILLINET Online) and others of them "virtual" (like the CIC[1] or Galileo). This situation is not unique to the United States, and it is a reality that also must shape our thinking.

Note

1. The Committee on Institutional Cooperation represents Indiana University, Michigan State University, Northwestern University, Ohio State University, Pennsylvania State University, Purdue University, University of Chicago, University of Illinois at Chicago, University of Illinois at Urbana-Champaign, University of Iowa, University of Michigan, University of Minnesota, and University of Wisconsin-Madison.

DISCUSSION

The panelists were questioned about the reason linkages are so expensive. They replied that, while storage is not much of an issue, system development and maintenance is costly. Costs depend on the kind of links being made and their use. Hard explicit links, which change as the records change, are more costly in system logic than links that are implicit, e.g., based on the index entry pointing to things that are different but have a common access point. It is difficult for vendors of local systems to accommodate two or three ways of handling linking records. Consensus on one method would reduce costs. One vendor noted that every system already links its proprietary items to bibliographic records, and there is much system level operational linkage that can be expanded. She predicted that system vendors will develop linkages that do not have to be created or maintained by human beings. The National Library of Canada is operating a bibliographic system on a relational database platform containing thirteen million records, all of which originated as MARC records. If the design and the thinking about the design are done in the beginning, there can be cost savings in the actual management of data.

A participant stated that the Dublin Core seems to be founded on the premise that *AACR2* is inherently unsuited to metadata and asked the vendors whether the Dublin Core can be compatible or integrated with *AACR2*. In reply, the OCLC Internet cataloging project was mentioned as an example; the study proved that *AACR2* was not inherently incompatible with electronic resources, that only a small number of changes were needed in *AACR2*. However, since there is no reasonable way to catalogue all the information now being generated in electronic form, it may be possible within the Dublin Core or some other structure to provide some level of bibliographic access. Cataloguers could then enhance selected records. Although the Dublin Core is a set of data elements that does not have any inherent descriptive standards for those elements and, therefore, the records are not *AACR2* compatible, the data can be mapped to USMARC and manipulated in the same way as other USMARC records. The usefulness of Dublin Core data will depend on whether any standards are used for the creation of data elements, e.g., authority control and rules for what is a title.

At the 1997 IFLA conference the ISBD review group was reconstituted and asked to look at all the ISBDs to determine if they are adequate to meet the needs of the present environment. One of the tasks is to examine the Dublin Core in detail to see how this can fit into the ISBDs as they are reconsidered.

Another topic raised was whether *AACR2* should be concerned with the whole bibliographic record which contains elements from subject heading lists, classification, MARC coding, OPAC displays in various systems, as well as *AACR2*. The JSC Chair replied that the Committee of Principals wanted the conference to fit

AACR2 into a broad context. Other JSC members felt that JSC should be taking a lead in setting standards, and that rule 0.1 merits some explicit rethinking.

A vendor reminded the participants that vendors respond not to cataloguers but to managers. The managers must understand the principles behind the system they want the vendors to provide.

The discussion ended with some comments about the necessity for specialist cataloguing manuals and the problems associated with using *AACR2* to meet the needs of special collections.

Demonstration of Super Records

On the final day of the conference Fattahi was asked to give a demonstration of his concept of super records. The following is a summary of his presentation followed by questions from the audience.

Fattahi began by describing some of the search, retrieval, and display problems in existing web-based catalogues, and demonstrated these problems with examples from some of the catalogues available on the web. He stated that some of the problems were related to software, some to incorrect implementation of *AACR2,* and some to *AACR2* itself.

Super records are different from work authority records or work records in that they incorporate a scope note or something like a scope note, e.g., different expressions, works for which the person is a coauthor, works for which the person is an editor. In addition to the person's works existing in a specific library collection, super records can relate to other collections and can note a priority among these collections.

The way to access super records is through a uniform title index. When a name is entered in an OPAC, only one name is retrieved, not, for example, 700 records for Shakespeare. When there is more than one instance of an identical name, advanced software should lead the user to the uniform title index or authority file. Then there is a categorization of that person's works according to types of expression, editions, and manifestations, all linked in a hierarchical structure to MARC records.

There are millions of MARC records, and many do not need to be linked together. It is understandable that there is some concern about the cost involved in the implementation of this concept. Priorities can be set for different collections. Libraries can identify different records for one author and link them through hypertext techniques so that no major change will be needed in either the MARC records or the MARC format. We do need to provide some MARC tags that can be identified for links. In the actual record some data elements can be linked to the upper level and added entries used for collocation purposes.

Notes will have a very important role in hypertext records. They can link to different web sites, to reviews about the work available in electronic formats, to the publisher's web site to see what is newly available from that publisher, or to similar bibliographic data. This is an area in which the cataloguer would have more flexibility to provide links.

DISCUSSION

In response to several questions about linkages, Fattahi said that, in order for linkages to be made automatically, the terminology used in bibliographic records would have to be standardized to a much greater extent than it is now. He disagreed with the suggestion that Library of Congress classification numbers could be used as a linking device because all works about a work do not have the same classification numbers. Fattahi believes that *AACR2* should have a specific chapter on work authority control with guidelines for different linkages which can make retrieval and display more understandable to the catalogue user. A clear display of records is very important. One participant claimed that SGML is a natural fit for super records. Several participants agreed with Fattahi that super records could be created from present MARC records without too much extra effort.

One participant pointed out that many catalogues include pre-*AACR2* records. While access points to these records may have been upgraded, the descriptions will never be up-to-date. This situation creates a problem for matching records with differing practices and making sense of any resultant super records. The problem is great enough for one catalogue, let alone linking these records to other catalogues. Fattahi stated that super records cannot be exchanged between systems.

3 ◆ **What Is a Work?**

MARTHA M. YEE

Introduction

There are three stages to the cataloging work required to represent a given entity, such as an author, a work, or a subject, in a catalog.

1. The entity must be defined.
2. The entity must be named.
3. Variant names for the entity must be identified, and syndetic apparatus provided that leads users from variants to the chosen name.

In the first stage of representing an author in the catalog, for example, the cataloger must determine whether the John Smith who writes poetry is the same John Smith who publishes texts on physics (see figure 1).

```
FIRST STAGE:
Poems / by John Smith
Physics : a text / by John Smith
```

FIGURE 1

In the second stage, the cataloger must determine how John Smith is commonly known, and, if necessary, add data, such as dates or initials, to his name to distinguish him from other John Smiths (see figure 2).

```
SECOND STAGE:
Smith, John, 1614-1733
Smith, John (John Aloysius), 1947-
```

FIGURE 2

In the third stage, the cataloger must determine whether John Smith has used other names in his publications, such as Jack Smith, and if he has, provide cross-references by means of an authority record (see figure 3).

```
THIRD STAGE:
Smith, John (John Aloysius), 1947-
x Smith, Jack, 1947-
```

FIGURE 3

These same three stages are necessary for representing a work in a catalog, although catalogers may be less conscious of this fact, since so much of the effort put into naming works goes into establishing the names of their authors, and the work on titles is only partially done, if at all, in most disciplines (a notable exception being the field of music). This paper will discuss each of these three stages in detail, covering current practice in *AACR2R*, problems with current practice, and suggested solutions. In addition, the paper includes a section on the structure of the catalog and methods of demonstrating relationships, as well as a summary of all of the recommendations made for change to *AACR2R*.

I. Defining the Work

A. Users

The following assumptions are based on common sense, on memory of my own experience as a naive library user, and on some experience as a reference librarian. They are the assumptions behind the objects of the catalog, and therefore the assumptions behind our cataloging practice. I would challenge those who disagree with them to do research to try to disprove them; I think, if such research were tried, it would be impossible to disprove the following:

Assumptions

- Most users seek particular works, not particular editions. Yet works are published in the form of editions; the fundamental duty of descriptive cataloging is to organize the resulting chaotic bibliographic universe to facilitate user access to works, and to allow them easily to select the edition of the work sought that best meets their needs as to language, illustration, currency, authority, nearness to original sources, availability to the user (not checked out and in the branch in which the user is located at the moment, for example), etc.

- Users assume that we display together all editions of a work held.
- Users usually don't know about editions they don't find.
- Users rarely have a way to protest or complain, and even when they do, they don't know how to analyze the problem beyond saying that they can't find what they are looking for.[1]

From the above, it should be apparent that in defining work, we want to aim at a definition that corresponds to most users' conceptions of work. While there are many types of work for which this is not difficult to do, there are some types of work concerning which users may differ in their conceptions depending on their subject backgrounds. It is apparent, for example, that users with a strong opera background will feel that Joseph Losey's film of Mozart's *Don Giovanni* is an edition or version of the work *Don Giovanni* by Mozart, while users with a strong film background will consider it a new work of mixed authorship to be cited and searched under title. When this kind of disagreement exists, a general set of cataloging rules like *AACR* must reach some sort of compromise, and then ensure that both sets of users can at least find the works they are looking for, even if we can't guarantee that in all cases they will be looking at the main entry for the work sought (where they would find *all* the editions of the work, as well as works about it and works related to it).

B. Definition implicit in *AACR2*

Giving two items the same main entry implies they represent the same work. One way to define main entry is as the citation or heading form for a work. Many works are still usefully identified using both author and title.

Figure 4 contains examples of current cataloging that illustrate this point. The main entry, identifying the work, is underlined.

In *AACR2R,* we have considered the following changes to be substantial enough to cause the creation of a new (but related) work (signalled by a change in main entry):

- rewriting of a text in another form, e.g., the dramatization of a novel
- filming of a play
- adaptation of an art work from one medium to another (e.g., an engraving of a painting)
- changing of the title of a serial work
- revision of a text accompanied by a change in representation of authorship[2]
- addition of commentary or biographical/critical material when the commentary or biographical/critical material is emphasized in title page representation
- free transcription of the work of a composer
- merely basing a musical work on other music, e.g., variations on a theme
- setting a preexisting text to music

EXAMPLE 1, TWO EDITIONS (OR "EXPRESSIONS") OF THE SAME WORK, GIVEN THE SAME MAIN ENTRY

Edition 1:

Wendt, Lloyd.
  Lords of the Levee : the story of Bathhouse John and Hinky Dink / by Lloyd Wendt and Herman Kogan. -- 1st ed. -- Indianapolis, Ind. : Bobbs-Merrill, 1943.
  384 p. : ill. ; 23 cm.

Edition 2:

Wendt, Lloyd.
  [Lords of the Levee]
  Bosses in lusty Chicago : the story of Bathhouse John and Hinky Dink / by Lloyd Wendt and Herman Kogan ; with an introduction by Paul H. Douglas. -- Bloomington, Ind. : Indiana University Press, 1967, c1943.
  xv, 384 p. : ill. ; 20 cm.

EXAMPLE 2, TWO EDITIONS (OR "EXPRESSIONS") OF THE SAME WORK, GIVEN THE SAME MAIN ENTRY

Edition 1:

Turgenev, Ivan Sergeevich, 1818-1883.
  [Ottsy i deti. English]
  Fathers and sons / by Ivan Turgenev ; translated by Barbara Makanowitzky ; with an introduction by Alexandra Tolstoy. -- Bantam classic ed. -- Toronto ; New York : Bantam Books, 1981.
  x, 208 p. ; 18 cm.

Edition 2:

Turgenev, Ivan Sergeevich, 1818-1883.
  [Ottsy i deti. English]
  Fathers and sons / Ivan Turgenev ; translated by Rosemary Edmonds ; with The Romanes lecture, Fathers and children / by Isaiah Berlin. -- Harmondsworth, Eng. ; Baltimore : Penguin, 1975.
  294 p. ; 19 cm. -- (Penguin classics ; L147)

FIGURE 4

EXAMPLE 3, TWO DIFFERENT WORKS, ONE RELATED TO THE
OTHER, GIVEN DIFFERENT MAIN ENTRIES, BUT RELATED BY MEANS
OF AN ADDED ENTRY ON ONE FOR THE MAIN ENTRY OF THE OTHER

Work 1:

<u>Mitchell, Margaret, 1900-1949.</u>
  <u>Gone with the wind</u> / Margaret Mitchell. --
Anniversary ed., with an introd. / by James A.
Michener. -- New York : Macmillan, 1975, c1936.
  xii, 947 p. ; 24 cm.

Work 2:

<u>Gone with the wind</u> [motion picture] / David O.
  Selznick ; director, Victor Fleming. -- Special
  CAV collector's edition. -- United States : MGM/UA
  Home Video, c1991.
  5 videodiscs (222 min.) : sd., col ; 12 in.

TRACINGS:

... I. Fleming, Victor, 1883-1949.
II. <u>Mitchell, Margaret, 1900-1949. Gone with the
wind.</u>

EXAMPLE 4, TWO DIFFERENT WORKS, NOT RELATED TO EACH
OTHER, GIVEN DIFFERENT MAIN ENTRIES

Work 1:

<u>Krogh, David.</u>
  <u>Smoking</u> : the artificial passion / David Krogh. --
New York, N.Y. : W.H. Freeman, c1991.
  xvi, 176 p. ; 24 cm.

Work 2:

<u>Gilbert, David G., 1947-</u>
  <u>Smoking</u> : individual difference, psychopathology,
and emotion / David G. Gilbert ; foreword by H.J.
Eysenck. -- Washington, D.C. : Taylor and Francis,
c1995.

FIGURE 4—Continued

In *AACR2R*, we have considered the following changes not to be substantial enough to cause the creation of a new work (signalled by the retention of the same main entry as the original work); rather such changes create "expressions," to use the term recommended by the IFLA Study Group on the Functional Requirements for Bibliographic Records:

- translation into another language
- addition of illustrations to a text

- revision of a text by the same author(s) as the original
- abridgement of a text
- editing of a text to produce a critical edition
- addition of commentary or biographical/critical material when the original work is emphasized in title page representation
- reproduction of an art work
- arrangement, transcription, etc., of the work of a composer
- improvisation by a performer on the work of a composer
- provision of a choreography for an existing musical work, such as a ballet
- addition of an instrumental accompaniment or additional parts to a musical work
- addition of words to music
- performance of a musical work on a sound recording
- republication with a different setting of type
- republication with a different title on the title page
- republication as part of a different series

The following types of criteria are invoked to produce the above results:

1. "The nature of the work itself," to use the language of 21.9A.

   21.10A, Paraphrase, rewriting, adaptation for children, version in a different literary form

   21.11, Illustrated texts

   21.12, Abridgement

   21.14, Translation

   21.16B, Reproduction of art work

   21.18, Arrangement or transcription (of music) vs. distinct alteration, paraphrase, or work merely based on

   21.19, Musical work that includes words

   21.20, Musical setting for ballet

   21.21, Added accompaniment

   21.16, Spirit communication

   21.23, Sound recordings

   21.27, Academic disputations

If the cataloger can determine that the work being cataloged is an "abridgement" or an "illustrated text," these rules will simply mandate a particular type of entry. However, if the cataloger has a work which does not quite fall into any of these categories, there won't be a form-based rule to indicate proper entry. These rules look suspiciously like the 1949 rules, which were criticized for including large numbers of rules for forms of publication, which grew as new forms of publication appeared, and which were riddled with inconsistency.

However, implicit in these rules seem to be more principled approaches based on primary and secondary authorship.

Writing of text as primary authorship:

- illustration of a text is subsidiary to writing the text (21.11)
- translation is subsidiary to writing the original text (21.14)

Creation of art work as primary authorship:

- reproduction of an art work is subsidiary to creating the art work reproduced (21.16B)

Composition of music as primary authorship:

- arranging music is subsidiary to composing it (21.18)
- writing lyrics is subsidiary to composing music (21.19)
- writing librettos is subsidiary to composing music (21.19)[3]
- writing the choreography, libretto, or scenario for a ballet or pantomime is subsidiary to writing its music (21.20)
- writing instrumental accompaniments and additional parts is subsidiary to composing music (21.21)
- performance is subsidiary to composition of music (21.23), except that
    a) all functions are subsidiary to performance by a group that "goes beyond mere performance, execution, etc." (21.1B2.e)
    b) when one performer performs the work of many composers, composing is subsidiary to performance (21.23C)

2. Change in the medium of expression (21.9A)

    21.16A, Adaptation from one graphic art medium to another

3. "Wording of the chief source" (21.9A)

    21.12, Revisions of texts

    21.13, Texts published with commentary

    21.15, Texts published with biographical/critical material

    21.17B, Reproductions of two or more art works with text

    21.14, Collaboration between artist and writer

4. Relative extent of content

    21.25, Reports of interviews or exchanges

5. Outside research establishing authorship (as a back-up approach)

    21.27, Academic disputations

C. Possibility of using fundamental content to help in making decisions about works, and possibly to reorganize the rules for description

The following are suggestions for analyzing the materials we catalog into pure types of fundamental content. My hypothesis in this exercise is that a work in one of the eight categories listed in section 1 cannot be transformed into a work in another of the eight categories without becoming a new work. This hypothesis needs testing by research.

The potential utility of this approach is as follows: if we can delineate the fundamental types of content, it might help in defining the concept of "work," and it might help us determine when a previously existing work has been modified so much it has become a new work. Incidentally, this approach might also provide a better means of organizing the rules for description, preventing the current problem of cross-classification in chapters 1-13, although that is a bit peripheral to the topic of this particular paper.

1. Pure types of fundamental content:

   a. text (a work fundamentally comprised of printed, typed, or handwritten words, or words read aloud)

   > Within the category of text, there may be subcategories which are also "pure" in the sense that a work cannot move from one category to another without becoming a new work. Consider the following possibilities, for example:
   >
   > - poetry
   > - fiction
   > - drama
   >
   > Drama may be a special case. For centuries the only things libraries could collect were the texts of works intended for performance. The performances themselves could not be recorded and thus could not be collected. However, there is a possibility that dramatic works, when seen as works intended for performance, rather than as literary textual works, are essentially works of mixed responsibility that cannot exist as performed works without the participation of many different people performing many different functions. This may also be true of dramatico-musical works intended for performance as well, such as operas and ballets (see below).

   b. music (a work fundamentally comprised of music, either musical notation (typed, printed, or handwritten), or actual sound, i.e., performed music)

   > There is a strong convention in Western classical music to consider performed music to be the work of its composer, even when the performer has improvised on the music as written, or an arranger has modified the original composition.

   c. still image (a work fundamentally comprised of image(s) that are stationary; includes original art (painting, drawing, art prints, dioramas), slides, posters, prints, photographs, architectural drawings)

   > Within the category of image, there may be subcategories which are also "pure" in the sense that a work cannot move from one category to another without becoming a new work. Consider the following possibilities, for example:
   >
   > - painting
   > - drawing
   > - engraving
   > - lithograph
   >
   > Photography presents a special case. Because slide collections are created and used as surrogates for art originals, which may be located at remote sites that are expensive or impossible to visit, current practice among slide librarians, codified in *AACR2R* rule 21.16B, is to treat a reproduction of an art original as if it were the art original itself, even though it is almost always different in scale and different in

medium (for any art original other than a photograph). This treatment of photography as sometimes being a "mere recording medium" is similar to the treatment of some kinds of moving image, to be discussed below. It seems to be a peculiarity of photographic image content that it can produce such a close likeness of a photographed work that the photograph can be useful to users as a surrogate for the photographed work. When photographic works are treated as surrogates in this fashion, they probably no longer function as pure content types, but rather as a method of reproduction that creates either a "manifestation," or, perhaps, an "expression," rather than a "work" (see below).

d. moving image (a work fundamentally comprised of moving images, which often (but not necessarily) has text and sound integrated to make a single work; includes dance as well as dance notation, since dance consists of movement (moving image) plus sound)

Film is a relatively new medium of expression (only one hundred years old) that is fundamentally a work of photography, in which meaning is expressed by means of the visual composition of frames, cutting, camera angles, and rhythm and timing of the action before the camera. While film draws on all previous art forms (painting, writing, sculpture, architecture, music, dance), it is fundamentally a new art form. As such, adaptation is necessary to turn any previously existing work into a work in this form.

The problem is, of course, that just as all text is not belles lettres, not all films are Films, i.e., cinematic works, such as those described above. Film can also be used as a "mere recording medium," as in the case of scientific record film, anthropological film, and so forth. In truth, film can be put to as many varied uses as text.

How can catalogers tell whether they are dealing with a cinematic work, or film as a "mere recording medium"? One clue lies in the functions credited on the film; if a cinematographer, an editor, a screenwriter, and/or a director are involved, it is highly likely that the work is a cinematic work, as these are the kinds of functions that result in the expression of meaning using visual composition of frames, cutting, camera angles, and rhythm and timing of the action before the camera.

If film is held to function sometimes as a "mere recording medium," this latter type of film would probably no longer function as a pure content type, but rather as a method of reproduction that creates either a "manifestation," or, perhaps, an "expression," rather than a "work" (see below).

Should choreographic works (in notation) be considered equivalent to the screenplay for a film, a kind of precursor to what is fundamentally a moving image work? Or should choreographic works form a separate category here (as a pure type)? Or are choreographic works a mixed type (see below)?

e. spatial data (includes maps, aerial photographs, remote sensing images, atlases, globes)

How does the concept of work function in the field of spatial data? Can a flat map be made into a globe and still be the same work? Note that any two-dimensional map is trying to represent a three-dimensional reality, so it is probably artificial to forbid a two-dimensional work from having a three-dimensional version that is the same work. When are two items considered to be two different versions or editions of the same work (i.e., when are they given the same main entry, despite intellectual or artistic differences between them that require making a separate record to express them)?

f. three-dimensional objects (includes realia, toys, specimens, sculpture, monuments, buildings, gardens)

Can a toy or a sculpture be an edition of a work that is not a toy or a sculpture?

g. numeric data (other than spatial data)

h. computer programs

2. Mixed types of fundamental content (aggregate works in the sense that the pieces are separable (can be published separately), and can have different authorship):

a. One type of content predominant (judgment will be required to determine primacy):

text with illustrations, which can now include musical and audiovisual illustrations

Traditionally, texts with illustrations have been entered under the author of the text. However, it is possible that in fields such as children's literature, this is somewhat artificial. As more and more visual and audio materials are added to electronic versions of previously existing texts, it is possible that it may become harder and harder to argue for the predominance of text.

music with words (opera, lieder, etc.)

As noted above, the field of Western classical music has a long tradition of considering composition primary authorship, and all other functions to be subsidiary. This has led to the practice of considering lieder with words by someone other than the composer to be the work of the composer. It has also led to considering an opera with a libretto by someone other than the composer, in a production unspecified by the composer (e.g., as to costumes, lighting, etc.), adapted into a cinematic work with frame composition, camera angles, cutting, etc., unspecified by the composer, to be the work of the composer. Operas, in fact, when performed, consist of more than just music with words, and perhaps (as suggested above) should be considered to be essentially works of mixed responsibility, along with other dramatico-musical works intended for performance.

dance (choreography and music)

The dance field has come to see performances of dance works as works of mixed responsibility to be entered under title, although this is not yet reflected in *AACR2*. Perhaps this would argue for including dance (both choreographic notation and recordings of dance performances) as moving image works, above.

b. Fundamentally mixed with no type of content predominant:

interactive multimedia and other electronic resources that mix text, sound, and image

When preexisting works are reissued with interactive multimedia commentary, biographical/critical information, and so forth, and are still represented as being the original work, it may be desirable to consider them to be expressions of the preexisting work. Also, when an existing print work acquires an online multimedia version (e.g., *Encyclopaedia Britannica* and *Britannica Online; New York Times* and *New York Times on the Web*), it may be desirable to treat them as expressions of the same work. Such tactics would argue against considering "interactive multimedia" to be a pure category.

kits

3. A work of any of these types (either pure or mixed) can:

a. be distributed in multiple copies or unique

b. be issued serially, issued in continuously updatable form, or issued "monographically" (Note: It is relatively rare for a particular work to be issued as both a monograph and a serial, but perhaps has happened, as in the case of Dickens' serialized novels. It is becoming more common for a serial work to be issued both serially (in print) and in continuously updatable form (online). Thus, it would not seem wise to consider a change in seriality to create a new work.)

c. be issued as part of a larger whole or not

d. be controlled archivally or not by the collection that holds it

e. exist on multiple physical carriers:

i) reproduced onto a number of different physical carriers as follows; such reproduction creates a "manifestation," to use the term recommended by the IFLA Study Group on the Functional Requirements for Bibliographic Records:

digitization: all (includes various types of digitization, including, for example: both Mac and Windows versions; both ASCII and Microsoft Word versions; scanned by optical character recognition software (thereby turned into text), vs. scanned as an image (bitmapped, jpeg, gif); CD-ROM vs. diskette vs. remotely accessed; etc.)

microfilming, photocopying, still and slide photography: text as print on page, musical notation, image, numeric data

audio reproduction (audiocassettes, sound discs, CDs, etc.): text read aloud, performed music

film and video reproduction (videocassettes, motion picture film, videodiscs, etc.): audiovisual works

ii) released simultaneously on a number of different physical carriers as follows; these simultaneous releases on multiple carriers are "manifestations," to use the term recommended by the IFLA Study Group on the Functional Requirements for Bibliographic Records:

digitization: all (includes various types of digitization, including, for example: both Mac and Windows versions; both ASCII and Microsoft Word versions; scanned by optical character recognition software (thereby turned into text), vs. scanned as an image (bitmapped, jpeg, gif); CD-ROM vs. diskette vs. remotely accessed, etc.)

microfilming, photocopying, still and slide photography: text as print on page, musical notation, image, numeric data

audio reproduction (audiocassettes, sound discs, CDs, etc.): text read aloud, performed music

film and video reproduction (videocassettes, motion picture film, videodiscs, etc.): audiovisual works

iii) reproduced and reissued on the same type of physical carrier; such reproduction also creates a "manifestation," to use the term recommended by the IFLA Study Group on the Functional Requirements for Bibliographic Records; e.g.:

resetting of type (text or musical notation)

reissue or republication using the same plates (text or musical notation)

prints and negatives (still photographic and moving image material)

D. Problem conditions not yet adequately covered in *AACR2R*

1. Collaborative works of mixed responsibility

There are no general rules for mixed responsibility in new works; therefore, most audiovisual materials are excluded from treatment as new works of mixed responsibility. Thus, catalogers of these classic works of mixed responsibility are thrown back to rules 21.1C1 and 21.6C2 for entry.

The rules for mixed responsibility are often based on format rather than on conditions of authorship.

The rules are not numbered logically—see indentations below.

Structure of the relevant rules in Chapter 21:

WORKS OF MIXED RESPONSIBILITY

21.8 WORKS OF MIXED RESPONSIBILITY:

   WORKS THAT ARE MODIFICATIONS OF OTHER WORKS

   21.9 GENERAL RULE

   Modifications of Texts: 21.10-21.15

   Art Works: 21.16-21.17

   Musical Works: 21.18-21.22

   Sound Recordings: 21.23

   MIXED RESPONSIBILITY IN NEW WORKS: 21.24-21.27

   [No general rule]

The section on "Works That Are Modifications of Other Works" includes rules that cover some new works of mixed responsibility, e.g., the rule for musical works that include words (21.19), some of which are new works.

Perhaps one of the sources of confusion in the current rules for "works of mixed responsibility" is that even though the section is defined by a condition of authorship, it is divided up based on types of modifications of work, not based on types of mixed responsibility. Note that a work could conceivably be made into a new work without introducing mixed authorship; for example, an author could dramatize his own novel. Also, of course, a new work of mixed responsibility can be created, without there being a preexisting work. To avoid such confusion in this paper, a number of categories which are currently subsumed by *AACR2R* into the section on works of mixed responsibility are discussed below independently of the discussion of mixed responsibility.

I would recommend that general rules for works of mixed responsibility be developed that can be applied to such works in any form or format, whether they are new works or are based on preexisting works. The rule for new works of mixed responsibility should call for entering such works under title.[4]

I would also recommend that the rules be restructured into two sections: rules covering new works of mixed responsibility, and rules covering various kinds of adaptation and other change to preexisting works. The latter category will be discussed further below.

2. Collaborative works of mixed responsibility produced in stages, with portions of the collaborative work existing as separable pieces

In 21.28 when the parts of a work of mixed responsibility are published separately, they are treated as works in their own right, rather than as parts of a greater whole. For example, the following may be published (or at any rate exist and be collected) separately: sound tracks of films; choreographies; librettos;[5] screenplays; set and costume designs; stills and posters connected with a particular motion picture. Some might argue that these should be considered parts of the preexisting works, even though published (or existing) separately.

Change in practice in this area could also affect 21.11B, according to which illustrations published with text are entered under the writer of the text, but the same illustrations published separately are entered under the illustrator.

One of the reviewers of the original outline of this paper suggested that this section should also cover "electronic resources, finding aids, digital supplements, guidebooks and manuals that accompany, and software/data." This suggestion may, in fact, cover a number of different problems:

a. Supplementary or related material that has a somewhat independent existence:

Past practice has sometimes been to enter materials such as supplements under the heading for the supplemented work in certain prescribed instances, for example, when they are by the author of the supplemented work, when they have dependent titles, when use of the supplement is dependent on a particular edition of the supplemented work, or when the supplement represents a clear continuation of the supplemented work.[6] It is possible that such approaches could be fruitful for dealing with supplementary or related electronic and other material.

b. Finding aids:

These represent a rather special case. Finding aids could be conceived as a fuller type of metadata that mediates between (i) the cataloging record metadata and (ii) the actual collection being cataloged in the cataloging record and described in the finding aid. Since the finding aid itself stands for the same "work" as the cataloging record, and since it does not actually appear in the catalog in the same sense that the catalog record does (it does not have headings linked to the authority file, etc.), perhaps it need not be dealt with by *AACR*. (Do any institutions catalog their finding aids, such that the cataloging record, too, needs to be linked in?) However, if it is felt useful to include in *AACR* rules for making hypertext links between cataloging records and the actual documents they describe (when the latter are in digitized form), then finding aids should not be ignored in such a context.

c. Guidebooks and manuals that accompany:

If "accompany" means physically bundled together, then I'm not aware that there are any problems with treating such accompanying material according to the existing rules in *AACR* for describing them in the physical description area. In effect, we treat them as being part of the expression being described in the bibliographic record, just as we would treat volume 2 of a multivolume work.

Could this refer, however, to guidebooks and manuals that are electronic and meant to be used in conjunction with works that are not electronic (or vice versa)? If that is the case, then the comments under section 1 above apply to these as well.

d. Software/data:

It is probably not possible to make sweeping recommendations about this type of relationship. It may be that we would want to devise different practices based on whether or not the software is meant to be used exclusively with the data, whether or not the data are meant to be used exclusively with the software, and so forth.

Changes in this area could represent a considerable shift from current practice and should probably be studied more closely before detailed recommendations are made.

3. Works intended for performance

When does performance create a new related work (akin to adaptation), rather than a version of the old (akin to translation, i.e., a type of subsidiary authorship)? (Subsidiary authorship refers to the type of authorship that can produce a new edition of a previously existing work; examples are editing, translation, illustration, and the writing of commentaries.)

Traditionally, music scholars have considered composing to be primary authorship and performance to be subsidiary authorship. Thus, musical performances are frequently given composer main entry. Traditionally, film scholars have been hesitant to assign primary authorship to any of the functions that go into the making of a film. Thus, films of performances have usually been given title main entry. Is there any way for these two fields to agree on which authorship functions involved in performance are primary (creating new related works) and which are subsidiary (creating manifestations of previously existing works)?

By the way, even within the music field, there is general acknowledgment that the primacy of composition over performance is culture-specific, and functions best when applied to Western classical music. Users are not as consistent in considering works of Western popular or folk music, or non-Western music of all kinds to be primarily the works of composers.

Works intended for performance raise general questions about the degree to which the rules should rank into primary and secondary responsibility the functions carried out in the production of a work of mixed reponsibility.

Do some types of performance create new works and some not? If so, what is a principled way to differentiate between the two (or more?) kinds of performance?

Is a work intended for performance and its realization the same work, or two different works?

If both are the same work, should the work be identified primarily by title, or by a primary author and a title? If the latter, how is the primary author to be identified? To the extent that this deals with the naming issue, it will be dealt with further below in section II.

Problems with specific rules in *AACR2R:*

a. 21.1B2e, in explicitly encouraging entry under performing groups for films and videorecordings, implies that all other functions carried out in the creation of a moving image work are subsidiary to the performance of a group. This approach is not consistent with the treatment elsewhere in the rules of performance of music as subsidiary to composition. The phrase "beyond mere performance, execution, etc." is ambiguous. Does this mean that if any improvisation on a preexisting work takes place, the preexisting work becomes a new work authored by the performing group? Music librarians have probably been inconsistent in practice on this point. If it does mean that improvisation creates a new work when carried out by a group, why does not improvisation create a new work when carried out by an individual performer?

b. There is potential cross-classification if some sound recordings are considered to be musical works. In general, there seems to be confusion about the meaning of "musical works"—does the category include videorecordings of musical performances or is it limited to graphic/textual representations of music intended for performance? The glossary definition ("musical composition . . . intended for performance") may imply that it is meant to cover only the graphic/textual representations of music. Further evidence that "musical works" might not be meant to cover sound recordings is provided by the fact that 21.23A1 refers back to rules 21.18-21.22, calling for use of the "heading appropriate to the work." If it is true that "musical works" is intended to refer only to graphic/textual representations of music, but not to the performances of music recorded on sound and videorecordings, the cataloging world is using the term "musical works" in an oddly narrow way compared to the way the rest of the world uses the term.

c. 21.23C1 calls for entering a sound recording compilation of works of multiple composers under performer. There are two functions carried out by the performer in the creation of such a compilation: (i) the compilation or assembly of the pieces to be performed and (ii) the performance of the pieces. Since we hold consistently elsewhere in the rules that performance is subsidiary to composition, the difference in this case seems to be the act of compilation. If that is the case, this current practice seems to be a throwback to the old rules for entering textual compilations under editor, and thus does not fit with the general principle of consistent treatment of underlying conditions of authorship regardless of format. Current practice is generally to enter under title when a subsidiary authorship function such as editing or compilation has been carried out, but there is no primary author.

d. 21.20 calls for entering musical settings for ballets under composer, even when the choreographic notation, scenario, libretto, etc., is present. The dance field has come to see performances of dance works as works of mixed responsibility to be entered under title, although this is not yet reflected in *AACR2*.

Recommendations concerning rules for works intended for performance:

Works intended for performance present the hardest problem to solve, since there are large groups of users who perceive of them as still being the work of the author of their original text, and large groups of users who perceive of them as being new related works once they are performed. The CC:DA Task Force charged with making recommendations concerning works intended for performance failed to reach consensus in an attempt to consider most works intended for performance the work of the author of the original text.[7] I lean toward another approach, perhaps based on my background in film. Note that there are actually three "layers" of creative activity going on in the creation of a dramatico-musical work which is then filmed: (1) There is composition of the original text (in the case of a play) or music (in the case of an opera; we will ignore the problem of the libretto for now). (2) There are the decisions that go into actually producing the play or opera in a live performance (lighting, sets, costume design, casting, various readings of the lines or voicings of the arias, and so forth). (3) Finally, there are the creative decisions that go into making a cinematic work: camera angles, composition of frames, cutting, etc. It is the third layer that I am convinced constitutes a kind of adaptation, such that the play or opera becomes a film, a different work—a photographic work, not a musical work (but one related to the play or opera on which it is based). I am willing to concede that when film is used as a mere recording medium, it is not a cinematic work. However, if a screenwriter, an editor, and/or a cinematographer are credited, I recommend that it be considered a new cinematic work. Note that if this approach were to be taken, it would be crucial to make an added entry for the main entry of any pre-existing work that is adapted into a new work in the course of performance.

There is a more logical (but very radical) approach that should be examined, at least. If it is desired to consider *all* performances of a particular dramatico-musical work as the same work, no matter what the medium, we could consider all dramatico-musical works to be inherently works of mixed authorship, unable to exist without the work of many different people carrying out many different functions, and therefore entered under title. Thus, all texts of *Macbeth* and all performances of *Macbeth* would be entered under title. We would then doubtless be committing ourselves to elaborate uniform titles to allow versions of versions to be linked up to each other. For example, the various versions of Orson Welles' *Macbeth* would need to be subcollated along with its sound track, its scripts, works about it, videodisc versions with additional material, etc. It is interesting to note in this connection that these works tend to have fairly distinctive titles (*Don Giovanni* vs. *5th Symphony*), and their performances are often advertised without using the names of playwrights or composers.

If my recommended approach toward cinematic works based on previously existing dramatic works is adopted, there is a way that users of online catalogs could be helped to find these performances fairly readily. It is possible that a change in the USMARC format to specifically identify related work added entries as performance added entries could lead to online catalog displays that might prevent undue confusion for users who consider a performance and a work intended for performance to be the same work. Currently, the second indicator of an added entry for a work can be set to 2 when the work is actually contained within the work cataloged, and an added entry for a work is contained in a 6XX field. If the same second indicator were given another value for performance, it would potentially allow for the following type of display:

Shakespeare, William, 1564-1616.

   1. All's well that ends well.

   2. Antony and Cleopatra.

   3. As you like it.

   4. Comedy of errors.

   5. Coriolanus.

   6. Cymbeline.

   7. Hamlet.

   8. Henry V.

9. Henry VI.

10. Macbeth.

When the user chooses line 10, for Macbeth, the following display could result:

Shakespeare, William, 1564-1616. Macbeth.

1. Editions of Macbeth.

2. Works containing Macbeth.[8]

3. Performances of Macbeth.

4. Works about Macbeth.[9]

5. Other works related to Macbeth.[10]

When the user chooses line 3, for performances of Macbeth, the following display could result:

1. Classic theatre. Macbeth. 1977.

2. Hallmark hall of fame. Macbeth (1954)

3. Hallmark hall of fame. Macbeth (1960)

4. Macbeth (1948)

5. Macbeth (1971)

6. Studio one. Macbeth. 1951.

7. Throne of blood. Akira Kurosawa's throne of blood. 1957.

Of course, this still dodges the question of which films are mere recordings of a performance (same work), and which are adaptations (new works), and whether this distinction should be made visible to users in displays. In figure 5 you can see what such a distinction could look like, if we decided to make it.

```
Shakespeare, William, 1564-1616. Macbeth.
1. Editions of Macbeth.
2. Works containing Macbeth.
3. Performances of Macbeth.
4. Films based on Macbeth.
5. Works about Macbeth.
```

FIGURE 5

"Performances of" would be for same main entry sound and videorecordings ("mere recordings"); "films based on" would be for films (i.e., motion pictures and videorecordings) with related work added entries for the preexisting works from which they were adapted.

Note that here the USMARC format calls for coding of types of relationships between works and editions of works not explicitly defined by *AACR2* (but implicit in the rules). In other words, some of the work to make relationships intelligible to users is being done by USMARC, not by *AACR2*. This may be an area in which better coordination between the two would be advisable, and may also point to the need to make explicit what is implicit in *AACR2*.

Also note the way that the encoding of relationships provides a method for helping users with unmanageably large OPAC displays.

By the way, I would like to take issue with those who might feel that it doesn't matter whether Shakespeare's *Macbeth* as a work includes all the film versions or all the performances. It does matter, because of the fact that a record can be retrieved many different ways, and the work it represents may need to be displayed with many other works. Polanski's *Macbeth* can be represented in the catalog as either an edition of Shakespeare's play (Shakespeare, William, 1564-1616. Macbeth) or as an adaptation of the play into a film (Macbeth (1971)). Whatever decision is made, that is the way the film will appear in the summary display to anyone who retrieves it along with ninety-five other hits, on say, a genre search, a subject search, a keyword-within-record search, a search for a particular actor or cinematographer, etc. The work heading must be able to stand on its own in representing the work among hundreds of other works in long displays. It is important to decide *what* is being named before naming it. One of the functions the main entry carries out in an OPAC is that of naming, defining, and differentiating the work entities of interest to users and making the relationships among them intelligible in complex displays representing hundreds of other works.

4. Preexisting works reissued with additional material

Here the fact that many rules of mixed authorship are based on format rather than on conditions of authorship is leading to the result that works with the same conditions of authorship, but in newer formats, are excluded from treatment under *AACR2R* rules. For example:

21.13 is defined as "Texts published with commentary." There are now lots of examples of musical performances and films (and probably other types of work) being republished with audio tracks containing commentary by people involved in the production, critics, etc. Many of these are works intended for performance, but the phenomenon is probably not limited to them. There are many videodisc examples in the UCLA Film and Television Archive; e.g., the interactive multimedia version of *The Magic Flute,* which, according to a summary on a cataloging record, contains "a complete performance of Mozart's The magic flute, enhanced by over one hour of commentaries and other music. Includes . . . long-form analysis of Mozart's music, story of the opera . . ."

21.15 is defined as "Texts published with biographical/critical material." The republications mentioned above can also include biographical/critical material. For example, *Microsoft Multimedia Mozart,* according to a summary on a cataloging record, contains "Multimedia information on Mozart and his Dissonant quartet, including a recording of the quartet, an examination of the historical and social context in which it was composed, a visual guide through the music."

21.11, Illustrated texts. It is now possible to publish discursive works which use fragments of preexisting performed works as illustration, e.g., musical performances or excerpts from films. *Cataloging Musical Moving Image Material,* edited by Lowell Ashley, recently published as *MLA Technical Report no. 25,* has an example (on p. 67) of a videocassette of lectures at Harvard by Leonard Bernstein that are illustrated by various musical performances.

Commentaries, biographical/critical material, and "illustrations" do not cover all of the categories of material that can be added to a preexisting work in a republication of it (or to a new work, as in the Leonard Bernstein example). For example, the multimedia version of *A Hard Day's Night* "features the complete, uncut movie, Alun Owen's original script, additional Beatles songs, an essay on the Beatles by critic Bruce Eder, the theatrical trailer and clips from Richard Lester's early work." Many people would consider this to be a version of *A Hard Day's Night*.

Perhaps the following could serve as a first draft of a general rule to cover these new situations: If a work consisting of a preexisting work accompanied by or interwoven with biographical or critical material, illustrations, commentaries, and other subsidiary material is represented as an edition of the preexisting work, enter it under the heading appropriate to that work. If it is represented as a new work, enter it according to the general rule for new works of mixed responsibility.[11]

5. Preexisting works transformed or adapted into new works

Are there other problems with decision-making about adaptations or other changes to preexisting works besides those discussed above?

To someone like myself who is not an expert music cataloger, it seems that it would be useful to have a more principled approach when arrangement or improvisation or other similar change to a musical work is extensive enough to justify considering it a new work (i.e., a type of adaptation). What is essential about a musical work that persists through arrangement or improvisation? Is it melody? Are there musical forms analogous to "play" and "novel" such that movement from one form to the other constitutes adaptation?

Is there adequate consensus yet about whether jazz improvisation creates editions of previously existing works, or whether, on the contrary, it constitutes a kind of composition on the fly, thereby creating new works? For example, the song "All of Me" was written by Gerald Marks (music) and Seymour Simons (lyrics). It has been performed by the following jazz artists: Billie Holiday, Erroll Garner, Frank Sinatra, Sidney Bechet, and Louis Armstrong, among others. If an analytical entry is being made for Erroll Garner's performance, should this be treated as an expression of the song by Gerald Marks (Marks, Gerald. All of me)? Or should it be treated as a new related work composed by Erroll Garner in the course of his jazz performance (Garner, Erroll. All of me)?

Is it really wise to consider musical works that include words (such as librettos or lyrics) to be primarily musical, rather than works of mixed responsibility? I recently had occasion to catalog a newsreel story about the famous Marian Anderson concert in front of the Lincoln Memorial. The newsreel includes her complete performance of "America" ("from every mountainside, let freedom ring"). I wanted to make an added entry for the song and was disconcerted to discover that the main entry for it is "God save the King," since it uses the melody of the latter. In other words, the change in the lyrics to the song was not considered significant enough to create a new related work.

What about spatial data? Map catalogers do seem to recognize the concept of edition. For example, the U.S. Geological Survey's 1939 map of Golden, Colorado, has an edition with revisions shown in purple compiled from aerial photographs taken in 1978. These two maps are given the same main entry, which would seem to imply that they are considered to be the same work. It would be useful to ask some map catalogers who were theoretically inclined to investigate whether or not a preexisting map can be changed to such a degree that it should be considered a new work related to the preexisting work and, if so, whether one can define the nature of such changes in a principled way.

And what about electronic resources? What types of "adaptation" of electronic works into new but related electronic works are likely to arise in this area? Will we be able to rely as heavily on representation to identify the relationships between two different but related electronic works as we have been able to do with current off-line publishing?

6. Represented works; for example, a series of photographs of a Frank Lloyd Wright house by an eminent photographer; the Frank Lloyd Wright house is the work represented, and the photographs are a work in which Wright's work is represented; also sometimes called a "surrogate" for Wright's work[12]

Image catalogers need to make a clear decision about what is being described in order to prevent the creation of a confusing record; the work that is not described must be treated as a related work of some type. *AACR2R* does not yet provide much guidance for decisions of this kind, although it does call for entering a reproduction under the heading for the original work (21.16B). Presumably a reproduction is of little interest in its own right. When a work is represented in another work that *is* of interest, such as a photographic work or the work of another artist, a decision must be made. For example, Michael Kenna's photographs of Le Notre's gardens, recently shown at the Huntington Library, should probably be considered to be primarily the work of Michael Kenna, but related to the work of Le Notre.[13] The current popularity of performance art is raising similar problems. When the work of a performance artist is documented by another artist, the latter a photographer or cinematographer, the problems are similar. Also, the proliferation of images of *Mona Lisa* in fine art, on T-shirts, in Wegman photos, reflected on magazine covers, on an apron, over and over by Warhol, etc., forces us to realize that reproduction of an image cannot always be held to be simply a copy ("manifestation") of the original.[14]

Ideally, *AACR2R* would contain rules for both options, (a) emphasis on the representation and (b) emphasis on the represented work, and leave it up to institutions to decide which was most appropriate for any given work. Possible criteria that could be applied might include (i) whether the intent was to create a surrogate for the original work, or whether the intent was to create a new work by the photographer; (ii) whether the image is presented as the represented work, or as a new work by the photographer.

It has been suggested by Sara Shatford Layne that it might be useful to explore the possibility of creating two records in one, one that describes the represented work and one that describes the representation, with the fields differentiated as to which work is being described by using USMARC linked-field techniques. Sherman Clarke suggests that another potential approach might be to create an authority record that describes the represented work and link all cataloging records for representations of it to that authority record. (Sara counters that in her view, that "authority record" should look more like a full bibliographic record; presumably she means, for example, that it should contain some physical description.)

7. Works of changing authorship[15] (serials and revised editions)

Currently, change of title of a serial work leads to the creation of a new main entry in *AACR2R;* in other words, change of title causes the creation of a new, related work. The various related works that make up the history of a given serial can only be assembled by a user who happens to be in a library that holds issues entered under each title the serial has held. If there are any missing links, the run cannot be assembled. Is this really the right way to conceive of a serial work? Does it really correspond to the way users conceptualize serial works?

Now that serials are beginning to be distributed electronically, their nature as works is beginning to change in rather profound ways. For example, a serial distributed as issues in text form can now exist simultaneously in electronic form as a continuously updated database consisting of all of the articles ever published in that serial, extending across title changes. In other words, such a database can easily contain articles from a serial which has changed its title several times. Users surely consider both the database and the journal they seek (under any title it has held) to be different versions of the same work.

Currently, rules 21.6C1 and 21.12 call for treating revised editions as new works whenever the representation of authorship changes, including simple transposition of the names of two authors on a title page. Such revisions are also treated as new works whenever the title changes. These practices, too, mean that a user can only be assured of finding the latest edition of a text (or other work subject to revision over time) in a library that has cataloging records for every earlier edition, so that the chained related work added entries can gradually lead the user from his or her citation to the latest edition. It seems likely that users consider all of these editions to represent the same work, and that they would find it useful to see the editions in one place. In this way they could be sure of getting the latest, most current edition, and scientific historians could more easily survey the library's holdings of earlier editions of a prominent text or other work subject to extensive revision over time. A definition of work that allowed for change in authorship, editorship, or title of a text without the text becoming a new work could help library users in a number of fields that make heavy use of texts (e.g., law and medicine).

E. Definition of work

There seems to be a certain amount of consensus in the field that it would be useful to at least explore the possibility of adding an explicit definition of work to *AACR2R*.[16] I did some dissertation work on at least trying to describe what such a definition might look like. Functions the definition should carry out:

1. It should include more than just works of single personal authorship, encompassing works of changing authorship, multiple authorship, and mixed authorship.

2. It should recognize that a work can change in either title or authorship without necessarily becoming a new work.

3. It should recognize that a work can be created by a group, whether named or unnamed and whether the group's name changes or not.

4. It should recognize that a work can be translated into a language other than its original language without becoming a new work.

5. It should recognize that a work intended for performance can be performed without becoming a new work.

6. It should recognize that a work can be reissued with subsidiary material, such as commentaries, illustrations, biographical/critical material, and other subsidiary matter, without thereby becoming a new work.

7. It should recognize that the intellectual and artistic content of a work can change without its necessarily becoming a new work, as in the case of revision, musical arrangement, and improvisation, etc.

8. It should recognize that a work can be reproduced photographically without necessarily becoming a new work.

With these functions in mind, the following definition is proposed:

Work: the product of the intellectual or artistic activity of a person or persons or of a named or unnamed group expressed in a particular way. A work has a name (or can be named[17]) and can stand alone as a publication; however, its name can change without its necessarily becoming a new work. The person(s) or group responsible can change without the work necessarily becoming a new work. The work can be translated into another language without necessarily becoming a new work. If two items are represented as the same work, consider them to be so, unless there is some overriding reason not to do so. As a rule of thumb, consider two items to be the same work if they would be considered interchangeable by most users, or if a user seeking one would actually find the other preferable (as in the case of a later revised edition).

Do not consider two items to be the same work if the particular way in which the intellectual or artistic activity is expressed has changed in order to adapt it to a new medium of expression. Examples would be the novelization of a film, the dramatization of a novel, an etching based on a painting, or a free transcription of a musical work.[18]

I feel I cannot in good conscience leave this topic without a warning, however. There are good reasons that our cataloging codes have never had a definition of work in their glossaries. Language can be treacherous. As soon as you write a rule or a definition, there is the potential for loopholes. There is the potential for practitioners to lose sight of the spirit or principle and seize on the letter of the "law" to do the exact opposite of the original intent. In some ways, it might be preferable to leave catalogers free to use their judgment in this area over time, as conditions change, rather than tying them down to the conception of work we are able to formulate in 1997. If we do attempt a definition, I would urge that we make it as principled a definition as possible to try to avoid this problem.

II. Naming the Work

Under our current system for naming works (using the main entry), we identify a work by means of its principal author (if it has one) in conjunction with its title. When there is a principal author, this usually results in a unique heading for the work, without the need for cataloger-added parentheticals to break conflicts. However, when the title alone must be relied on, it is frequently necessary for catalogers to add qualifiers to break conflicts, to ensure that all of the editions of one work come together independently of another work with the same title. Serials catalogers are very familiar with this phenomenon (see figure 6).

Once catalogers start tinkering with the titles in this fashion, the titles become much less predictable for users, especially in systems that are incapable of ignoring parenthetical qualifiers in the arrangement of records retrieved, as most of our OPACs are. If we are really serious about trying to implement the objectives of the catalog and helping users find the works they seek (demonstrating the relationships between works), we ought to try to find a way to roll back *AACR2*'s move toward title main entry, so as to create stronger collocation points for the editions of a work, as well as works related to it and works about it.

Unfortunately, OPACs are at their worst when it comes to helping a user find a work of which both author and title are known, probably still the most common search done in research libraries.[19] Systems can't seem to handle an identifier that sometimes occurs in two fields (e.g., 100 and 245) and sometimes in one field broken into subfields (e.g., 700 with a $t subfield) (see figure 7), and that sometimes consists of a uniform heading (that can be

---

Using the title alone for main entry:

```
Report (Aerojet-General Corporation. Liquid Engine
    Division)

Report by the Railway Board on Indian railways.

Report covering the operation and enforcement of liquor
    laws in Manitoba.

Report (Forest Products Laboratory (U.S.))

Report from the Select Committee on Abortion.

Report (National Severe Storms Project (U.S.))

Report of Chief Inspector of Locomotive Boilers.

Report of the Banana Board and statement of accounts.

Report of the California party boat fleet.

Report of the Millinery Stabilization Commission, Inc.

Report on freedom.

Report on sunspot observations.

Report on the Kenya Post Office Savings Bank.

Report on the macaroni and kindred products industry in
    Canada.

Report on tourism statistics in Tanzania.

Report to the legislature on Brown Bag Network Program.

Report (United Kingdom Atomic Energy Authority. Research
    Group)

Report upon forestry.
```

527 screens of journal titles listed in ORION as of September, 1997

FIGURE 6

```
Work identified using two fields:
100 1_ $a Shakespeare, William, $d 1564-1616.
245 00 $a Macbeth.

Work identified using one field:
700 12 $a Shakespeare, William, $d 1564-1616. $t Macbeth.
```

FIGURE 7

dynamically updated, e.g., 130) and sometimes consists of a transcribed field (that must be protected from dynamic updating, e.g., 245). They never offer users a search for a known work, and they often force the user to choose either author *or* title (see figure 8);

```
Searches offered on initial search screen on MELVYL's new
web site:
Title
Author
Subject
Power

Searches offered on the initial screen of DRA's web
catalog:
Any word or words
Search by subject
Search by author
Search by title
```

FIGURE 8

even when an author-title search is available, it tends to be treated as an expert or power search, and it tends to be done as a keyword-within-bibliographic-record search, such that the authority file is not searched for name and title variants (see figure 9),

```
Keyword-within-bibliographic-record search:
FNT Cummings 1
Cummings, E. E. (Edward Estlin), 1894-1962.
    1 x 1 / with an introduction by Lloyd Frankenberg. --
London : Horizon, 1947.
```

FIGURE 9

and the only possible display is a display of bibliographic records in main entry order. Thus, any work *added entries* that may have been retrieved will not be apparent in the display (see figure 10).

```
Bibliographic record that displays as:
Search done: FIND NAME TITLE Cummings 1
Hollander, John. An entertainment for Elizabeth ... 1972
... not revealing the reason for its retrieval:
Hollander, John.
   An entertainment for Elizabeth / with designs for
costumes by Anne Hollander ; and introduction by Irving
Cummings ... (English literary renaissance monographs ; v.
1, no. 1) ...
```

FIGURE 10

Also, retrieved records are not summarized as to whether they are editions of the work itself, related works, or works about the work, producing the unmanageably large results sets that plague OPAC users. However, rather than letting the failures of our systems determine our cataloging practices, I would urge that we figure out a better way to force our systems to behave as catalogs. It is the business of *AACR2* to cause the creation of catalogs that meet the cataloging objective of allowing the user to find a particular work of which the author and/or title is known.

It is very important to separate issues concerning the *form of name* we give an entity from issues concerning the *definition* of the entity (covered in the section above). The film *Seven Samurai* has been released under three different titles:

> *Seven samurai*
>
> *Shichinin no samurai* (a transliteration of the Japanese script)
>
> *Magnificent seven*

The question of whether to use a uniform title to bring together all of the editions of a work is different from the question of what that uniform title should be (e.g., whether it should be in the language of the library users, English in most of the U.S., for example, or the language of the country of origin of the work in question, Japanese, for example, for a Japanese film). A number of commentators have pointed out the possibility of developing international authority records that identify the language of each heading contained in them, allowing libraries to designate their own language forms as the preferred forms for display in their OPACs. This could potentially free us from the tyranny of language that led commentators like Eva Verona to oppose the use of uniform titles because her users didn't like having to deal with foreign languages. Allowing an English-language-speaking population to search for works under their English-language titles, regardless of their titles in their countries of origin, would allow us to come closer to our principle of trying to enter authors and works under the names by which they are commonly known.

III. Providing Access to Works under Their Variant Names

Provision of access to works under their variant names is haphazard and in a state of confusion at the present time. In current practice, some of the variant names for a work may be found only in the form of title added entries on bibliographic records, while others may be found only in the title subfields of name-title cross-references in authority records (see figure 11).

Variant names for a work may be found:

1. In title added entries and contents notes on bibliographic records:

        245 1_

        246

        505

        740

2. In name-title cross-references found on authority records.

FIGURE 11

Given the yawning gap between authority records and bibliographic records maintained by most OPACs (described above), this ensures that users' searches for works using variants of author name and/or title will be highly likely to fail in most systems, or to succeed only partially (as when only editions carrying the variant forms are retrieved, not *all* editions). (See figure 12.)

This is an area in which work to clarify our concepts of "work" and "edition," and to implement cleanly defined record structures based on these concepts (authority records for "work" (chapters 21, 25, and 26) and bibliographic records for "edition" (chapters 1-13)),

---

When the title variant sought by the user exists as a name-title cross-reference, users searching for a work by title (rather than author and title) may find the work only if a keyword-within-heading search of authority record headings is included as part of the title search (not done in any existing OPACs) and only if the search results are small.

User searches on FTI Nutcracker

<00>400-7 10 $a Tchaikovsky, Peter Ilich, $d 1840-1893.

FIGURE 12

could be most fruitful in making our catalogs work better for users, although OPACs will have to be better designed to make use of these records as well.

Other problems for users stem from the fact that our OPAC software lacks hierarchical sensitivity. For example, the cross-reference from "FBI" to "United States. Federal Bureau of Investigation" needs to be applied not just to that heading, but to those hierarchically beneath it, including, for example, "United States. Federal Bureau of Investigation. Intelligence Division." (See figure 13.)

```
Two authority records:
United States. Federal Bureau of Investigation.
     x FBI

United States. Federal Bureau of Investigation.
Intelligence Division.

The second authority record lacks the cross-reference from
FBI.
```

FIGURE 13

A search for "FBI Intelligence Division" should not be allowed to fail, as it would in all current OPACs. Perhaps a statement of principle in chapter 26 of *AACR2* might help convey the need for better searching software. For example, the principle might be stated as: "A cross-reference to a heading should also be made available to users who access any subset of that heading. For example, a cross-reference to an author should be available to any user seeking one of his works identified by means of his name and the title of the work."

IV. Structure of the Catalog and Methods of Demonstrating Relationships

On the AACRCONF listserve[20] and at the Toronto meeting in October of 1997 there was considerable discussion of whether or not we need to change our current record structures and methods of demonstrating relationships in a computerized and networked environment. This topic applies to more than just works, but much of the discussion centered on the need for a work-based record, as opposed to the current practice of creating edition- or expression-based records.

First of all, let me point out that in many ways we are *already* doing most of what some commentators have described as a radical new approach (and therefore impractical). Let me explain. We already differentiate one work from another (in making main entry decisions). (See figure 14.)

We already name works (again, by means of the main entry). (See figure 15.)

And we already create work-based records whenever we create an authority record for a work. Music catalogers, who create more of these authority records than anyone else, will

```
Two works differentiated by their main entries:
Health (New York, N.Y.)
Health (San Francisco, Calif.)
```

FIGURE 14

```
A work named using author and title:
Beethoven, Ludwig van, 1770-1827. Symphonies, no. 5, op.
67, C minor.
```

FIGURE 15

probably feel that this hardly needs to be said, but I think it does need to be said for people who work in fields in which such records are rarely made (see figure 16).

We already implement a "superwork" concept whenever we make a work (i.e., name-title or uniform title) added entry on the bibliographic record for another work. For example, when I make a name-title added entry for Margaret Mitchell's novel on the film *Gone*

```
A work-based authority record:
<00>010-0 __ $a n80056438
   <00>100-0 10 $a Tchaikovsky, Peter Ilich, $d 1840-1893.
$t Shchelkunchik
   <00>400-1 10 $a Tchaikovsky, Peter Ilich, $d 1840-1893.
$t Casse-noisette
   <00>400-2 10 $a Tchaikovsky, Peter Ilich, $d 1840-1893.
$t Di|bot|hor|no
   <00>400-3 10 $a Tchaikovsky, Peter Ilich, $d 1840-1893.
$t N|hotkn|happar
   <00>400-4 10 $a Tchaikovsky, Peter Ilich, $d 1840-1893.
$t Nussknacker
   <00>400-5 10 $a Tchaikovsky, Peter Ilich, $d 1840-1893.
$t Schiaccianoci
   <00>400-6 10 $a Tchaikovsky, Peter Ilich, $d 1840-1893.
$t Sp|farg|fator de nuci
   <00>400-7 10 $a Tchaikovsky, Peter Ilich, $d 1840-1893.
$t Nutcracker
```

FIGURE 16

with the Wind, I am treating the novel as a superwork, from which new works, such as the film, have spun off over time (see figure 17).

```
Superwork concept:

Related work:

245 00 $a Gone with the wind $h [Motion picture] / $c
Metro-Goldwyn-Mayer.

700 1_ $a Mitchell, Margaret, $d 1900-1949. $t Gone with
the wind.

Original work (Superwork):

100 1_ $a Mitchell, Margaret, $d 1900-1949.

245 00 $a Gone with the wind / $c Margaret Mitchell.
```

FIGURE 17

What is needed most, I think, is clarification and statement in the code of the principles behind what we are doing now, more consistent application of those principles, and an examination of how far our current practices can be extended to help library users find the multiple-edition works that are probably the most commonly sought works in our libraries.

Note that these decisions about when an item is a new work cannot be avoided. It is a fact of life that works exist in the form of editions, and as soon as there is more than one edition, there is the possibility for variation in both the author name and the title by which the work is known, cited, and sought by users. Cataloging is essentially the act of decision-making about issues like these, and all catalogers should be taught to make such decisions effectively. Those who think they are avoiding such decision-making are simply representing two items that are the same work as if they were two different works; in other words, they are not cataloging (doing professional work), they are creating the equivalent of a publisher's catalog or a web search engine (doing clerical work). The only difference is that our work costs more. It is a waste of the taxpayers' money for people who add no more value than that to be paid out of the public purse for cataloging in libraries.

On the AACRCONF listserve, and at the Toronto meeting, a number of participants suggested that we begin to move data from bibliographic records for editions ("expressions") of works to the authority record that stands for the work itself. I would have no objection to our studying the possibility of moving toward such an approach for all of the *access points* that apply to the work as a whole, with some important qualifications:

1. as long as the distinction can be made cleanly (i.e., this access point is not needed for this particular edition ("expression"), only for the work as a whole); consider, for example, what is to be done with data that applies to more than one edition, but not to all editions, e.g., some editions may be illustrated by Gustave Dore, but not all.

2. as long as descriptions of editions of a particular work are readily available to anyone who selects that work.

3. when and only when OPACs routinely integrate authority records with bibliographic records such that all searches (including keyword searches) are done on both (as far as I know, no OPAC can claim to do this now).

However, I would strongly oppose moving any of the *descriptive elements* from the bibliographic record to the authority record. Consider the following. A work exists only as the set of all of its editions (or "expressions"). If all of the copies ("manifestations" or "items") of all of those editions were to be destroyed, the work would thereby be eliminated from our cultural record. The marks that we transcribe from an edition (or "expression") into our bibliographic record constitute historical evidence of how the abstract work manifested itself concretely. After the main entry, all of the bibliographic description in a bibliographic record serves to identify a particular edition of a work, distinguish it from other editions of that work, and characterize it as an edition. All of this data serves to help a user select the particular edition of the work that best meets her needs.

Remember that all of the following can vary between editions of a work:

- title, as when a work changes title between editions (see figure 18);

```
Title:
Smollett, Tobias George, 1721-1771.
   The expedition of Humphry Clinker ...
Smollett, Tobias George, 1721-1771.
   Humphry Clinker ...
```

FIGURE 18

- statement of responsibility, as with translators, editors, illustrators (subsidiary authors), and as with an author who uses different pseudonyms across the various editions of one work (see figure 19);

```
Statement of responsibility:
The expedition of Humphry Clinker / by the author of
Roderick Random.
The expedition of Humphry Clinker / by Dr. Smollett.
The expedition of Humphry Clinker / by Tobias Smollet,
M.D., with 10 plates by T. Rowlandson.
L'expedition d'Humphry Clinker / traduction de Jean Giono
et Catherine d'Ivernois.
```

FIGURE 19

- publisher and publication date (see figure 20);

```
Publisher and publication date:

The expedition of Humphry Clinker / by Tobias Smollett ,
M.D. ; with 10 plates by T. Rowlandson. -- London :
Printed for H.D. Symonds and T. Kay, 1793.

The expedition of Humphry Clinker / Tobias Smollett ;
edited by Peter Miles. -- London : Everyman, 1993.
```

FIGURE 20

- illustration statement in the physical description, as when one edition of a work is illustrated and another is not (see figure 21);

```
Illustrations:

The expedition of Humphry Clinker / Tobias Smollett. --
Ware : Wordsworth Classics, 1995.
333 p. ; 20 cm.

The expedition of Humphry Clinker / Tobias Smollett ;
introduction and notes by Thomas R. Preston ; the text
edited by O.M. Brack, Jr. -- Athens, Ga. : University of
Georgia Press, c1990.
ix, 500 p. : ill., map ; 24 cm.
```

FIGURE 21

- paging, which is often the *only* indicator of a change of edition in the classic sense of a resetting of the type; in this example, these two items probably represent the *same* edition of the work (see figure 22);

```
Paging:

The expedition of Humphry Clinker / by Tobias George
Smollett. -- New York, Century, 1902.
372 p.

The expedition of Humphry Clinker / by Tobias George
Smollett. -- New York, Century, 1904.
372 p.

(Same edition of the same work (same setting of type),
```

FIGURE 22

• series, as when one edition of a work is in a series and others are not (see figure 23).

```
Series statement:

The expedition of Humphry Clinker / Tobias Smollett ;
edited by Peter Miles. -- London : Everyman, 1993.
xxxiii, 444 p.

Humphry Clinker : an authoritative text, contemporary
responses, criticism / Tobias Smollett ; edited by James
L. Thorson. -- 1st ed. -- New York : Norton, c1983.
  xxi, 436 p. : ill. ; 22 cm. -- (A Norton critical
edition)
```

FIGURE 23

The edition entity has been dangerously neglected by major writers on the work, in three major ways.

First, there seems to be a failure to recognize that the entire bibliographic description functions to identify, describe, and characterize a particular edition of a work, not a particular work. There are many editions that do not have either edition statements or notes that specifically identify them as editions; see the examples in figures 18-23. Barbara Tillett's dissertation research on the derivative relationship, including editions, looked only at edition statements and notes, not at the rest of the description. Her "derivative relationship," which includes editions, translations, adaptations, and changes in genre, was studied using only the following USMARC fields: 041, 250, 775, 534, and the only fields in the body of the descriptive record that she characterizes as "devices to express these relationships in the catalog" are dash entries, edition statements, and notes.[21] What Tillett fails to recognize is that what makes explicit the fact that two items are two different editions of the same work is (1) the fact they have the same main entry (same work) and (2) the fact the description differs in some way (different editions). It is not necessary for the description to explicitly state "2nd edition" or for there to be a reference to a previous edition in the notes. The same type of error seems to have been made by the IFLA Study Group on the Functional Requirements for Bibliographic Records, which seemed to define "edition" as "expression" in the introduction, but then failed to associate all areas of the bibliographic description with the function of identifying an "expression" in the tables that make up the bulk of their work,[22] by Leazer, who includes date, edition, and language as attributes of work (and does not treat of editions at all),[23] and by Howarth (p. 154) who seems to imply that elements of the bibliographic description describe the work, rather than an edition of the work.

Secondly, there seems to be a failure to recognize that there is a layer between work and item, here called "edition," and that some changes in text do not necessarily create a new work, but rather create a new edition of the same work. Thus, for example, Patrick Wilson seems to consider even the most minute change to create a new work,[24] and, following him, Smiraglia states that "any change in either ideational or semantic content results in the creation of a new work,"[25] while Leazer adopts Smiraglia's definition.[26] See the examples in figures 18-23 for examples of change in semantic or ideational content that create new editions of a work, not new works. Note also that the changes that can occur between editions can be more complex than simple changes in the text.

And thirdly, there is a dangerous tendency to conflate the concepts of edition (same work) and adaptation (new related work) into one category. In fact, these are two quite distinct conditions, and they have been treated quite differently in Anglo-American cataloging practice. Two editions of the same work are given the same main entry. A work and its adaptation are given different main entries, with the latter given an added entry for the main entry of the first in order to demonstrate the relationship. As I have tried to argue above, there are good reasons to treat these two conditions differently; Polanski's *Macbeth* can be represented in the catalog as either an edition of Shakespeare's play (Shakespeare, William, 1564-1616. Macbeth) or as an adaptation of the play into a film (Macbeth (1971)). Whatever decision is made, that is the way the film will appear in the summary display to anyone who retrieves it along with ninety-five other hits on, say, a genre search, a subject search, a keyword-within-record search, a search for a particular actor or cinematographer, etc. It is important to aim at a representation of the work in a heading that corresponds to users' perceptions of the work, so that they can recognize and choose the heading for the work they seek. Unfortunately, Barbara Tillett lumps editions and adaptations together in the derivative category,[27] and then Smiraglia[28] and now Vellucci (p. 110) follow Tillett in lumping adaptations (new works) and translations (editions of the same work) together as "derivative relationships."

Another reason to avoid moving edition-specific information to a work-based record is that this edition-specific data represents our primary source material for determining how an author or a work (or a subject, for that matter) is commonly known. When determining the form of name for any of the three major entities (author, work, and subject), we need to know how the entity is usually named on the title pages of particular editions of works.

To lose this information descriptive of a particular edition, or to muddle it up with information applying to the work as a whole, would be a bibliographic disaster. The user may begin by seeking a particular work, but most users end their search by selecting a particular edition of it (e.g., the latest one, the illustrated one, the one from an authoritative publisher, the one with an editor known to the user). In the ideal catalog, once the user had selected an edition of the desired work, he or she could then select a physical format for that edition (e.g., electronic form, microform, or text; or electronic form, audiocassette, or CD; or electronic form, videocassette, or 35 mm. nitrate film).

Finally, consider the fact that the work develops over time by means of the accrual of editions. In a sense, the work cannot be described completely ahead of time.

A web-based world offers a new type of linking device to be used to demonstrate various types of relationships. Now we have the following potential linking devices for demonstrating relationships among our bibliographic, authority, and holdings records:

1. Hot links using web addresses

2. Standard numbers such as ISBNs and ISSNs

3. Record numbers such as an authority record number in the national Name Authority File or an LCCN

4. Uniform headings

I would like to suggest that in our current shared cataloging environment, in which we are maintaining numerous local catalogs with no linkages between catalogs, uniform headings, such as authorized forms of name for authors and works (including uniform titles), are still the most functional linking device. My reasons are as follows:

All are equally bad in terms of stability. All can change over time, and we have no reliable methods for proliferating these changes into all the catalogs which are using the linking device.

Uniform headings have the following advantages:

1. They are the only type of link that is humanly readable. Thus, they can represent an author, a work, or a subject to a user, enabling the user to recognize and select (or not select) a particular heading. Thus, they also have the effect of explaining something about the nature of the link (although various people have suggested ways in which to categorize relationships in a more detailed manner than we have done so far). Thus, a link that consists of an author name and a title carries the information that it represents the work named.

2. Since the uniform heading link is humanly readable, when it gets out of synch, that fact is more likely to be recognizable to catalog editors who can then put the link back in synch.

3. Certainly all links are prone to error, but it seems probable that humanly readable links are less likely to contain errors than meaningless strings of numbers or, at least, more likely to be spotted and corrected eventually.

4. And finally, uniform headings strike me as being more sharable. Unlike the other types of link, a uniform heading actually can sit in a catalog that does not have any other records with that heading and still function perfectly well. Once more records with that heading arrive, they should automatically link (assuming no errors and assuming adequate system design).

I think it would be helpful if we put more thought into detailing the types of linking that would be helpful in our catalogs. It seems to me that we most commonly need one-to-many links. Consider the following list:

1. Work to its editions (one-to-many, if authority record for work is linked to bibliographic records for its editions)

2. Edition to all copies of it in various physical formats (one-to-many, if bibliographic record for the edition is linked to holdings records for its near-equivalents or "manifestations" in various physical formats)

3. Author to his or her works (one-to-many, if authority record for author is linked to authority records for his or her works, and thence to bibliographic records attached to the work authority records)

4. Subject heading to the works about that subject (one-to-many, if authority record for subject is linked to bibliographic records using that subject heading)

5. Work to related work links (one-to-one, if authority records for the works were linked; many-to-many if all the editions of one work were linked to all the editions of the other work)

That latter category should perhaps give us pause. In my opinion, any link between bibliographic records should be considered to be at least potentially a link between two particular editions of two particular works, not a link between works, since the object of a bibliographic record is a particular edition of a particular work. It seems to me that linking of works would be much more efficient and logically explicable if it could be done as much as possible on a one-to-one basis (work record-to-work record), rather than on a many-to-many basis (bibliographic records-to-bibliographic records). If we do bibliographic record-to-bibliographic record linking, we risk increasing the number of linking added entries on each bibliographic record exponentially.

Currently, when we make a related work added entry on a bibliographic record, in effect, we link that bibliographic record to two different work authority records; its main entry links it to the work of which it is an edition; its related work added entry links it to the work to which it is related. Each of those work headings then provides one-to-many links to both editions of itself, and works related to it. Chained entries, such as those made between successively entered serials records, and revised editions of texts with authorship changes lose the power of the one-to-many linking.

We also need to develop methods of creating hierarchical links between entities that could be used in smart systems to signal to the computer (1) that a cross-reference to one element in a hierarchy also applies to all elements beneath it in the hierarchy; (2) that an editing change to one element in a hierarchy should also be applied to all elements beneath it; and (3) that a search that retrieves one element in a hierarchy should display that element and all elements beneath it. One possibility might be to try defining this hierarchy to the computer using the fact that our headings are already designed to be treated this way; thus, one could define the elements beneath as being those that begin with the same heading, but have subsequent subfields attached. (This assertion is probably oversimplified and would benefit from some research! For example, one would probably not often want to exercise hierarchical power over all authors with the same surname. You might want to sometimes, though, e.g., for names beginning with "Mc"....)

Consider the following hierarchical relationships that are currently ignored in OPACs:

- A corporate body to all of its subdivisions
- An author to all of his or her pseudonyms
- An author to all of his or her works represented by author-title headings
- A work to all of its editions; consider, for example, works such as the Bible that are subarranged by edition information such as language, date, etc., using uniform titles that include such edition-related elements.

(If we weren't limiting discussion to descriptive cataloging rules here, we could also list the hierarchical relationships between subject headings and their subdivisions, and between class numbers and all numbers included underneath them in classification hierarchies.)

It is because OPACs ignore these hierarchical relationships that we have the problem described earlier in this paper: a search on FBI Intelligence Division would fail in all current systems because the cross-reference from FBI occurs only on the authority record for "United States. Federal Bureau of Investigation," not on the record for "United States. Federal Bureau of Investigation. Intelligence Division."

The real problem with all linking devices in a shared cataloging environment, however, lies with the shared cataloging environment itself. Because our thousands of local catalogs are not linked together, or linked upward to the national name authority file, any change in a uniform heading will be made in only three places: the national name authority file; the Library of Congress catalog; and the local catalog of the cataloger who made the change.

All other catalogs will henceforward be out of synch until that heading happens to be worked on locally for some other reason.

The real solution, and admittedly it's a radical one (but we live in radical times), is that instead of sharing cataloging records, we need to re-reexamine the possibility of sharing a catalog!

I have tried to make this point elsewhere,[29] but will try to reformulate it a bit for this context. If the development of the information superhighway eventually means cheap and ubiquitous telecommunication, could we not begin to envision a single catalog, accessible to all users, and updatable by all catalogers?

Advantages for linking:

1. Any link could be made once and would be permanent (but editable), and immediately ubiquitous, i.e., visible to all users.

2. We could demonstrate complex hierarchical relationships using both uniform headings and, when necessary, mechanical linkages, and presenting authority, bibliographic, and holdings records in seamless hierarchical integration.

3. Changes in headings to keep them in line with commonly known forms and current vocabulary could be made once and would be immediately ubiquitous.

4. System design for the OPAC interface (display of records, arrangement of headings, compression and expansion of large displays), so important for supporting the demonstration of relationships, could be done once and shared by all libraries and library users. I have long had the suspicion that the complexity of programming necessary to build an OPAC that is a true catalog is so expensive that the library market cannot support it in the current world of multiple private-sector vendors. However, I wonder if it could not be supported by tax dollars, as a public good, if it were, in fact, going to be used by *all* libraries and library users. This would have the effect of standardizing the catalog interface, as we all long to do. Perhaps we could then teach students to search The Catalog in kindergarten, along with their ABC's.

Other advantages:

1. Such an approach has got to be more cost-effective than our current approach of maintaining thousands of local catalogs. Adding an item to a collection would consist of either adding a holdings symbol to an existing record in the catalog (which requires professional judgment, in my opinion, but could be done extremely quickly by a well-educated professional) or adding new record(s) for that item when necessary.

2. We could take all the money we save on heads of technical services, copy cataloging departments, cataloger updating of multiple catalogs, OPAC vendors, planning for new OPAC software, etc., and spend it on hiring more well-educated (not just trained) professional catalogers who would, perhaps, then be able to create analytic records for the individual cuts on sound recordings, full cataloging records for series with the full panoply of added entries, etc., all of which added value would immediately be available to all users of the catalog.

Maybe when Bill Gates finally discovers the limits of "intelligent assistants," we could talk him into funding such a catalog and becoming thereby the Carnegie of the twenty-first century. After all we have the expensive part already—the USMARC records; the software design would probably cost him about what he spends every year on shoes.

V. What *AACR2* Should Do

In Toronto there was a good deal of support for the position that *AACR2* should more explicitly state the objectives and principles that already underlie our current practice, in order to make the rules more understandable, teachable, and extensible. The following are my recommendations:

1. State the objectives and principles of cataloging clearly in the introduction to the code, and direct anyone using the code to refer to these whenever a bibliographic condition not covered by a particular rule is encountered. Ensure that these principles are applied consistently, and examine how far current practice can be extended to apply the principles consistently to all kinds of materials.

2. Include in the objectives a statement that one of the major goals of the catalog is to ensure that a user who does any kind of a search leading to the selection of a particular work should be shown in an organized display all available editions of that work, as well as works that contain it, works that are based on it, and works about it.

3. Include in the objectives a statement that a work should be named using the name of its principal author (if there is one) and the title by which it is commonly known to the users of the library.

    Consider also stating that two works with the same name should be given uniform headings that differentiate one from the other whenever one is represented by more than one bibliographic record.

4. Include in the objectives a statement that the user should be led to a desired work from any variant of its author's name or its title that the user might employ in his or her search.

5. Include a statement of principle concerning the degree of change to a preexisting work that causes the creation of a new edition of that work, and the degree of change that causes the creation of a new work related to the preexisting work.

6. Make explicit the types of relationships between works, and the types of relationships among the editions ("expressions") of a work that are implicit in *AACR2*.

7. Consider defining work as follows:

    the product of the intellectual or artistic activity of a person or persons or of a named or unnamed group expressed in a particular way. A work has a name (or can be named[30]) and can stand alone as a publication; however, its name can change without its necessarily becoming a new work. The person(s) or group responsible can change without the work necessarily becoming a new work. The work can be translated into another language without necessarily becoming a new work. If two items are represented as the same work, consider them to be so, unless there is some overriding reason not to do so. As a rule of thumb, consider two items to be the same work if they would be considered interchangeable by most users, or if a user seeking one would actually find the other preferable (as in the case of a later revised edition).

Do not consider two items to be the same work if the particular way in which the intellectual or artistic activity is expressed has changed in order to adapt it to a new medium of expression. Examples would be the novelization of a film, the dramatization of a novel, an etching based on a painting, or a free transcription of a musical work.[31]

8. Clarify our concepts of work and edition ("expression") and tie them to clean record structures, e.g., the authority record should always stand for the work, and the bibliographic record should always stand for the edition.

Recommendations for Chapter 21

1. Develop general rules for works of mixed responsibility that can be applied to such works in any form or format, whether they are new works or are based on preexisting works. Restructure the rules into two sections: rules covering news works of mixed responsibility and rules covering various kinds of adaptation and other change to preexisting works.

2. Create a new rule for new works of mixed responsibility that calls for entering such works under title unless only two functions are carried out and a more specific rule calls for considering one function primary and the other secondary. Ensure that this rule covers choreographic works.

3. Study the problem of collaborative works of mixed responsibility produced in stages with portions of the collaborative work existing as separable pieces, and consider whether it might be possible to collocate all of the portions of a single work.

4. Reconsider 21.1B2e. If the phrase "beyond mere performance, execution, etc." refers to improvisation on the part of a group, consider extending this approach to performance of individual performers who improvise as well; if it does not, drop this rule, or rationalize it better.

5. Use a different term than "musical works" if it is desired to refer to printed music, but not to performances of musical works recorded on sound recording or videorecording formats.

6. Clarify in 21.23C1 whether the function carried out by the performer leading to main entry is that of compilation or that of performance, and rationalize this practice in the context of the treatment of compilation/performance elsewhere in chapter 21.

7. Consider any preexisting work that is adapted to create a cinematic work as a new work related to the preexisting work.

8. Try to get rid of rules in chapter 21 that are tied to format; instead, analyze the underlying conditions of authorship. For example, consider replacing 21.11, 21.13, and 21.15 with the following more general rule: If a work consisting of a preexisting work accompanied by or interwoven with biographical or critical material, illustrations in any format, commentaries, and other subsidiary material is represented as an edition of the preexisting work, enter it under the heading appropriate to that work. If it is represented as a new work, enter it according to the rules for new works of mixed responsibility.

9. Study music, spatial data, electronic resources, and other special types of material to identify the nature of adaptation in those materials, i.e., what types of change to a preexisting work cause the creation of a new related work, and what types of change simply produce a new edition ("expression").

10. Reexamine rule 21.16B; study represented works, and consider including rules in *AACR2* that allow institutions cataloging these works to either (a) emphasize the representation or (b) emphasize the represented work in their cataloging, depending on what is most appropriate in any given case.

11. Reconsider the rules for entry of works of changing authorship such as serials and texts to see if the various expressions of these works can be better gathered together and represented as one work to users.

12. Consider rolling back *AACR2*'s move toward title main entry, i.e., consider entering more works under corporate and personal authors in order to create unique headings to identify the work without having to resort to uniform titles.

Recommendations for Chapter 26

State in the introduction to chapter 26 the general principle that a cross-reference to a heading should also be made available to users who access any subset of that heading. For example, a cross-reference to an author should be available to any user seeking one of his works identified by means of his name and the title of the work.

Notes

1. An elaboration of this point may be in order for those who are puzzled about what it is doing here. I have heard catalogers make remarks such as, "Our library doesn't use uniform titles and none of our users has ever complained." One of the major reasons we call ourselves a profession is that we have a kind of expert knowledge our users do not necessarily have that allows us to help or harm them without their realizing it. Thus, we have a professional and social responsibility to do everything we can to help rather than harm, *even though* they cannot evaluate our work. I particularly want to make this point because we are a profession under attack by a society that has never grasped the nature of our expertise and thinks that Bill Gates' intelligent assistants are going to solve all the problems they are having finding things on the Internet. Unfortunately for us, the fact users don't observe when we have helped them means that our work is largely invisible to them. Now is a time when, rather than trying to make cataloging so easy that low-paid clerks can do it without training (only putting things up on the Internet can really be that easy), we need to focus our energies on practicing our special expertise, and perhaps on trying to educate the public (and other librarians!) more thoroughly in what that is, and what its value is.

2. See both 21.6C1 and 21.12 in *AACR2R*.

3. Actually, U.S. practice follows the alternative rule in the footnote to 21.28 which leads to the libretto being entered under the heading for the musical work.

4. It should be noted that the CC:DA Task Force on the Cataloging of Works Intended for Performance made the following recommendation in October of 1996:

   1. Develop general rules for works of mixed responsibility that can be applied to such works in any form or format, whether they are new works or are based on preexisting works.

   On the basis of discussions of various approaches at the 1996 ALA Annual Meeting in New York, the Task Force roughed out the following approach for the part of recommendation 1 dealing with new works for consideration by the cataloging community (the various approaches are outlined in section 2 of the discussion paper prepared by the Task Force, which can be found at the following web site: Committee on Cataloging: Description and Access, CC:DA documents, CC:DA Midwinter and Annual Conference documents, ALA Annual, San Francisco,

CA, CC:DA meetings, 6/28/97 and 6/30/97, Draft document of the Task Force on the Cataloging of Works Intended for Performance for discussion by CC:DA and the cataloging community (18 December 1997)):

> New works of mixed responsibility in which creation of a text is just part of the collaborative production of the work should be entered under title, unless there are only two authorship functions involved, and a more specific rule assigns primacy to one of the functions.

5. Actually, as noted above, U.S. practice follows the alternative rule in the footnote to 21.28, which leads to the libretto being entered under the heading for the musical work. If librettos are considered to be parts of the original work, why not consistently apply this treatment to screenplays, set and costume designs, etc.?

6. Martha M. Yee, "What Is a Work? Part 3: The Anglo-American Cataloging Codes," *Cataloging & Classification Quarterly* 20, no. 1 (1995): 33-36.

7. The CC:DA Task Force on the Cataloging of Works Intended for Performance made the following recommendation in October of 1996:

> 2. Develop rules for works realized through performance that can be applied to such works in any form or format.

On the basis of discussions of various approaches outlined in section 2 of the discussion paper prepared by the Task Force, at the 1996 ALA Annual Meeting in New York, the Task Force roughed out the following approach for recommendation 2 above for consideration by the cataloging community (discussion paper is located at the following web site: Committee on Cataloging: Description and Access, CC:DA documents, CC:DA Midwinter and Annual Conference documents, ALA Annual, San Francisco, CA, CC:DA meetings, 6/28/97 and 6/30/97, Draft document of the Task Force on the Cataloging of Works Intended for Performance for discussion by CC:DA and the cataloging community (18 December 1997)):

> Realizations of preexisting texts which consist of instructions for performance should be entered as follows:
>
> If the instructions are detailed, and if they are closely followed in the performance, the performance should be considered the same work as the preexisting text, and creation of the text should be considered the primary function in the creation of the work, with performance being subsidiary.
>
> If, however, the original instructions are not detailed and/or are not closely followed in the performance, the performance should be considered a new work, but one related to the preexisting text; i.e., if improvisation and/or adaptation and/or creative or intellectual work beyond mere performance occur, the performance should be considered a new work. This new work should be entered under title, unless there are only two authorship functions involved, and a more specific rule assigns primacy to one of the functions.

The Task Force agreed that it should be emphasized in the rules for added entries that it is crucial to make an added entry for the main entry of any preexisting work which is adapted into a new work in the course of performance.

Some clues that might be taken to point to adaptation having occurred in the course of making a film based on a preexisting work might be a screenplay credit and/or a cinematography credit.

Subsequent to the above recommendations having been made, it became clear that the principle of "detailed instructions closely followed" was in conflict with current practice in the music field of considering works that have been either arranged (prior to the performance) or improvised (during the performance) as being still the work of the original composer (in other words, the same as the preexisting work). If the Task Force's approach is desired, a loose approach to the definition of "detailed instructions" would have to be taken, such that when improvisation was intended as part of the original instructions or is accepted as a standard method of performance of a particular kind of music, it would have to be considered to be part of the instructions. In fact, this same kind of looseness of definition of "detailed instructions" could be used to justify considering production elements of dramatic works (costumes, lighting, etc.) to have been understood as part of the original instructions, or intended by the composer of the opera or the writer of the play. Several comments received from the field based on the CC:DA document posted on the web indicate that catalogers who are not expert in music or film feel they would have a hard time carrying out the decision-making required by the Task Force's approach.

8. In the USMARC format, work added entries with second indicator 2.

9. In the USMARC format, 6XX fields contain subject added entries for the work.

10. In the USMARC format, added entries for the work with second indicator 1 or blank.

11. It should be noted that the CC:DA Task Force on the Cataloging of Works Intended for Performance made the following recommendation in October of 1996:

> 3. Develop a general rule covering preexisting works reissued in any form or format with the addition of matter of all kinds, including commentaries, and biographical/critical material, as well as non-textual matter such as posters, film trailers and new sound tracks. Usually, inclusion of such material should not be held to create a new work.

The document containing this recommendation can be found at the following web site: Committee on Cataloging: Description and Access, CC:DA documents, CC:DA Midwinter and Annual Conference documents, ALA Annual, San Francisco, CA, CC:DA meetings, 6/28/97 and 6/30/97, Draft document of the Task Force on the Cataloging of Works Intended for Performance for discussion by CC:DA and the cataloging community (18 December 1997).

12. For a much fuller discussion of this problem, see: Sara Shatford, "Describing a Picture," *Cataloging & Classification Quarterly* 4, no. 4 (summer 1984): 13-30.

13. The relationship is rather a special one, in which one work "depicts" another. Our practice has probably not been consistent between considering this a subject relationship (6XX fields in the USMARC format) or a descriptive relationship (7XX fields in the USMARC format). Perhaps it needs definition as a separate type of relationship in its own right.

14. Sherman Clarke and Jenni Rodda moderated a discussion on the Mona Lisa phenomenon at the 1997 conference of the Visual Resources Association.

15. This was the phrase Seymour Lubetzky used to describe works that continue to exist and change over time, with the change including change in authorship, such that they are most usefully entered under title.

16. The CC:DA Task Force on the Cataloging of Works Intended for Performance made the following recommendation in October of 1996 (Committee on Cataloging: Description and Access, CC:DA documents, CC:DA Midwinter and Annual Conference documents, ALA Annual, San Francisco, CA, CC:DA meetings, 6/28/97 and 6/30/97, Draft document of the Task Force on the Cataloging of Works Intended for Performance for discussion by CC:DA and the cataloging community (18 December 1997)):

> 4. Add a definition of "work" to the glossary.

17. Care must be taken not to exclude pictorial and other types of frequently untitled works.

18. Unfortunately, there just wasn't room in this paper to include an extensive justification for the proposed definition. Considerably more extensive examination and discussion of past Anglo-American cataloging practice, and of criteria proposed by cataloging theoreticians, as well as other justifications for the proposed definition of "work" may be found in the following series of articles:

> Martha M. Yee, "The Concept of *Work* for Moving Image Materials," *Cataloging & Classification Quarterly* 18, no. 2 (1993): 33-40.
>
> ———, "What Is a Work? Part 1, The User and the Objects of the Catalog," *Cataloging & Classification Quarterly* 19, no. 1 (1994): 9-28.
>
> ———, "What Is a Work? Part 2, The Anglo-American Cataloging Codes," *Cataloging & Classification Quarterly* 19, no. 2 (1994): 5-22.

————, "What Is a Work? Part 3, The Anglo-American Cataloging Codes," *Cataloging & Classification Quarterly* 20, no. 1 (1995): 25-46.

————, "What Is a Work? Part 4, Cataloging Theorists and a Definition," *Cataloging & Classification Quarterly* 20, no. 2 (1995): 3-24.

19. User studies are very difficult to interpret in this regard, due to the propensity for users to do subject searches or include subject terms in their searches when looking for a known work, and due to the tendency of OPACs to force users to search under *either* author *or* title; probably most author searches should be counted as known-work searches for this reason.

20. International Conference on the Principles and Future Development of AACR, Discussion list archives, July-October 1997 (9 December, 1997).

21. Barbara B. Tillett, "Bibliographic Relationships: Toward a Conceptual Structure of Bibliographic Information Used in Cataloging" (Ph.D. diss., University of California, Los Angeles, 1987), 43-56, Appendix B. In a personal communication (December 22, 1997), Barbara states "it looks to me that the identification of the significant data elements needed to identify an edition is what you are after rather than identifying a relationship to another edition or work, which makes it a different exercise from the one I conducted in my dissertation, which looked at the devices that had been used to show the relationships—recognizing full well that there are many other indicators that the human uses to distinguish."

22. International Federation of Library Associations (IFLA), *Functional Requirements for Bibliographic Records. Draft Report for World-wide Review* (Frankfurt: IFLA, 1996).

23. Gregory H. Leazer, "A Conceptual Schema for the Control of Bibliographic Works," in *Navigating the Networks: Proceedings of the ASIS Mid-Year Meeting, Portland, Oregon, May 21-25,* ed. D. L. Andersen, T. J. Galvin, and M. D. Giguere (Medford, N.J.: Learned Information, 1994), 125.

24. Patrick Wilson, *Two Kinds of Power* (Berkeley, Calif.: University of California Press, 1968), 6.

————, "The Catalog as Access Mechanism: Background and Concepts," *Library Resources & Technical Services* 27, no. 1 (January 1983): 5.

————, "The Work and the Work Record in Cataloging," *Annual Review of OCLC Research* (1986-1987): 43.

————, "The Objectives of the Catalog and the Means to Reach Them," in *The Conceptual Foundations of Descriptive Cataloging,* ed. Elaine Svenonius (San Diego: Academic Press, 1989), 11.

————, "Interpreting the Second Objective of the Catalog," *Library Quarterly* 59, no. 4 (October 1989): 339-53.

25. Richard Smiraglia, "Derivative Bibliographic Relationships: Linkages in the Bibliographic Universe," in *Navigating the Networks: Proceedings of the ASIS Mid-Year Meeting, Portland, Oregon, May 21-25,* ed. D. L. Andersen, T. J. Galvin, and M. D. Giguere (Medford, N.J.: Learned Information, 1994), 169. It is confusing to find later on in this paper references to "edition" without any definition of it. His use of the term seems to conflict with the definition of work quoted here.

26. Leazer, "A Conceptual Schema for the Control of Bibliographic Works," 116.

27. Tillett, "Bibliographic Relationships," 43-56. In a personal communication, December 22, 1997, Barbara continues to argue that "the entities that are in derivative relationships populate a continuum from the same work to different works."

28. Smiraglia, "Derivative Bibliographic Relationships: Linkages in the Bibliographic Universe," 177.

29. Martha M. Yee, "Editions: Brainstorming for AACR2000," in *The Future of the Descriptive Cataloging Rules: Papers from the ALCTS Preconference, AACR2000, American Library Association Annual Conference, Chicago, June 22, 1995,* ed. Brian E. C. Schottlaender, ALCTS

Papers on Library Technical Services and Collections, no. 6 (Chicago: American Library Association, 1998), 40-65.

30. Care must be taken not to exclude pictorial and other types of frequently untitled works.

31. Unfortunately, there just wasn't room in this paper to include an extensive justification for the proposed definition. Considerably more extensive examination and discussion of past Anglo-American cataloging practice, and of criteria proposed by cataloging theoreticians, as well as other justifications for the proposed definition of "work" may be found in the following series of articles:

Yee, "The Concept of *Work* for Moving Image Materials."

———, "What Is a Work? Part 1, The User and the Objects of the Catalog."

———, "What Is a Work? Part 2, The Anglo-American Cataloging Codes."

———, "What Is a Work? Part 3, The Anglo-American Cataloging Codes."

———, "What Is a Work? Part 4, Cataloging Theorists and a Definition."

Bibliographic Relationships

SHERRY L. VELLUCCI

Introduction

Bibliographic relationships exist when bibliographic entities—i.e., any instances of recorded knowledge—are associated with each other in some way. For more than a century, bibliographic relationships were discussed by implication within the context of the collocating function of the catalog. It was not until the late 1970s, however, when the move toward online catalogs sparked hopes for a more sophisticated catalog structure, that bibliographic relationships became an independent topic of discussion.[1] Theoretical and empirical examination of the concept began in earnest in the 1980s and continues to the present day.

For the purpose of defining the role of bibliographic relationships within the principles and future development of the *Anglo-American Cataloguing Rules (AACR),* it is important to understand the types of relationships that exist in the bibliographic universe as they have been identified to date, and the means currently used for identifying and linking bibliographic records for related bibliographic entities. It is also crucial to have a contextual understanding of this topic as it relates to the functions of the catalog; the functions of the bibliographic record; the concept of the work; the concepts of main entry, added entries, and references; bibliographic and authority record structure; and catalog design. As several of these topics will be presented as independent position papers at this conference, there is no need for this paper to explore them all in depth. But it is important to comprehend that bibliographic relationships do not exist as an isolated concept. They are enmeshed in almost every aspect of the cataloging process, are alluded to throughout the *AACR,* and are an important factor in the structure and design of the catalog.

Bibliographic relationships should also be distinguished from other relationships that exist in the bibliographic universe, e.g., the relationship of one name to another, or the relationship of one subject to another. While both names and subjects may be related to a bibliographic entity, and both name entities and subject entities may be used to help identify bibliographic relationships and link related records, it is primarily those relationships between two bibliographic entities that are included in the study of bibliographic relationships.

Background and Context

In her groundbreaking study of bibliographic relationships, Tillett noted that in the library catalog established bibliographic relationships are pathways that provide a systematic display of related materials. These pathways direct the user to associated materials, and that direction "helps to fulfill the stated objectives of the library catalog."[2] Because identification of bibliographic relationships is integral to the fulfillment of the objectives of the catalog, a brief discussion of these objectives as they pertain to bibliographic relationships is appropriate.

One of the first detailed discussions regarding the functions of a library catalog was occasioned by Panizzi's need to defend the systematic cataloging rules that he developed to create a catalog for the library of the British Museum. In the hearings before a Royal Commission, Panizzi stated that "A reader may know the *work* he requires; he cannot be expected to know all the peculiarities of different *editions* . . ." (emphasis in the original).[3] Panizzi strongly believed that it was the job of the catalog to collocate these related editions of the work, so that the user had all information at hand when making a selection. In 1848 Panizzi posited five basic characteristics for a library catalog: it should provide enough detail that users could identify a specific book; it should have only one entry for each bibliographic item; it should use a normalized form of an author's name for that entry; it should arrange all the editions and translations of a work together; and it should provide cross-references to lead users to the appropriate forms of names and titles.[4] It was Panizzi's fourth and fifth characteristics—i.e., the collocating function for related works and references to appropriate titles—that linked bibliographic relationships with the functions of the library catalog.

Thirty years later, Cutter clearly stated the objects of the catalog in his landmark work *Rules for a Printed Dictionary Catalog.* These objects, which are ubiquitously quoted today, read:

1. To enable a person to find a book of which either
   a) the author is known
   b) the title is known
   c) the subject is known;

2. To show what the library has
   d) by a given author
   e) on a given subject
   f) in a given kind of literature;

3. To assist in the choice of a book
   g) as to its edition (bibliographically)
   h) as to its character (literary or topical).[5]

The objects of a catalog, as detailed by Cutter, essentially served the same identifying and collocating functions that were delineated by Panizzi, and added the evaluating function that was implicit in much of Panizzi's writing. Cutter's second object, collocation, depends upon gathering together material that is related by virtue of author, subject, or form. He does not, however, include gathering all editions of a work under this rubric. Nevertheless, this first set of explicitly stated objects did signal that identifying bibliographic relationships and linking records for related materials were intrinsic functions of a catalog, and marked the beginning of the "second objective" as the focal point for those concerned with collocation and bibliographic relationships.

Almost half a century later, the Library of Congress (LC) asked Lubetzky to examine and define the underlying principles of cataloging that would form the basis of a new and simplified code. As a starting point Lubetzky examined the functions of the catalog, for he believed that the defined functions of the catalog determine the direction and purpose of any new code. In his draft, Lubetzky cited the following two purposes that the catalog should serve: "First, to facilitate the location of a particular publication, i.e., of a particular edition of a work, which is in the library. Second, to relate and display together the editions which a library has of a given work and the works which it has of a given author."[6] Lubetzky's functions did not include the treatment of subjects or form. While his functions were more sophisticated than Cutter's in that they introduced the concepts of the item and the work as separate entities and called for collocating various manifestations of the work, they did reiterate Cutter's objects of identifying and collocating. The evaluating function was implied but not explicitly stated. Although a final code was never published, Lubetzky's work served as a basis for the *Statement of Principles* adopted at the International Conference on Cataloguing Principles (ICCP), Paris, 1961, known thereafter as the "Paris Principles."[7]

The developers of the "Paris Principles" reaffirmed that the catalog served a dual purpose: it identified and located specific items (the identifying, or finding function) and enabled related items to be identified and located (the collocating function). The following objectives were included in the report of the "Paris Principles":

> The catalog should be an efficient instrument for ascertaining
>
> 1. whether the library contains a particular book . . . and
> 2. which works by a particular author and which editions of a particular work are in the library.[8]

Again it is the "second objective" that focuses on the collocation of related items and works. Since the 1961 Conference, each successive publication of the *Anglo-American Cataloguing Rules* has acknowledged Lubetzky's contribution to the formulation of cataloging principles, but the ICCP objects of the catalog have never been explicitly stated in the code.

More recently, Svenonius noted that the three decades since Lubetzky reformulated the catalog's objectives have witnessed "more dramatic changes to the cataloging infrastructure than the preceding seven. Not only have catalogs been automated but also an unprecedented amount of cooperative cataloging has led to the emergence of international standards, global catalogs, and linked systems."[9] Expanding on Svenonius' reference to global systems, O'Neill and Vizine-Goetz stated that "the information that was sufficient to identify particular items and bibliographic relationships within a local collection is inadequate in this new [global] environment."[10] They questioned whether the objectives of the catalog as stated in the "Paris Principles" were still valid for future library catalogs within the broader context of a global environment.

Wilson responded to this question not by proposing new objectives, but by suggesting a different *priority* for the established objectives.[11] He maintained that through technological advances the storage of documents would be separated from their medium of display, and libraries would provide access to what he termed *virtual copies* that were not actually present in the local collection, but could be downloaded from some distant database.[12] In view of this global access, Wilson believed that a reordering of the relative priorities of the objectives of the catalog was in order. Since the time of Cutter, priority had been given to the first objective, i.e., the identifying function, which provides access to the specific physical item in the library. Wilson deemed this priority more valid for an emphasis on a local collection, but believed that the *work,* rather than the physical *item,* was of primary bibliographic interest in the global online environment where the physical item had little meaning. Thus, he postulated that the second objective, i.e., providing access to the work through collocation, should receive first priority. It is the identification of bibliographic relationships and linking of related records that furthers this second objective of collocation.

The next step is to determine whether the functions of the catalog will hold as appropriate for the restructured bibliographic systems of the future. Within the context of restructuring the catalog, Green's seminar class conducted a requirements analysis to determine the functions of a bibliographic database that would be designed using an entity-relationship model. Results of the analysis provided the following statement of purposes of a bibliographic database:

Identification
> Verify that a bibliographic unit exists
>
> Verify information about a bibliographic unit so as to make accurate and distinguishing reference to it
>
> Ascertain whether a bibliographic description matches a bibliographic unit
>
> Ascertain whether two bibliographic units are the same
>> a) bibliographic entity ("book")
>> b) intellectual entity ("work")

Selection
> Determine the (absolute) appropriateness to a user's situation of
>> a) a bibliographic entity
>> b) an intellectual entity
>
> Determine the (relative) appropriateness to a user's situation of two
>> a) bibliographic entities
>> b) intellectual entities

Availability
> Determine the physical location of a bibliographic unit
>
> Determine (restrictions on) availability (e.g., hours facility is open, document delivery delay, required user authorization) of a bibliographic unit for
>> a) local use
>> b) loan (including interlibrary loan)
>> c) purchase

Relationships (based on Tillett, see below)
> Determine the relationship between a work and any of its bibliographic manifestations . . . . ("equivalence")
>
> Determine the relationship between a work and any works produced by modifying it . . . . ("derivative")

Determine the relationship between a work and a work that describes it . . . . ("descriptive")

Determine the relationship between an intellectual or bibliographic entity and its components . . . . ("whole-part")

Determine the relationship between a bibliographic unit and another bibliographic unit that accompanies and either complements or augments it . . . . ("accompanying")

Determine the relationship between a work and a predecessor work . . . . ("sequential")

Collocate works or bibliographic units that have some characteristic . . . in common . . . . ("shared characteristic")[13]

Examination of this statement shows that the overall functions remain much the same as the traditional catalog functions, but the details have been altered to incorporate a clear distinction between the item and the work, to express and expand the concept of availability, and to delineate specifically the concept of expressing relationships. This new statement enables the functional requirements of a catalog to be discussed within the context of a new database structure and the broader global environment.

The adequacy of the traditional functions of the catalog still remains to be decided by the cataloging community. It appears that while the original functions are still valid, they could be reworded, redefined, and expanded to accommodate better the needs of today's catalog users. Additional concepts related to the functions of the catalog also must be reexamined, i.e., the physical item versus the abstract work, and the local library collection versus the global electronic library environment. Should the catalog continue to represent only the physical holdings of a given library's collection? In fact, with the addition of bibliographic records for remotely accessed electronic resources and consortia holdings, catalogs already go beyond the limited scope of local holdings. The real questions to be answered are "what are the parameters of the catalog?" and "what level or levels of description and access, vis-à-vis the item or work, should the catalog include?" In order to accommodate bibliographic relationships within a global environment, the parameters of the library catalog should be expanded to include records for those entities to which the library wishes to provide access; and, if new database structures are to be considered seriously, the catalog must provide description and access at the abstract level of the work, as well as the lower level of the physical item.

Types of Bibliographic Relationships

While the need to clarify relationships among bibliographic entities in library catalogs has been acknowledged for many years, the formal study of bibliographic relationships is relatively new. One of the first attempts to define and categorize types of bibliographic relationships can be found in the *UNIMARC Format* (1980) published by the International Federation of Library Associations and Institutions (IFLA). The format identified three main categories of relationships:

Vertical—the hierarchical relationships of the whole to its parts and the parts to a whole . . . ;

Horizontal—the relationship between versions of an item in different languages, formats, media, etc. . . ;

Chronological—the relationship in time between issues of an item. . . .[14]

The IFLA committee that developed the *UNIMARC Format* approached the identification of bibliographic relationships at a highly theoretical level. While these three broad categories are comprehensive in that all relationships can be fitted into them, they do not contain the degree of detail necessary to describe, distinguish, and classify all types of more complex bibliographic relationships.

Goossens and Mazur-Rzesos offered a second attempt at the analysis of relationships, but limited their examination to whole-part relationships, identified as vertical by the *UNIMARC* document.[15] In this study Goossens and Mazur-Rzesos created a three-tier schematic representation to express both simple and complex hierarchical relationships as tree structures. Their objective was to create a theoretical model for expressing such relationships in both manual and automated systems. The limitations inherent in confining the model to one type of relationship, however, do not allow it to be used for nonhierarchical relationships such as the horizontal relationships identified by the *UNIMARC* publication. Thus, this type of analysis cannot be used to identify and classify all types of bibliographic relationships.

Relationships Defined by Current Research

Recent research into bibliographic relationships has had a more practical focus, identifying specific relationships in detail, investigating the frequency with which bibliographic relationships occur, and examining the ways in which these relationships are expressed in the catalog. While each study made its own unique contribution to the knowledge base, it was Tillett's vanguard research of bibliographic relationships that succeeded in presenting the first detailed analysis of relationship types.[16] Her study began with the creation of a taxonomy of bibliographic relationships that she discovered by examining twenty-four different cataloging codes from Panizzi's 1841 *Rules* to the 1978 second edition of *AACR*. Tillett's definitions for the seven categories of relationships identified in her taxonomy are presented in the following list, along with a summary of her examples for each category:

Equivalence Relationships, which hold between exact copies of the same manifestation of a work, or between an original item and reproduction of it, as long as the intellectual content and authorship are preserved. Included here are copies, issues, facsimiles, photocopies, microforms, and other similar reproductions;

Derivative Relationships, called horizontal relationships in UNIMARC, which hold between a bibliographic item and a modification based on that same item, including variations, versions, editions, revisions, translations, adaptations, paraphrases, etc.;

Descriptive Relationships, which hold between a bibliographic item or work and a description, criticism, evaluation, or review of that work, including annotated editions, casebooks, commentaries, critiques, etc.;

Whole-Part Relationships, called vertical relationships in UNIMARC or hierarchical relationships by Goossens, which hold between a component part of a bibliographic item or work and its whole, including a selection from an anthology, collection, or series;

Accompanying Relationships, which hold between a bibliographic item and the bibliographic item it accompanies, such that the two items augment each other equally or one item augments the other principle or predominant item, including supplements, concordances, indexes, catalogs, etc.;

Sequential Relationships, called chronological relationships in UNIMARC, which hold between bibliographic items that continue or precede one another, including successive titles in a serial, sequels of a monograph, parts of a series, etc.;

Shared Characteristic Relationships, which hold between a bibliographic item and other bibliographic items that are not otherwise related but coincidentally have a common author, title, subject, or other characteristic used as an access point.[17]

In addition to bibliographic relationships, Tillett examined the cataloging codes to identify the various types of linking devices used to establish each type of relationship on the bibliographic record. These will be discussed later in the section "Past and Current Linkage Systems."

The second part of Tillett's work included an empirical study designed to examine the extent of bibliographic relationships as reflected in their frequencies of occurrence in MARC records entered in the Library of Congress machine-readable database between 1968 and July 1986. One of the important findings in this portion of the study indicated that bibliographic relationships were widespread throughout the bibliographic universe, for Tillett found that almost 75 percent of the records in the database contained some type of relationship information.[18] The study included records for materials in a variety of MARC formats, including books, serials, maps, visual materials, and music. Although the overall proportion of Tillett's sample exhibiting each type of relationship is not known, she does provide figures that represent the proportional breakdown of all relationships found. Thus, 62.32 percent of the relationships were whole-part, 16.14 percent were sequential, 14.29 percent were derivative, 3.91 percent were accompanying, and 3.34 percent were equivalence. When distribution by format was examined, it was found that accompanying relationships predominated among music and visual materials, with high proportions of sequential and equivalence relationships discovered among serials, and a high degree of whole-part and derivative relationships found among maps. This particular discovery was significant for it suggested that different formats—and in some cases different disciplines—have a propensity for certain relationship types, and, therefore, care must be taken not to make general statements about relationships that are based on observations of largely monographic collections.

Tillett's study had two major strengths. First, her taxonomy was derived from examination of the cataloging rules, thus identifying those relationships that fell within the scope of the codes' underlying principles and merited treatment in the rules. Second, her study extended to constructing a profile of the means provided by the cataloging codes to identify and link the specific relationships in the catalog. With this code-based taxonomy in place, there was still a need for empirical research to verify these relationships in the bibliographic universe, and to document further the extent of these relationships in the real library environment.[19] Tillett's landmark study became the starting point for two further investigations that focused on the bibliographic universe represented in library catalogs, both of which were narrower in scope.

The study conducted by Smiraglia examined bibliographic families found in the academic library catalog of Georgetown University. The purpose of the study was to discover the characteristics and extent of derivative relationships among works (rather than items) represented in an online catalog.[20] In an article describing his dissertation research, Smiraglia defined derivative relationships as those "bibliographic relationships that exist between any new conception of a work and its original source, or its successor, or both."[21] After examination of the *AACR,* he defined the following seven categories of derivative relationships:

Simultaneous Derivations. Works that are published in two editions simultaneously, or nearly simultaneously. . . . Often such simultaneous derivations will exhibit slightly different inherent bibliographic characteristics;

Successive Derivations. Works that are revised one or more times, and issued with statements such as "second [third, etc.] edition," "new, revised edition," works that are issued successively with new authors, as well as works that are issued successively without statements identifying derivation;

Translations, including those that also include the original text;

Amplifications, including only illustrated texts, musical settings, and criticisms, concordances and commentaries that include the original text;

Extractions, including abridgements, condensations, and excerpts;

Adaptations, including simplifications, screenplays, librettos, arrangements of musical works, and other modifications;

Performances, including sound or visual (i.e., film or video) recordings.[22]

He later added an eighth category—*predecessor derivations*—that included the work from which the progenitor clearly derived. Smiraglia went on to suggest that it was this network of related works that constituted a bibliographic family, which he defined as the "accumulation of works that deliberately share ideational and semantic content, and that are derived from a progenitor work."[23]

Smiraglia's study contained several important findings for the study of bibliographic relationships. First, 49.9 percent of the works in his sample exhibited a derivative relationship, a proportion that is more than twice as large as the percentage discovered by Tillett for this relationship category.[24] Smiraglia attributed this discrepancy to methodological differences between the two studies.[25] Specifically, he examined the documents themselves, rather than relying exclusively on information found in the bibliographic records, and he examined the bibliographic universe beyond the catalog of one library's holdings. Second, data from Smiraglia's study suggested that derivative relationships were most strongly associated with the characteristic of age of the progenitor work—i.e., bibliographic families with older progenitors tended to be larger. This finding has implications for catalogs of libraries with large humanities collections where older literature remains relevant for longer periods of time than scientific literature. Third, between 40 and 63 percent of the derivative relationships found to exist in the study did not have any explicit linkages in the Georgetown catalog. In other words, the existence of the known relationship was not indicated on the record, nor could it be inferred by the user from collocated records.[26] Smiraglia attributed this, in part, to the progenitor work not having information relating to derivative works that succeeded it. In addition, he noted that unless a given library owned all manifestations of a work, it was impossible to identify all derivative relationships from that one catalog. Smiraglia observed that "when the catalog of any institution contains only a portion of a bibliographic family, implicit linkage is even more likely to fail to make the relationship apparent."[27] The results of this study indicate a need to provide the user with explicit bi-directional linkages among related bibliographic works, rather than relegating this function to the user's deductive powers.

A third study, conducted by Vellucci, focused on the bibliographic relationships that exist among musical bibliographic entities represented in library catalogs.[28] The basis for the study was a sample of music scores drawn from the catalog of the Sibley Music Library, Eastman School of Music. This research included three major goals: to identify general characteristics of music scores found in a library collection; to describe and classify the bibliographic relationships that exist among musical bibliographic entities and other bibliographic entities found in the bibliographic universe of library catalogs; and, to identify and categorize the devices used to identify and link related musical bibliographic entities in the library catalog. In order to provide contextual rather than theoretical information, the research design used existing musical entities as the basis for determining the bibliographic relationships.

Vellucci identified the same relationship categories for music as those found by Tillett, but the subgroups within each category varied because of the nature of musical entities. The following six categories of bibliographic relationships were defined based upon their application for musical entities:

Equivalence Relationships that exist between exact copies of the same manifestation of a work, or between an original item and a reproduction of it, when the reproduction is intended to function as a substitute for the original. Subgroups include exact copies; microform copies; manuscript reproductions; issues, reissues, and impressions; and photocopies;

Derivative Relationships that exist between any new conception of a work and its original source (the progenitor), or a successor, or both. Subgroups include performances (audio and visual); derivative editions; amplifications; adaptations; arrangements; forms of musical presentation; translations; and notational transcriptions;

Descriptive Relationships that exist between a bibliographic entity or work and a description, criticism, or evaluation of that work, including annotated editions, commentaries, analyses, etc. Subgroups include description included with printed musical work; separate text; audio description; visual description; filmstrips, kits, etc.; and performance programs;

Whole-Part Relationships that exist between a segment or component part of a bibliographic entity or work and its whole. Subgroups include physical inclusive; physical extractive; abstract inclusive; and abstract extractive;

Accompanying Relationships that exist between the primary musical item or work and the complementary material that occurs with it, such that the two augment each other equally, or the secondary material augments the primary musical item or work. Subgroups include supplemental and inclusive; and,

Sequential Relationships that exist between bibliographic items or works that precede or continue one another, embodying the aspects of chronology and sequence, but are not derivative. Subgroups include series, sequels, and serials.[29]

Among the more important findings of this study was the high degree of relatedness found among musical entities. Vellucci discovered that 97 percent of the scores in the sample exhibited at least one relationship, a considerably higher figure than that discovered by Tillett. This was probably due to several reasons including the methodological differences identified by Smiraglia that also held for Vellucci's study, and factors stemming from the inherent nature of music that requires performance for its aural realization. Included among the musical factors are the concept of the *performable unit,* which allows sections of a musical work to be published separately; the need for performing editions and performance parts; the preponderance of western art music standard repertoire and its continued demand regardless of age; and specific genres of music that tend to be produced and published in groups, anthologies, or collections. In addition, the international scope of music and the music publishing industry, with its focus on specific sales markets, contributes to the extent of relatedness. Not surprisingly, therefore, the whole-part, derivative, and accompanying relationship categories each had a high frequency of occurrence, exhibited by 86 percent, 85 percent, and 71 percent of the sample, respectively. The remaining three categories of relationships examined in this study—sequential, equivalence, and descriptive—were discovered for 31 percent, 29 percent, and 22 percent of the sample, respectively. Vellucci also found that 33 percent of the sample exhibited some type of relationship that was not identified on the bibliographic record. In addition, the age of the composition was found to be the only characteristic that had a statistically significant association with every type of relationship (although other characteristics showed significant associations with specific relationships). This supported Smiraglia's finding that the older the literature, the greater the chance that bibliographic relationships will exist.

Several observations can be generalized from these three studies. The seven types of relationships identified by Tillett's conceptual analysis of cataloging codes—i.e., equivalence, whole-part, derivative, accompanying, sequential, descriptive, and shared characteristics—appear to be valid in the bibliographic universe; bibliographic relationships are widespread among items and works found in the bibliographic universe; and, the most reliable predictor of relationships in general appears to be the age of the work, although other characteristics may be associated with specific relationships. It also appears that certain categories of entities—e.g., music scores, serials, and nonprint materials—tend to exhibit a higher than expected frequency of relationships. In addition, it seems that not all existing relationships are identified and linked in the catalog by our current methods of creating, storing, and displaying bibliographic records. This last aspect of bibliographic relationships will be discussed below in the section "User Needs: Navigating the Relationship Universe."

Relationships Defined by the IFLA Study Group on the Functional Requirements of the Bibliographic Record

The IFLA Study Group on the Functional Requirements of the Bibliographic Record adopted a different approach to the examination of bibliographic relationships than the empirical research just discussed.[30] First, it used the functions of the bibliographic record as the starting point for analysis, rather than the functions of the catalog. Second, the IFLA study used an entity-relationship model to analyze the bibliographic record, thus structuring the study to emulate recent research into relational database and object-oriented database modeling for online catalogs.[31] Previous bibliographic relationship research provided a descriptive analysis of relationships, but did not attempt a structural model. Third, the study was broader in scope than the previous studies, in that it first included a detailed analysis of three entity groups described in the bibliographic record. These entity groups were: (1) entities that represent the products of intellectual or artistic endeavor (*works, expressions, manifestations,* and *items*); (2) entities responsible for the intellectual or artistic content of such products (*persons* and *corporate bodies*); and (3) entities that form the subject of intellectual or artistic endeavor (*concepts, objects, events,* and *places*).[32] The previous studies focused primarily on the bibliographic relationships exhibited by the entities defined as items and works, with the responsible entities included only in the examination of certain linkages, and very limited inclusion of subject entities in the discussion of descriptive relationships. Finally, the IFLA Study Group attempted to place a relative value on data in the bibliographic record, basing its weighting on a conceptual analysis of user needs as perceived by the Study Group. Although the previous studies attempted to identify, through empirical research, entity characteristics that could be used to predict the occurrence of specific relationships, no attempts were made to place value on bibliographic data. The user needs for bibliographic data identified by the IFLA Study Group were, in fact, a rewording of the four primary functions of the catalog that have been discussed for over a century—finding, identifying, selecting, and obtaining. This may dispel the criticism that the study did not take the functions of the catalog into account, but will support the criticism that the study did not base user needs—and therefore the relative value of bibliographic data—on information verified by empirical research.

Before discussing the IFLA report's treatment of bibliographic relationships, a few words must be said about the definitions and the terms used to represent the products of intellectual or artistic creation—i.e., *work, expression, manifestation,* and *item*—for the relationship modeling is based on these entities. Since the document was disseminated for worldwide review, there has been considerable criticism, a portion of which centered on these entity definitions and their application. The problem is perhaps more semantic than substantive, and while the intention was clarity, the result was confusion. At times the application of the definitions does not always appear to be consistent throughout the document (which may be due in part to a lack of clarity and inappropriate examples). More importantly, these definitions confuse because they have modified certain concepts of long standing, and have applied to different entities previously used entity definition terms. For example, the *work,* as referred to in most previous studies of bibliographic relationships, has been defined as the intellectual or artistic content of a bibliographic entity; the *work* consisted of two properties: the ideational content and the semantic content, and existed in the abstract. The IFLA study defines work as "a distinct intellectual or artistic creation," but does not define the properties of a work.[33] The definition implies, however, that the *work* contains only ideational content, for the property of semantic content appears to be the defining factor for the new second-level entity, *expression*—"the intellectual or artistic realization of a work in the form of alpha-numeric, musical, or choreographic notation, sound, image, object, movement, etc., or any combination of such forms."[34] The report goes on to state clearly that the *work* is an abstract entity; however, *expression* is not explicitly defined as an abstract entity. Nevertheless, it is stated that the *expression* entity excludes aspects of physical form, thus implying that it is an abstract concept. To further obfuscate the issue, some examples given of the *expression* entity are physical objects, e.g., "the specific score used for the performance of a musical composition,"[35] and the term "object" is actually used in the definition. It is not surprising that there has been a bewildered reaction from the cataloging community.

The confusion is exacerbated because the cataloging community also has been unclear in its definitions and terminological usage. For many years, the *item* has been viewed as a physical manifestation of the work, with the terms *item* and *manifestation* frequently used interchangeably.[36] The individual exemplar of the physical item has been referred to as a *copy*. The IFLA Study Group has defined the *manifestation* entity as the physical embodiment of an *expression* of a *work*[37]—what the cataloging community understands alternately as the *item* or the *manifestation*—and has defined the *item* as a single exemplar of a *manifestation*[38]—what the cataloging community understands as the *copy*. To add to the confusion, other researchers have described this hierarchical entity grouping by various other clusters of terms, including *work, text, edition, printing,* and *book,*[39] *impressions, editions, texts, works,* and *superworks,*[40] *uniform work, work, bibliographic set, bibliographic copy,* and a super-entity called *bibliographic unit,*[41] and *text* or *abstract work, publication,* and *copy.*[42] Additionally, Yee subdivided the *manifestation* entity into *manifestation, title manifestation,* and *near equivalent.*[43] Thus, with the variation in hierarchical cluster terms and definitions that already exists within the cataloging community, the IFLA study has further compounded the semantic problems with its new definitions, murky explanations, and inadequate examples. Since the cataloging code with its glossary is most often referred to as the arbiter in defining cataloging terms, it would benefit the cataloging community to come to consensus on the concepts and terminology that are so integral to the future development of the descriptive cataloging code. Once agreed to, the definitions could then be incorporated into the future code to provide a common language. In this respect, the IFLA study has furthered the process by providing a detailed document to initiate discussion, and a conceptual analysis that may yet prove viable once terms are further clarified.

Generalized-Level Relationships

The IFLA study defined the relationships used in the model at two different levels, those operating at a generalized level and those operating at a lower level between specific instances of entities.[44] The relationships defined at the generalized level are broader in concept and incorporate bibliographic relationships as well as other types of relationships that represent logical operations or functions in the entity-relationship model. These generalized-level relationships are considered the logical structural framework upon which the specific-level relationships are based.

Modeled on the three entity groups, the generalized, or high level, accommodates three relationship clusters: relationships between *work, expression, manifestation,* and *item* (i.e., bibliographic entities); relationships to *persons* and *corporate bodies* (i.e., responsible parties); and *subject* relationships. The relationships are binary—in that they only operate between two entities, and they are bidirectional, in that the relationship, when expressed as its own reciprocal, operates in two directions. The first cluster—relationships between *work, expression, manifestation,* and *item*—links the hierarchical levels between these entities, each of which incorporates the attributes of its superordinate entity. The following statements illustrate this relationship cluster, with the relationship statements enclosed in angled brackets:

> A *work* <is realized through> an *expression;* an *expression* <is a realization of> a *work*.
>
> An *expression* <is embodied in> a *manifestation;* a *manifestation* <is the embodiment of> an *expression*.

A *manifestation* <is exemplified by> an *item;* an *item* <is an exemplar of> a *manifestation.*

This first cluster can be referred to as the bibliographic entity cluster, for lack of a better collective term. The seven categories of bibliographic relationships identified by previous research operate among this group of bibliographic entities, and may exist at both this generalized level or the specific instance level, depending upon the specific relationship type. Due to the lack of relationship statements in most current catalogs, this relationship cluster employs both descriptive elements and access points on the bibliographic record to identify the relationship at each level of the entity hierarchy.

The second relationship cluster—relationships to *persons* and *corporate* bodies—links the entities in the first group (i.e., bibliographic entities) with the entities in the second group (i.e., responsible parties), using two operational relationships. The following statements exemplify this relationship cluster:

A *work* <is created by> a *person* or *corporate body;* a *person* or *corporate body* <created> a *work.*

An *expression* <is realized by> a *person* or *corporate body;* a *person* or *corporate body* <realized> an *expression.*

Due to the cumulative nature of data in the bibliographic record as entities lower in the entity hierarchy are described, these responsibility relationships for the *work* and the *expression* are often incorporated into the records for *manifestations* and *items.* Other aspects of responsibility also could be included at these two lower levels, if the responsibility relationship were redefined to include activities other than creation of the content, to which it is currently limited by definition.[45] For example, if the definition were expanded as the Study Group implied it could be under the relationship definition,[46] the following operational relationships may apply:

A *manifestation* <is published by> a *person* or *corporate body;* a *person* or *corporate body* <published> a *manifestation.*

An *item* <is owned by> a *person* or *corporate body;* a *person* or *corporate body* <owns> an *item.*

The second relationship group is primarily concerned with access points for the bibliographic record, although at the expanded *manifestation* and *item* level, this information is currently contained in the bibliographic description. Additionally, this relationship cluster could be expanded easily beyond bibliographic data, to include, for example, *circulation data* (<is borrowed by>) and *acquisitions data* (<is bought from>) in an integrated database model.

The third relationship cluster—subject relationships—links the *work* entity with all the entities included in all the entity groups by the operational relationship <has as subject>. This indicates that any entity may be the subject of a work, including those entities defined as subject—i.e., *concepts, objects, events,* and *places*—as well as *persons* or *corporate bodies,* and *works, expressions, manifestations,* and *items.* While the relationship is accommodated in the model because the study examined all aspects of the bibliographic record, subject relationships are generally not part of the descriptive cataloging process, with the exception of descriptive relationships and certain instances of derivative relationships such as when subjects are used as linkages to bibliographic records for authors of texts set to music.

Lower-Level Relationships

The second level of relationships operates between specific instances of entities. While these relationships may occur between instances of the same entity type or different entity types, the goal of the study was "to show how the relationships operate in the context of the four primary entities in the model (i.e., *work, expression, manifestation,* and *item*),"[47] and, therefore, the examples were confined to this primary entity group. Again, the relationships are binary, in that they only operate between two entities, and they are bidirectional, in that the relationship, when expressed as its own reciprocal, operates in two directions.

In defining the relationship types, the study deconstructed the seven higher-level relationship categories established by empirical research—i.e., whole-part, derivative, equivalence, accompanying, sequential, descriptive, and shared characteristics—and used instead the more specific subclasses within the relationship categories.[48] For example, the study includes successor, supplement, and adaptation among the relationship types. In fact, successor is a subclass of the higher-level sequential relationship category, supplement belongs to the higher-level accompanying relationship category, and adaptation is a subclass of the higher-level derivative relationship category.

This deconstruction approach has both strengths and weaknesses. Deconstruction is necessary to categorize accurately the nature of the subclasses of relationships, for it is primarily at the subclass level that relationships operate between instances of entities. Each subclass will exhibit its own unique relationship characteristics, and each will vary as to its entity-relationship statement. For example, <is adaptation of>, <is translation of>, and <is aural performance of> are all types of derivative relationship statements, yet the higher-level relationship statement <is derivation of> is not adequate to explain the exact nature of the relationship. The problem with the deconstruction approach is that the subclasses within each higher-level relationship category are often numerous and tend to vary depending on the nature of the discipline.[49] This, no doubt, is one reason why the study does not claim to be exhaustive. Further analysis must be done at this level, both in general terms and within specific disciplines, before a comprehensive entity-relationship model is completed. This deconstruction approach, however, is a great step forward in converting the theoretical higher-level relationship research into a more pragmatic structure useful for database design.

Another useful aspect of the relationship definition model developed by the study is the classification of relationship types by their degree of autonomy. Two categories of relationship autonomy were defined: referential, where one entity is so closely connected to another entity that the relationship has little value outside the context of the other entity; and autonomous, where one entity does not require reference to another entity in order to be useful or understood.[50] While certain relationship types (i.e., successor, supplement, and complement) have greater potential to be included in the referential category than other types, the final decision on autonomy will depend on the characteristics of the specific entity. In addition, it appears that the degree of autonomy applies only among entities at the upper level of the hierarchy—i.e., *work* and *expression*—for autonomy is not discussed in relation to *manifestations* or *items*. The study used this autonomy characteristic in determining the relative importance of identifying a given relationship in the catalog, with greater weight given to those relationships that were dependent, i.e., referential, since the meaningful use of one entity will be dependent on the content of the other entity in the relationship.

The treatment of relationships in the IFLA study is somewhat uneven, for although the report claims to use deconstruction analysis in lieu of describing specific higher-level relationships, one higher-level relationship type—the whole-part relationship—is singled out and discussed separately for each entity type. In reviewing the whole-part relationship, the study identified one important characteristic associated with this relationship type—the degree of dependency of the part to the whole.[51] A part can be either an *independent* component of the whole, in which case it does not depend to any significant extent on the context provided by the larger part for its meaning, or it can be a *dependent* component that is intended to be used in the context of the larger work and thus depends on the context provided by the larger work for its meaning. The degree of dependency characteristic does not appear to operate at the lower end of the entity hierarchy among *manifestations* and *items*. This may be because the relationship type at these levels is mostly limited to reproductions, which by their nature are equivalent, and thus preclude a dependent relationship. The dependent whole-part relationship is further divided into two subcategories: discrete components whose content exists as an identifiable segment with distinct boundaries, such as chapters, sections, etc.; and integral components without distinctly identified parameters, whose content is interwoven throughout the whole work, such as illustrations.[52]

While in the past it was not usually necessary to identify or create access to dependent parts of a work, this should be reexamined within the context of catalogs that provide direct links to electronic texts, and electronic documents that provide direct access to parts (e.g., chapters) of the work. It may be that access to the whole work is all that is necessary to create the initial linkage, and once linked, the text itself will identify the parts for the user; however, the cataloging of electronic texts should be studied empirically to document the most efficient and effective use of bibliographic records in this environment.

The IFLA study discusses indirectly most of the remaining higher-level relationship types—i.e., derivative, accompanying, descriptive, sequential, and equivalence—through certain of their subclasses; the higher relationships are not mentioned specifically by name. The separate treatment for whole-part relationships may be justified, however, for unlike other relationship types that have several specific subclasses, each of which has its own separate characteristics, the whole-part relationship contains only whole entities or parts of entities, and thus is best discussed at the higher level. As in other bibliographic relationship research, the shared characteristic relationship category is not addressed in the IFLA discussion, for a shared characteristic is ubiquitous and may be found among any entity attributes in all three relationship entity groupings.

In summary, the IFLA study of relationships has provided a model for the structural analysis of data, in order to determine which data elements are necessary to include in bibliographic records that will meet user needs. While problems with the definition of specific entities, attributes, and relationships have created confusion that will engender further discussion, the relationship model succeeds in presenting a cogent structure for converting the theoretical research in the area of bibliographic relationships into a more pragmatic structure useful to a variety of database designs. In order to be useful in the development of a new cataloging code, however, the means used to identify bibliographic relationships in the catalog and the methods prescribed by the rules to link records for related entities must be examined.

User Needs: Navigating the Relationship Universe

From the time of Panizzi onward, a syndetic structure has been a standard feature of most library catalogs, and has provided the pathways employed by users to navigate among the complex array of related bibliographic records. Traditionally, linkage of related records was accomplished through the combined efforts of the cataloging code—which governs the descriptive elements and access points of the bibliographic record—and the structure and arrangement of the bibliographic records in the catalog or database.[53] Thus, the collocating function of the catalog is dependent upon the symbiotic relationship between the code and the catalog structure. This dependence continues today, and any discussion of linkages used to express bibliographic relationships must consider both the role of the cataloging code and the structural environment of the catalog.

Dual Function of Linkages

While implying connectivity, the *linkage* frequently serves two distinct functions in the expression of bibliographic relationships. A linkage helps to *identify* a specific or potential relationship among bibliographic entities, and it also serves to *link* the bibliographic records for the related entities. Not all current linkages successfully accomplish both functions, placing the burden upon the user to infer relationships from the combination of information presented in the bibliographic record and the proximity of records in the catalog or database display.

Linkages are divided into two categories: explicit and implicit. Explicit linkages can be either directional links that provide instructions to lead searchers from one heading to another (e.g., cross-references) or mechanical links made by a computer that automatically identify related records in some way for the searcher. Explicit linkages serve the linking function well. For example, a directional name-uniform title *see* reference that leads the user from the heading for a part of a work to the heading for the whole work explicitly links the part to the whole. The user, however, must infer the type of relationship—in this case, a whole-part relationship—from the information presented in the reference heading, because the relationship is not explicitly identified. It is the cataloging code that governs this reference linkage.

Mechanical links offer the opportunity to provide both explicit identification of the relationship type and explicit linking of the related records. For example, the 76x-78x linking entry fields in the MARC format, used primarily for serials, may be coded to identify the nature of the relationship—e.g., preceding or succeeding entry—and provide the means for a direct link between the two records. In this case the cataloging code prescribes the information necessary to identify the details of the relationship, but the encoded record structure identifies the specific relationship type and the database structure enables the direct linkage.

Implicit linkages, on the other hand, are not specifically identified as links in the catalog; they are usually achieved by one of two methods. Either they can be indicated through collocation, when records with the same heading are placed adjacent to one another in a file or display (*entry*-level linkage); or they can be provided on a bibliographic record through a specific reference or citation (usually in a note) that is not directly linked to another record (*data*-level linkage). In the case of implicit links achieved through collocation, the linking function is served indirectly by the structure of the catalog and the arrangement or display of the bibliographic records. The user must infer that some relationship exists based on the proximity of records in the catalog or entries in the display. The identifying function is rarely served by collocation, however, for proximity alone cannot indicate the specific nature of a relationship.

Most implicit links that appear as specific citations on the bibliographic record—e.g., a bibliographic history note citing an earlier edition—are in fact more of an *identifier* of the relationship than an actual link. The potential exists, however, for computers to convert these implicit identifiers and links into explicit identifiers and linkages. A variety of options are available, including expanding the number and usage of linking fields in the MARC record, linking relationship statements in a relational database structure, or by standardized mark-up language encoding in a hypertext environment.

In summary, it is the function of the cataloging code to ensure that relationships are identified and related records linked by prescribing rules to create bibliographic records that contain the access points and identifying data necessary for the task. The information required will vary depending upon the relationship type. It is also the function of the cataloging code to define the level at which the entity is described—*work, expression, manifestation,* or *item*—and to prescribe whether descriptions for the various levels will be contained in one bibliographic record (as is generally the case now), or whether separate records should be created for each level. The task of creating the explicit linkages, and in many cases the explicit identifiers, is allocated to the structure and encoding of the bibliographic record, and the design of the catalog database.

Past and Current Linkage Systems

Two research studies on bibliographic relationships included a detailed analysis of the types of linkages that have been used to express relationships in catalogs. Tillett based her linkage analysis on the cataloging codes, and identified the following linking devices for each relationship category:

Equivalence—Dash entry; notes; uniform title;[54]

Derivative—References; dash entries for added editions; edition statements; notes; uniform titles; cross-references; subject headings; common main entries; filing titles; added entries;[55]

Descriptive—Notes; common main entry; added entries; subject entries;[56]

Whole-Part—Contents notes; analytical entries; added entries; multilevel description; dash entries; uniform titles; explanatory references;[57]

Accompanying—Addition to physical description; notes; dash entries; multilevel description; separate record with linking notes;[58]

Sequential—Notes; added entries; uniform titles;[59]

Shared Characteristic—Same access point; language; publisher; date.[60]

In a later article, Tillett provided a history and in-depth analysis of linking devices grouped into three primary categories: catalog entries, uniform titles, and other devices incorporating linking information.[61]

Vellucci's research, which was based on literary warrant rather than code analysis, found a similar distribution of linkage types among relationship categories, but grouped the linkages found for musical bibliographic entities into the following four categories:

References—See references; *see also* references; *explanatory* references;

Access Points—Name-title; uniform title; name; title; series title; subject headings; dash entries;

Notes—Contents; accompanying material; form and medium of performance; language; edition and history; "with"; relationship to reproduction; physical description; responsibility; local holdings; summary; notation; other formats; series; and

Other Information Found on the Bibliographic Record—Title and statement of responsibility; edition statement; publication statement; physical description; series statement; musical presentation statement; MARC 040 field; MARC holdings data.[62]

The findings of these two studies show that while the primary linking devices are access points, the information necessary to identify and link bibliographic relationships is embedded throughout the entire bibliographic record including the ISBD areas of description. The lack of explicit relationship identifiers and direct linkages often forces the user to refer to other data on the bibliographic record to deduce relationship information. For example, name-title entry collocation may alert the user that two records are related in some way because of proximity, but the specific nature of the relationship—in the case of a successive derivative relationship, for example—may only be inferred by comparison of information found in the edition and publication statements of the two bibliographic descriptions.

Linkage Types and Associated Relationships

References, which are separate from bibliographic records and consistently provide the most explicit connectivity of all linkage types (other than direct mechanical links), are the only linkages that operate solely at the higher entity level, connecting *works* and/or *expressions*. All other linkages, even when linking *works* and/or *expressions* via access points, are also linking at the lower entity level, for they are connecting bibliographic records for specific *manifestations* or *items*. This is due to the underlying principle of the present code to "describe the item in hand," which limits the creation of bibliographic records to the description of lower level (i.e., physical) entities. As the IFLA study explained, however, the data on the bibliographic record is incorporative of several entity levels in that it concatenates "attributes of a particular *manifestation,* with the attributes of the *expression* that is embodied in that *manifestation* and with the attributes of the *work* that is realized through that *expression.*"[63] In the current linkage system, therefore, references provide solely higher-level entity linkage, while bibliographic records—which include both higher- and lower-level entity descriptive information—are linking at the higher- and lower-level entity simultaneously.

When examining the specific linkages associated with a given relationship type, it should be remembered that the findings of both Tillett and Vellucci are dependent on the linkage treatment prescribed by the cataloging code. Tillett's findings resulted from a direct analysis of the code's treatment of linkages, while Vellucci's findings were based on the examination of bibliographic records that were created according to the conventions of the cataloging codes. It is possible, therefore, that in a theoretical model, other linkage-relationship associations may operate as well.

Both Tillett and Vellucci found reference linkages to be associated exclusively with whole-part and derivative relationships.[64] This, no doubt, is because the cataloging rules do not make specific provision for references for other types of bibliographic relationships. Examination of the IFLA higher-level relationship structures confirms that the vast majority of relationships at the higher entity level are indeed whole-part and derivative; however, the IFLA analysis also identified sequential and accompanying relationship possibilities at this level. Although not currently used as linkages for these two relationship types, the rules do allow for references to be made instead of added entries (26.6A), and for references to be made for relationships other than whole-part (26.4C1), although the example given in the code is for the more commonly found derivative relationship. Depending on the structural design of the catalog, the expanded use of references in lieu of added entries for linking higher-level entities may merit further exploration. In this regard, some cataloging theorists believe that many aspects of collocation have been abandoned by the substitution of added entries for references, and that the user would be better served by a return to references.[65] This view warrants further discussion, and should be examined in relation to its impact within various catalog environments.

Access point linkages, including main, added, and analytical entries, are probably the most common form of linkage used in today's catalog. They provide implicit links for most relationships by collocating and displaying common headings together in the catalog. Identification of the relationship type is implicit, and depends on the user's ability to infer relationship information from record proximity and cataloging conventions. Access points in one form or another are found as linkages for every relationship type. Although name-uniform title access points are used to identify *works* and *expressions* that are abstract in nature, the linkage does not exist solely at the abstract level, since, as explained earlier, these access points occur as part of bibliographic records for specific *manifestations* or *items*.

Among the several types of access points, the name-uniform title *citation* access point, which is used to identify the *work* and is presently associated with the concept of main entry, is common for all types of relationships, and reflects the current catalog structure's reliance on entry-level linking. Even when another linkage is used to identify the relationship type, the function of actually linking the related records usually falls to the *citation* access point.

Within the citation construct, the uniform title plays a major role in identifying and linking related records. The *AACR2R* glossary defines a uniform title as "the particular title by which a work that has appeared under varying titles is to be identified for cataloging purposes," providing the clue as to why it is so heavily used among derivative relationships.[66] When a work appears under varying titles, it implies that derivative manifestations of the work exist. The uniform title by definition, then, is the means of collocating derivative entities in the catalog. Additionally, it is used to collocate equivalent entities, to identify the whole-part relationship, and to link a part to its whole in the catalog. The potential importance of the uniform title in a variety of future catalog structures will be discussed later in the section "New Catalog Environments."

Even though uniform titles play a major role in the expression of bibliographic relationships, there are certain situations in which the cataloging rules fail to provide even this implicit level of linkage. For example, the rules state that a uniform title should not be used for a revised edition of a work when it is in the same language as the original (25.2B). In cases where the title has changed in the revised edition, the related works will not be collocated in the catalog; and while a note on the record for the revised edition should direct the user to the previous edition, there is no reciprocal link from the earlier edition that will lead the user to the later edition. Yee provides several detailed examples of this problem in her discussion of the work, the user, and the objectives of the catalog.[67] As descriptions of electronic documents become a larger part of the catalog, the difficulties of describing and relating numerous versions of these entities will magnify the predicament.

Additional problems arise because the rules, with their focus on item-level cataloging, do not require normalization of the heading for a work. The rules for construction of a uniform title have limited application (as seen above), and their application is not required even when a particular condition for use may be met. General rule 25.1A states that "Although the rules in this chapter are stated as instructions, apply them according to the policy of the cataloging agency." This creates inconsistencies both among catalogs and within a specific catalog, weakening the collocation of records for related material. If the focus of descriptive cataloging shifts from the item to the work level, consistent application of the rules for uniform titles as work identifiers will be necessary.

Other access points that appear with regularity as linkages include series added entries for whole-part and sequential relationships; title entries for derivative collections and media materials; subject headings, primarily for descriptive relationships, but also used for derivative relationships; and name access points for shared characteristics.

While the strength of access points is in providing a level of implicit linkage in the catalog rather than identifying relationships, the notes linkage category is generally more successful at identifying relationships than linking related records (with the exception of the MARC linking entry fields previously discussed). The *AACR* calls for the use of notes to provide information not contained in other areas of the bibliographic description. While the function of notes extends well beyond their use as relationship identifiers or links, they are among the more important linkages for bibliographic relationships. This is due to their overall function within the bibliographic record, i.e., as supplemental information to the bibliographic description. Since the main body of the current bibliographic record is designed for description of the item, the information necessary to identify related entities is provided within the supplemental information in notes. Notes with a formal construct, such as those prescribed for contents and summary notes, are more explicit in identifying the type of relationship.

Among the wide variety of notes prescribed by the *AACR,* those most commonly used to identify bibliographic relationships include the contents note, frequently used for whole-part relationships; accompanying material notes, used for both accompanying and derivative relationships; language, bibliographic history, and statement of responsibility notes, most often associated with derivative relationships; reproduction detail notes, primarily used to indicate equivalence relationships; and summary notes that express the descriptive relationship. These are not exclusive associations, however, and most note types are associated with several relationship categories.

Many changes needed in the notes linkage category to enhance the treatment of bibliographic relationships depend more on improvements to the record and catalog structures than on code revision. Nevertheless, one problem area that is also related to the code is the contents note, an important identifier for whole-part relationships and a popular bibliographic data element for users.[68] Currently, access to information in most note fields depends on the success of keyword searching, which is hindered to some extent by the lack of authority control for names and titles appearing in such notes. Names with variant forms and works requiring uniform titles create collocation problems for catalog searches in fields without authority control. The problem arises because the cataloging rules call for presenting contents notes data in the form in which it is found on the item being cataloged (2.7B18).[69] Thus, in most current catalogs, the use of notes to fulfill the linking function depends largely on the keyword search capabilities of individual OPACs using a hit-or-miss combination of controlled and uncontrolled data. If the *AACR* moved away from the "item in hand" principle, and allowed authority data to replace data transcribed from the item in the contents note area, this would improve retrieval for keyword searches in the short term, and would pave the way for direct linking of bibliographic records at the data level, or direct linking of bibliographic records and authority records at the data level. If this concept were applied to name and title information presented in other notes areas, such as bibliographic history or statement of responsibility notes, it would improve the identification and linkage for several types of bibliographic relationships.

In addition, with the move toward minimal-level cataloging and core bibliographic records, the cataloging community should be aware of how the lack of certain notes will affect the identification and linkage of records for related materials. For example, without the bibliographic history note citation to an earlier edition, the identification and linking of revised editions with title changes in current catalog structures would be severely curtailed.

Several of the ISBD areas of description provide the necessary detail to identify relationships when other means are lacking, but generally cannot provide explicit linkage to related records. One frequent use of ISBD data is the addition of information to the physical description to denote an accompanying relationship. Other uses include edition statements that are often used to alert the user that other editions exist without specifically identifying those other editions; and series statements that tell the user of sequential and whole-part relationships without creating the linkage provided by a series added entry.

In summary, the primary linkage categories currently in use to express bibliographic relationships in catalogs include references, access points, and notes, with additional information provided by other ISBD areas of description. Only references and a few direct linking notes provide any explicit linkage of related bibliographic records, and with the possible exception of formally structured notes, few currently used linking devices clearly identify the type of relationship. The two processes necessary for the successful treatment of bibliographic relationships—identification and linkage—are accomplished through the combined efforts of the cataloging rules and the bibliographic record and catalog structures. Identification is primarily dependent on information prescribed by the code, while linkage is usually dependent on record structure and catalog design. Because of the dependence on catalog design, most bibliographic relationships currently rely upon implicit entry-level linking through record or citation display proximity, implicit relationship identification through descriptive information in the bibliographic record, and the user's ability to infer relationship meaning from a combination of the two.

Relationships Important to Catalog Users

It is clear from this discussion of linkages that the lack of explicit identifiers and linkages places a great deal of responsibility for determining relationships on the catalog user and his or her ability to infer relationships from record proximity and data in the record. Deducing the type of bibliographic relationship based on the type of linking device used is made more difficult because the cataloging rules often prescribe the use of one device to express several different relationship types, while at the same time several different linking devices are used to identify the same relationship. Consequently, there is not a one-to-one correlation between linkage type and relationship. An additional confusion for the user is that linking devices used to show relationships often have other uses as well in bibliographic description.

This may explain the problems faced by users who need to understand a given relationship, but it does not identify the catalog users' needs regarding bibliographic relationships. In order to redesign catalog structures and provide cataloging rules that create effective tools for access and description, the relationships that are most important to the user must be identified.

User Studies

In a paper presented at a Seminar on Bibliographic Records, Svenonius discussed how the data elements on bibliographic records fall into two categories: "those that describe the entity in hand and those that relate the entity to other entities." The former she termed descriptive elements and the latter were referred to as organizing elements. The organizing elements included the normalized forms of names and titles, including uniform titles, main entries, and added entries. Svenonius stated that the purpose of these organizing elements "is to convey information about bibliographic relationships and in so doing to organize the catalog."[70] These two categories of data elements have each been the focus of catalog user studies, but unfortunately not within the context defined by Svenonius.

Although dozens of studies have examined various aspects of catalog use,[71] the resulting empirical data generally are inadequate to clarify user needs in terms of bibliographic relationships. Methodological problems have contributed to this lack of applicable user data. With the increasing number of OPACs, transaction log analysis has become the data collection method of choice, and while this does provide an unobtrusive window from which to examine catalog use activity, it does not answer questions about whether the user is searching for a work (represented by more than one record) or an item (represented by one specific record), or if and how the data elements in the bibliographic record are used to identify a specific relationship. Another problem is the users' lack of a vocabulary to discuss their information needs, their search processes, and the bibliographic data used.[72] This creates problems for methodologies that employ interview techniques. A user unfamiliar with the concept of bibliographic relationships, the means used to identify relationships, and the technical terms used to describe the parts of a bibliographic record, will find it difficult to converse about such needs and data uses.

Many studies have investigated how users search the catalog, focusing on the access points employed. A large portion of these studies have examined subject access, which is not part of the descriptive cataloging process, and therefore only marginally associated with this discussion of bibliographic relationships. When subject access is omitted, almost all studies examined for this paper found that the most used access points were title and author,[73] both of which operate as linkages for bibliographic relationships. For several reasons, however, caution must be exercised when interpreting these results to infer user need for the bibliographic relationships associated with these access points. First, most user studies identify author and title access point searches as "known item" searches, assuming that a searcher uses these access points when a specific *item* is known and sought. This would preclude the need to identify any related materials. None has taken into account the possibility that the user was actually performing a *work* search, to determine what editions or versions of a work might exist and then use the collocated list of related records to select an appropriate item; nor has any study provided data on the proportion of "known item" searches that retrieved multiple records for one work. Once categorized as a known item search, most user studies did not delve further into the user's motives and goals in performing the search. Such a follow-up might have discovered that the searcher was actually employing the "second objective" of the catalog (collocating), to identify specific relationships of importance, or in Svenonius' terms, was using the organizing elements of the bibliographic record to convey information about bibliographic relationships. As it stands, it can only be conjectured that some proportion of these known item searches were work searches that necessitated identification of relationships among entities represented by the retrieved record set.

A second problem with studies that focus on access points is that several relationship types use the same access points for linkage. Even if it were assumed that an author, title, or author/title search was conducted to view the record set for a *work* rather than a known item, it would be impossible to determine which specific relationship was sought by the user without an interview.

A third problem with many user studies is the lack of differentiation between title proper and uniform title. Such a distinction might indicate whether the search was for an item or a work, and might indicate the user's need for specific relationships to be identified. This is a particularly thorny problem to solve because the user might not understand the distinction between the two types of titles, and the indexing of many catalogs will retrieve data from both title proper and uniform title fields when the titles are identical or similar, depending on the search method employed.

It is interesting to note that the form of the catalog has affected how its use is studied and what aspects of use are examined. While the focus of more recent research has been on access points and user searching as determined by transaction log analysis, earlier user studies —primarily of card catalogs—focused more on the use of various elements of bibliographic data in the catalog record, employing survey, interview, and observation methodologies. No studies, however, have provided data on the use of data elements in the catalog record within the context of bibliographic relationships. Palmer summarized twenty-two catalog use studies prior to his own research in 1972, and discovered that overall the most heavily used data elements were author's name, title, call number, subject headings, and date of publication.[74] The moderately used elements included place of publication, publisher's name, edition statement, and contents note. All remaining elements were used infrequently. Palmer's own study largely supported these findings. Among the few recent studies that examined the bibliographic record, Hufford's examination of reference librarians' use of data elements indicated that 20.6 percent of all data elements accounted for 96.6 percent of the total uses of all elements, with title proper, author, location information, call number, serial chronological designation, date of publication, and serial alpha/numeric designation accounting for the most heavy use.[75] The study by Lundgren and Simpson, which examined faculty opinion on the usefulness of specific data elements of the bibliographic record, also supported similar findings.[76] Those elements rated as the highest degree of usefulness included title, primary author, date, subject, other authors, and series; those rated as a moderately high degree of usefulness included summary notes, contents notes, standard numbers, publisher, pagination, and related titles. Since these studies did not indicate how the information was used, one can only guess that some portion of these data elements were employed to assist in the identification of a relationship.

Additional problems exist with many user studies. Most examined a limited user population (i.e., staff, faculty, academic library users, etc.), providing data that is not generalizable to a larger population, or to users within specific disciplines who may have different needs. For example, Hufford's study of reference staff use concluded that "accompanying material" data were not used very frequently; however, it is likely that a similar study in a music library would find this data element heavily used to identify a musical score with accompanying parts.

Studies in the area of information retrieval have focused on the cognitive and behavioral aspects of catalog use, considering various factors that might affect the search, and trying to determine the users' criteria for successful catalog searches.[77] While the methodology employed in these studies would be helpful in determining a user's need for identification and linking of bibliographic relationships, none has examined that particular aspect of catalog use.

What then, if anything, can be learned about bibliographic relationships from the user research conducted thus far? Two of the most important linkages for derivative, whole-part, and equivalence relationships—author and title—are among the most heavily used access points. Of the data elements discovered to be heavily or moderately used, the date of publication, place of publication, publisher's name, and edition statements might be used primarily to demonstrate derivative relationships; contents note use would mainly indicate a need to identify whole-part relationships; and serial data elements would associate with sequential and whole-part relationships. It is also likely that the importance of various data elements and relationships will vary depending on the discipline, the type of library, and the type of user. Individual testimony, for example, has indicated that historical research scholars rely heavily on data elements that relate editions, relate and distinguish various states and versions of a work, link original works with their facsimiles, and link parts of a work with the whole.[78]

If these relationship linkages and identifiers were ranked in order of importance based upon the data gathered in these user studies, it would appear that those relationships that served an access function would rank highest, followed by those relationships serving a distinguishing or differentiating function, and those that identify the nature of a relationship. All of this is highly speculative, however, and is based on data culled from studies that were not designed to investigate bibliographic relationships.

IFLA Study

The final portion of the IFLA report attempted to place the bibliographic record within the context of user needs by mapping each entity attribute and relationship to the user tasks that they support.[79] Although the origin of the user task categories was not stated, they are clearly based on the functions of the catalog rather than any specific empirical user studies. These functions, identified by the IFLA group, included the following four generic user tasks: to find, to identify, to select, and to obtain. Each attribute and relationship was then assessed a value based on the Study Group's decision of its importance for supporting each of these four user tasks.[80] In many cases, information named as entity attributes in the IFLA study currently serves as a relationship identifier, for it provides the information necessary to distinguish between two entities, thus enabling the nature of the relationship to be understood.

The report assigned the highest value to those relationships that provided information needed for access; information needed to identify, distinguish, or differentiate bibliographic entities; or information about restricted use or access. Within these categories, relationships that were applicable to the largest number of records were assigned the highest value. Additionally, dependent relationships that linked referential entities and component parts were assigned the highest value. Thus, the IFLA study ranked the importance to the user of a given relationship first on the function served, then on its frequency of occurrence, and finally on the nature of the relationship.

This IFLA document is the first to provide a set of criteria to rank the importance of bibliographic relationships to users, and as such must be commended. One potential concern with these criteria, however, is the high ranking associated with frequency, for this creates problems for material that does not bulk large in the catalog. Research has shown that certain relationships are discipline or format specific, and even though a relationship may be important primarily to a subgroup of material within a specific discipline or in a specific format, it may still be vital to the user requiring that material. Thus, frequency of occurrence is a less than ideal means of ranking relationship importance to the user, if it means that lower frequency relationships will receive less than optimum treatment in the catalog. This, in effect, would create a caste structure of preferred users based on discipline. It is possible, however, that entities with low frequency relationships will also exhibit a relationship characteristic that would override the lower ranking. For example, an accompanying relationship occurring with lower frequency might still be ranked of high importance because of a dependent relationship to another entity. Perhaps, then, these ranking criteria might serve the user better if frequency were a secondary criterion, with function and the nature of the relationship taking precedence in rank. It is also noteworthy that the IFLA user criteria—function, nature of the relationship, and frequency—reflect the interpreted findings of the user studies. It would be preferable, however, if these criteria could be verified by user studies designed specifically to test the importance of bibliographic relationships, rather than relying on inference and speculation.

Relationships Important to Authority Record Users

Closely allied to the conceptual model of bibliographic relationships is the authority control process as manifested in the authority record. Authority control promotes the concept of one authoritative form of a name or title based on the choice and form of entry as prescribed by the *AACR,* with variant forms linked to the authorized form through references. Both the authorized form and its variants are recorded in the authority record. Thus, the authority record controls two important linkage categories for bibliographic relationship: access points and references. As part of the descriptive cataloging process authority records are associated with two types of relationships: *bibliographic relationships,* between two or more bibliographic entities; and *name relationships,*[81] between two or more names or forms of a name. While name relationships are important because names are an attribute of most bibliographic entities, authority records for names alone are not the nucleus of concern for bibliographic relationships.

Bibliographic relationships are primarily associated with authority records for *works.* These work authority records contain the citation heading for the work as the authorized heading, which usually consists of name and uniform title components—or a uniform title alone—depending on the origin of the work. The uniform title is an inextricable part of these work authority records, for currently the very existence of an authority record for a work depends in large part on that work's need for a uniform title as determined by the cataloging code and library policy.[82] But just as uniform titles are not created and used for all works, authority records have not been created for all works, even those requiring uniform titles. For example, Vellucci's study of music bibliographic relationships found work authority records for only 26.1 percent of the musical works in her sample,[83] even though 83.3 percent of the sample had a uniform title, and 62.9 percent of the sample used the uniform title as a linking device for a bibliographic relationship.[84] Theorists have predicted an expanded role for the uniform title in the online catalogs of the future due to its crucial function as a work identifier,[85] for in order to develop a fully linked, work-based catalog environment, authority records must be created for all works, which means that uniform titles must be constructed and applied consistently for all works.

Other than Vellucci's research, few empirical studies have examined the use of authority records within the context of bibliographic relationships, although a considerable body of research exists on the authority control of name relationships. An early study by Smiraglia that examined the use of uniform titles for music as one aspect of derivative relationships showed that virtually his entire sample yielded multiple manifestations, and that the majority of these had titles proper different from that of the first edition of the work.[86] From these results Smiraglia concluded that uniform titles were a necessary part of the description of musical works and were needed to serve as authority controlled collocating devices. He also cited the need for more references as part of that authority control.

In reporting her replication of Taylor's classic study of the value of authority files for name searching in an online catalog,[87] Bangalore reiterated that "the authority file is not only for the benefit of users, but also acts as a resource for library staff in technical as well as public services."[88] Name authority records are an important time-saver for catalogers and therefore are useful even when references are not required for a given name. While discussed within the context of name authority records only, these views could be extended to authority records for works and their usefulness for the identification and expression of bibliographic relationships.

Authority records for works are associated most frequently with four types of bibliographic relationships—derivative, whole-part, equivalence, and sequential. These associations stem in part from the *AACR2R* general rule (25.1A) that defines the use of uniform titles, i.e., to identify the work, to differentiate works with similar or like titles, and to collocate works.[89] As discussed earlier, name/uniform title references—determined by chapter 26 of *AACR2R* and controlled by authority records—serve as linking devices for both derivative and whole-part relationships. When included in bibliographic records, the name/uniform title citation headings controlled by authority records help identify relationships and link the records for related entities. Thus, several of the component parts of the work authority record—including names, uniform titles, and references—play an important role in the expression of bibliographic relationships in the catalog.

Recently there has been growing support to replace *authority records* with *access control records,* a change that reflects a shift in concept as well as terminology. Begun by Gorman twenty years ago with the idea of *information packages* as an alternative to the concept of main entry,[90] the term *access control* was first applied by Tillett a decade later.[91] Since then the body of literature on access control has continued to expand, as interest in work-based cataloging and direct-linkage databases has increased.[92]

Access control records were described by Barnhart as the next generation of authority records. These records remove the notion of "authority" and link variant forms of names and titles without declaring any one the "authorized" form. One form may be selected as the default form for display, but this can be varied by the user or the library. In a direct-linkage database structure, these access control records would be connected to bibliographic records—which would collocate all manifestations of a work—and to other related access control records—which would collocate related works. The access control record would become the locus for all information obtaining to the work, and could be expanded to include much information that is presently encoded in the bibliographic record for the manifestation.[93]

The use of access control records could greatly enhance the expression of bibliographic relationships in the catalog; however, in order to be fully implemented, certain inconsistencies in the cataloging code and its application for different formats of material must be addressed. For example, the previously discussed problem of revised editions of a work must be resolved so that there is a bidirectional link between the old and new editions. This type of linkage could be accomplished in a variety of ways through the use of relator codes in the MARC record and by linking access control records with each other and with the appropriate bibliographic records.

Another problem exists with the varying treatment of translations for nonmusic and music materials. As Barnhart pointed out, the *AACR2R* rule for references from variant titles (26.4B1) states that "In the case of translated titles, refer to the uniform title *and the appropriate language subheading . . .*" (emphasis added).[94] This rule, in effect, results in the creation of separate authority records—one for the original work and one for each language into which that work was translated, thus scattering information about the work among several records. For example, Thomas Mann's *Magic Mountain* has the following two authority records:

```
010        n 79077983
100  10    Mann, Thomas, $d 1875-1955. $t Zauberberg


010        n 94017974
100  10    Mann, Thomas, $d 1875-1955. $t Zauberberg. $l English
400  10    Mann, Thomas, $d 1875-1955. $t Magic Mountain
```

If these name/uniform title authority records are both considered *work* records, then this practice essentially treats the translation as a new work with its own work authority record. While some might agree with this idea for semantic reasons, for purposes of entry the code has adopted the view that they are the same work and the translation should be entered under the same heading as the original (21.14A). An alternative view would be to consider the first record an authority record for the *work* and the second record an authority record for an *expression* of the work, which is a more accurate interpretation; however, like bibliographic records, lower-level authority records of necessity include cumulative data for the superordinate level. Thus, citation information for the *work* is included in the *expression* record. This still results in multiple authority records that are only implicitly linked by collocation.

A Library of Congress Music Cataloging Decision (MCD) for rule 26.4B1 allows music catalogers to refer to an authority record for the original work that contains a uniform title without the addition of elements that would be used for derivative manifestations in most cases.[95] This interpretation of the rule allows music catalogers to create one authority record for the work that includes references from the variant forms of the title in many other languages. For example, the following is the work authority record for Brahms' *Zigeunerlieder:*

```
010        n 82040719
100  10    Brahms, Johannes, $d 1833-1897. $t Zigeunerlieder
400  10    Brahms, Johannes, $d 1833-1897. $t Gypsy songs
400  10    Brahms, Johannes, $d 1833-1897. $t Chants tsiganes
```

When used on a bibliographic record, the language element $l is added as appropriate to the uniform title for the original work. This practice allows one work authority record to be created that collocates all information appropriate to that work, without the creation of separate authority records for each expression. Although in these two examples the discrepancy is between the rules and an interpretation of the rules, rather than within the rules themselves, the impact on the creation of authority records and the catalog remains the same.

One final example of inconsistency in the rules to be discussed here is the treatment of entry for whole-part relationships. Rule 25.6A1 states "if a separately cataloged part of a work has a title of its own, use the title of the part by itself as the uniform title. Make a *see* reference from the heading for the whole work and the title of the part as a subheading of the title of the whole work."[96] The separate part is entered as a subheading of the title of the whole work only if the part does not have a distinctive title (rule 25.6A2). In a work-based environment, this practice essentially treats the part as a separate work with its own independent heading and authority record; and the determination of that separateness is not based upon the nature of the work, but rather whether or not it has a distinctive title. Special types of material are treated differently, however, and for both sacred scriptures and music, parts of a work with either distinctive or non-distinctive titles are entered under the heading for the whole work, with the title of the part entered as a subheading of the title of the whole work (rules 25.18A1, et al.; 25.32). The end result of these discrepancies is that for some materials there are authority records with the title of the part as the authorized heading and the whole-part title construct as the reference, and with other authority records the opposite is true. The authority records below illustrate this:

```
010       n 82257989
100  10   Dickens, Charles, $d 1812-1870. $t Bagman's story
400  10   Dickens, Charles, $d 1812-1870. $t Pickwick papers. $p Bagman's story

010       n 86130956
100  10   Bach, Johann Sebastian, $d 1685-1750. $t Matthäuspassion. $p Komm,
          süsses Kreuz
400  10   Bach, Johann Sebastian, $d 1685-1750. $t Komm, süsses Kreuz
```

In the catalog, the bibliographic records for the work and all its separate parts will be collocated for some material, while for other materials the user will retrieve a mixture of bibliographic records and references, but the bibliographic records for the parts will not collocate with those for the whole work. A consistent approach to the entry of parts of works would make the cataloger's work easier and bring uniformity to the treatment of whole-part relationships in the catalog for the user.

In summary, authority records for *works* are a critical part of the bibliographic relationship environment. While little empirical research exists that verifies the importance to users of authority records for the control of bibliographic relationships, observation indicates their importance for maintaining citation headings for works and providing the reference structure necessary for certain types of bibliographic relationships. These authority records are dependent upon the cataloging code to prescribe guidelines for constructing the citation headings—an important part of which is the uniform title—and the necessary references. The present creation of name/uniform title authority records is erratic at best, and does not represent the systematic process that is necessary to support a work-based catalog structure capable of treating bibliographic relationships with greater precision.

Underlying most of the problems discussed in this section is the code's lack of a conceptual foundation for describing a work and creating work authority records, a deficiency that stems in part from the focus on item-level cataloging and in part from the code's lack of a clear definition for a work. This results in inconsistencies in the construction and application of uniform titles and their authority records. It also leads to a proliferation of specialized rules and rule interpretations for materials that exhibit numerous relationships and are, therefore, more dependent on the concept of the work for their description, access, and expression of relationships.

Improved Methods for Expressing Bibliographic Relationships in the Online Environment

By now it is evident that while the rules often provide for the descriptive detail and access points necessary to identify a particular relationship, linkage—and in many cases explicit identification—is dependent upon the record and catalog structures. For better or worse, the MARC communications format is the most prominent record structure in use, and is the structure upon which most of today's OPACs are based. Since vast amounts of money have been invested in the MARC format in terms of the huge number of encoded records and the various library systems and utilities designed specifically for compatibility with the present formats, the *Realpolitik* of the situation suggests that the MARC structure will not be discarded lightly, if at all. Consequently, discussions of catalog improvements are often within the context of revamping the MARC record structure to accommodate better a direct-linkage database environment, rather than abandoning its use altogether.

The MARC Environment

A good starting point for discussion of bibliographic relationships within the MARC environment is Leazer's analysis of the USMARC formats for bibliographic, authority, and holdings data, conducted to determine the degree to which the structure adheres to a conceptual design schema as defined by database design theory.[97] With a view towards supporting future catalogs capable of formally expressing bibliographic relationships, Leazer analyzed the compactness, efficiency, and expressiveness of the MARC record format. He discovered a high degree of redundancy among the data elements and their functions, with twenty-six specific fields to handle bibliographic relationships, and a total of twenty-two fields designed to link related records. Much of the overall redundancy was due to the use of the MARC format within an antiquated linear computer environment. For example, much redundancy was caused by the expression of the same data in both encoded and narrative form, which could be eliminated by exploiting the computer's ability to store data in one format and display it in another. In other instances the same data were repeated in two different linked records, when a direct-linkage database structure could have connected the records without repeating the data. Both of these shortcomings have implications for the explicit expression of bibliographic relationships. For example, a relationship type could be identified by encoded data that could then be displayed as a textual label; or records for related material could be linked using a record control number and coded to display textual information from a specific field without rekeying the data. Leazer concluded that a new conceptual schema for the organization and structure of bibliographic databases was needed in addition to a reconceptualization of the MARC format. This dual theme of revamping MARC and developing a new database structure in order to improve the catalog's relational capabilities has become the "ground bass" for many articles on this topic.

As Leazer noted, the current MARC record structure already accommodates certain bibliographic relationships and record linkages; with revision, it is capable of providing the more sophisticated record linkages, data linkages, and explicit identifiers that are needed to create more formal expressions of bibliographic relationships in the catalog. MARC revision can be discussed on a continuum ranging from slight modifications, such as increasing the number of specialized note fields that deal with bibliographic relationships and expanding their record linking capabilities, to creating an entirely new MARC framework designed for direct-linkage database systems and hypermedia structures.

To this end, Tillett proposed a "slow evolution" in which current MARC fields could be mapped into a new MARC structure, with traditional linking devices, such as notes, combined with nontraditional next-generation hypertext links that would not only connect records, but identify relationships.[98] In her vision of the new "MARC III" format, there are no separate access fields, but rather text within the descriptive fields that is intended for access would be "marked" in such a way that it would be connected to the appropriate access control record for that data element. Tillett's "MARC III" structure requires direct links between access control records and bibliographic records, and a holdings format that links item-specific information to the appropriate bibliographic record. The entire structure is designed to "provide ways for users of online systems to discover the relationships and interconnections inherent in bibliographic information and those accidental, incidental, or perhaps even mystical relationships that derive from sharing an attribute. . . ."[99] Again, this idea represents MARC revision coupled with database restructuring, but Tillett's vision of the new "MARC III" catalog structure is grounded in the belief that the cataloging rules and principles should transcend the format used to communicate or store the bibliographic data. In her view, the cataloging code should be an underlying constant for the creation of cataloging records and, as such, should remain separate from the record format.[100]

Other theorists have advocated a more radical approach, suggesting totally revamped MARC and database structures, and cataloging rules that integrate MARC coding with description and access. Gorman described the current MARC format as a unitary record that contains complex information with few and weak links to other related unitary records.[101] He proposed that this structure be replaced by a system with many records containing simple data, wherein the records could be linked in a variety of ways to create a complex structure expressive of all types of bibliographic relationships. Gorman's view recasts both the cataloging rules and the MARC format into "The HYPERMARC Record Preparation Manual— Bibliographic," which integrates the rules for description, access, and record formatting into a single document. Significant features of this new manual include the provision for "levels" of description (in terms of analysis), guidelines for linking these descriptions, instructions for creating authority packages, and guidelines for linking authority packages to bibliographic descriptions and other information packages. Once again, the expression of bibliographic relationships is a key factor in the revision of MARC and the restructuring of the database.

Ultimately, the record structure should provide an economic and efficient way to store bibliographic data, show the relationships among that data, and present the information in a useful way to the catalog user. Revising the MARC format to accomplish this may be the most financially viable path when the extent of existing investment is considered. Web-based bibliographic systems have already found ways of using hypertext mark-up language to link bibliographic records with index entries, and to establish direct links between information in bibliographic records and the electronic documents that they describe. All of this has been accomplished within the framework of the MARC format. Some researchers, however, do not consider this "band-aid" approach to MARC revision the best or most efficient approach to database design, even when augmented by hypertext mark-up language linking capabilities.

New Catalog Environments

As long as the structure of the catalog remains modeled on the linear card catalog, improvement in the expression of relationships in the online environment will continue in piecemeal fashion by combining revision of MARC content, codes, and structure with a hypertext mark-up language. But as Tillett noted, current hypertext mark-up languages are excellent for direct connections but do not explicitly identify relationships;[102] and as Leazer found, the current MARC format is riddled with redundancy, and would require extensive reconceptualization to become a truly efficient data structure in a relational database. Several researchers, therefore, have begun to explore the possibility of other database models for future catalogs, some of which use a modified MARC format as an interim data structure, while others focus solely on the database structure without reference to MARC.

Heaney used object-oriented modeling to conceptualize a three-tiered catalog design independent of any particular method of implementation.[103] The three-tiered structure consists of the abstract work, the publication, and the copy. Based on the principle that objects can pass on their characteristics to other related objects, the record for each level of the hierarchy consists of bibliographic data pertinent only to the object at that specific level, with data pertinent to objects at other levels associated with the related object by links. The precise nature of the relationship can then be modeled as a link attribute. Thus, unlike the current MARC structure that includes data for all three tiers in each record, there is no redundancy among the database records. This model "involves a fundamental shift away from the *AACR2* philosophy of description of, plus access to, physical items," and requires cataloging rules that focus on the work.[104] Uniform title authority records for works are a critical component of the structure, and act as a means of linking works with their related bibliographical items. Heaney also suggests that relator codes, similar to those already authorized for use in $4 of MARC name fields, be used to identify a specific relationship or association, and provides examples of how the MARC format could be adapted as an interim structure for the model. Heaney's object-oriented model is similar to the entity-relationship model presented in the IFLA study.

The importance to the basic database structure of uniform title authority records for works was echoed by Wainwright, who suggested that a consistent means of linking related versions of works through an authority record for the primary work was needed. Wainwright also noted that "the most recent version of UNIMARC allows for pointers to the authority control records for the work, but unless the various types of relationships can be separately tagged, in any sizeable catalog the user is likely to be confronted with a confusing group of hits for many author or author-title searches."[105] Creating a link between records without identifying the precise nature of the relationship solves only half the problem. Thus, the combined use of specific relationship identifiers and direct linkages to access control records would be one viable method for identifying and linking related records.

Leazer has explored a different catalog model based on a bicameral system of description that contains one file for descriptions of items and one file for descriptions of works.[106]

The individual records in both files are linked to express explicitly three possible types of relationships: work-to-work, item-to-item, and item-to-work. In this system Leazer views all relationships as binary, one-to-one entity relationships, which may be repeated as often as necessary to describe the full array of possible relationships between any two entities. Leazer's model does not address the use of authority or access control records within this bicameral bibliographic system, but he does suggest computer data recognition routines to identify relational information resident in current MARC records.

Because the concept of a relational database design for catalogs has been growing in popularity,[107] Green's seminar class conducted an examination of the full-relational structure for use with bibliographic, authority, holdings, and classification data.[108] Building on a detailed analysis of the functions of a bibliographic database,[109] a conceptual database was designed based on an entity-relationship model. The study found that the complexity of bibliographic data created database efficiency problems when the normalization process of record deconstruction was applied to create the relational design. Due to the single-value attribute structure of a relation, any multivalue attribute must generate additional relations. With the high number of multivalue attributes for bibliographic data identified by the analysis (almost one-third of the relations), it would be necessary to access dozens of relations to assemble the complete bibliographic information for a specific physical item. It was determined, therefore, that the cleanness of the full-relational database design was immaterial in the face of the processing inefficiencies discovered. The group concluded that a full-relational approach, while semantically sound, resulted in inefficient processing, and that use of a MARC-based data storage format retains efficiency at the expense of semantic integrity.[110] Green goes on to suggest more efficient alternative structures, including a MARC-based structure with increased relational links between records, and an object-oriented database structure that accommodates multiple values, and, as Heaney noted, has the added advantage of hierarchical characteristic inheritance.

Thus, while it appears that a new catalog structure would enable bibliographic relationships to be identified and linked in a more direct and logical manner than the current MARC format allows, it is still unclear as to which database design would be most efficient. It is likely, therefore, that for the immediate future the MARC structure will be retained—while increasing its linking capabilities—and any major shift in database structures will occur only after further research has been conducted.

Local versus Global Bibliographic Universe

Until recently, the role of the local catalog has been to provide access to physical items owned by the local library, justifying to some extent *AACR2R*'s emphasis on description of, and access to, the physical item. As Wilson predicted, however, the role of the local catalog is expanding to incorporate information about objects neither owned by the local library nor traditionally accessed through the local catalog, with a resulting emphasis on the retrieval of works rather than physical objects.[111] This shift in focus from a local to a global bibliographic universe has distinct implications for the treatment of bibliographic relationships in catalogs. Three areas in particular deserve further consideration: the impact of network access to, and simultaneous searching of, multiple catalogs and databases; the ability to catalog within an international arena; and the effect of hypertext linkages on surrogate/document relationships.

Network technology offers many opportunities to expand the OPAC on several levels by providing remote access to local and union catalogs via local, regional, national, or international networks. Web-based OPACs using the Z39.50 information retrieval protocol are becoming commonplace, and projects are under way to provide simultaneous searching of multiple catalogs via the World Wide Web.[112] The extended local catalog presents a paradox for the expression of bibliographic relationships. On the one hand, since the catalog of any one institution contains only a portion of the bibliographic universe, relationships are likely to exist that are not apparent to users of a local OPAC. Thus, for a more accurate picture of any given work and all of its relationships, bibliographic records in the local catalog should be considered as only one part of the broader bibliographic universe. On the other hand, as the ability to perform simultaneous searches of multiple catalogs allows users greater access to the broader bibliographic universe, the complexity of relationships among records will increase, and users are likely to be overwhelmed by large retrieval sets and OPACs that provide inadequate means of interpreting the nature of relationships among myriad records.

One solution to this problem is under development by researchers at the University of Bradford, who have created a user-friendly PC-based front-end system for manipulating large retrieval sets,[113] and are currently working on a similar web-based system.[114] Based on the concept that works often appear in many versions or with complex multipart relationships, the Bradford OPAC "groups together into sets items that are manifestations of the same work."[115] A manifestation set is created around a manifestation entry consisting of a uniform title and author(s) for the work—essentially the equivalent of a work access control record. All manifestations of the work are linked under this heading to create the set, and users are then able to sort, search, and display these sets in various ways. The expression of bibliographic relationships is the primary function of this catalog, and therefore the difficulties encountered during its development process deal directly with the practical problems of creating a global catalog fully expressive of bibliographic relationships. Many difficulties occurred because of inconsistencies and redundancies in the MARC record. Additional obstacles were caused by the division between main and added entries in *AACR2R* and the MARC record, as well as the lack of analytical records for works. Thus, the Bradford OPAC project provides an example of how the shortcomings of *AACR2R* and the MARC format made the identification and linking of related records problematic.

The growing emphasis on networked access to library catalogs has engendered an increased awareness of the importance of bibliographic relationships for cataloging on an international scale. Tillett's access control record concept for names and works, which includes controlled forms of all pertinent data for the entity without identifying one authorized form, could become the pivotal data structure upon which the international cataloging community could develop their global catalogs. The access control record could compensate for differences in language and language scripts by allowing all variant forms of names and titles of works to be equally accessible. Additionally, access control records could provide the vertical and horizontal linking structure necessary for any relationship-based database.

The UNIMARC/Authorities format may be an appropriate structural basis for developing an access control record. In a comparison of the USMARC and UNIMARC authorities formats for the purpose of international data exchange, Truitt noted that "many of the most valuable links that UNIMARC seeks to establish are not presently coded in USMARC records."[116] Linkages important to bibliographic relationships in an electronic environment include language specification—i.e., language of cataloging, primary and alternate character sets, and script of cataloging—collective uniform title identification, and explicit inter-record links. Truitt attributed the lack of structural links between related records and headings in the USMARC format to a separate manual authority system mentality focused on the local catalog. He posited that the creators of UNIMARC/Authorities had a better understanding of the need for the identification of linkages and relationships because of the complexity of authority control at the international level. As discovered by the Bradford OPAC project, not only is there a need to improve the bibliographic relationship linking capabilities of UK and USMARC, but greater compatibility is needed among the various national MARC formats to facilitate the creation of new catalogs based on international data transfer.

A final area of consideration in the local versus global bibliographic universe is the effect of hypertext linkages on surrogate/document relationships. In a discussion of methods for organizing electronic resources, Vellucci noted that the transformation of the catalog into a "gateway" for accessing electronic resources has created conceptual problems for librarians by blurring the boundaries between the catalog and the bibliographic universe.[117] Until now, linkage concerns have focused on connecting two bibliographic records in the catalog, or in a few more advanced systems, connecting related authority and bibliographic records. With the advent of web-based catalogs, however, the linking function has been expanded to connect information in the bibliographic record to the actual related document when it is available in a digitized format. This example of connectivity represents linkage at the *document* level, and raises new issues about relationships between the surrogate record and the document represented by the surrogate. While this type of linkage is currently made by encoding the data with a hypertext mark-up language, the bibliographic record must contain the necessary information in order to make the link. It is the function of the cataloging code to ensure that the required information is contained in the bibliographic record.

The hypertext environment also affords the opportunity to go beyond connections between the bibliographic record and the electronic document. For example, links can be made from the bibliographic record to descriptive information about the document such as an abstract, summary, or online review of the work. In addition to text, these descriptions may be in graphical, video, or aural form, and the descriptions may be linked as separate objects or embedded in the bibliographic record itself. These types of descriptive relationships will become more common as the technology advances, and the next cataloging code must consider the possibility for including such relationship data in the bibliographic record.

In summary, it appears that no matter which specific database structure ultimately is deemed best for future catalogs, certain issues must be addressed in order to develop an efficient bibliographic system capable of serving the global community of the twenty-first century. Based on information gleaned from the Bradford OPAC project and other research into direct-linkage database structures, bibliographic relationships are the focal point of many important issues. Some concerns primarily deal with the MARC format's capacity to handle relationships—i.e., its redundancies, structural linkage deficiencies, and inconsistencies among different national structures. At the heart of many other issues, however, lies the cataloging code that determines the content, access points, and philosophical basis for what is described.

General Principles for Bibliographic Relationships in Catalogs

This paper has shown that bibliographic relationships do not exist as an isolated concept, but are integrated into almost every aspect of the descriptive cataloging process and are critical to the structure and design of catalogs. It is vital, therefore, that the cataloging rules clearly and directly address the expression of bibliographic relationships as part of the underlying principles that guide the cataloging code. These principles of description for bibliographic relationships are designed to support an expanded version of the catalog's functions, in which the expression of relationships is an integrated goal, the provision of access to bibliographic entities stored locally or remotely is an intended aim, and the description of bibliographic entities at multiple levels is considered useful. In order to fulfill these functions, the following four principles for bibliographic relationships should guide the cataloging code.

1. *The Principle of Relationship Identification.* The bibliographic record should identify all important bibliographic relationships that exist between the entity being cataloged and other entities. These relationships include both independent and dependent relationships. Identification should be bidirectional.

2. *The Principle of Enabling Linkage.* The data elements of the bibliographic record should enable related bibliographic records to be linked, and should permit the bibliographic record to be linked to related documents. To this end, the bibliographic record should provide enough information to identify the relationship and create a linkage. Linkages between bibliographic records should be bidirectional.

3. *The Principle of Multilevel Description.* The cataloging code should provide for the independent description of an entity at several levels, including the abstract work, the abstract expression, the physical item, and the specific copy. These hierarchically related descriptions should be linked.

4. *The Principle of Consistency.* The identification and linkage of like bibliographic relationships should be treated in a consistent manner, regardless of physical format. This includes the consistent application and use of uniform titles.

These principles provide a logical direction for the treatment of bibliographic relationships in the cataloging code. They encourage a consistent and uniform approach that would enable all formats of material to treat relationships in the same manner. The application of these principles would facilitate record restructuring and catalog design, expedite the international transfer of bibliographic data, and enable the design of a bibliographic system with specific relationship identifiers and direct linkages. Above all, they would allow the construction of catalogs that provide users with an overall picture of the work sought, its many and varied manifestations, and any works or manifestations of a work that are related in some way. In conclusion, "Cataloging is an art, not a science. No rules can take the place of experience and good judgement, but some of the results of experience may be best indicated by the rules."[118]

Notes

1. Gorman saw the definition of bibliographic relationships as the basis upon which the catalog file structure depended. He viewed the links between bibliographic records as critical to file design, and called for studies of the universe of bibliographic relationships in order to ensure that these links were both comprehensive and practical (see Michael Gorman, "Authority Files in a Developed Machine System," in *What's in a Name? Control of Catalogue Records through Automated Authority Files,* ed. N. Y. Furuya (Toronto: University of Toronto Library Automation Systems, 1978), 193).

2. Barbara B. Tillett, "Bibliographic Relationships: Toward a Conceptual Structure of Bibliographic Information Used in Cataloging" (Ph.D. diss., University of California, Los Angeles, 1987).

3. Antonio Panizzi, [Response to Question 9814], in *Report of the Royal Commissioners Appointed to Inquire into the Constitution and Government of the British Museum: With Minutes of Evidence* (London: Her Majesty's Stationery Office, 1850), 695.

4. Antonio Panizzi, "Mr. Panizzi to the Right Hon. the Earl of Ellesmere. British Museum, January 29, 1848," in *Foundations of Cataloging: A Sourcebook,* ed. Michael Carpenter and Elaine Svenonius (Littleton, Colo.: Libraries Unlimited, 1985), 15-47.

5. Charles A. Cutter, *Rules for a Printed Dictionary Catalog,* 4th ed. (Washington, D.C.: Government Printing Office, 1904), 12.

6. Seymour Lubetzky, *Code of Cataloging Rules, Author and Title Entry: An Unfinished Draft for a New Edition of Cataloging Rules, Prepared for the Catalog Code Revision Committee* (Chicago: American Library Association, 1960), ix.

7. International Conference on Cataloguing Principles, *Report: International Conference on Cataloguing Principles, Paris, 9th-18th October, 1961* (London: Organizing Committee of the International Conference on Cataloguing Principles, 1963), 91-96.

8. Ibid., 91.

9. Elaine Svenonius, "The Objectives of the Catalog and the Means to Reach Them," in *The Conceptual Foundations of Descriptive Cataloging,* ed. Elaine Svenonius (San Diego: Academic Press, 1989), 2.

10. Edward T. O'Neill and Diane Vizine-Goetz, "Bibliographic Relationships: Implications for the Function of the Catalog," in *Conceptual Foundations of Descriptive Cataloging,* ed. Elaine Svenonius (San Diego: Academic Press, 1989), 172.

11. Patrick Wilson, "The Second Objective," in *Conceptual Foundations of Descriptive Cataloging,* ed. Elaine Svenonius (San Diego: Academic Press, 1989), 5-16.

12. Ibid., 6.

13. Rebecca Green, "The Design of a Relational Database for Large-Scale Bibliographic Retrieval," *Information Technology and Libraries* 15, no. 4 (December 1996): 209.

14. *UNIMARC Format,* 2nd ed. (London: IFLA International Office, 1980).

15. Paula Goossens and E. Mazur-Rzesos, "Hierarchical Relationships in Bibliographic Descriptions: Problem Analysis," in *Hierarchical Relationships in Bibliographic Relationships: INTERMARC Software Subgroup Seminar 4, Library Systems Seminar, 1980* (Essen: Gesamthochschulbibliothek Essen, 1982).

16. Tillett, "Bibliographic Relationships."

17. Ibid., 24-25.

18. Ibid., 190.

19. Attig was concerned with the development of structures for communicating information about bibliographic relationships when he expressed his opinion that "Before decisions can be made or data structures designed, . . . there must be some solid conceptual analysis of the biblio-

graphic universe" (see John C. Attig, "Descriptive Cataloging Rules and Machine-Readable Record Structures: Some Directions for Parallel Development," in *The Conceptual Foundations of Descriptive Cataloging,* ed. Elaine Svenonius (San Diego: Academic Press, 1989), 145). More recently Gorman called for bibliographic system records that contained simple data with articulated, complex, and sophisticated linkages expressive of all the pertinent bibliographic relationships (see Michael Gorman, "After *AACR2:* The Future of the Anglo-American Cataloguing Rules," in *Origins, Content, and Future of AACR2 Revised,* ed. Richard P. Smiraglia (Chicago: American Library Association, 1992), 92-93).

20. Richard P. Smiraglia, "Authority Control and the Extent of Derivative Bibliographic Relationships" (Ph.D. diss., University of Chicago, 1992).

21. Richard Smiraglia, "Derivative Bibliographic Relationships: Linkages in the Bibliographic Universe," in *Navigating the Networks: Proceedings of the ASIS Mid-Year Meeting, Portland, Oregon, May 21-25,* ed. D. L. Andersen, T. J. Galvin, and M. D. Giguere (Medford, N.J.: Learned Information, 1994), 172.

22. Ibid., 177.

23. Ibid., 172.

24. Smiraglia, "Authority Control," 60.

25. Ibid.

26. Smiraglia, "Derivative Bibliographic Relationships," 175.

27. Smiraglia, "Authority Control," 61.

28. Sherry L. Vellucci, *Bibliographic Relationships in Music Catalogs* (Lanham, Md.: Scarecrow Press, 1997).

29. Ibid., 80-81.

30. International Federation of Library Associations and Institutions, *Functional Requirements for Bibliographic Records: Draft Report for World-Wide Review* (Frankfurt: IFLA, 1996).

31. Since the publication of Fidel and Crandall's article in 1988, interest has increased in developing new catalog structures, primarily based on databases that employ data linking based on relationships (see Raya Fidel and Michael Crandall, "The *AACR2* as a Design Schema for Bibliographic Databases," *Library Quarterly* 58, no. 2 (April 1988): 123-42). Leazer's doctoral research was concerned with developing a relational database model to accommodate better the bibliographic relationships associated with works (see Gregory H. Leazer, "A Conceptual Plan for the Description and Control of Bibliographic Works," D.L.S. diss., Columbia University, 1993). Heaney discussed the cataloging process in terms of an object-oriented database model for catalogs (see Michael Heaney, "Object-Oriented Cataloging," *Information Technology and Libraries* 14, no. 3 (September 1995): 135-53).

32. International Federation of Library Associations and Institutions, *Functional Requirements for Bibliographic Records,* 9.

33. Ibid.,11.

34. Ibid., 12.

35. Ibid., 13.

36. To further cloud the issue, manifestations are frequently called versions or editions, and catalogers usually disagree with bibliographers on the definitions of these terms.

37. International Federation of Library Associations and Institutions, *Functional Requirements for Bibliographic Records,* 14.

38. Ibid., 15.

39. O'Neill and Vizine-Goetz, "Bibliographic Relationships: Implications for the Function of the Catalog," 172.

40. Elaine Svenonius, "Bibliographic Entities and Their Uses," in *Seminar on Bibliographic Records: Proceedings of the Seminar Held in Stockholm, 15-16 August 1990, and Sponsored by the IFLA UBCIM Programme and the IFLA Division of Bibliographic Control,* ed. Ross Bourne (München: K. G. Saur, 1992), 5-6.

41. Green, "The Design of a Relational Database for Large-Scale Bibliographic Retrieval," 210-11.

42. Heaney, "Object-Oriented Cataloging," 152.

43. Martha M. Yee, "Manifestations and Near-Equivalents: Theory, With Special Attention to Moving-Image Materials," *Library Resources & Technical Services* 38, no. 3 (July 1994): 246.

44. International Federation of Library Associations and Institutions, *Functional Requirements for Bibliographic Records,* 7-8.

45. Ibid., 16-17.

46. Ibid., 47.

47. Ibid., 48.

48. Ibid.

49. Note, for example, the variation in subclasses defined by Vellucci in the study of music bibliographic relationships (see Vellucci, *Bibliographic Relationships in Music Catalogs,* 310-11). It is highly likely that relationship subclasses are discipline specific, and while common subclasses will be found to occur in most disciplines, each discipline will also have subclasses of its own.

50. International Federation of Library Associations and Institutions, *Functional Requirements for Bibliographic Records,* 50.

51. Ibid., 52.

52. Ibid., 53.

53. The author acknowledges the role of subject access in the linkage system, but has excluded it from this discussion since it is not part of the descriptive cataloging process.

54. Tillett, "Bibliographic Relationships," 42.

55. Ibid., 56.

56. Ibid., 58.

57. Ibid., 71.

58. Ibid., 77.

59. Ibid., 82.

60. Ibid., 83.

61. Barbara B. Tillett, "The History of Linking Devices," *Library Resources & Technical Services* 36, no. 1 (January 1992): 23-31.

62. Vellucci, *Bibliographic Relationships in Music Catalogs,* 242-44.

63. International Federation of Library Associations and Institutions, *Functional Requirements for Bibliographic Records,* 43.

64. References are also used heavily to link variant forms of names and to provide the syndetic structure of subject access; however, neither of these uses are considered bibliographic relationships because they are not linking to a bibliographic entity. In the first instance they link name entity to name entity and in the second instance they link subject entity to subject entity.

65. For a discussion of the role of references versus the role of added entries see Seymour Lubetzky, *The Principles of Cataloging* (Los Angeles: Institute of Cataloging Research, 1969), 20-22; Elaine Svenonius, "References vs. Added Entries" (paper presented at OCLC's *Authority Control in the 21st Century: An Invitational Conference, March 31-April 1, 1996,* available at: http://www.oclc.org/oclc/man/authconf/svenoniu.htm), and Barbara B. Tillett, "Bibliographic Structures: The Evolution of Catalog Entries, References, and Tracings," in *The Conceptual*

Foundations of Descriptive Cataloging, ed. Elaine Svenonius (San Diego: Academic Press, 1989), 149-65.

66. *Anglo-American Cataloguing Rules, Second Edition, 1988 Revision,* prepared under the direction of the Joint Steering Committee for Revision of AACR, ed. Michael Gorman and Paul W. Winkler (Ottawa: Canadian Library Association; London: Library Association Publishing; Chicago: American Library Association, 1988), 624.

67. Martha M. Yee, "What Is a Work? Part 1: The User and the Objects of the Catalog," *Cataloging & Classification Quarterly* 19, no. 1 (1994): 9-28.

68. In several studies that surveyed catalog users about the use of data elements or ways to improve the catalog's ability to meet their information needs, contents information was cited as an important element. See, for example, Arthur Maltby and A. Duxbury, "Description and Annotation in Catalogues: Reader Requirements," *New Library World* 73 (April 1972): 260-62, 273; Danuta Nitecki, "User Criteria for Evaluating the Effectiveness of the Online Catalog," in *Research in Reference Effectiveness* (Chicago: American Library Association, 1993), 8-28; and Richard Palmer, *Computerizing the Card Catalog in the University Library: A Survey of User Requirements* (Littleton, Colo.: Libraries Unlimited, 1972), 88-92.

69. Although MARBI has approved separate subfield codes for names, titles, and other types of information within the 505 contents note field, authority control will not be imposed on any of these subfields at this time.

70. Svenonius, "Bibliographic Entities and Their Uses," 7-8.

71. Many authors have presented an overview of catalog use studies or incorporate details of such studies into literature reviews. Those referred to by this author include:

Carol L. Barry, "User-Defined Relevance Criteria: An Exploratory Study," *Journal of the American Society for Information Science* 45, no. 3 (April 1994): 149-59.

Carol A. Hert, "User Goals in an Online Public Access Catalog," *Journal of the American Society for Information Science* 47, no. 7 (July 1996): 504-18.

Jon R. Hufford, "Use Studies and OPACS," *Technical Services Quarterly* 9, no. 1 (1991): 57-70.

Palmer, *Computerizing the Card Catalog in the University Library.*

Sharon Seymour, "Online Public Access Catalog User Studies: A Review of Research Methodologies, March 1986-November 1989," *Library and Information Science Research* 13 (April-June 1991): 89-102.

Charles W. Simpson, "OPAC Transaction Log Analysis: The First Decade," in *Advances in Library Automation and Networking: A Research Annual,* ed. J. Hewitt (Greenwich, Conn.: JAI Press, 1989), 3: 35-67.

D. Kathryn Weintraub, "The Essentials or Desiderata of the Bibliographic Record as Discovered by Research," *Library Resources & Technical Services* 23, no. 4 (fall 1979): 391-405.

Martha M. Yee, "System Design and Cataloging Meet the User: User Interfaces to Online Public Access Catalogs," *Journal of the American Society for Information Science* 42, no. 2 (March 1991): 78-98.

72. Yee, "System Design and Cataloging Meet the User: User Interfaces to Online Public Access Catalogs," 90.

73. See, for example:

Terry Ballard, "Comparative Searching Styles of Patron and Staff," *Library Resources & Technical Services* 38, no. 3 (July 1994): 293-305.

Lynn Silipigni Connaway, John M. Budd, and Thomas R. Kochtanek, "An Investigation of the Use of an Online Catalog: User Characteristics and Transaction Log Analysis," *Library Resources & Technical Services* 39, no. 2. (April 1995): 142-52.

Jon R. Hufford, "Use Studies and OPACS," *Technical Services Quarterly* 9, no. 1 (1991): 57-70.

Jimmie Lundgren and Betsy Simpson, "Cataloging Needs Survey for Faculty at the University of Florida," *Cataloging & Classification Quarterly* 23, no. 3/4 (1997): 47-63.

Brendan J. Wyly, "From Access Points to Materials: A Transaction Log Analysis of Access Point Value for Online Catalog Users," *Library Resources & Technical Services* 40, no. 3 (July 1996): 211-36.

74. Palmer, *Computerizing the Card Catalog in the University Library.*

75. Hufford, "Use Studies and OPACS," 59.

76. Lundgren and Simpson, "Cataloging Needs Survey for Faculty at the University of Florida."

77. See, for example, the following among others:

Barry, "User-Defined Relevance Criteria: An Exploratory Study."

Hert, "User Goals in an Online Public Access Catalog."

Carol C. Kulthau, *Seeking Meaning: A Process Approach to Library and Information Services* (Norwood, N.J.: Ablex Publishing, 1993).

Dee A. Michel, "What Is Used during Cognitive Processing in Information Retrieval and Library Searching," *Journal of the American Society for Information Science* 45, no. 7 (August 1994): 498-514.

Nitecki, "User Criteria for Evaluating the Effectiveness of the Online Catalog."

78. Henry L. Snyder, "End Users'/Researchers' Functions," in *Seminar on Bibliographic Records: Proceedings of the Seminar Held in Stockholm, 15-16 August 1990, and Sponsored by the IFLA UBCIM Programme and the IFLA Division of Bibliographic Control,* ed. Ross Bourne (München: K. G. Saur, 1992), 48-60.

79. International Federation of Library Associations and Institutions, *Functional Requirements for Bibliographic Records,* 63.

80. Ibid., 64.

81. For a taxonomy of name relationships see Barbara B. Tillett, "Considerations for Authority Control in the Online Environment," *Cataloging & Classification Quarterly* 9, no. 3 (1989): 10-11.

82. These *work* authority records would be considered *expression* records according to the IFLA Study Group definitions. They are created at the expression level when the work has appeared under varying titles, which indicates that more than one expression of the work exists. In addition to the citation form of heading for the *work,* these *expression* records contain references from the variant forms of titles that are found on different expressions of the work.

83. Vellucci, *Bibliographic Relationships in Music Catalogs,* 182.

84. Ibid., 191-92. The lack of authority records found in the LC Authority File was in large part due to the Library of Congress' past policy not to create an authority record for works when no references were required, even though a uniform title may be used. This presented special problems when cataloging music with nondistinctive form titles (e.g., quartets, symphonies, etc.), for each cataloger had to construct the multielement uniform title from scratch for such works, a time-consuming and often redundant task that could be eliminated by the creation of a work authority record. LC has recently changed this policy for music materials and will provide such uniform title authority records in the future (as per communication with Barbara Tillett, July 17, 1997).

85. F. H. Ayres, "Bibliographic Control at the Crossroads," *Cataloging & Classification Quarterly* 20, no. 3 (1995): 5-18.

Michael Gorman, "Cataloging and the New Technologies," in *The Nature and Future of the Catalog: Proceedings of the ALA's Information Science and Automation Division's 1975 and 1977 Institutes on the Catalog,* ed. Maurice J. Freedman and S. Michael Malinconico (Phoenix, Ariz.: Oryx, 1979), 127-36.

Heaney, "Object-Oriented Cataloging."

Sherry L. Vellucci, "Uniform Titles as Linking Devices," *Cataloging & Classification Quarterly* 12, no. 1, (1990): 35-62.

Eric Wainwright, "Implications of the Dynamic Record for the Future of Cataloguing," *Cataloguing Australia* 17, no. 3/4 (September-December 1991): 7-20.

Patrick Wilson, "The Catalog as Access Mechanism: Background and Concepts," *Library Resources & Technical Services* 27, no. 1 (January-March 1983): 4-17.

———, "Interpreting the Second Objective of the Catalog," *Library Quarterly* 59, no. 4 (October 1989): 339-53.

86. Richard P. Smiraglia, "Uniform Titles for Music: An Exercise in Collocating Works," *Cataloging & Classification Quarterly* 9, no. 3 (1989): 97-114.

87. Arlene G. Taylor, "Authority Files in Online Catalogs: An Investigation of Their Value," *Cataloging & Classification Quarterly* 4, no. 3 (spring 1984): 1-17.

88. Nirmala S. Bangalore, "Authority Files in Online Catalogs Revisited," *Cataloging & Classification Quarterly* 20, no. 3 (1995): 75-94.

89. *Anglo-American Cataloguing Rules, Second Edition, 1988 Revision, Amendments 1993* (Ottawa: Canadian Library Association; London: Library Association Publishing; Chicago: American Library Association, 1993).

90. Gorman, "Cataloging and the New Technologies."

91. Barbara B. Tillett, "Access Control: A Model for Descriptive, Holding and Control Records," in *Convergence: Proceedings of the Second National Conference of the Library & Information Technology Association, October 2-6, 1988, Boston, Massachusetts,* ed. Michael Gorman (Chicago: American Library Association, 1990), 48-56.

92. Linda Barnhart, "Access Control Records: Prospects and Challenges" (paper presented at OCLC's *Authority Control in the 21st Century: An Invitational Conference, March 31-April 1, 1996*), available at: http://www.oclc.org/oclc/man/authconf/barnhart.htm#8.

Gorman, "After *AACR2:* The Future of the Anglo-American Cataloguing Rules."

Heaney, "Object-Oriented Cataloging."

Tillett, "Access Control: A Model for Descriptive, Holding and Control Records."

———, "Considerations for Authority Control in the Online Environment."

———, "International Shared Resource Records for Controlled Access" (paper presented at OCLC's *Authority Control in the 21st Century: An Invitational Conference, March 31-April 1, 1996*), available at: http://www.oclc.org/oclc/man/authconf/barnhart.htm#8.

93. Barnhart, "Access Control Records: Prospects and Challenges."

94. *Anglo-American Cataloguing Rules, Second Edition, 1988 Revision,* 558.

95. The MCD reads as follows: "Generally the heading referred to should include only the basic uniform title of the work, without additions such as 'arr.' (25.35C), 'Vocal score' (25.35D), 'Libretto' (25.35E), language (25.35F), etc., even if such additions are used in the uniform title in the bibliographic record for the item being cataloged. If, however, the title being referred from is specific to the arrangement, format, language, etc. brought out by an addition to the uniform title, and the title would not logically be used for a different manifestation of the work, refer to the uniform title with the addition." (*Music Cataloging Bulletin* 21, no. 6 (1990): 4).

96. *Anglo-American Cataloguing Rules, Second Edition, 1988 Revision,* 491.

97. Gregory H. Leazer, "An Examination of Data Elements for Bibliographic Description: Toward a Conceptual Schema for the USMARC Formats," *Library Resources & Technical Services* 36, no. 2 (April 1992): 189-208.

98. Barbara B. Tillett, "Future Rules and Catalog Records," in *Origins, Content, and Future of AACR2 Revised,* ed. Richard P. Smiraglia (Chicago: American Library Association, 1992), 110-18.

99. Ibid., 116.

100. Ibid., 117.

101. Gorman, "After *AACR2:* The Future of the Anglo-American Cataloguing Rules," 91.

102. Tillett, "Future Rules and Catalog Records."

103. Heaney, "Object-Oriented Cataloging," 135-53.

104. Ibid., 152.

105. Wainwright, "Implications of the Dynamic Record for the Future of Cataloguing," 13.

106. Gregory H. Leazer, "A Conceptual Schema for the Control of Bibliographic Works," in *Navigating the Networks: Proceedings of the ASIS Mid-Year Meeting,* ed. D. L. Anderson, T. J. Galvin, and M. D. Giguere (Medford, N.J.: American Society for Information Science, 1994), 115-35.

107. One of the earliest suggestions for the use of a relational database design for library catalogs came from Gorman (see "Authority Files in a Developed Machine System" and "Cataloging and the New Technologies"). Since then other researchers have examined the relational database concept in various contexts including the following, to name a few:

    Roy Chang, "dBase, Relational Data Models, and MARC Records," *Technical Services Quarterly* 10, no. 2 (1992): 81-91.

    Robert G. Crawford, H. Sue Becker, and Janet E. Ogilvie, "A Relational Bibliographic Database," *Canadian Journal of Information Science* 9 (June 1984): 21-28.

    Green, "The Design of a Relational Database for Large-Scale Bibliographic Retrieval."

    J. Llorens and A. Trénor, "MARC and Relational Databases," *The Electronic Library* 11, no. 2 (April 1993): 93-97.

108. Green, "The Design of a Relational Database for Large-Scale Bibliographic Retrieval."

109. See pages 108-109 for a list of the functional requirements identified by the seminar group.

110. Green, "The Design of a Relational Database for Large-Scale Bibliographic Retrieval," 213.

111. Wilson, "The Second Objective."

112. For example, the Europagate Project has developed gateway software that implements multiple-target catalog searches using a World Wide Web front-end interface. Project information is available at URL: http://europagate.dtv.dk/.

113. F. H. Ayres, L. P. S. Nielsen, and M. J. Ridley, "Bibliographic Management: A New Approach Using the Manifestations Concept and the Bradford OPAC," *Cataloging & Classification Quarterly* 22, no. 1 (1996): 3-28.

114. Information on the current Bradford OPAC 2 is available at: URL: http://www.comp.brad.ac.uk/research/database/bopac2.html.

115. Ayres, Nielsen, and Ridley, "Bibliographic Management," 3.

116. Marc Truitt, "USMARC to UNIMARC/Authorities: A Qualitative Evaluation of USMARC Data Elements," *Library Resources & Technical Services* 36, no. 1 (January 1992): 37-58.

117. Sherry L. Vellucci, "Herding Cats: Options for Organizing Electronic Resources," *Internet References Services Quarterly* 1, no. 4 (1996): 13.

118. Cutter, *Rules for a Dictionary Catalog,* 6.

DISCUSSION ABOUT YEE AND VELLUCCI PAPERS

The discussion began with access control records and the possibility of having both an authoritative form of citation for a work plus entries under original title and varying titles, thereby allowing local libraries to decide which type of authority control record to use. Several participants voiced the belief that this would be difficult to implement in a cooperative cataloguing environment where agreement beyond the local level is essential.

Access control records were also suggested as a solution to the problem of title changes in serials. These title changes would be more meaningful if brought together on one record rather than in the linked manner now used. This problem is not limited to serials; it pervades all cataloguing, e.g., the various versions of motion pictures and videorecordings.

It was noted that the MARC formats, rather than *AACR2,* are making bibliographic relationships intelligible. Several participants believed that if the relationships are important enough to be made in MARC records, the justification for them needs to be outlined in *AACR2* in rules and principles about when to make and the form in which to make them. *AACR2* should make explicit many things that are now implicit.

In card catalogues uniform titles were used to provide a type of classification ("works" first,

then "selections," etc.). Guide cards helped the user to understand this arrangement. Nonalphabetic arrangement is not suited to OPACs. While a cataloguer's impulse is to organize something that is in disarray, the organization only works for people who know what is being done, the terminology used, and where the records can be found. It was suggested that perhaps Fattahi's proposed super records function as guide cards.

The problem of terminology arose in discussing several topics: the meaning and usefulness of "main entry," "primary access point," and "added entry"; reference librarians who opposed "authority records" as a means of access to the catalogue; and the terms used in dealing with people outside the library profession, e.g., programmers. *AACR2* needs to change its terminology in order to make rule changes understandable and acceptable.

One participant described a project, eventually abandoned, that dealt with the concept of creating an SGML/MARC record which could map over into the OPAC to display a catalogue record, but could also display an access mechanism in the digital catalogue. It proved difficult to take many different pieces out of some very complicated MARC records and display them in a meaningful manner.

Content versus Carrier

LYNNE C. HOWARTH

1. Introduction

Acting as a surrogate for an actual item or object, the bibliographic record must present as accurate and full a description of the physical, intellectual, and/or artistic properties of a work as will facilitate its identification and access by an individual with an information need.[1] The inherent value or usefulness of the bibliographic surrogate resides in its ability to represent each entity (item or object) uniquely, permitting different manifestations or formats of the title to be distinguished one from another. Determining what is appropriately "accurate" and "full" so as to be "useful" has been the challenge for designers of descriptive cataloguing codes, particularly since the proliferation of both published materials and libraries accessible to a wide range of users or clients necessitated a systematic and consistent approach to the creation of bibliographic surrogates.

2. Content versus Carrier: Some Issues and Problems

Rule 0.24 of the *Anglo-American Cataloguing Rules, Second Edition, 1988 Revision* (with 1993 amendments) *(AACR2R)* establishes the framework for the descriptive cataloguing endeavour. "It is a cardinal principle of the use of part I that the description of a physical item should be based in the first instance on the chapter dealing with the class of materials to which that item belongs. In short, the starting point for description is the physical form of the item in hand, not the original or any previous form in which the work has been published." (*AACR2R,* p. 8). Descriptive cataloguing is thus based, in the first instance, on the physical format of the material—the carrier—rather than on the intellectual or artistic content of the work. Chief sources of information for various elements of the bibliographic record (title and statement of responsibility area; edition area; area 3 data, where applicable; publication, distribution, etc., area) are format-dependent. Part II of the code deals with the choice and form of access points for the item, with rule 20.1 advising that: "The rules in part II apply to works and not to physical manifestations of those works, though the characteristics of an individual item are to be taken into account in some instances" (*AACR2R*, p. 305). The creation of a complete bibliographic record for an item or object will begin with the application of part I, with the choice and form of access points subsequently based on that description and as directed in part II (see *AACR2R*, rule 20.1, p. 305).

As Delsey[2] and Heaney[3] have observed, the structure of *AACR2* (and *AACR2R*) is itself problematic in ensuring consistent application of rules 0.24 and 20.1—arguably the defining elements of the "content versus carrier" discussion. In his "Object-Oriented Cataloging," Heaney explains:

> Even within *AACR2* there are sleights of hand which disguise the centrality of the issue of description versus access. Theoretically, access points should arise from the description of the physical item, but in some instances they depend upon decisions about the "nature" of a work: for example, the text versus commentary aspect or the original author versus revising author in *AACR2* rule 21.12B. *AACR2* does give guidance which uses the layout of the physical object as a touchstone, but in the end the decision is based on the cataloguer's conception of what the work "really" is.
>
> Another important example is the case where a known author is not named in the work. Here the cataloguer is instructed to give the known author as the main entry and to add a note identifying the person. Adding the note to the record is access determining description.[4]

While the code makes explicit that descriptive cataloguing is physical object-focused, and access points are work-dependent, nonetheless the process involves using the chief source of information for the item-in-hand as a starting point for the choice and form of main and added entries. As Delsey summarizes:

> It is clear that the notion of the work as an entity distinct from any given "physical manifestation" of the work is operative in the rules applying to works for which a single person is responsible, and also in the rules for establishing uniform titles. But as we move into dealing with works of shared and mixed responsibility, there is a clear tendency to skew the concept of the work, to judge who is responsible for the work and whether or not the work is a new work entirely on the basis of what is in effect "product labelling" information derived from the item in hand. In those cases the characteristics of a single "physical manifestation" effectively displace the notion of the work as an entity or object in its own right.[5]

These apparent inconsistencies underscore the problem of drawing clear distinctions, or a definite demarcation, between content and carrier in the application of *AACR*.

As new media types have proliferated, in essence to acquire "literary warrant," the cataloguing codes have evolved to incorporate the particular or unique physical properties of the material. Appropriate rules have been added to existing chapters, or complete chapters have been inserted into the code as a whole. Increasingly, the same work in multiple formats or with parts comprised of different media types have emerged to challenge the concept of the single carrier. Likewise, the evolution of electronic media, including Internet resources which contain multimedia formats (e.g., audio and/or video clips to complement text and graphics) have, in some cases, made the interpretation and application of rule 0.24 less clear, if not problematic.

Why has rule 0.24 proved to be problematic? Because it makes the physicality of a work the focus and the starting point for the creation of the descriptive portion of the bibliographic record, its application leads to apparent duplication since the same work (title) can appear in many formats, and separate bibliographic records can be created for each item. In some cases determining the "class of materials to which that item belongs" is less than straightforward. For some kits or multimedia manifestations it may be unclear as to which component should be designated the primary medium and the starting point for the descriptive cataloguing, per se. Devising guidelines for representing interactive multimedia proved challenging because of the packaging of several distinct media—videorecordings, sound recordings, computer files, printed text, each with their own separate chapters for descriptive cataloguing in *AACR2R*—into one work. In that case, the determination of primary medium was sufficiently daunting to raise the question of creating a separate chapter in the code to deal exclusively with interactive multimedia. For the time being, *AACR2R*, chapter 9, suffices along with a companion manual, *Guidelines for Bibliographic Description of Interactive Multimedia*,[6] to assist with interpretation and application of the rules.

While the cataloguing code is explicit in its directives for handling different manifestations of the same title or work, *application* of those rules has been less than consistent. Deviation from the letter of *AACR* has occurred, for example, with the Library of Congress practice with microforms. Rather than using chapter 11—"the class of materials to which the work belongs"—as the basis for describing works reproduced in microform, the Library of Congress reserves that chapter for materials that have only been published in microform format, applying chapter 2 for the original text and making a note of the format. While the National Library of Canada follows both the letter and spirit of *AACR2R,* chapter 11, the wide availability and use of Library of Congress cataloguing copy ensures the proliferation of "nonstandard" bibliographic records for many titles published in microform.

Most recently, the explosion of information resources accessible via the Internet, and particularly through the World Wide Web, has called into question the usefulness of the bibliographic record as a whole, and of the application of chapter 9, more specifically. Should a catalogue record be created for resources that change content or location unpredictably and with some frequency, particularly when those resources exist in a relatively freewheeling, uncontrolled, and largely uncontrollable arena, such as the web? Is a bibliographic record with its imperatives for structure and consistency a contradiction in terms relative to the amorphous and ever-changing nature of Internet resources? Is chapter 9 merely a "shoe horn" rigorously applied to force "boundary-less" digital fragments into a predetermined structure initially devised in the book-centered nineteenth century? Can we appropriately apply the provisions of rule 0.24 to a "carrier" where physicality is an intangible, and not readily definable? The *International Standard Bibliographic Description for Electronic Resources (ISBD (ER))*, recently published, omits a physical description area for remote access electronic resources in recognition of the lack of "physicality." In short, is descriptive cataloguing attempting to follow fashion with outmoded tools, rather than readily accommodating a logical bibliographic fit?

These are questions which will persist and likely intensify as digital formats, in particular, continue to evolve. More common will become instances where, as with the publication of *City of Bits*,[7] the same work appears in both print and electronic formats simultaneously. The latter, which is accessible via the World Wide Web and readable with a web browser that supports a graphical user interface (e.g., Netscape, Explorer, Mosaic), offers the reader all the content of the printed monograph, and more. For example, through the use of hyperlinks, the table of contents which appears "up-front" on the electronic title page links to other content pieces in the document. Providing consistent access to such "in tandem" publications through the application of *AACR2R,* part II, may prove less challenging than providing descriptive cataloguing for two carriers or manifestations—one tangible, the other intangible. In these instances, will the descriptions resulting from the application of *AACR2R,* part I, call into question the equivalency of the work itself as the same bibliographic entity but in different formats?

3. To Change the Code(?): Some Considerations

a) *AACR* as a Robust Framework

The previous section attempted to highlight some of the issues and problems associated with the application of *AACR2R* rule 0.24, specifically, and also as it relates to rule 20.1 and the choice and form of access points for the "work." The work is or *represents* the content, or is the *expression* of the content as determined by the author(s) or creator(s) (whether known or anonymous; whether a person or a corporate body), while the item-in-hand, the physical entity, or the "carrier" is the vehicle or vessel for that content. As further elaborated by the IFLA Study Group on the Functional Requirements for Bibliographic Records: "The entities defined as *work* (a distinct intellectual or artistic creation) and *expression* (the intellectual or artistic content) reflect intellectual or artistic content. The entities defined as *manifestation* (the physical embodiment of an *expression* of a *work*) and *item* (a single exemplar of a *manifestation*), on the other hand, reflect physical form." The apparent primacy of physical form[8] in the creation of the complete bibliographic record (description and access points) has proved sufficiently problematic to support calls for a review and substantial revision of the *Anglo-American Cataloguing Rules.* Are significant changes demanded, or is there a place for an *AACR* with modest revisions or reinterpretations?

The eight areas of description derived from the International Standard Bibliographic Description (ISBD) provide a simple yet robust framework for the capture and expression of data pertaining to the item-in-hand. The inclusion of optional additions, while confounding to overall record consistency and to those who would prefer a more prescriptive code, provide for flexibility of application across a variety of physical formats and within different cataloguing environments. While one might argue that the eight areas of description have more readily accommodated some new formats (e.g., videorecordings) than others (e.g., electronic resources), overall the framework has proved a good fit. Research[9,10] has suggested that catalogue users would favour enhancements to elements (such as table of contents, summary notes, critical reviews) that provide a better picture of the intellectual content of an item, while downplaying the usefulness of aspects related to physical format (for example, pagination, dimensions, illustrations).[11] Modifications of this magnitude could appropriately and readily be incorporated into the code as it currently exists, but would not address the more fundamental concerns regarding the interpretation and application of *AACR.*

In spite of whatever concerns may have been identified in the application of *AACR2R* rule 0.24, there is no getting around the fact that some types of items have distinctive physical characteristics that need to be described in a record to make individual entities and their respective surrogates unique. Certain properties pertain to certain types of materials, properties that can serve as particular identifiers of an item. In some cases, where interpretation or use of an item is dependent on its physicality, it will be important to capture and describe those characteristics. Some material formats may require special equipment, particular software, or certain other specifications. Given the rapid changes in hardware and software technologies, there may be a greater necessity than previously for detail and precision in description. What is required for interpretation and/or use of the item? For example, is readability of electronic resources based on different operating systems, or restricted because of incompatible generations of software, changes in standards, etc.? Is a proprietary hypertext browser required to display particular web sites? This is information which will be essential to catalogue users and which can be provided using the existing framework of *AACR*.

b) Same Content, Different Physical Representation

At the same time, there is an increasing call for a descriptive cataloguing structure which "collocates" all physical manifestations of a work within one bibliographic record, effectively putting the work, or the "content," ahead of "carrier" in the creation of the surrogate. Why might this be considered an effective approach? Proponents argue that this brings all manifestations of an item together under the same basic framework, and provides an entry more representative of the "intellectual" nature and content of the work. While providing a description that incorporates different physical formats, the initial approach to creating the record is independent of the carrier. Furthermore, the "convenience of the user" may be better addressed by having all physical manifestations (or versions) of the same intellectual or artistic work attached to one master record. On a more pragmatic level, less disk space is required to store a unit record with multiple physical descriptions than multiple records for the same title.

A two-tier hierarchical model was advocated as the preferred option among three proposed in the *Multiple Versions Forum Report*[12] emanating from a meeting held in Airlie, Virginia, in December 1989. The model proposed an independent bibliographic record for one version of an item at the first level of the hierarchy, with dependent partial records representing equivalent versions of the item described in the level-1 record (USMARC bibliographic record) included in the second level (USMARC holdings record). A complete description of versions included in the second level would be achieved only by combining data from both the first- and second-level records. The *Report,* while widely discussed in the cataloguing community, was never adopted. It has remained a kind of contrapuntal framework hovering in the background while discourse on the need for changes to the cataloguing code has continued.

While the collocation of multiple versions of the same intellectual work within one record may have some appeal, there are some inherent limitations to the approach, notwithstanding a fundamental shift from carrier to content in the interpretation of *AACR*. Would the descriptions for each material format be sufficient to uniquely identify an individual item? While not a concern specific to descriptive cataloguing, given the current state of automated systems and bibliographic displays, would the presentation of information concerning each physical manifestation of the same intellectual work prove confusing to catalogue users? In cases where there were extensive listings under the same item, would the unique distinctions between and among formats be readily apparent in the display? On a pragmatic level, the limited implementation of the USMARC holdings format was, and continues to be, a barrier to implementing a model, such as the two-tier hierarchical model described above.

c) *AACR* in the Broader Context

Added to the above practical concerns are the present realities of bibliographic databases containing millions of records representing individual works (and several records for the same manifestation of an individual title in many cases); the use of the code within various sizes and types of libraries with different collections; the fact that not all libraries and collections are automated; and the current state of electronic resources which are not necessarily widely distributed nor available. Given that *AACR* is applied in countries around the world, fundamental changes to descriptive cataloguing must take into account potential impact on the international bibliographic community, as well as on the Anglo-American cataloguing cohort. Also important to consider are the relatively recent incorporation of the *AACR* framework into rules for archival description and implications of major revisions to the code for archives and burgeoning databases of archival records. Code revision becomes more problematic when an international bibliographic and/or archival community of catalogue creators and/or users may be impacted.

On a more fundamental level, there is the question of why we are revisiting the "content versus carrier" question at this time. Is there, indeed, a major flaw in the code which is rendering, or has rendered, *AACR* in general and rule 0.24 as an approach in particular substantially impractical, unwieldy, or obsolete? Or is the call for change based primarily on the appearance of formats of materials that confound interpretation of rule 0.24 or invalidate its application (for example, "physicality" cannot be, and therefore is not, described for Internet resources)? Or is a rethinking of *AACR* founded on automated systems functionality or limitations that changes to the code would override/overcome? If that is the case, is the tail then wagging the dog? Instead of rethinking our approaches to descriptive cataloguing, why are we not concentrating on enhancing computer-based technologies to better manipulate the vast storehouses of bibliographic information currently available?

Perhaps another kind of question is in order. Given advances in information technology and in computer-based information storage and retrieval systems, and with the evolution of sophisticated tools and methods for displaying information in both stand-alone and extensively networked environments, why are we limiting our vision to current configurations? Are there creative opportunities to combine the best of *AACR* description with cutting-edge information interfaces, displays, and technologies, while also preserving a code that is readily applicable in nonautomated environments and across different constituencies? Is it time to think in mutually "inclusive" terms of "content" *and* "carrier," rather than the mutually exclusive "content *versus* carrier"? How might this be accomplished?

4. Deconstructing *AACR* and Reconstructing Cataloguing: A Proposal for a Linked Four-Tier Record Structure

The *Anglo-American Cataloguing Rules* contains a framework for describing, and providing access to, a variety of items or objects. The MARC formats for bibliographic, authority, and holdings records supply a structure for recording data related to manifestations or versions, works, and discrete items or copies. The technological limitations, which may have discouraged the implementation of the two-tier hierarchical model for multiple versions and most certainly the three-tier hierarchical model rejected at the Multiple Versions Forum in 1989, have been remedied to a large degree by the increasing availability and functional enhancement of web-based catalogues supporting both the display of individual records and the dynamic linking of fields across multiple records, or records across databases.

Given this backdrop, it may be useful to conceive of the code as a kind of metadata "shell," supplying the data for the MARC format records which could be linked to provide a user with a "holistic," all-inclusive surrogate, which would not only identify and provide access to an object or item, but which would also assist in the retrieval process. By "deconstructing" part I of *AACR2R* one can isolate those elements which provide a framework of intellectual/artistic or "content" information common to any work (title, statement of responsibility, series, generic notes about bibliographic or intellectual content). With the addition of access points (including subject headings derived from standard lists and, perhaps, class numbers based on standard classification systems) which represent the work independently of the physical format, a first-tier, "work level" record would be created (see figure 1).

Each of the work-specific access points (title, author(s), series—if associated with the work and not with a particular format—subject headings, and classification numbers) would be linked to their respective authority records, where the linked authority records would constitute the second-tier, "authority level" record of the whole record structure (see figure 1). Within the web-based catalogue, one could click on the access point, connect with the authority record, and extend the search based on variant or additional authority data, as appropriate. The second-tier record reflects on *AACR2R* insofar as the construction of the personal and corporate author, (uniform) title, and series authority records would continue to be based on the current form of entry guidelines now contained in chapters 22-26 of the code.

From each of the first-tier work-level records could hang separate descriptions of unique physical properties or of format-specific details: general material designation; edition statement; current area 3 information for designated material types; publication, distribution information; physical description; notes relating to physical format (including responsibility for a particular material type, such as "Credits"); numbers (standard and other) associated

4-Tiered Record Model

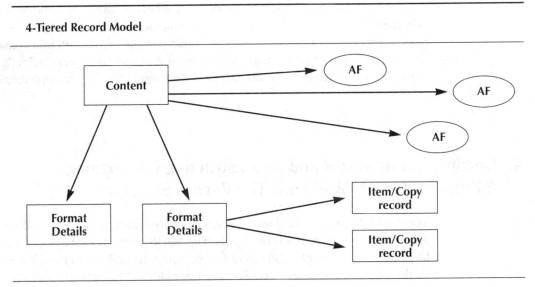

FIGURE 1

with format type, e.g., ISBN, ISSN, URL, URN, etc. This approach would essentially re-order the existing areas of descriptive cataloguing, but allow for a greater separation of the intellectual core of a work from its physical manifestation. In essence, a "chapter 1" would serve to provide guidelines for identifying and recording intellectual content common to any format with subsequent chapters detailing elements unique to the physicality and use of the item. No one medium would be designated as "primary" and, therefore, the basis for the description. "Sources of information" would pertain, as currently, to elements within the physical description component of the record. This third-tier "manifestation level" record (see figure 1) would also include access points specific to the manifestation-in-hand, and might include information derived from "Credits" or other notes indicating responsibility, variant titles, series unique to the format, etc. As with the first-tier "work-level" record, access points within the third-tier "manifestation-level" record could be linked to second-tier authority records for enhanced identification, search, and retrieval.

The fourth tier would be an "item-level" record (see figure 1), containing copy-specific information as defined by, though not necessarily limited to, the data structures of the MARC holdings format. This mimics, to some degree, the concept of the "second level" in the proposed two-tier hierarchical model, and is a replication of the "H" level (holdings level or copy level) of the three-tier hierarchical model proposed for the Multiple Versions Forum. In fact, with the exception of the addition of a linked authority-level (my "second-tier") record, the linked four-tier record structure proposed in this paper fully incorporates the three-tier hierarchical model proposed for the Multiple Versions Forum. The four-tier record structure (see figure 1) can be "operationalized" utilizing a web-based catalogue, supports dynamic links, and adds a layer of "retrieval" to the identify and access components now supported by *AACR* and its communications companions, MARC record formats.

While changes to the MARC record formats would clearly be required to accommodate a four-tiered record, the process of creating such records and record structure would be readily accommodated in nonautomated environments, as currently. "Manifestation-level" and "item-level" records could be added to "work-level" records, and authority records would continue to be created and maintained as currently in manual environments. Where an institution had the benefit of access to networked information technologies, greater enhancements could be realized. For those with a web-based catalogue, links additional to those described above could be made to the full-text of an electronic resource through a TEI header, or a Universal Resource Locator (URL).[13] With a MARC record running in the background, links to remote access sites through field 856 could be made and, with the provision of XML, SGML, or HTML tagging, searches of discrete parts of the item facilitated. Given the remarkable depth and richness of the current "carrier" of the bibliographic record, the MARC record format, there exist a wealth of opportunities for innovative and imaginative linkages to enhance bibliographic displays, to facilitate information search and retrieval, and to add considerably to "the convenience of the public" when combined with mark-up language provisions—Standard Generalized Mark-up Language (SGML); Hypertext Mark-up Language (HTML); Virtual Reality Mark-up Language (VRML); or the most recent XML and Dynamic HTML—with textual and graphical interfaces, and with object-oriented environments, such as those supported in some Internet-accessible applications. There are clearly substantial resource implications associated with the proposal for a four-tier record structure which could deter its implementation. Benefits to users in terms of seamless and item-level (and potentially within-item-level) information access and retrieval must surely be included in the "cost-benefit" equation.

As computer-based technologies and computer-supported applications continue to evolve, and as electronic and other "virtual" resources proliferate, the boundaries that separate the physical formats in which information is packaged will become increasingly blurred. Some of the most dramatic developments in bibliographic control occurred in the latter quarter of the nineteenth century. With the pending dawn of the second millennium, it seems an appropriate symmetry to shake the foundations of *AACR,* to rethink the structure and rejig the pieces, and to create a code for the twenty-first century that, while cognizant of twentieth-century realities and respectful of nineteenth-century requirements, is sufficiently visionary to accommodate the "fuzzy sets" of information resources.

Notes

1. In the words of the *Final Report* of the IFLA Study Group on the Functional Requirements for Bibliographic Records, those who search and use national bibliographies and library catalogues require data to *find* materials, to *identify* and to *select* an entity, and to *obtain* access to the entity described (pp. 8-9).

2. See pp. 1-16 of this volume.

3. Michael Heaney, "Object-Oriented Cataloging," *Information Technology and Libraries* 14, no. 3 (September 1995): 135-53.

4. Ibid., 137.

5. Tom Delsey, "Modelling the Logic of *AACR*" (draft 1997), typescript, 6.

6. Interactive Multimedia Guidelines Review Task Force, *Guidelines for Bibliographic Description of Interactive Multimedia* (Chicago: American Library Association, 1994).

7. Available at: http://www.mitpress.mit.edu/City of Bits

8. IFLA Study Group on the Functional Requirements for Bibliographic Records, *Functional Requirements for Bibliographic Records: Final Report* (Frankfurt am Main: Deutsche Bibliothek, 1997), 12.

9. Annie T. Luk, "Evaluating Bibliographic Displays from the Users' Point of View: A Focus Group Study" (Master of Information Studies Research Project Report, Faculty of Information Studies, University of Toronto, 1996). Also available at: http://www.fis.utoronto.ca/research/displays/index.htm

10. Richard W. Kopak and Joan M. Cherry, "Bibliographic Displays and Web Catalogues: Responding to User Preferences," in *Communication and Information in Context: Society, Technology, and the Professions,* ed. Bernd Frohmann (Canadian Association for Information Science, Proceedings of the 25th Conference, June 8-10, 1997, Learned Societies Congress, Memorial University of Newfoundland, St. John's, Newfoundland), 241-52.

11. Jimmie Lundgren and Betsy Simpson, "Cataloguing Needs Survey for the Faculty at the University of Florida," *Cataloging & Classification Quarterly* 23, no.3/4 (1997): 47-63.

12. Multiple Versions Forum, *Multiple Versions Forum Report: Report from a Meeting Held December 6-8, Airlie, Virginia* (Washington, D.C.: Network Development and MARC Standards Office, Library of Congress, 1990).

13. Or to a Universal Resource Name (URN) once this scheme has been formalized.

DISCUSSION

When Howarth was asked how she envisioned serials records with their title changes at the work-level record, she replied that she had no answers for this problem and offered two possibilities: to choose a key title for an item or change the title within the work record. *AACR* would have to address this matter.

Another participant thought that, because a key title has a distinct connotation and a relationship with ISSN, a cataloguer-supplied title would be more stable than a key title. It is also possible to create a summary note for a changing serial just as it is possible to create a summary note for a changing collection of archival materials by writing the note in open-ended language.

The participant stated that it is not the publisher's job to provide uniform headings and syndetic structure, but rather the cataloguer's job to clean up a publisher's language and put it into an organized structure in a catalogue that shows people all the different editions of a work. Howarth replied that work-level records and manifestation-level records would be renderings of what is represented in the item itself. Transcriptions of information and restructuring into formats that we find useful for syndetic structures would be in that authority-level record. It is an attempt to preserve the natural language representation that publishers, creators, etc., have and that may be more familiar to users while at the same time recognizing we need to have some control over forms and representations of that data elsewhere, perhaps through an authority record.

A participant asked whether Howarth meant bibliographic, authority, and holdings formats or USMARC, UKMARC, and UNIMMARC, etc., when she stated that all MARC formats were supported. She replied that she was talking about the former, and trusting in the process of harmonization for the latter.

The Anglo-American Cataloguing Rules, Second Edition

Their History and Principles

MICHAEL GORMAN AND PAT ODDY

History and Context

It is possible that the *Anglo-American Cataloguing Rules, Second Edition,* is the most spectacularly misnamed bibliographic standard in history. *AACR2* has far less in common with its titular predecessor—the *Anglo-American Catalog[u]ing Rules* of 1967 *(AACR1)*—than that code had with its predecessors, the *A.L.A. Cataloging Rules for Author and Title Entries* of 1949, the Library of Congress *Rules for Descriptive Cataloging* of 1949, and the *Catalog[u]ing Rules, Author and Title Entries* of 1908. The description of *AACR2* as a "second edition" arose first from its history—in the early 1970s, the idea was nothing much more than a harmonization of the American and British texts of *AACR1* and some less than fundamental modifications—and then from political expediency. In the later stages of the creation of *AACR2,* it became obvious that this code was to be a radical departure—one that was going to be vociferously opposed by many administrators and bibliographic reactionaries. It is entirely possible that an entirely new name—say, "Integrated Cataloguing Rules for English-Speaking Countries"—would have scuppered the whole enterprise. It is also entirely possible that such a new name would have meant that a conference such as this would have been unnecessary and that regular revisions of the code could have taken place in an orderly, nondisputatious manner freed from the idea that change means a new code, an "AACR3." We adhere strongly to the latter view and wish that the significance of the break from the past had been recognized by a new name.

In order to understand *AACR2* fully, one needs to understand that there have been three ages of modern English-language descriptive cataloguing codes.

The first was the nineteenth-century age of the single-person codes—notably those of Panizzi and Cutter. These first-age codes had the intellectual coherence that comes from a single controlling intelligence and experience and tended to be based on a combination of principle and of cases.

The second age, which began at almost the same time as the new century was born, was the age of the committee code. In the span of time between the *Catalog[u]ing Rules* of

1908 and *AACR1* in 1967, the rules became longer and more elaborate and more and more case based.

The prophet of the third age, the age that was ushered in by *AACR2*, was, of course, Seymour Lubetzky. In his writings and draft rules[1] and in his work for the International Conference on Cataloguing Principles (Paris, 1961), we see a radical departure foreshadowed; a departure that combined the best feature of the first age—a single controlling intelligence—with a rejection of the "case-law" approach of the second age. Many features of *AACR2* were, as it turned out, compromises based on political and practical exigencies but, as we shall demonstrate later, these compromises do not alter the Lubetzkyan ideas that are at the core of the rules. Moreover, all those compromises can be detached from *AACR2* surgically—that is, without compromising the basic principles and integrity of the rules.

Principles

The principles on which *AACR2* is based are:

- that descriptions are to be formulated in accordance with the specifications of the *International Standard Bibliographic Description (ISBD)*
- that all media of communication are treated equally
- that descriptions are based on the bibliographic item
- that access points are to be derived from the nature of the work being catalogued, *not* the nature of the bibliographic entity being described.

These principles are as valid today and for the foreseeable future as they were when *AACR2* was created. Any revision of *AACR2* must recognize the centrality of these principles and will, therefore, be something that is different from *AACR2* in degree rather than kind.

The Importance of *AACR2*

Because it is based on these principles and uses them as the basis for rules, *AACR2* represents a major change, comparable to that of Panizzi's rules and the 1908 *Rules*. The following are the most significant reasons why *AACR2* is the first code of the third age of cataloguing.

1. *AACR2* was the first code to integrate all media in both description *and* access points. It is a well-known and lamented fact that the *ISBD(M)* preceded the *ISBD(G)*—a classic example of the dangers of proceeding from the special to the general. *ISBD(M)* was flawed in that it continued the "book-centric" descriptions of previous codes, whereas the later *ISBD(G)*—the basis of part 1 of *AACR2*—provided, for the first time, a comprehensive, media-neutral descriptive framework.

2. As far as the rules on access points are concerned, part 2 of *AACR2* is the first instance of any cataloguing code dealing with names and titles on a medium-neutral basis—for

example, names are based on the forms found in "chief sources of information," which are determined, medium by medium, with reference to the framework of *ISBD*.

3. *AACR2* is the first cataloguing code that *clearly* delineates the distinction between *description* (of bibliographic items—now including defined electronic assemblages) and *access* (relating to works and not to manifestations of those works). The language of *AACR2* is not always clear and consistent when it comes to this distinction, but the principle is clear and, if the explication of the principle is flawed, that is an editorial, not conceptual, failing and one relatively easily remedied. In this context, the placing of parts 1 and 2 of *AACR2* is of significance. The cataloguer is led to proceed from the description of the bibliographic item (book, serial, set of maps, assemblage of electronic data, etc.) to the consideration of the work rather than the other way round.

4. Access points in *AACR2* are based (not always entirely successfully) on the Lubetzkyan principled approach rather than the case-law method that had hobbled previous codes. It is true that political/strategic considerations again rear their ugly heads and that *AACR2* contains some hangovers from the past. It is important to note, though, that those "case-law" hangovers are isolated in special rules that could easily be detached in a future revision (we will return to this point later).

5. *AACR2* is consciously internationalist, albeit from the English-language point of view. That internationalism has not only made *AACR2* the most widely used cataloguing code in history and the basis for a number of non-English-language codes but has also imposed the burden of remaining responsive to that global use. Proposals to change the *nature* of *AACR2* should be greeted with considerable caution and a clear appraisal of the consequences of such change for libraries and catalogues throughout the world. This is the first global cataloguing code—something to be welcomed, not feared, in an era of globalization in bibliographic control as in so many other areas of life.

6. Though *AACR2* preserved the main entry (yet more of the politics of bibliographic fear reinforced, in this instance, by the existence of the 1xx field in MARC), it showed the way toward the concept of authority records *of equal value* attached to descriptions and, thus, presages the ultimate elimination of this unnecessary complication of little relevance to the computerized catalogues of today. We stress that the ideas of authorship and of the work remain central to the choice of name and uniform title access points but that this conceptual framework need not dictate the structure of the catalogue and does not call for the selection of one access point over another.

7. *AACR2* is the first code to embody the concept of one person having two or more bibliographic identities—that is, an "author" not necessarily being coextensive with a person. This is not a purely theoretical point. There is, for example, a book about the police novels of "Ed McBain" and, in framing the subject heading for that work, it is crucial to distinguish one bibliographic persona from others created by the same individual. This innovation is of considerable theoretical importance and represents one of the most radical breaks with past codes.

8. *AACR2* provides an infinitely expandable framework (in both description and access) to accommodate new media and media yet to be and has, hence, eliminated the need for "new" AACRs to deal with the problems such new media may pose.

Implementation of *AACR2*

Those who are old enough to remember the War of *AACR2* in the late 1970s will understand the way in which the weight of existing library practice influenced the implementation of the *Rules* and delayed that implementation in the United States for a full year. Those who are, mercifully, too young to recall that squabble may need to be reminded that substantial change has serious economic and political consequences. This is even more true today than it was twenty years ago because of the gigantic number of MARC records (based on *AACR2*) that there are in the world and because of the multitude of online systems that have been designed to manipulate those *AACR2*-derived MARC records. The implementation of *AACR2* in the "author" countries (Australia, Canada, the United Kingdom, and the United States) differed from country to country—the weight of history falling especially heavily on U.S. libraries. Today, however, each of these countries has a major investment in its respective national bibliographic infrastructure and, in this era of reduced resources, neither the desire nor the capacity to implement profound change in the cataloguing rules, particularly profound change that is not justifiable on objective cost-benefit grounds.

Description/ISBD

In many ways, the *ISBD* program represents the most successful international endeavour in bibliographic standardization. The study that was used as the basis for the conference that gave rise to the first *ISBD* clearly showed wide variance between national cataloguing agencies and cataloguing codes in the order of descriptive data, the data included and excluded, and the abbreviations used in descriptions. *ISBD* addresses all of these issues and prescribes content, order, and presentation of all descriptive data. Since *AACR2* led the way in incorporating this international standard into cataloguing codes, every single cataloguing code throughout the world (existing and contemplated) has used the *ISBD*s as the basis for its rules on description. This is a major part of the progress that we have made toward Universal Bibliographic Control and it is unthinkable that any revision of *AACR2* should step back from that commitment. If the English-speaking cataloguing community were to decide that there is a need for change in any descriptive detail, its only recourse would be to work with other international interests to change the *ISBD*s. Unilateral change within *AACR2* itself would be a major retrogressive step.

The discussion of part 1 has been clouded to some extent by the confusion over what is being described, in particular by the belief that the cataloguer is always describing a physical object. In many, if not most, instances a physical object will be coexistent with the bibliographic item, but this is not always the case. To take two obvious examples, a serial as a whole is a bibliographic item without being a physical item available to the cataloguer; and an electronic document may or may not be present as a physical item and, even if it is, descriptive data are not all drawn from that physical item. Descriptive data are made up of elements that relate to the physical carrier, elements transcribed from that carrier, elements that describe the recorded knowledge and information, and elements that describe how the carrier is to be used and how to gain access to the recorded knowledge and information it contains. Once the twin concepts of the bibliographic item and the different elements of the description are understood, it is easy to see that discussion of the applicability of part 1 to electronic documents is, at best, a diversion. The plain fact is that electronic documents can be assimilated into *AACR2* cataloguing in exactly the same way as other media of communication have been and media yet unknown will be.

Access Points

Part 2 of *AACR2* deals with assigning name and title access points to descriptions with the simple aim of making those descriptions retrievable and capable of being grouped together meaningfully. The essential difference between parts 1 and 2 is that, when cataloguers are creating access points, they are doing so with reference to the *work*, not the bibliographic item or the physical item (even though the three may overlap to a great extent). The concept of "work" is elusive and hard to define with legal rigour, but it is not hard to understand the idea of a defined piece of expression created by a person, persons, or group of persons and possessing a name. There is a world of cultural and bibliographic difference between Sartre's *Being and Nothingness* on the one hand and the online *Annual Report* of the National Library of Canada on the other, but it is not difficult to recognize them both as works. It is also not difficult to understand that the book of Daphne du Maurier's *Rebecca,* the 1940 Hitchcock film, the video of the 1996 BBC television adaptation, and the Claire Bloom audiotape abridgement are all manifestations of the same work. In creating access points, then, the cataloguer is concerned with identifying a work, establishing its standardized name ("uniform title") and the standardized forms of the name(s) of its author(s), and in creating links to other works to which it is related. This process is medium-neutral because the idea of a work is unrelated to any particular form of carrier, even though evidence that goes toward the creation of standard access points may be derived from the carrier (by definition, a work that can be catalogued must have or have had at least one physical carrier).

The fundamental importance of the application of part 2 of *AACR2* lies in the standardization that it promotes and in the authority work and authority files that it necessitates. All attempts to provide coherent, accurate access to large numbers of net and web resources have been dismal failures, failing to provide either recall or relevance. There is a simple reason why this is and will remain so—keyword searching has proven to be inadequate for decades, especially when compared to standardization of access points and the creation of internally consistent authority files.

Where Are We Now?

Some have said that there is a need for radical, structural change to *AACR2*. Others, among whom we count ourselves, believe that there is a need for some change but that the change should be gradual, evolutionary, and within the structures and principles of *AACR2*. If we are to evaluate the need for change and the nature of the change, it is imperative that we understand the real-world context of the cataloguing rules. The context is: the need for standardization because of cooperation and copy cataloguing; the emerging importance of the authority control concept as central to electronic bibliographic systems; other standards;

and, in North America, the Library of Congress rule interpretations (LCRIs). Most of these factors and influences are self-explanatory, but we will comment on the LCRIs. When it comes to LCRIs, North American cataloguers are humble petitioners looking to a mysterious Higher Authority for guidance, and LC is a burdened giant accepting the unwanted duty with increasing reluctance. We complain when the word from on high is complicated or not to our liking. This is not LC's fault. They produce LCRIs *because we ask them to* and would be happy to get out of the interpretive business. Until North American cataloguing matures to the point when we can distinguish between necessary and foolish consistency, the LCRIs will be always with us.

There have been calls from various quarters for "simplification" and some nebulous consequent cost-cutting. Some recommend the use of minimal-level records and have implemented less than full descriptions (often ignoring the standardization offered by *AACR2* rule 1.0D). The fact that rule exists at all is proof that shorter descriptions do not violate *AACR2* principles or practice and, more importantly, do not affect adversely the vast majority of catalogue users. Whether the use of shorter descriptions is a major cost-saver is much more problematic. We believe such savings are marginal at best. "Simplification" is also used, however, in a much more sinister meaning. When one strips away the weasel words and obfuscation, it turns out that what is being advocated is the abandonment of authority work in, for example, the use of "title page" forms of name without verification. We cannot state too strongly that "simplification" in this sense is a stake through the heart of *AACR2* and cannot be countenanced by any rational interpretation of cataloguing principles. We owe a duty to the users of our libraries and to the cooperative endeavours in which we all participate to provide the highest level of authority control and standardization that we can provide. Anything less is dereliction of duty.

In addition, there has been some extraordinarily misguided and misinformed discussion on the need to create "master records" for works that are manifested in many different physical forms. It is hard to believe that this proposition has been put about by people who are cataloguers. Let us repeat. Descriptions are of bibliographic items (including, nowadays, defined assemblages of electronic data). Descriptions are made up of data derived from the physical means by which the bibliographic item is carried, data transcribed from the carrier, and data descriptive of the carried recorded knowledge or information. It is literally impossible to have a single description of two or more different bibliographic items. Once described, the cataloguer looks at the manifestation in the light of the *work* (an intellectual construct that, by its nature, cannot be described) in order to assign access points (including uniform titles) and create authority files. This process, which should be understood by anyone who has taken an introductory cataloguing class, clearly demonstrates that the idea of a "master record" for several manifestations of the same work is cataloguing nonsense.

An Agenda for Managed Change

As we have stated before, we believe in evolutionary change (revisions of *AACR2* that enhance and do not compromise its principles) and not in revolutionary change (the creation of an "AACR3"). There are some things that could and should be done to improve *AACR2* without changing its structure and principles. In order to illustrate the nature of evolutionary revision and to make specific recommendations, we propose the following ten-point agenda for managed change that is based on a comprehensive review of *AACR2* aimed at ensuring the pervasiveness of its principles.

First, we should get rid of all the "special" case-law rules that were imported into part 2 of *AACR2* for political reasons after Lubetzky resigned as editor (for example, the numerous cases of special religious materials and laws).

Second, we should prune descriptive rules of the over-elaborations in particular cases— those that are insufficient for the specialist cataloguer and too much for the general cataloguer (for example, in the rules for music and maps). The needs of the specialist cataloguer and special collections could be catered to by specialist manuals created by the relevant cataloguing bodies and overseen and certified as true interpretations of *AACR2* by the Joint Steering Committee.

Third, we should resolve the issue of "unpublished" items (printed and electronic texts, videos, sound recordings, etc., etc.) in a completely uniform manner across the chapters in part 1.

Fourth, we should develop new or revised chapters of part 1 to accommodate new media (especially electronic—including those accessible only remotely).

Fifth, we should study access issues for new media (especially electronic) with a view to seeing how the general rules hold up or need elaboration without creating new case-law rules.

Sixth, we should review part 2 with the authority record concept in mind (including addressing the main entry issue). The aim should be a catalogue that is based on descriptions of bibliographic items linked to access points of equal weight. This is not the easiest issue to address in concrete terms and is peculiarly unlikely to be addressed effectively by the ponderous committee process. We recommend the commissioning of a consultant to review the whole main entry issue and to come up with specific rule recommendations for review and disposition by JSC.

Seventh, we should resolve the microform issue, not only by persuading LC to drop its "interpretation" that directly contradicts the letter and the spirit of the rule but also to avoid a similar debacle over the question of parallel print and electronic texts.

Eighth, we should do a comprehensive review of the examples with a view to amending those that are no longer relevant and adding examples of new media and problems.

Ninth, we should create a consolidation of the unified MARC format and *AACR2* and bear in mind the possibility of a principle-based subject term code to be added to create a complete cataloguer's resource.

Tenth, we should ask LC to review and curtail the LCRI program (for instance, have them cease issuing those not concerned with important questions of access).

The Future of the Revision Process

The revision mechanisms put into place after the first publication of *AACR2* have served us well. They have allowed considered, gradual, democratic change. It appears, though, that principles on which that mechanism was based have faded from the collective memory. Let us review the process; delineate clearly the respective roles of the Joint Steering Committee, the Committee of Principals, the national libraries, and the national committees; and, using a reinvigorated revision mechanism, ensure that the next manifestation of *AACR2* is even better than its predecessors.

AACR2 represents not just an historic achievement in the Anglo-American cataloguing tradition but also a pioneer and exemplar in the new age of global cataloguing. We should celebrate and consolidate what we have accomplished and work toward making an ever-improving *AACR2* the basis for international cooperation devoted to attaining Universal Bibliographic Control.

Note

1. Notably his *Cataloging Rules and Principles* (1953) and his *Code of Cataloging Rules* (1960).

International Panel Responses

HELENA COETZEE
University of Pretoria, South Africa

Introduction

Since its publication in 1978, the *Anglo-American Cataloguing Rules* has been the recognized standard for use by South African libraries. After the appearance of the revised edition in 1988, a survey showed that virtually all libraries use this code. Although uniform application is desirable, many libraries apply the rules to suit individual needs. The Joint Catalogue, maintained by the State Library in Pretoria making it possible for all libraries to make use of this database for interlibrary loans, showed discrepancies clearly. With the creation of SABINET (South African Bibliographic and Library Network, now called SABINET Online) in 1983, *AACR2* was accepted as the cataloguing standard for members. The SABINET union catalogue (now called SACat), founded to serve its members for all cooperative efforts, was created by members each adding their own records. This practice also led to a significant variation in the completeness and quality of records in the database. The newly created regional consortia, however, intend compelling members to adhere strictly to *AACR2* in order to develop much more useful databases for its members. Although *AACR2* is the only cataloguing standard used for the creation of bibliographic records in South Africa, application of the rules is by no means as uniform as it should be. The importance of standardization and the consistent application of internationally accepted bibliographic standards is generally supported by all members of the library and information community, but there are a number of reasons, such as a shortage of qualified and experienced staff, leading to a lack of uniform and consistent application of the code.

There are eleven languages in South Africa, most very different from one another and many not related at all. Each of the nine provinces selects its official languages; only the national library deals with all South African languages. Publications issued by the central government appear in these eleven languages. The diverse languages present a special problem for consortia and the national library because the catalogue record must indicate the specific language of many items. Fortunately, MARC coding makes it possible to indicate languages.

Creation of National Bibliographic Tools

The bibliographic tools created by the State Library, which is the national agency for South Africa, adhere strictly to the rules and provide guidelines for other libraries to follow. These tools are:

- South African National Bibliography;
- Periodicals in South African Libraries, a union catalogue of all periodicals received by libraries in South Africa, with holdings;

- Joint catalogue of collections in South African libraries, also with holdings.

The last two are used mainly for interlibrary loans.

SABINET Online

SABINET Online, the South African national bibliographic network created in 1983, is responsible for a variety of services and products to its members, one of which is the maintenance of SACat, the union catalogue of the holdings of its members. It currently also provides access to a vast number of electronic databases local and international. SABINET Online initially used the WLN system, but has since changed to ERUDITE, a local system.

Regional Consortia

This is a comparatively new development, where a number of libraries in a region cooperate in collection building and sharing of bibliographic data. The main reason for the creation of these consortia is resource sharing. No library can any longer afford to buy everything its users might need. The poor exchange rate of the South African rand makes all sources extremely expensive. The consortia visualise the creation of a virtual library, consisting of the stock of all its members and freely available to all members. They are still in the process of being developed and shortage of funds will probably make it more difficult to get all of them operational in the near future. The future role of SABINET Online is also not yet clear. Examples of consortia are:

- GAELIC (Gauteng and Environs Library Consortium), consisting mainly of academic libraries in the northern part of the country. This consortium has decided to use Innopac, an American system.
- CALICO (Cape Library Consortium), consisting mainly of libraries in the Western Cape. This consortium has decided to use Aleph, a system developed in Israel.
- FRELICO (Free State Library Consortium), consisting mainly of libraries in the Free State and Northern Cape. They have yet to decide on a system.

Although the intention was that all members of all the consortia should use the same system to facilitate the creation of a nationwide union catalogue, financial problems encountered by some of the smaller members might cause serious problems in this regard. The ideal was also that regional consortia should be able to combine their union catalogues or provide mutual access, but even this seems to have become increasingly difficult.

Libraries Participating in Cooperative Efforts

All major libraries, such as university and technikon libraries, provincial library services, government libraries, and libraries of research bodies, apply *AACR2* relatively consistently. Cataloguing copy is derived mainly from records created by the Library of Congress and available on SACat and other cataloguing services through SABINET Online. Many smaller libraries of all kinds are also members of SABINET Online and have access to SACat.

Education and Training in *AACR2*

Education and training in *AACR2* is provided by all library schools at universities and technikons in South Africa. A number of continuous education programmes such as short courses are also offered to practicing cataloguers. Close contact is maintained with the profession, in order to prepare students adequately for entrance-level cataloguing and all possible efforts are made to employ lecturers with practical experience in cataloguing.

Efforts to Promote the Consistent Use of Bibliographic Standards

The Interim Committee for Bibliographic Organization has a Subcommittee for Bibliographic Standards, giving guidance and coordinating training courses for cataloguers. Professional organizations also have interest groups on a regional basis to promote standardization and offer training in specific areas.

Issues Affecting South Africa Regarding *AACR2*

South Africa has been a user country of *AACR* since its publication in 1978. When the invitation was received to send a national representative to this conference, the possibility of also taking part in a revision process was received with enthusiasm by the library community and cataloguers in particular. A request for comments made by the Subcommittee for Bibliographic Standards on the issues to be discussed at the conference led to an avalanche of contributions, many of them on specific rules. In general the following recommendations were made:

- principles should be more clearly defined;
- rules should be formulated more clearly;
- options and exceptions should be reduced to a minimum;
- the use of qualifiers for all countries should be possible;
- a web address should be made available to all users of *AACR2* where comments and suggestions can be exchanged.

Conclusion

Thank you for the opportunity to give a very brief overview of the status of *AACR2* in South Africa. We would welcome any opportunity to contribute to the improvement and adaptation of the rules, by becoming not only a user country, but also a participating member of the revision of the rules.

STUART EDE
The British Library

The brief given me before the conference was to:

- react to Michael Gorman and Pat Oddy's keynote paper

- set the framework for the conference, and
- provide a British perspective with regard to cataloguing now and in the future.

My support for Pat Oddy and Michael Gorman's thesis should become obvious as I address the other two aspects.

The British Perspective

Starting with the British perspective, I hesitate to claim I represent the UK view. What I can relate is my personal perception of the climate in the UK.

The technical and economic environment in the UK cataloguing field is much the same as in other partner countries:

- steadily improving database and OPAC design (improving but still not perfect)
- growing electronic publishing
- most libraries are struggling with resourcing
- consequential pressures to increase record sharing are making this perhaps the key objective of a common cataloguing code
- resource discovery, providing access to other libraries' catalogues and collections, is a hot topic, e.g., plans for the National Resource Discovery Network in the university sector and pressure on government to implement the recommended Public Network linking public libraries.

There are voices in the UK calling for a review of *AACR,* but there is not the same clamour as in North America. There may be parallels with the stance the UK community took to the MARC harmonisation process:

- a recognition of the benefits of easier record exchange
- a willingness to change—up to a point
- drawing the line where change would have a too radical impact and associated high cost.

In essence, there is an appetite for change, but we do not want to change too far. I suspect the same applies to *AACR* revision and is not restricted to just the UK community.

Framework for the Conference

Does the British perspective help us set a framework for the review of *AACR?* I think it does, especially as I have been hearing comments by various attendees and speakers which echo my perception. The main tenets of that framework would be:

1. Changes should show obvious—and preferably quantifiable—benefits. It is not just the vendors that have to construct a business case for change; we all do, collectively.
2. An obvious benefit should be the streamlining of the cataloguing process. By this I do not mean the much vilified term "simplification" used as a cypher for a reduction in record content. Quite the contrary; I think we should increase content wherever possible. What we

need to do is to make it easier for the cataloguer to decide how to catalogue an item. By streamlining we might release some resource to cope with the increasing workload electronic publishing will bring. And, as has been suggested by other speakers, a more streamlined approach to the thinking process in cataloguing might benefit the user, too.

3. In constructing the business case a large cost element will be the cost of change. If we have to reconstruct our databases—especially if it means human intervention—the community will balk at the cost. No matter how seductive the future benefits, libraries do not have the resources for massive change. There were a lot of worries about the cost of the change from *AACR1* to *AACR2;* the scale of change will be much bigger next time if we decide on radical revisions.

What does that lead us to conclude?

1. We should avoid a step change to an AACR3. A better target would be a fine-tuned *AACR2*. It has served us well; let's keep the best of it.
2. We must strive for backwards compatibility, as Sherry Vellucci suggested. Records we create in the future should be capable of coexisting with those we have created in the past.
3. By all means let us improve our understanding of the logical framework on which the code rests by employing entity modelling or object-oriented analysis techniques. If an improved understanding helps extend the code to the electronic environment, that would be an excellent outcome, but if it means scrapping large parts of *AACR2* then it would be a step too far.

To put it another way, using Tom Delsey's analogy, we do need to understand the foundations of the house before we build an extension. (Actually from my own construction experience it is even more important to find out where the sewer pipes run, but I wasn't sure where that analogy would lead me!) If through entity modelling we can convince ourselves that we have a sound foundation for both the house and extension, that would be superb. That is, the records we produce in the future under a revised code will look pretty much like those we are creating now under the present code. However, if the conclusion of the analysis is that the house needs to be knocked down first, then I would want us to reconsider.

In any future development of the code we need to keep our feet on the ground. At the end of the day we need a practical working tool. We do need guiding principles, but the pursuit of a Unified Field Theory of the catalogue is likely to be fruitless in the real world. Whatever model we adopt, the fit is going to be less than perfect somewhere. Those of you that are fans of *The Hitchhiker's Guide to the Galaxy* will know that quests for the Meaning of Life, the Universe, and Everything tend to lead to answers like 42.

We need to undertake a radical review once in a while, and that is why the Joint Steering Committee and the Committee of Principals convened this conference, but we also need to apply a sanity check at the end of the process. There is no better sanity check than constructing a business case. This forces one to address the questions:

- Do the changes achieve the strategic objective set?
- What are the benefits and savings?
- What are the costs?
- What are the risks?
- What is the bottom line?

If we apply that to ourselves in the conference, and JSC members apply it to their subsequent deliberations, I don't think we shall go too far wrong.

MONIKA MÜNNICH
Universitätsbibliothek
Heidelberg, Germany

I am very honoured to be one of the few people from outside the AACR community to have been invited to the conference and, in addition, to have been asked by our Russian colleagues, Irina Tsvetkova and Irina Klim, to speak also on their behalf.

The German and Russian Cataloguing Environment

Before I comment on the Gorman/Oddy paper I shall provide some information about cataloguing in Germany and Russia. Both countries applied the Prussian Instructions until the 1970s when they changed to the current rules, which are based on the International Standard Bibliographic Description (ISBD) and the Paris Principles.[1] It is interesting to note that three different codes (*AACR,* the German and Russian codes) have been built on the same bases, all calling themselves international.

Because of the wish and the necessity to exchange bibliographic data, OCLC has sponsored projects in both Germany and Russia.[2] Both projects have shown that a complete adaptation to *AACR* does conflict with our users' needs. Therefore, we hope for a mixture of harmonizing with *AACR* and *AACR* development toward internationally agreed standards.

The migration of three regional networks and the national Serials Database caused the Germans to discuss the introduction of some rule changes in the hope of harmonizing with *AACR* and becoming more online-oriented. Proposed changes that are steps to harmonization with *AACR* include: changes in transcribing the title proper; changes in headings for names with prefixes; dropping additional hierarchies for subseries, but not giving up all hierarchies in part/whole statements; introducing differentiation for identical names (at present there is one record for persons with identical names). Harmonization and online adaption will be reached by encoding form titles, etc. (see below). We hope that further online adaption will be reached by giving up redundancies of titles in the bibliographic description and entries (with the possibility of ISBD reconstruction) and, last but not least, in simplifying the rules for entries and references.

The Gorman/Oddy Paper

I want to congratulate Michael Gorman and Pat Oddy on their paper, especially from the viewpoint of outsiders. We agree in general with the following:

- We agree that ISBD is the most successful endeavour of international cataloguing.
- We concede that *AACR* is an international code—though from the point of view of the English-speaking community—as the authors confirm.

- We are confident that a revision of *AACR* will not step back but come even closer to universal bibliographic control (UBC). This is a crucial point for the non-English-speaking community.

- We strongly agree with Pat and Michael that "we owe a duty to the user and thus must cooperate worldwide"—as the user is surfing worldwide—"in order to achieve good service to our users" and cutting costs by cooperation instead of minimizing information.

- Thus—I quote again—"we must evaluate the need for changes . . . it is imperative to understand the real world context of the cataloguing rules . . . the need for standardization"—I would like to add "a worldwide standardization." We do have a unique chance to undertake this task.

International Standards

The standards that should be internationally accepted and applied are:

- common definitions of what we describe (work, manifestation, etc.);
- common definitions of what we describe (in terms of ISBD, hopefully revised);
- type and number of access points (at least minimal standards for multiparts);
- same terms for transcribing titles (treatment of punctuation marks, abbreviations, etc.);
- common authority files with clearly defined entities and in the sense of Barbara Tillett's access control,[3] i.e., allowing national name headings;
- common form headings.

Rules for a Computer Age

I think it is agreed that *AACR* as well as RCR (Russian Cataloging Rules) and RAK (German Cataloging Rules) are codes of a precomputer age and need to be redesigned. We Germans await the publication of the *Functional Requirements for Bibliographic Records* and the impact of this conference and hope for worldwide acceptance of conceptual models and general definitions. Discussions in Germany have evolved some modest and practical ideas about adaptation to the online environment. A few of these are:

- a modernized ISBD avoiding duplication between ISBD and access points;
- international authority files with the above-mentioned criteria;
- more and better links using the web technique;
- removal of references not needed in the online environment (in names and titles—added entries included);
- internationally agreed form access points (again on the basis of access control).

Let me illustrate what I would like included in internationally agreed access points, some of which are already part of different codes or formats. Encoding these in a uniform way would be of great help to the worldwide surfer user:

- (collective) uniform titles ("works," "selections," etc.);
- uniform titles and/or form headings as made for legal and liturgical works, for treaties, constitutions, festschrifts, etc.;
- document and literary type information (so far partly general and specific material designations), or part of format labels, such as:
  - bibliographical information (serials, theses, conference proceedings, etc.);
  - material information (book, microform, electronic resource, etc.);
  - literary type information (prose, bibliography, etc.);
- within this context adapting treatment of dates (e.g., in conferences) and languages (e.g., in qualifiers of uniform titles) as encoded information, that is, as a renunciation of qualifiers or additions, which is usually a duplication.

I think we must react before managers adopt "standards," such as the Dublin Core or others. Most of all we must act because we want to accept the online environment when designing—allow me to say—International Cataloguing Rules. Wouldn't ICR be a nice acronym?

Notes

1. International Conference on Cataloguing Principles, *Report: International Conference on Cataloguing Principles, Paris, 9th-18th October 1961* (London: Organizing Committee of the International Conference on Cataloguing Principles, 1963).

2. The final report of the German Project REUSE can be found at http://www.oclc.org/oclc/cataloging/reuse_project/index.htm and additional information in Monika Münnich, "Approach of *AACR2* and RAK-WB or: No Problems in Future Data Exchange?" *Cataloging & Classification Quarterly* 24, no. 3/4 (1997): 3-16.

3. Barbara B. Tillett, "Access Control: A Model for Descriptive, Holding, and Control Records," in *Convergence: Proceedings of the Second National Conference of the Library and Information Technology Association, October 2-6, 1988, Boston, Mass.* (Chicago: American Library Association, 1990), 48-56; Barbara B. Tillett, "21st Century Authority Control: What Is It and How Do We Get There?" in *Reconciling Change and Continuity in Authority Control: Proceedings of the OCLC Symposium, ALA Annual Conference, June 23, 1995* (Dublin, Ohio: OCLC, 1996), 17-21; and Barbara B. Tillett, "International Shared Resource File," in *Authority Control in the 21st Century: An Invitational Conference, March 1996* (http://www.oclc.org/oclc/man/authconf/tillett.htm).

INGRID PARENT
National Library of Canada

I would like to give you some brief comments from a Canadian perspective on a few of the issues that are being discussed over these three days, which were in most cases also referred to by Michael Gorman in his presentation.

I'd like to begin by saying how impressed I was by all the papers prepared for the conference. The authors articulated their personal visions for the direction the catalogue code should take, and they succeeded in stretching our minds to see the code in a different light, and to visualize its development in different ways.

I have also sifted through the rather voluminous comments from subscribers to the electronic listserve. These comments, coming generally from cataloguers who use the rules day to day, brought a more practical perspective to some of the issues raised in the papers. The result of all this analysis is a wealth of ideas and information that, just as in hypertext links, can lead the reader through various paths of discovery and thought.

So where did this path lead me? It led me right to the catalogue users, the people who depend on cataloguers to help them identify and retrieve information, a particular item, or a group of items. And, as we have heard, there is no typical user. But we do know that this user is becoming increasingly sophisticated in his/her search methods, and is searching for information not only in one library, but across libraries and other information providers, and even across countries. In addition, the Internet and current telecommunications technologies are presenting new opportunities for the exchange and sharing of bibliographic records beyond national boundaries. In order for libraries to take full advantage of these new trends and to better serve users, adherence to bibliographic standards is of prime importance. The implementation of the harmonized CAN/MARC-USMARC format will be a significant step towards the facilitation of record sharing. Standardization of record content, or uniform application of the cataloguing rules, is another key component to the sharing of records nationally and internationally.

This is particularly true in the Canadian context. The reality is that the shelves of Canadian libraries contain not only Canadian publications, but also much material that is published elsewhere, especially in the United States, and to a lesser extent, material published in Great Britain, in France, and in other countries. Therefore, there is also strong reliance on catalogue records produced elsewhere, especially those produced by the Library of Congress. Through some user focus studies undertaken by the National Library of Canada, we have heard that divergence between NLC and LC cataloguing practices is problematic, with differences in form of headings most often cited as being particularly difficult. We have been working with LC for several years to minimize the differences in our cataloguing description and headings and have agreements in place that establish mechanisms to avoid the creation of conflicting headings.

However, we have found that pragmatism sometimes wins out over principle. A case in point is the treatment of microform reproductions. As the national bibliographic agency, the National Library is sometimes caught between its role as the creator of the "authoritative" record for listing in the country's national bibliography and the needs of its users. NLC made the decision to follow *AACR2* and the principle of cataloguing the item in hand.

It sought and received the support of the Canadian library community. However, while Canadian libraries endorsed the NLC decision to follow the standard, many of them, in practice, chose to follow the LC Rule Interpretation on practical grounds since much of their derived cataloguing comes from LC. My question, as an administrator, is: "What is the point of leading if no one is following?"

This rather frustrating conflict between following a principle and responding to practical situations needs to be resolved as soon as possible. With the growing number of digital reproductions we are now seeing, the issue of bibliographic descriptions for such reproductions needs to be quickly addressed so that the library community does not have to contend with more than one major standard or practice.

Although I find the LCRI dealing with microform reproductions particularly problematic, I think that, in general, many LCRIs serve a very useful purpose. A cataloguing code must consist of sound principles, based on logic and user needs, clearly formulated, and widely accepted. But no code, no matter how well constructed, can comprehensively address all current and future situations. Therefore, we do appreciate the work that LC has done in developing guidelines for ambiguous or difficult situations not adequately covered in the rules and sometimes to make explicit what may be implicit in the code. In fact, many of the LCRIs for headings contribute to standardization, as they can be seen as the underpinnings of cooperative cataloguing programs and increased record sharing.

The challenge, of course, is to identify what are acceptable extensions to the rules and what are differences that will result in the development of nonstandard implementations. I also see changes to *AACR2* being made in an evolutionary way rather than through a radical restructuring. And when I say evolutionary, I don't mean glacial. The process of rule revision should be timely and responsive to changing needs. While it is true that interim guidelines could be developed by national cataloguing agencies or associations to deal with new technologies or new formats until such time as things "settle down" and the rules can be officially revised, the danger is that these interim guidelines become the *de facto* standard as thousands and perhaps millions of records are created based on interim guidelines. I would wish that one of the action items that will result from this conference is a review of the entire rule revision process, both within the author countries and at the JSC level. The objective would be to ensure that appropriate changes are approved and implemented in a timely way, in order to be both responsive to user needs and to avoid the proliferation of various interim guidelines.

I would also like to see more emphasis put on factoring in the cost of change when rule revisions are discussed. As we all know, cataloguing is still a labour-intensive activity, and any proposed major changes should be evaluated not only on the usual economic argument of millions of retrospective catalogue records that would need to be updated, but also on the impact on the cataloguer's workload. For example, how much will it cost in time and effort to create a work authority record in all cases? Will there be any cost savings if this is implemented? I think it is fair to say that the cost of cataloguing is decreasing in large part through increased sharing of standard bibliographic records and innovative and widespread use of technology. Let us not reverse that trend.

Finally, to come back to the user, I think that the cataloguing code alone does not determine whether a user will be successful in his or her search for the right information. There have been a lot of ideas put forward in the discussion leading up to this conference about the impact of MARC, OPAC display, SGML coding, and Z39.50 retrieval on the rules and vice versa. I believe that the rules should not be tied to any particular format or online display. However, the cataloguing rules must be built on solid principles and consistently applied so that they can be adapted to different uses and displays. At a session organized by the Section on Cataloguing at the last IFLA conference, there was a presentation on a bibliographic retrieval project for a union catalogue in Denmark based on the use of "fuzzy logic." The search methods used may have been fuzzy, but the results were not. This research project would not have been a success were it not for consistent data found in the catalogue records.

I would like to see the custodians of the code work more closely with other information specialists and system providers. Libraries with their databases and catalogues are not the sole providers of information, and, therefore, we should work in partnership with the other players to ensure some compatibility in interfaces to the ultimate benefit of the end-user.

I hope that the results of the discussions at this conference will confirm the necessity for a sound and evolving cataloguing code, based on logical principles, that will form the consistent foundation needed for further manipulation of the data in online systems and networks.

I too feel that the present rules have served us well and have resulted in a very mature cataloguing tradition in North America and elsewhere. However, there are major issues and trends which have been brought forward in the conference papers that the rules do not adequately accommodate. If we can address these issues and can determine a direction which will lead to judicious rule revision, I firmly believe the rules will continue to serve us well into the next century.

VERNA URBANSKI
University of North Florida

Preparation of bibliographic records has a love/hate relationship with the rest of professional librarianship. Those who are not catalogers may or may not understand the product, but they do understand that they are not in full control of the product. This lack of control makes them suspicious of the product, the process, and the producers of the product, leading to varying degrees of criticism, disbelief, and distrust. The result is low status for professional catalogers and a confused response to efforts to change either what catalogers do or how cataloging is done. Many of the current efforts at simplification of the cataloging process and many of the disjointed OPAC displays are evidence of this distrust. Sometimes, we catalogers are our own worst enemies with our endless navel-gazing over minor details. We are not nurtured in our profession. We find ourselves too often in a defensive posture, trying to appeal to the reason of people who barely understand why we do what we do, much less how we do it. So why start with this sour critique? Because I believe this lack of understanding on the part of administrators and noncataloging librarians leaves catalogers and all their rules and tools exposed to the form of explicit criticism that can dampen progress toward new goals.

In many U.S. libraries we are learning to live on our own, knowing that the leaders at the Library of Congress must struggle with their own institutional goals and limitations. They are there; they know very much; they are willing to share, but their priorities must of necessity be more inwardly directed at this time. Meanwhile in most libraries much of the routine cataloging continues to be done by low-paid but highly trained technical assistants. Professional catalogers continue with original cataloging, training paraprofessionals, updating and revising written instructions, supervising and evaluating workers, participating in committee work, and adapting to an endless improvement in technology. We want to do our best for our employees, satisfy our supervisors, contribute in a meaningful way to our profession, and participate in innovation and change. It is no wonder we are always tired.

This conference will help us begin to organize our future, but we must realistically balance what can be done against what we might want to do. I don't believe the profession as a whole will be sympathetic to an extended period of rule revision. Those who think that *AACR2* is pointless, goofy, and convoluted, and there are many of them, will assume that we are about the business of making it more pointless, even goofier, and perfecting convoluted to the point of the obtuse. I am not deaf to the attractions of defining the difference between "work," "manifestation," "expression," and "item." At the multiple versions forum at Airlie House in 1989 many of us were enchanted by the prospect of a three-tier-level record. We settled for two, and I have not seen any progress in adopting even the two-level record. If this new way of looking at bibliographic information is such a barnburner, why hasn't it been done in the intervening years? I don't think that there is support for striking out into such new territory at this time. I may not be the sharpest blade in the knife drawer, but much of the description and discussion of bibliographic relationships leaves me saying "Yah, but so what?" While this may show my intellectual poverty and my unprofessional discipline, I don't think this reaction would be too far off the mark for most of our colleagues.

I like much of what Michael Gorman and Pat Oddy have said in their paper. They have a good measure of what can be done that will be helpful with the resources available at this time. I am especially supportive of the notion of letting special materials cataloging groups develop cataloging manuals for their own special needs. JSC does have a role to play in coordinating and monitoring these efforts.

It must be remembered that *AACR2* is not a manual of examples. It is a set of rules. We need to look at *AACR2* in a different way, not expecting it to provide all our answers, but rather to provide an intelligent pattern of bibliographic information that can be a reasonable guide to us. It is not efficient to expect *AACR2* to answer every quibble and every niggly question that can be asked. Catalogers of the world should use their brains and get on with it.

With regard to some other Gorman/Oddy suggestions: we all, not just the Library of Congress, need to look at the function of rule interpretations. Perhaps rule interpretations should be seen to tell us what they do at the Library of Congress, not necessarily what we must do. As Emily Littell would say "What's all this about main entry?" Talk about something that is capable of diverting enormous amounts of energy into the black hole of cataloging inner space! Ask me whether I would rather spend time devising a uniform work title or deciding on a main entry. Something must be done to expedite the handling and identification of electronic media. Crystal Graham and Jean Hirons are right about the rules needed to accommodate serials in a sensible way.

These are all reasonable efforts, and solving these problems would not only be possible but would also have the support of the profession as a whole. If the role of cataloging in a modern library is to maintain its rightful place, we must have the support of our colleagues profession-wide. There is much to be done, and much of our future lies in the hands of those who understand communication formats, the power of metadata to inform, and the flexibility of Unicode to describe. Their development is essential to our future, and an effective, efficient *AACR2* is part of the drama that is the future of libraries. We must not be discouraged or overwhelmed, but keep in mind something I have thought when sitting through hours of long cataloging meetings. Cataloging is a lot like sex: the more you talk about it the worse it gets.

ANDREW WELLS
National Library of Australia

The opening words of *AACR2* state that "these rules are designed for use in the construction of catalogues in general libraries of all sizes." In Australia, the creation and supply of catalogue records has been largely dominated by the Australian Bibliographic Network (ABN), operated by the National Library of Australia. *AACR* is the underlying descriptive standard for all records added to the ABN database.

The introduction of *AACR2* in Australia fortuitously coincided with the development of the ABN in 1981. This, to a high degree, smoothed the transition from the first to the second edition of *AACR*. The cooperative environment created by ABN accelerated Australian cataloguers' expertise and understanding of *AACR*. The flexibility of the standard has enabled libraries of many types to contribute data to ABN. For example, rule 1.0D has been used to ensure a minimum level of contribution, enabling small and special libraries that may not have cataloguing expertise to add records to the ABN database. Over one million records have been created by Australian cataloguers on ABN using *AACR2*. Another good example of the flexibility of *AACR2* has been its ability to incorporate rules for new formats.

Australia's means of commenting on and contributing to the development of *AACR2* is through the Australian Committee on Cataloguing (ACOC), a tripartite body representing the National Library of Australia, the Australian Council of Library and Information Services, and the Australian Library and Information Association. A recent review of bibliographic advisory mechanisms recommended the continuation of the committee's chief functions, one of which is involvement in the revision of *AACR*. The recommendation has been accepted by the Committee's parent bodies and will be implemented in new advisory structures in the next two years. ACOC is included in the rules as an author of *AACR* and has one representative on the Joint Steering Committee for Revision of AACR. While Australia is the smallest of the author countries, the nation's cataloguers are committed to the rules and their revision.

The combination of Australia's size, dependency on cataloguing data created in other countries, and the legacy of Australian catalogue records constructed in a networked environment using *AACR* puts Australia into the category of those who would prefer gradual change and evolution of the rules. One of Australia's national characteristics is pragmatism, and this is increasingly accompanied by an appreciation of the forces of globalisation. A recent good example of this is the decision made on the future of the nation's MARC format, AUSMARC. Instead of embarking on a process to achieve harmonisation or compatibility with the dominant USMARC format, Australia decided seven years ago to adopt USMARC as its national standard. This mirrors the use of *AACR* in Australia: it is an international standard, which needs little amendment to meet the needs of Australian libraries. The inclusion of an Australian voice on the JSC adds to national commitment to the standard.

However, the forces of pragmatism and globalisation do not mean that Australia in not interested in change. ACOC has put forward many proposals for rule revision. I recommend that the revision process be reviewed. In my period as chairperson of ACOC, many small revisions took several years to accomplish as the proposals went through extended periods of occasionally aggressive debate. The revision process needs to proceed in a spirit of good will and with an increased focus on all users of catalogue records. The process proposed in Tom Delsey's paper suggests a way forward on the latter issue.

The National Library of Australia supports all of the recommendations in the Gorman and Oddy paper. In particular, issues in the description of microforms must be resolved, and a consolidated *AACR* and MARC holds the promise of reducing redundancy in the standards and improving the productivity of cataloguers. There are three additional areas the Library puts forward for consideration:

Uniform titles. Their rationale is far from explicit and their rules for construction are complex. The role of collective uniform titles in the online environment needs to be considered. Uniform titles could play an important role in the developing concept of "work authority records"; however, their current form seems applicable to physical manifestations in some cases, and abstract concepts of the "work" in others. Uniform titles in *AACR* are worthy of examination, and Delsey's paper should provide a useful starting point.

The treatment of single works which update their content needs to be considered by *AACR*. Adele Hallam's work on loose-leaf publications needs to be in the rules, not an accompanying manual.[1] The proliferation of this category of publication on the Internet makes this inclusion an urgent candidate for rule revision.

Serials. There are far too many title changes in serial records. Mechanisms to reduce these are needed, and the suggestions included in the paper by Jean Hirons and Crystal Graham merit serious consideration. All stakeholders in the bibliographic control of serials need to be involved, and agreement on standard practice achieved. The National Library supports full implementation of the recommendations in the Hirons/Graham paper.

Australian libraries look forward to continuing their involvement in the revision and development of *AACR*. The standard has sufficient flexibility to adapt to new environments and formats, but as several papers at this conference reveal, the conceptual foundations need clarification. Australian librarians will be eager to participate in this process.

Note

1. Adele Hallam, *Cataloging Rules for the Description of Looseleaf Publications,* 2nd ed. (Washington, D.C.: Office for Descriptive Cataloging, Library of Congress, 1989).

Issues Related to Seriality

JEAN HIRONS AND CRYSTAL GRAHAM

Introduction

According to the Ken Burns documentary, Thomas Jefferson claimed that the ideas expressed in the Declaration of Independence were not new; it was simply the first time they had been formally set down. In this paper we hope to similarly formalize certain concepts long held to be "self-evident" by serialists. These concepts lack the magnitude of those expressed in the Declaration of Independence and we lack Jefferson's eloquence; nevertheless, we believe them to be critical to the success of our cataloging code. And while the ideas we espouse are somewhat revolutionary, we'd rather think of them as evolutionary.

What are these ideas?

First, that publications[1] have three dimensions: (1) their intellectual and/or artistic content; (2) their physical carrier(s); and (3) the susceptibility of content to change over time, both extensively, by the supplementing of content through additional carriers, and intensively, through the alteration of content within the existing carrier. We will refer to the third dimension as the *publication status,* which can be *static* (i.e., complete as issued) or *ongoing* (not complete as issued).

Second, that the publication status will have a growing influence on cataloging decisions with the gradual migration of bibliographic resources from the comparatively stable world of print to a more malleable electronic form. More and more, this susceptibility to change over time will be a potential characteristic of all electronic publications, and not simply of the subset that we customarily refer to as serials. Thus, publication status must play an integral role along with content and carrier in determining the application of rules for the description of and access to a publication.

Third, that the cataloging code as it stands is not adequate to deal with these particular aspects of the changing bibliographic universe and that the principles associated with ongoing publications need to be fully integrated into the code.

Serials are truly in a state of flux! Though traditionally issued in a succession of numbered parts, serials are now beginning to appear in new ways that call into question their continued status as serials. Is seriality becoming a thing of the past? Do we need to redefine our definition of *serial* or do we need new terminology to cover the broad spectrum of today's publishing world?

Our rules and definitions were crafted in a time of bibliographic stability and do not accommodate changing formats and new forms of publications. How can we reshape them to fit the increasingly dynamic world in which we now work?

In this paper we will address these issues as follows:

Part I will introduce the concepts of publication status and ongoing publications and examine how these concepts relate to the *Functional Requirements for Bibliographic Records.*[2]

Part II will provide a summary of the current environment in which we are working and the challenges posed by that environment.

Part III will present a conceptual approach to the categorization of publications through models that represent the gradual redefinition of *serial*.

Part IV will propose broad concepts and principles that can be applied to ongoing publications and discuss how these principles are applied to the cataloging of these publications.

Part V will examine the impact of the redefinition of *serial* on *AACR2*, MARC, ISSN, and ISBD and summarize the major issues for discussion.

Part I. Introducing the Concepts of Publication Status and Ongoing Publications

A. Defining Ongoing Publications

The debate over "content versus carrier" is one of the primary reasons for this conference. *AACR2* favors carrier as the starting point for the description (rule 0.24); others feel that the content should play a more important role, particularly in the cataloging of reproductions and digitized publications. We contend that there is a third dimension: the *publication status,* which relates to completeness and the degree to which content will be added or changed over time. A publication which is complete as issued is considered to be *static* in this paper; a publication which is intended to be continued in any form is considered to be *ongoing*.

Ongoing publications may be *determinate* (i.e., intended to be completed) or *indeterminate* (i.e., intended to be continued indefinitely). The degree to which a publication is ongoing may require special cataloging considerations in the form of special rules or in the ways in which rules are applied. For instance, the ongoing nature is currently manifested in *AACR2* in the rules for title changes found under rule 21.2. But it is also manifested in ways not always covered by the rules. For instance, when selecting the title proper, a cataloger who considers a publication to be ongoing evaluates the stability of data and may select different words as the title than a cataloger who catalogs the same publication thinking it to be a static item.

Ongoing publications, as defined in the broadest sense, include (but are not limited to):

- Multivolume monographs, for which all volumes have yet to be issued
- Monographs accompanied by regularly or irregularly issued supplements
- Loose-leaf publications

- Serial-like publications issued in conjunction with a limited-time event (e.g., a newsletter associated with the 24th Olympic Games)
- Databases,[3] web sites,[4] online services, and discussion lists
- Numbered serials, including monographic series
- Unnumbered monographic series

Note: We are distinguishing *ongoing* publications—those that are intended to continue—from electronic publications, which because of their format are capable of change. Thus, a report issued in electronic form and later corrected would not be considered an ongoing publication.

B. Attributes of the Content, Carrier, and Publication Status

In this paper we will use terms for attributes of each dimension as described below.

Content

Scope of content: whether the subject matter is broad or limited in nature, and thus, indicating whether the publication is likely to be determinate or indeterminate.

Mode of expression: whether the contents consist primarily of text, music, cartographic data, graphic material, etc.

Dynamic nature of contents: whether the contents are characterized as additive (i.e., new information with each issuance), updating (i.e., part of the contents is added, changed, or deleted by way of updates), or replacement (each issuance completely replaces all others). Note: Updating and replacement publications have no distinction in the online environment and are collectively referred to in this paper as "updating publications."

Genre or type of publication: whether a publication is a periodical, a newsletter, an online service, a web site, an atlas, a newspaper or news service, etc.

Equivalency: whether what is contained in one publication is the same or differs significantly from what is contained in a related publication.

Carrier

Type of physical carrier: whether a publication is issued as paper, microform, electronic, sound recording, film, etc.

Form of issuance: whether an ongoing item is issued in successive parts (i.e., each with its own chief source), in one constantly updated part (i.e., with a single chief source), or in other configurations.

Tangible vs. intangible nature of the carrier: whether a publication is issued tangibly (e.g., print, sound recording, CD-ROM) or intangibly (e.g., via the Internet). Note that publications issued on tangible CDs once loaded on a computer appear intangible to those who use them.

Publication Status

Static publications: those that are complete as issued.

Ongoing publications: those that are not complete as first issued. Ongoing publications may be *determinate* or *indeterminate*.

Determinate publications: ongoing publications that are intended to be complete in a finite number of parts or over a finite period of time.

Indeterminate publications: ongoing publications that are intended to continue indefinitely.

All three dimensions of a publication are important and need to be accommodated in our rules. Furthermore, as the bibliographic universe becomes increasingly digital, each dimension can have a profound impact on the other. None can be completely separated or omitted from our consideration. As an example, Tom Delsey notes that "the effort to extend the MARC formats to accommodate serials in nonprint form and multimedia items have stumbled against the inconsistent grouping of attributes related variously to intellectual form, physical medium, and publication type."[5] What we need is a three-dimensional approach to cataloging that encompasses all dimensions in the most appropriate ways.

The challenge for catalogers is to be able to meaningfully express in catalog records the similarities and disparities between publications that look different but whose content is essentially the same, and between publications that look very similar but whose content is quite different. We can only accomplish this by giving careful attention to each dimension of the publication and its attributes.

RECOMMENDATION 1: Adopt a three-dimensional approach to the cataloging rules.

C. Benefits of Defining the Concepts of Publication Status and Ongoing Publications

By introducing the broad concept of "ongoing publications" we hope to:

1. *Raise the consciousness of all catalogers to applying the appropriate levels of specificity to ongoing publications.*

   This paper does not presume to say *who* should be cataloging certain types of publications, only *how* they should be cataloged. Nevertheless, we are aware that those who have never cataloged serials tend to approach such publications very differently from those who have. In the digital world many more publications will be ongoing and will require the application of principles long associated with traditional serials.

By grouping such publications under a common category we can facilitate the education and training of all catalogers.

2. *Assure that the attributes of such publications are adequately addressed in the rules.*
   Cataloging decisions that must be made for ongoing publications should be fully integrated into the rules. Furthermore, by looking at such rules collectively, we can take a more principled approach to their formation that will provide more consistency and assure that new forms yet unknown can be accommodated.

3. *Ensure that all types of publications are covered by the rules.*
   The rules should be inclusive, covering ongoing nonprint materials, loose-leafs, and other categories currently omitted.

4. *Assure that ongoing publications are cataloged in a way that will accommodate their special needs for control.*
   In today's automated library systems, accurate bibliographic records are essential to the overall control of the publications. Serials and most ongoing publications require special types of control, such as subscriptions and standing orders, licensing, claiming, and check-in. Being able to accurately define the nature of the publication is crucial.

5. *Create rules for description that are compatible with form of issuance.*
   This is a basic premise of this paper. One form should not be shoehorned into the rules for another. We do not want to create a situation in which new forms of publication are forced into the rules for old forms. Nor should we throw out rules that are working perfectly well in order to accommodate new types of publications. In this paper we will suggest that how we label a publication will not necessarily limit it to a single set of rules.

RECOMMENDATION 2: Incorporate the concept of the "ongoing publication" into the cataloging code.

D. The FRBR Model and Its Relation to Ongoing Publications

The model proposed by the IFLA Study Group on the Functional Requirements for Bibliographic Records (called hereafter the "FRBR model") presents four entities: the *work* as an abstract idea, its *expression* in various forms, its physical *manifestations,* and the actual *item* held within a library.

The FRBR model is most useful in determining the levels in which a publication exists and the attributes that exist at each level. It also helps in our understanding of the problems related to seriality, as currently defined.

Whether a publication is ongoing occurs at the level of the *work*. To be sure, a publisher may issue a one-time publication, find that it is quite popular, and decide to continue its publication each year with a new annual volume. More often, however, the nature of the content of the work determines whether it is determinate or indeterminate, and this is one of the first decisions made at the publication's inception.

The *expression* involves differences in content and mode of expression. While this level is common in literature and music, it is less likely to occur with most serials. Indeed, for serials this is the most difficult entity to envision or explain and perhaps is not relevant at all. If content is a factor, to what degree do differences in the content constitute new expressions, and at what point is the content so different that one has a new work? Perhaps a more difficult question is, in the fluid world of the Internet, how exact can we be in defining differences in content, and how much do these differences matter if the patron can directly access the publication through a hypertext link in the catalog record?

Seriality, as currently defined, occurs at the *manifestation* level because both the aspects of successive issuance and numbering may be dependent on the physical manifestation of the work or work/expression. Having a clear concept of manifestation will be useful to standardize the cataloging of reproductions and simultaneously issued physical versions (now sometimes treated differently), assure that physical versions are kept together in the catalog, and separate the problems of describing the physical publication from the more conceptual aspects of defining the work and its content.

The *item* level is critical to serials because of the importance of holdings. For serials, the item level includes the extent of the run of each copy of the serial that is held by a library.

Thus, while clarification is still needed, the FRBR model provides a useful framework in which to understand the problems of seriality, multiple versions, and the concept of a work.

Part II. The Current Environment and Its Challenges

A. Problems with *AACR2*

For serials and ongoing publications in general, *AACR2* presents problems with definitions and with the overall structure of the code. While some of these problems have always existed, the emergence of the Internet has highlighted the code's weaknesses to a point where they can no longer be ignored.

1. *Definitions*

AACR2 offers very little to aid the cataloger who is trying to determine the ongoing nature of a publication and how that publication should be treated according to the code. There is no descriptive text such as that found at the beginning of the serial chapters in the earlier *AACR1* and ALA codes. *AACR2* offers two definitions: that of a serial and that of a monograph, and it has become increasingly clear that these definitions are no longer adequate.

a. The serial as defined by *AACR2*

AACR2 defines a serial as "a publication in any medium issued in successive parts bearing numeric or chronological designations and intended to be continued indefinitely." While the majority of serials are primarily textual and issued in print, microform, and electronic formats, there are serial sound recordings, videorecordings, maps, posters, and slides.[6]

Publications that have traditionally been treated as serials fall into two categories. The first category includes primarily *additive* publications, i.e., those which present new information with each issuance. These include periodicals (publications that contain articles, whether scholarly or popular), regularly issued reports (such as annual reports), newsletters, newspapers, reports of societies, numbered monographic series, and some conference publications. There are also publications such as abstracting and indexing services and book catalogs, such as *New Serial Titles,* the contents of which is additive but which also cumulate annually, quinquennially, etc. The primary characteristic of additive publications is that the scope of their content is broad enough to support additional new material for an indeterminate period of time.

The second group of publications is those for which the content requires *updating* to some degree. Updates may be issued in the form of replacement volumes, sometimes called "editions," which is the case for many directories, travel guides, and other reference publications. When the updates are frequent and regular, the publications are cataloged as serials. Many of these publications have been treated as serials for matters of convenience, since they require the same type of inventory control needed for additive publications, and they meet the criteria for a serial. Updates may also be issued as separate parts in themselves, as is the case with loose-leaf publications, which we will discuss below. The primary characteristic of the content of updating publications is the need to be current.

A library may choose to discard the old versions of updating reference publications, give them to other institutions, retain them for historical purposes, or, in the case of CD-ROMs, may be required to return them to the publisher. Whatever their disposition, they are issued in a succession of parts and are therefore currently cataloged as serials.

b. The monograph as defined by *AACR2*

A monograph is defined as "a nonserial item (i.e., an item either complete in one part or complete, or intended to be completed, in a finite number of separate parts)." Thus, the primary distinguishing difference between a serial and a monograph is whether or not the publication is intended to be continued indefinitely. Monographs range from publications that are complete in one part, such as *A Year in Provence,* to multivolume publications that are issued over a long span of time, such as Mansell's *National Union Catalog, Pre-1956 Imprints,* published 1968-1981.

We should note here that to some extent, treatment as a serial or as a monograph can be determined by an individual institution, based on the desire for economic processing or maximal access to specific data. This is particularly true for analyzable publications, such as conference publications and monographic series, where the individual issues may or may not be cataloged separately.

c. Loose-leafs and other misfits

A category of publication that has never fit into the monograph/serial dichotomy presented in *AACR2* is the loose-leaf. In her *Cataloging Rules for the Description of Looseleaf Publications,* Adele Hallam notes that "the Library of Congress concluded that by the strict definitions of a monograph and a serial, loose-leaf publications constitute neither; instead their unique characteristics need to be considered outside established cataloging formulae."[7] For years, catalogers have relied on Hallam's separate set of cataloging rules to catalog these publications. (Note: The only mention of "loose-leaf" in *AACR2* is in rule 2.5B9, which allows for the addition of the parenthetical "(loose-leaf)" following the number of volumes, i.e., 1 v. (loose-leaf)).

The current treatment of loose-leafs depends on the regular or irregular issuance of the base volume or binder. If a new binder is regularly issued, the publication is treated as a serial. If a new binder is not issued on a regular basis, as is more often the case, the publication is cataloged as a monograph. The decision to treat such loose-leafs as monographs was somewhat arbitrary, since they are not covered by the definition of monograph. This decision has also been problematic because serial bibliographic records may be required by serials control systems for the check-in of the updates.

Unnumbered series, though ongoing and issued in successive parts, lack designations and thus do not meet the definition of a serial. But neither are they monographs! Another problematic category includes publications that look and act like serials but are limited to a particular duration of time. This category includes the regularly issued newsletters and journals associated with limited term events and quarterly progress reports of a limited term project.

The biggest omissions from our current definitions are the new formats and types of publications that have emerged with online publishing. We will address those in Section B below.

2. *Structure of the code*

a. Descriptive portion

AACR2 is structured so that the cataloger uses the general chapter 1 and one or more specific chapters when creating cataloging records. For printed serials, chapters 1 and 12 are used; for nonprint serials, the appropriate nonprint chapter is also consulted. Thus, for computer files, rules in chapters 1, 12, and 9 are used. While the idea of universally applicable rules is a noble one, the current code does not achieve its full potential. This is because chapter 1 is too specifically based on books and chapter 12 is too specifically written for printed serials.

And although the definition acknowledges that a serial can be published in any medium, this principle is not carried through in the rules for nonprint media. For example, notes are highly specific in the special chapters, such as rule 9.7B1, the system requirements note. The rule instructs the cataloger to record the exact make, model, and version of computer hard- and software required to access the publication. When serials catalogers began cataloging computer file serials they tried to follow this rule as written but soon realized the folly of including such highly volatile information in serial records. Yet there are no instructions on how such a note might be made less specific and suitable to a serial record.

Furthermore, chapter 12 doesn't go far enough in addressing the needs of traditional printed serials. The rules almost always presuppose that one has the first issue, and there is little guidance on how to handle changes that appear on later issues. For example, there is no mention in rule 12.7B6 (notes relating to statement of responsibility) of when and how to record changes in the issuing body. Nor is there clear instruction on what to do about the publication date when the first issue is not in hand.

b. Access portion

In the rules for title changes there are no rules that govern a change in title for a continuously updated single-part publication such as the loose-leaf. Only in Hallam's work does one find rule 1B10, which says to use the latest title proper and note the earlier titles. There are also no rules for constructing the entry for an unnumbered series; these are only covered in LC rule interpretations.

B. The Impact of the Internet and Online Publishing

In the past several years we have witnessed the rapid evolution of the online serial and we know that it will continue to evolve. What began as rather ephemeral publications, published in an experimental environment in plain ASCII text and available via gophers or e-mail, has blossomed into sophisticated, multimedia publications available on the World Wide Web, such as *Postmodern Culture*. A rapidly growing trend is for publishers of scholarly journals to make available "online versions" such as those published in Johns Hopkins Press' Project Muse (http://www.muse.jhu.org) and Academic Press' IDEAL (http://192.215.52.3/www/ap/aboutid.htm). Digital reproductions of journals have been the focus of projects such as JSTOR—the Journal Storage Project (http://www.jstor.org). Many other publishers have created sites that include only the tables of contents and abstracts, e.g., *Cataloging and Classification Quarterly* (http://ccq.libraries.psu.edu/index.html), or late-breaking news, e.g., *LJ Digital* (http:www.ljdigital.com/). It is not hard to imagine the day when virtually every serial published in technologically advanced countries will have some form of online site, and we envision the eventual demise of the paper copy for at least some of these titles.

Not only are the numbers increasing but in some cases the formatting of the online versions is changing as publishers realize the possibilities inherent in the Internet and World Wide Web. Just as our early online catalogs mirrored the card catalog, so the "early" online journals (i.e., those issued in 1993 as opposed to 1996!) mirrored their printed counterparts, appearing in volumes and issues that paralleled the print publication. Others, however, are taking on new formats that are more indicative of the realm in which they reside. The *Journal of Electronic Publishing* (http://www.press.umich.edu/jep) is an example of a journal whose articles are contained in a database which the user accesses through author, title, and subject searches. Others have developed a format that includes the most recent issue for browsing and a database of searchable articles from previous issues.[8] An example of a popular journal is *Slate* (http://www.slate.com), Michael Kinsley's experiment with a general-interest online journal. The current issue looks like a print journal, having a magazine-style layout and even including page numbers, but the older articles are "composted" in a database. These publications still contain articles but lack issues. We continue to think of them as periodicals, but are they still serials?

Perhaps most affected are updating publications, such as directories, catalogs, and indexes, for which the online format is ideal. What was once issued in a succession of printed editions—in a loose-leaf format or in monthly cumulative issues—can now all be issued in a single updating database. There is no longer a succession of parts and the only designation is the date of last updating.

In addition to the changes to traditional publications, there are new forms of publications and electronic resources that never existed before that are currently treated as monographs because they lack successive parts, but which are truly ongoing publications. Web sites, electronic forums, and online services are among the new types of resources that are stretching our old conceptions of what constitutes a serial and, indeed, a "publication." To be sure, these new forms are serving very different functions than traditional publications and we can hope that embedded metadata will eventually provide a certain level of access, but we may still want to include the more important ones in our catalogs.

What does the future hold in store? Ann Okerson observes two trends: "1) blurring boundaries between the different types of electronic serial, so that it is difficult to categorize them by the same taxonomies as those used for paper serials; and 2) blurring boundaries between formats. That is, some electronic serials are electronic only, but various of them either index or review paper publications, and others move between electronic and more traditional formats. . . ."[9]

The only thing that we can be certain of is that we will continue to witness many variations of the traditional serial as publishers test the waters to determine how they can best attract and meet the needs of their readers. To quote Erik Jul, "The electronic journal seems poised to rewrite our sense of periodicity, . . . if technology will allow it, serials will do it."[10]

C. The Shared Cataloging Environment

One of the difficulties of using *AACR2* is that it assumes that each cataloger is always doing original cataloging. There is no acknowledgment that most catalogers now work in a shared cataloging environment and use existing records whenever possible. Two factors come into play. The first is the factor of what actually exists. The second is the factor of what an individual library owns. For ongoing publications, what exists and what a library owns will be dependent on the point in time that the publication is given initial cataloging and the library's holdings at that time.

For publications that are complete in a single part, working in a shared environment is relatively easy, since all catalogers have the same data before them. For multipart ongoing publications, however, working in a shared environment is more complicated because different catalogers can have different parts of the publication on which they are basing the cataloging. Ideally, our rules would fully accommodate the level of knowledge brought to the cataloging process; however, in a shared environment, this accommodation is difficult to accomplish. In order to create and use records cooperatively, all catalogers must follow the same conventions.

Some accommodation may be possible, however. As an example, a recent addition to LCRI 12.0B1 allows catalogers to choose a chief source other than the title page, when cataloging retrospectively and when doing so would eliminate records for needless title changes. Another accommodation for retrospective work might be to reinstate the concept of the "title of short duration," which was dropped from *AACR2*.

To do this in a cooperative environment, catalogers need to be able to communicate with one another. The CONSER Program has found it useful to use the local 936 field to indicate the latest issue consulted (LIC). Perhaps rule 12.7B23 might be changed to include such information in the "description based on note," e.g., Description based on: Vol. 2, no. 3; latest issue consulted: v. 5, no. 1. Such information could be deleted once the final issue is recorded in area 3.

Online publications are further complicating the ability to share cataloging. Many of these publications have a single source for the title and other bibliographic details, such as publisher. The title can be changed on this source, leaving no trace of the earlier title and making it difficult to determine whether a record already exists when only the current title is known.

D. The Online Cataloging Environment

1. *Discarding the remnants of the card catalog*

Our rules are still based on an environment that is fast disappearing—that of the 3x5 catalog card and the printed card catalog. With the online catalog we have new opportunities never dreamed of by the creators of our earlier codes, upon which so many of *AACR2*'s concepts are still based. The most obvious change is that we are no longer limited to the space on a 3x5 card! Nor do we have to display data in the traditional format. The labeled displays popular in online public catalogs offer a metadata style listing that is considered by many to be more legible and understandable than the compact paragraph with its ISBD punctuation. However, the fact that each local system displays data differently means that we can no longer set rules with one format in mind. And the terms used to label the data could be improved. We should continue to explore new ways of presenting cataloging data that will be both efficient and understandable to our users.

As an example of how outdated *AACR2* has become, consider the linking entry fields. For over twenty years serial catalogers have been using linking entry fields to link the records for bibliographically related serial publications. With format integration, linking fields may now be used in any format. *AACR2* still refers to these as notes (12.7B7) and provides no guidance for the construction of the entry in these "notes." The only guidance has been in the form of an LCRI and instructions given in the *CONSER Editing Guide.* In a web-based catalog the concept of the linking entry field could be enhanced with a direct hypertext link to the related record or the item itself, when online.

We also have the ability to combine description and access, as is currently done in the USMARC fields 245 and 246, and more of this would be welcome. Gregory Wool notes that we might "abandon transcription from the item in most cases, in favor of a well-labeled list of searchable terms either chosen from, or created for, an authority file." He also points out, however, that such an approach might "make catalog records less useful for identifying specific bibliographic items."[11]

Since not all libraries have the same level of technical sophistication, Barbara Tillett suggests customized cataloging manuals that would incorporate subsets of rules "augmented by guidelines for record creation appropriate to the technology available to the library."[12]

2. *Multiple versions*[13]

While the dream of a multiple versions "solution" seems to be elusive in the world of communicated records, we should never give up. The more sophisticated integrated systems of today are better equipped to handle complex bibliographic relationships than their predecessors, and the FRBR model is an important step in developing the conceptual model.

Multiple versions, the FRBR model, and the definition of serial are all closely connected. Applying the FRBR model to multiple versions, we see that at the level of the *work* all that is required of a serial is that a publication be intended to continue indefinitely. If all of the physical manifestations are to be tied in some way to the work, they must be recognized as having intrinsically the same intellectual or artistic content.

3. *Alternatives to cataloging*

When discussing electronic publications, we cannot ignore those who ask "why catalog them at all?" or "aren't there alternatives?" Yes, there are alternatives, and there are a number of varying practices, depending on the types of electronic serials (called hereafter "e-serials"). Some libraries are citing e-serial versions and reproductions on the record for the original according to interim guidelines issued by the CONSER Program (http://lcweb.loc.gov/acq/conser/). Many libraries are including lists of e-serials on their institutional web pages, but these will soon become unwieldy. Eventually, metadata within the publication itself may offer some form of basic access. While this paper addresses *AACR2* and traditional cataloging, it is important to keep alternatives in mind when we look at the ramifications of our proposals.

E. The Importance of the Concept of "Serial"

1. *The need for control: the serials infrastructure*

Because serials have always been issued as multipart publications, they have required certain types of control that have not been needed, at least not to the same degree, by monographs. Serials management and control is important within libraries and is a critical aspect of any automated library system. Serials control in its broadest sense can include subscriptions and standing orders; holdings and routing data; claiming and binding records; bibliographic records; circulation and interlibrary loan policies; and often special shelving for unbound and bound volumes.

It should be noted that libraries use their serials control mechanism for many ongoing publications that are not officially defined as "serials," such as loose-leaf services and multivolume sets that are issued over a period of time in order to provide tracking/inventory control over the sequentially received pieces.

In addition, the hierarchical nature of serials, particularly periodicals, requires multiple levels of access. Because patrons most often are seeking information on a topic, they will approach periodicals through abstracting and indexing (A&I) services that give citations to specific articles. Some library systems have instituted a method known as "hooks to holdings" which employs the ISSN to tie the citation in the online A&I service to the library's bibliographic and holdings records. Thus, upon finding the citation to an article, the patron can learn whether the library subscribes to that journal and whether the specific issue is available, its location, call number, etc.

In addition to libraries, there are subscription agents, abstracting and indexing services, and the ISSN community that are all dealing with various aspects of serials control. Publications such as *The Serials Directory,* published by EBSCO, or the R. R. Bowker publication *Ulrich's International Periodicals Directory,* both of which are available in print and as databases, provide information relating to subscriptions, frequency, available formats, abstracting and indexing services, and document delivery. Both have sections listing online serials, including many directories and databases, which may or may not also be available in print. The point is that these are all referred to as "serials" because they are performing the same function as their print counterparts. The actual form of issuance is of minor importance in this context.

While online publications may not require the same degree of control, they can still be listed, subscribed to, and indexed in the same way as their print counterparts. Thus, we feel that publications that serve the function of serials should be considered serials, regardless of their form of issuance.

2. *The need to inform users: user perceptions and the function of serials*

Do our carefully crafted distinctions between monographs and serials make sense or even matter to those outside the cataloging community? While catalogers think of serials in terms of publication pattern and descriptive cataloging rules, the user is more likely to think in terms of the various genres of serials, such as journals, newsletters, newspapers, and monographic series, each of which has a specific function. For example, users recognize journals because of their intrinsic characteristics, i.e., an assemblage of articles on various topics, usually with some unifying purpose, subject, slant, or field of enquiry. On the other hand, users are more apt to think of reference publications, such as directories or guidebooks, as books, since they are generally only interested in the latest volume.

Journals serve a certain societal function, particularly in the area of scholarly communications. The association of an article with a specific journal is a measure of its credibility, quality, perspective, and target audience. An article about "Life on Mars" appearing in the *National Enquirer* does not carry the same weight as a peer-reviewed article on the same topic in *Science*. The scholarly journal serves a gatekeeping function, selecting the best and most appropriate articles for publication. Editorial quality and copyright protection are assured by a reputable journal.[14]

Likewise, newsletters, newspapers, annual reports, and directories all have a certain function within the bibliographic universe. These fundamental functions, though potentially enhanced, will not change in the electronic environment. Whether one refers to the latest volume of *Ulrich's* from the shelf, or logs into the CD-ROM database, one is seeking and will retrieve the same type of information. Using the FRBR terminology, these are both essentially the same work, just different manifestations.

Ed Jones reminds us that "publishers do not consciously set out to create serials as defined by *AACR2*."[15] Users will care little about whether a journal is issued in successive parts or in a searchable database; their main concern is to find the article they are looking for.

Publishers also have a hard time with our distinctions. Regina Reynolds, head of the U.S. ISSN Center at the Library of Congress, reports that she frequently receives requests from publishers for ISSN for publications that under the *AACR2* definition cannot be considered a serial. In one telephone conversation the astonished publisher said "but surely it's not a book!"

3. *The need to group and distinguish records in online catalogs*

For users, the primary concern is access. In online catalogs, searches can be limited to serials, and thus treating some versions of a publication as a serial and others as monographs may cause problems for retrieval. Serials may reside in a discrete database, such as CONSER, or appear on periodical union lists and local finding aids. For instance, in the Library of Congress, patrons go to the Serial and Government Publications Division to access a wide variety of printed, microform, and electronic publications. Many of the journals, newspapers, and indexing services are now available electronically and lists of such titles are maintained in house. To suggest that some of these aren't really serials because they no longer consist of successive issues would be counterproductive to the overall identification of and access to these publications.

Part III. The Model for Ongoing Publications and the Redefinition of Serial

While we currently separate the bibliographic universe into monographs and serials,[16] in reality there is a continuum from publications that are very static to those that are very ongoing. Where we draw the line between monograph and serial within this continuum has changed little over time. In the following discussion, we will present a model that divides the bibliographic universe between publications that are static and those that are ongoing. We will first discuss what each category includes, then look at the current practice. Then we will proceed to examine what would happen if we removed various elements of the definition of serial, incorporating a larger category of materials under the category of "serial." In the final model we will look at the possibility of removing the terms "monograph" and "serial" altogether!

A. The Model for Ongoing Publications

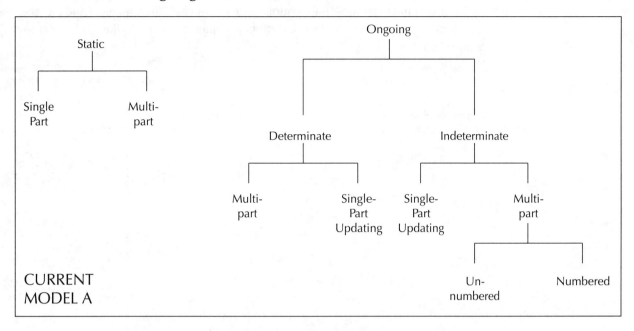

CURRENT
MODEL A

We have already defined *static, ongoing, determinate,* and *indeterminate* publications. In order to better understand the impact of the models that follow, we will briefly discuss the types of publications that fall under the multipart and single-part updating categories given in the model.

1. *Static publications*
   Static single-part publications include books, sound recordings, videos, CD-ROMs, maps, etc., issued in a single physical part. This could also include an electronic text. Static multipart publications include multivolume monographs complete as issued, a set of musical CDs, an interactive multimedia publication that consists of multiple components, and so forth.

2. *Ongoing publications*
   The primary difference between single- and multipart is the fact that one has a single chief source that can be revised, while the other has a succession of chief sources, each of which remains stable, but on which information can change from one to another.

   a. Determinate publications
      An ongoing multipart determinate publication is a multivolume set that is incomplete as first issued and is intended to be completed over a period of time. The expected number of parts and the length of time in which they will be issued will determine how the parts are noted on the catalog record and controlled internally. However, all are finite in nature.

      An ongoing determinate single-part publication would include a loose-leaf with limited duration and the web site for this conference.

   b. Indeterminate publications
      Single-part indeterminate publications include serials that have migrated to an online format and are now issued as databases, plus any loose-leaf or updating publication

that is not intended to be completed, such as the *CONSER Cataloging Manual.*

Multipart indeterminate publications include journals, newspapers, and all other categories of traditional serials and monographic series, including those that are unnumbered.

B. The Current Practice

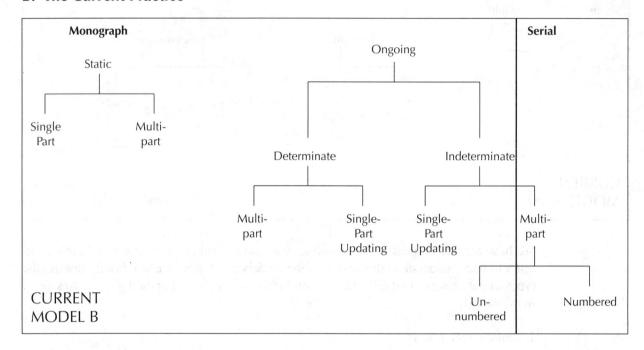

Looking at the model above, we see how restricted the current definition of serial is in relation to the spectrum of ongoing publications. We have already discussed the problems with our current definitions and the fact that some of the categories aren't included in the rules at all, so we will move on to Model A.

C. Future Practice: Model A

1. *Explanation of Model A*

Model A would retain the *AACR2* definition of serial with the exception that numbering would not be required, thus including unnumbered series.

Because serials would only include successively issued publications, updating publications would be excluded from the category. They would either have to be done as monographs (as is the current practice) or form a new category of their own.[17]

In this model, a serial would be defined as:

A publication in any medium that is intended to continue indefinitely and is issued in successive parts.

2. *The significance of removing the requirement for numbering*

Requiring a designation makes the job of the serials librarian much easier, since designations are important for the check-in and retrieval of the individual parts of a successively issued publication. For updating and replacement publications, when the updates or

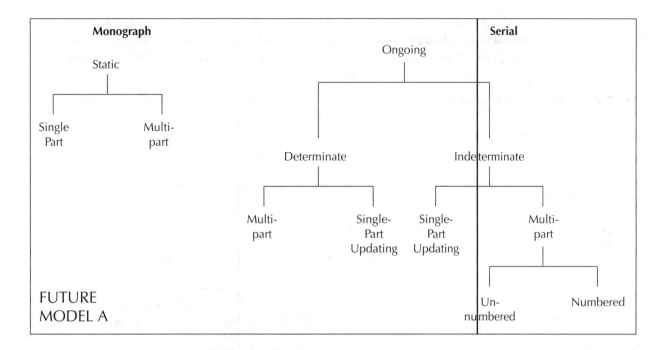

FUTURE
MODEL A

replacements are issued in a tangible form such as a printed loose-leaf or CD-ROM discs, a designation is needed to identify the individual update or replacement.

The primary category of unnumbered indefinitely issued publications is the unnumbered series.

Catalogers need to know how to formulate the heading and uniform title qualifier for unnumbered series and how to relate the series headings when the title changes. Presently these instructions are contained only in an LC rule interpretation. We do not need to change the way in which we are handling unnumbered series. But we need to acknowledge the existence and special needs of such bibliographic entities within *AACR2*.

An additional benefit of loosening the requirement for a designation would be to acknowledge that publications that are clearly intended to be issued on an ongoing basis are serials, even though the publisher has supplied nothing more than a copyright date on the first issue. (An example is the *Annual Bed and Breakfast Directory,* which was first published with no designation.) In such cases, the publisher will normally add a date on subsequent issues.

Other unnumbered publications that are not obviously intended to continue indefinitely and are unlikely to carry a designation would continue to be treated as monographs.

3. *Advantages and disadvantages of Model A*

Under Model A, unnumbered series would be brought into the serial fold. In all other respects it would maintain the status quo. Neither determinate nor indeterminate single-part items, such as loose-leafs, would be cataloged as serials. Needless distinctions regarding the intention to continue would not have to be made since they would all be cataloged as monographs. A further advantage is that one set of rules for serials would suffice, with additional provisions for unnumbered serials.

Removing the requirement for numbering may create problems for check-in and make the distinction between "serial" and "monograph" more difficult to make. The primary disadvantage of Model A, however, is that it is not in keeping with the FRBR model and separates publications that are issued successively in one format from those issued as updating publications in another format. It also negates the ongoing nature of a large group of publications, many of which require some form of serial control.

D. Future Practice: Model B

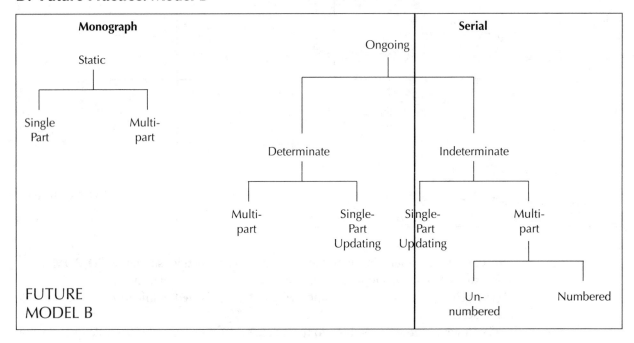

1. *Explanation of Model B*

   With Model B we remove the requirement for successive issuance and move the line farther to the left in order to include indeterminately issued updating publications, such as continuing loose-leafs and databases. In this model, "serial" is defined as:

   A publication that is intended to continue indefinitely.

   Model B divides the bibliographic universe of ongoing publications between those that are determinate and those that are indeterminate. It recognizes that this intention is determined at the level of the work and in addition to the content itself may be the unifying feature for all expressions and manifestations of the work.

2. *The significance of removing the requirement for successive issuance*

   Successive issuance is perhaps the most important characteristic of serials because it has the greatest impact on the cataloging rules. It is also a basic premise for ISSN assignment. However, successive issuance has been a matter of practicality in a world of tangible printed serials. By removing this requirement we are acknowledging that an electronic journal or a database with a single chief source and additive or updated contents is also a serial. The basic function is the same, as is the degree to which it is ongoing; the major difference is the form in which it is issued.

   Perhaps the largest ramification of removing the criteria for successive issues is that we would no longer be able to describe all serials according to the same cataloging conventions. This will be addressed in Part IV.

3. *Advantages and disadvantages of Model B*

Model B has the advantage of being more in keeping with the FRBR model in that it brings together the various physical versions of the same publication under the same category. This would be advantageous for identifying the work, linking records, and multiple versions.

However, a disadvantage is that it imposes a distinction between updating publications that are intended to continue indefinitely and those that are finite in nature. Looseleafs and databases intended to continue indefinitely would be categorized differently from those with a foreseeable end. This distinction is one that is not generally made now and may not be a very useful one. Many loose-leaf publications, which have been arbitrarily called monographs, would now be called serials. For online resources, such as web sites, calling them serials would be less of a recataloging problem because so few have been cataloged.

E. Future Practice: Model C

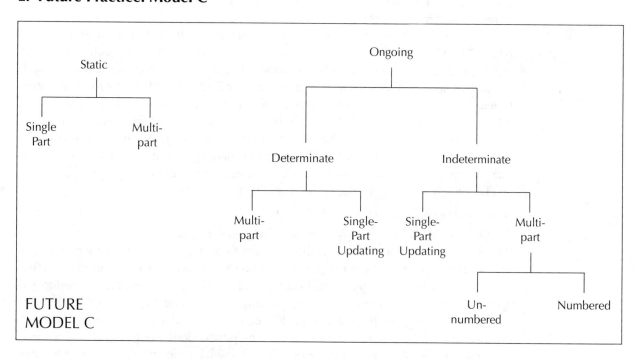

FUTURE
MODEL C

1. *Explanation of Model C*

In Model C we have taken a large leap—back to where we started with the basic model for ongoing publications! In Model C we have not only removed the requirement to be continued indefinitely, but also the terms "monograph" and "serial" as well. With this model we are suggesting a more global and principled approach to the cataloging of ongoing publications, and thus we have also left out the line. This does not suggest that all ongoing publications should be treated as "serials" but that all ongoing publications exhibit a degree of seriality or "ongoingness." And where is the "serial" in this model? One possibility is that "serials" might be the subset of ongoing publications that require serials-type control.

2. *The significance of removing the requirement for indeterminacy*

As noted above, the requirement that a serial be intended to continue indefinitely is the primary distinction between monograph and serial, as currently defined. As we've also acknowledged, making this distinction may be difficult and irrelevant for many online publications. In addition, there are multivolume sets that continue over many years that are best treated serially, and serial-like publications associated with an event that would also benefit from such treatment. The fact that a publication is continuing—that it will need certain aspects of library control, that it has the potential for change, that its coverage is broad and ongoing—is an essential aspect of identifying the work. The fact that the distinction between determinate and indeterminate may not always be clear requires a flexible approach but does not negate the basic purpose of providing this information to our users and organizing our catalogs according to such distinctions. Making a determination between "static" and "ongoing," however, is much easier and more meaningful than "monograph" and "serial" and would no doubt save time.

This is not to say that there will no longer be "serials." But what we think of as serials now might be better described for our users in terms of genres, and for librarians in terms of the need for control.

Interestingly, others seem to be coming to similar conclusions. The latest revision of NISO Z39.71 for holdings statements takes a similarly flexible approach saying "furthermore, a clear-cut distinction between 'serial' and 'non-serial' is difficult to make in the case of such publications as conference proceedings, loose-leaf materials, and electronic publications. Not all libraries treat them the same way. For these reasons, the NISO Standards Committee AL determined that one standard for holdings would be more appropriate than two."[18] Another example is the emerging standard for metadata, called the Dublin Core Record, which does not identify "serials" or "monographs" but does accommodate genres. Using the Dublin Core, one might identify a publication as an electronic journal, web site, or electronic text, for instance.

3. *Advantages and disadvantages of Model C*

By adopting Model C, we would be grouping together a broad category of publications that are ongoing. Various manifestations of serials and updating publications would be kept together and distinctions that are not helpful would not have to be made. The primary advantage of Model C is that it recognizes the similarities and the need for consistency of approach for ongoing publications. For example, we would be acknowledging that a numbered multipart publication has much in common with a numbered journal or monographic series. It does not mean that all ongoing publications would be cataloged identically, but that where there are similarities, the rules will be consistent. A further advantage is its flexibility, and given the rapid changes in publishing, a certain degree of flexibility is essential. Furthermore, it is possible that by categorizing publications broadly in a way that can be universally acknowledged (i.e., that they are ongoing), they can be treated more flexibly at the local level as to their needs for serials control.

If Model C were to be adopted as part of the cataloging code, it might be necessary for national agencies or programs such as CONSER to determine how certain groups of publications would be treated for the sake of consistency and sharing of records. But even CONSER has relaxed control lately by allowing its participants to catalog conference publications as monographs or serials as best fits their needs (LCRI 12.0A, rev. Feb. 1997).

RECOMMENDATION 3: Adopt Model B as a short-term solution. Work towards the adoption of Model C as a longer-term approach.

Part IV. Cataloging Serials and Ongoing Publications

If we redefine *serial* or speak primarily in terms of *ongoing publications,* how do we provide rules for the cataloging of such a broad group of publications? One of the goals of defining ongoing publications is to provide a more principled approach to the cataloging of such publications. In Part IV we will offer principles and examples of their application. Next, we will examine three important aspects of the cataloging of ongoing publications—determining the basis for the description, accommodating changes in the entry, and accommodating changes in the description—how they have traditionally been handled and how this treatment might be changed.

A. Principles

1. *Consider the whole publication rather than a single issue*

   We cannot require that catalogers of ongoing publications be psychics! There is no way to know what changes will occur on later issues. Nevertheless, by keeping in mind that the record represents all current and future issues (until there is a change in entry), catalogers are mindful of the types of information and the level of specificity that are appropriate to the record.

   An example is rule 1.0F1 for transcribing inaccuracies. According to the current rule, in areas where transcription is necessary, inaccuracies are to be transcribed as they appear. Serial catalogers recognized years ago that transcribing an obvious error in the title of one issue in the title statement of the record that is to represent all issues does not make sense, theoretically or practically. Instead, they follow LCRI 12.0F and give the corrected title in the title statement (field 245), while providing the incorrect title in an added entry (field 246).

   Giving what will presumably be the predominant title (i.e., the corrected title) as the title proper is also in keeping with the use of predominance for title changes of multivolume monographs. According to rule 21.2B2, the title is based on the first issue, but a later title which predominates may be substituted for the earliest.

2. *Emphasize identification rather than transcription*

   As evidenced from the above, one of the problems is the concept of *transcription. AACR2*'s emphasis on carefully transcribing from one issue of an ongoing publication is counterproductive to the overall identification of the publication. For online publications, of course, carefully transcribing a chief source which may completely disappear seems particularly futile! If there were more of an emphasis on *identifying* ongoing publications rather than *transcribing* them down to the exact punctuation, we wouldn't end up with meaningless designations, such as: "1992-1993-1994-1995," but could give "1992/1993-1994/1995."[19]

   An example of transcription that doesn't work well for serials is the concept of the statement of responsibility. Unlike books, which have personal authors, most serials are either the product of a commercial publisher or a corporate issuing body. The placement of the body's name on the chief source of the first issue determines whether it is recorded as a statement of responsibility or as the publisher. The placement often changes on subsequent issues, while in reality the body is continuing to serve the same function. The record should reflect the function of the body rather than its position on one issue. In addition, we question the wisdom of displaying so prominently in the catalog record the name of a body which may change or sever affiliation with the publication.

More importantly, if we focus on identifying aspects of the work rather than transcribing from an individual item, we might be able to select more stable titles and reduce the number of records created due to title changes.

While this principle might represent the most substantial change for *AACR2,* it is probably the most critical for our ability to adequately and efficiently describe online publications.

3. *Focus on constants rather than variables*

This principle is particularly important when determining what will constitute the title proper. One of the best rules in *AACR2* chapter 12 is rule 12.1B3, which allows a cataloger to look for other presentations of the title within the serial when in doubt as to whether the corporate body's name should be given as part of the title proper. This rule acknowledges that one source alone, particularly one that is at the whim of designers, may not be sufficient. With LCRI 12.1B3, LC has extended this concept to include any word or phrase found in conjunction with the title, when in doubt. Perhaps we should apply this concept in *all* cases, regardless of whether there is doubt.

B. Determining the Basis for the Description

By focusing on *identification* rather than *transcription* we are not negating the need to *describe.* By *describing* we mean providing important bibliographic details of a publication that aid in its identification and distinction from other publications. While we do not want to be overly detailed in the description of a single issue, neither do we want to say so little about it, in fear that the information might change, that the resulting record is inadequate for the identification and distinction from other publications. This is particularly important in the shared cataloging environment.

There are two aspects to determining the basis for the description. The first is to determine which part to use and the second is to determine which source within that part will be used as the source of the title, and thus the chief source.

1. *Which part to use?*

a. Multipart publications

Both *AACR2* 1.0H2 (for multipart items) and *AACR2* 12.0B1 (for serials) call for the first or earliest available part to be used as the basis for the description. Under the 1967 edition of *AACR,* the latest issue was used for the description of serials, while the earliest was used for the description of multivolume monographs.

Using the first issue rather than the latest is a matter of practicality and stability, since the first issue is always the earliest, whereas what constitutes the latest constantly changes. By basing the description on the first issue, the basic description need not be changed, since information that appears on later issues is handled by notes when considered significant. Interestingly, the concept of "first" issue has become more complicated with the introduction of CD-ROMs where later releases can contain earlier issues that have been newly digitized. Thus, the disc that contains vol. 1, no. 1 may be issued quite some time after the initial disc was first issued.

When using the earliest issue approach, however, the information given in the description can become quickly out of date, which is not conducive to brief record displays in public catalogs. Basing the description on the latest issue is more useful to catalog users because the most recent publishing information and other aspects of the description can be given prominently.

b. Single-part publications

By contrast, Hallam's rule 0B2 for loose-leafs says to use the latest item in hand. For a continuously updated database, this is realistically the only approach that can be applied, since earlier versions of the chief source will have completely disappeared!

Electronic journals, even when displayed in a successive array of volumes and issues, may have a single home page containing the title and publishing information. Such information may or may not appear on the individual issues. Thus, basing the description on the "latest issue" translates to the "latest iteration of the home page" and the concept of "issue" may have to be reevaluated in such cases.

c. Reconsidering description based on the latest issue

If one group of publications that are cataloged as serials will have to be cataloged based on the latest issue, might we want to change the practice for all serials? We could return to the *AACR1* practice of combining successive entry with description based on the latest issue. It could alleviate some of the distinctions between serials cataloged according to latest and successive entry conventions and reduce the number of special rules and instructions needed. Certainly, being able to give the current publisher prominently, rather than in a note, has much appeal.

However, would we want to limit the approach to elements other than the entry? For instance, we probably would not want to change the title proper when a variation occurs that does not constitute a title change. Nor, probably, would we want to change a uniform title that is qualified with a place of publication when the place changes.[20] Making such changes in the entry would create havoc among catalogs and in files where the entry is used apart from the description.

Thus, changing the base of the description to the latest issue may not be the answer if it couldn't be applied to the entire record. Aside from the title, the areas of the description that are most volatile are the statement of responsibility and publishing information. Perhaps a better solution would be to combine such information into one area within the record, as we will discuss below under "Accommodating Changes in the Description."

RECOMMENDATION 4: Retain description based on the earliest issue for publications issued successively; for publications issued in a single updating part, base the description on the latest iteration.

2. *Which source to use as the chief source?*

AACR2 introduced the concepts of "chief" and "prescribed sources of information." The chief source of information is defined as "the source of bibliographic data to be given preference as the source from which a bibliographic description (or portion thereof) is prepared." In actual fact, the chief source is the source from which the title is taken.

For textual monograph and serial publications, the title page is the first choice as chief source. This is an example of how applying a general set of book-based rules to all materials does not work very well. For serials, the emphasis on title page has long been problematic, since many serials (e.g, periodicals, newsletters, and newspapers) rarely or never have a title page. *AACR2* rule 12.0B1 acknowledges this fact and gives a preferred order for choosing "title page substitutes," such as the cover, masthead, or caption. There is also the problem of the insignificant or doubtful title page—the single sheet of paper inserted inside the cover with an official-sounding title that differs from the catchy title on the cover. The problem is that this "title page" tends to come and go and is not terribly reliable.

Providing preferred sources of the title is critical for serials, since the title is most often the main entry. For purposes of consistency and for sharing cataloging records, it is important that catalogers working in a shared environment follow a preferred order when choosing the source of the title.

One problem with preferred sources, however, occurs with CD-ROMs, for which the internal title screen is currently the preferred source. When catalogers cannot readily load the CD and examine the title screen, they resort to using the label on the outside. This particular source requirement seems to be more problematic for ongoing CDs because of the potential for title changes and the inability for check-in staff to catch the changes.

The rules already require that a source of information be specified in all records for computer files, but improvements could be made in the terminology used in these notes. Rather than always citing "title from title screen," it would be more beneficial to define sources within computer files, such as home pages, splash screens, menu screens, etc.

We do not need to be as specific for the other bibliographic attributes, however. Once the title has been selected (and perhaps the edition, when this applies), the cataloger should be free to use any other source in which to "identify" issuing bodies, publishers, and other bibliographic attributes of the publication. Thus, we suggest that the concept of "chief source" be replaced with that of "source of title" for ongoing publications.

RECOMMENDATION 5: For ongoing publications, replace the concept of "chief source" with that of "source of title." Allow greater flexibility in the selection of title within the parameters of the prescribed sources. Define new terminology for sources within online publications.

C. Accommodating Changes in Entry

1. *Methods for handling change*

a. Serials

The three methods for handling title changes that have been employed by various codes are:

i) Earliest entry: With this method, prescribed prior to ALA rules, the title of the earliest piece was retained, with later titles given as notes and added entries. The entry remained the same, though possibly long out of date.

ii) Latest entry: All of the ALA rules called for latest entry, which used the current title (or author) as the entry. Each time the title changed, the old title was shifted to a note and added entry (USMARC field 247) and the new title assumed the role of the title entry (or author/title entry).

iii) Successive entry: Introduced with *AACR1,* successive entry requires a new record each time the title (and/or entry element) changes and the records are linked with notes (USMARC field 78X) to the immediately preceding and succeeding titles. The records for the old title are revised to add the linking note.

While all of these methods require some form of further annotation on catalog cards or MARC records, successive entry has the advantage of requiring only a link, rather than substantial changes to the description and entry elements.

Up to now, our rules have mandated that a single convention be applied to all serials. However, the Library of Congress has for some time been applying a form of earliest entry cataloging to session laws according to LCRI 21.2C, and LC plans to extend this practice to certain rare serials. Is there any reason all three types of conventions might not be applied?

b. Multipart monographs

The *AACR2* rule for multipart monographs calls for a single-record approach. *AACR2* 21.2B2 says to use the title of the first part as the title for the whole monograph, but if a later title predominates, to use that title. This is an example of one of the practical differences in the current cataloging of determinate and indeterminate ongoing publications.

c. Loose-leafs, databases, and other ongoing single-part publications

For loose-leafs, following the Hallam guidelines, the latest title is given as the title proper and changes are noted on the same record. For databases and web sites, for which all earlier titles can totally disappear, giving the latest title (i.e., the title at the time of cataloging) is again the only practical approach, although there are currently no rules to this effect.

d. Reconsidering latest entry

In recent years, with the advent of the MARC record, which is more easily updated than catalog cards, some have called for a return to latest entry for serials in order to reduce the number of records representing the serial and to enhance public access. The primary advantage of latest entry is that all holdings for a serial are kept together and that patrons often think of the serial in terms of one work (rather than as a succession of different works under different titles). Latest entry cataloging has been controversial and not widely accepted, however, because it does not adhere to international standards and is not conducive to use of the ISSN.

However, as we noted above, there is a growing number of publications for which latest entry conventions are the only ones that can be applied. With such conventions being applied for one group of ongoing publications, might we want to consider applying them to all?

If we were starting all over again, we might say yes; however, the implications of this change for existing records are prohibitive. In addition to all of the successive entry records for serials, there are the numerous monographic series analytics that are tied to the succession of series authority records, as well as notes and entries on related bibliographic records, all of which would require revision. Our past experience with use of latest entry records for cooperative cataloging also suggests that this would not be a wise approach for successively issued publications because it requires catalogers to research the bibliographic history of titles they do not own and may result in entries in a library's catalog for titles not held. Libraries that shelve serials by title are faced with the dilemma of shelving the titles differently than they are recorded in the catalog or putting blocks in the stacks directing the user to a different location. A further compelling reason is the deviation from the standards used to assign the ISSN, which is used to facilitate "hooks to holdings," automated check-in, online ordering, and unambiguous identification of each serial title.

RECOMMENDATION 6: Adopt an approach that allows for multiple cataloging conventions for handling title changes in the rules. Following the principle that the method for cataloging should be appropriate to the form of issuance, apply successive entry to changes of entry for successively issued publications and a latest entry approach to changes of entry for updating publications.

2. *Thoughts on title changes*

The problems of title changes will always be with us. While we favor successive entry for successively issued publications, we also hope that the principles given above will aid us in future refinements to the rules. We learned quickly that the "any change in the first five words" prescribed by *AACR2* when it was first issued was not a practical way to approach title changes. Yet we must also curb our innate desire to resist making new records. While multiple records for seemingly insignificant changes do not serve any of us well, neither does the record that is so generalized in order to avoid change that the work it describes cannot be identified.

But improvements can be made. Can we find ways to better handle meaningless changes, such as *Bowling* to *Bowling Magazine* and back to *Bowling* again, while providing adequate access? Can we find a way to reinstate the concept of the "title of short duration" within a cooperative environment, at least when cataloging retrospectively? Must we also consider all titles to be equal? Might we not give more credence to the title of a journal (which is entered under title main entry) than to that of an annual report or conference publication (which is entered under corporate body)? In the latter cases, the corporate or conference headings are the truly significant part of the entry, as evidenced by the frequent arbitrary and capricious changes to the titles. Perhaps we might adopt a method of making successive entries only for changes in the corporate/conference heading while recording all title variations and changes within those records. Or perhaps some form of uniform title might work. We know of a number of libraries that are currently using such an approach in their local catalogs. These are but a few ideas for further exploration following the initial work of this conference.

RECOMMENDATION 7: Modify the rules for title changes to reduce the number of meaningless changes.

3. *Problems of linking multiple versions*

What are the implications of cataloging versions of the same work under multiple sets of conventions? One problem immediately apparent is that of linking records for physical versions of the same work. Maintaining the links on the successive entry records will be difficult because the entry on the latest entry record can change. A possibility would be to omit the title from the link, as CONSER has done for microforms, and just give "Online version" or some such phrase and the record number, from which the user can go directly to the related record. Explaining this in a cataloging code that is divorced from the automated environment and MARC record would, of course, be difficult!

D. Accommodating Changes in the Description

When the description is based on the earliest piece, changes in the description that occur on later issues are recorded in notes. For loose-leafs and updating publications the latest information is recorded in the body of the description and earlier information is given in notes, when it is available.

The need to describe an ongoing publication from one issue is obviously problematic. While we don't want a cluttered record that is difficult to decipher, giving all related information in one place in a different type of display might be very beneficial. For example, a possible change would be to record all changes in place and publisher in the same area of the record using the same or similar tags, e.g., multiple 260 MARC fields,[21] or 260/26x for current and former publishers. Coding all publishing information in the same field might be beneficial for display and retrieval, and users might be more apt to see it. With places and publishers changing at different times, we would need to take an approach similar to that used for series in which a change of publisher, rather than a change of place, would result in a new field.

By taking such an approach, we might also alleviate some of the differences that will result from applying both latest and successive entry conventions to different manifestations of the same work.

> **RECOMMENDATION 8:** For ongoing publications, create rules that focus on *identification* rather than *transcription*. Consider new displays and arrangements of data that might result from and facilitate such a focus and that would keep similar information together in the record.

Part V. Potential Impact of the Concept of Ongoing Publications on *AACR2* and Other Standards

A. *AACR2*   The concept of "ongoing publication" and the three-dimensional approach to publications could be implemented in the cataloging code in three ways: (1) by developing a conceptual chapter as the initial chapter in the code; (2) by broadening the rules for serials to cover differing types of ongoing publications; and (3) by integrating principles related to ongoing publications in all chapters.

1. *The conceptual chapter*

We envision a conceptual chapter that would incorporate the principles agreed to at this conference. This chapter would give the cataloger an idea of what he or she is trying to accomplish and why. It would include the concepts based on the FRBR model that would govern the creation of new records based on differences in the content. It might also incorporate alternatives to cataloging and when they are appropriate. The conceptual chapter would provide a basis for future rule revision and enhancement, particularly as new forms of materials evolve.

A separate section explaining ongoing publications would discuss the basic principles behind the rules for the basis of description and accommodation of change in ongoing publications. It would provide guidance on what constitutes an ongoing publication and how the description of that work may differ from static publications. The concepts of identification rather than transcription, focusing on constants, and the idea of describing the work would all be included. It would also discuss how the terms "monograph" and "serial" apply within the framework of static and ongoing publications and discuss aspects of control, access, and cataloging efficiencies as appropriate.

Convenience and judgment must also be incorporated in some way. The chapter should express the idea that catalogers need to use the rules as a tool in order to best describe materials so as to meet the needs of their users and use judgment in doing so. We should acknowledge the need to deviate from time to time. The first edition of *AACR,* in setting out its "principles of descriptive cataloging," noted that "by their use it is possible for the cataloger, when faced with problems not specifically provided for, to solve them in the spirit and intent of the rules."[22] The words "spirit" and "intent" are particularly meaningful here.

The chapter should also acknowledge that the environment in which most catalogers are working is shared. Contributing to and using records from shared databases has become the norm in most of the Anglo-American world, at least, and in many other countries as well.

And lastly, this chapter should address the purpose and functions of the bibliographic record in the world of automated library systems.

RECOMMENDATION 9: Create a conceptual chapter that will be the first chapter in a new or revised code.

2. *The individual chapters*

Aside from the conceptual chapter, deciding how best to arrange the individual chapters is problematic. If we agree that content should be the starting point, we would need separate chapters for text, music, cartographic data, and so forth. But textual and cartographic data can be issued in print, microform, and electronically, and we wouldn't want to repeat the rules for each carrier under each of the content-based chapters. Furthermore, not all publications consist of a single mode of expression. Art books rarely have been single mode, and in the online environment we are likely to see wide blending of moving image, text, and sound.

If we are going to take a three-dimensional approach, as we have advocated, we will need chapters in three categories: (1) the content and its expression in the record, e.g., authors, title, bibliographic relationships, nature of contents note, etc.; (2) the physical carrier and its expression in the record, e.g., publishing data, physical description, system requirements note, etc.; and (3) the publication status (static or ongoing) and the type of control (monograph or serial) and how the status and treatment is expressed in the record in terms of specific data elements and in the level of specificity given. This type of code would integrate description and access as appropriate.

The ideal format for such a code would be an automated desktop version in which a cataloger could specify the specific attributes of the publication to be cataloged and the programmed code would generate a customized list of rules! While this may initially seem far-fetched, it is certainly possible; and though complex to produce, it would make the process of cataloging much easier, particularly for catalogers who will be faced with a broad spectrum of publications. Such a code would also have the advantage of being easily updatable, a must for any new version!

A far more conservative and less exciting approach would be to move the current serials chapter to the front, following the general and books chapters, and make the serials chapter less specific to print. An additional chapter would also be needed to accommodate single-part updating publications.

RECOMMENDATION 10: Explore new ways of arranging the rules that will facilitate a three-dimensional approach to cataloging. Incorporate rules for single-part updating publications into the code.

B. MARC   In view of the automated environment in which we do our cataloging, we must explore the relationship of the cataloging rules and the current MARC format.

The implementation of format integration gave us the ability to code all attributes of a publication, regardless of its mode of expression. Thus, an open entry monograph and a serial may contain the same variable fields and look essentially the same at one level. But format integration was unsuccessful in eliminating the concept of a primary format and bibliographic level. The cataloger must code the leader/07 (bibliographic level) as monograph, serial, collection, monographic analytic, or serial analytic. While one can add an 006 fixed-length field for aspects of seriality on a monograph record, the fact remains that a primary bibliographic level is required.

If we redefine "serial" as described in Model B, we will be able to collocate print serials and their electronic equivalents, facilitating one-record and "multiple versions" approaches. The coding for latest entry conventions is already present in the serials 008 and 006 fixed-length fields, accommodating the need to differentiate the cataloging conventions used for updating publications and successively issued serials.

In reality, any change in the coding of the bibliographic level has far-reaching effects. The Type of Record (leader/06) and Bibliographic Level (leader/07) are deeply imbedded in our systems. They are used for identifying duplicate records, mapping records to different files, limiting/filtering searches, creating serial union lists, and underpinning serials control systems. If redefining the concept of *serial* requires the recoding of existing records, the effects on record processing and the cost of conversion must be weighed.

The main problems are with the category of updating publications. While the number of records for web sites, databases, and online systems is small (and coding inconsistent), there are many more records for loose-leaf publications. Loose-leafs have been somewhat arbitrarily coded as monographs since they didn't meet the *AACR2* definition of serial. Recoding them as serial publications could be time consuming and without obvious rewards. An exception could be made to continue coding printed updating publications as monographs while cataloging online updating publications as serials. Such a treatment separates them from their online versions, as loose-leafs often become databases on the Internet. This is a matter for further discussion among members of the law library community (where loose-leafs are ubiquitous), MARC experts, and system designers.

If we adopt the broader approach in Model C, we would need to make more substantial changes to MARC, such as changing the codes in the bibliographic level (leader/07) to "static" and "ongoing," redefining the serial type code (008/21) to ongoing type and adding values for other types of ongoing publications. We might also want to reconsider adding "serials control" to leader/08, the type of control code now used only for archival materials. In early drafts for this byte, serials control was included and this could provide a useful mechanism for local application to indicate whether an ongoing publication would require serials control.

C. International Standard Serial Number (ISSN)

The ISSN is extremely important to the identification and control of serial publications and is being used in many ways. In addition to its use for check-in, and the "hooks-to-holdings" feature noted above, the ISSN is being considered as an important part of a uniform resource name (URN) that would provide stable access to remotely issued publications.

The ideas expressed in this paper would in some ways bring *AACR2* closer to ISSN and in some ways cause a divergence. One of the biggest problems would be the reintroduction of latest entry for some serial and ongoing publications. To begin with, the ISSN Network would need to decide whether or not to enlarge its scope to include more ongoing publications. Another challenge would be whether and how to apply latest entry principles to those ongoing publications for which it is suggested in this paper, since a basic principle of ISSN is one ISSN per key title. On the one hand, keeping the same ISSN despite title changes for titles cataloged on one record has some appeal; on the other hand, it would create two sets of rules for ISSN assignments. But if the ISSN principles remained the same and separate ISSN numbers and their corresponding records were required in all cases, serious problems might result for the increasing number of countries which are using a single *AACR* record to serve both as the catalog record for their national bibliography and as their national ISSN records. Thus, it is essential that the ISSN International Centre and JSC work closely together in order to assure such compatibility.

D. International Standard Bibliographic Description (ISBD)

We recognize that our vision for a new code is not in keeping with the structure of ISBD, and we wonder how the multilevel entity-attribute-based FRBR model will impact future revisions of these standards. However, we also recognize that our current code is based on the various ISBD standards and the problems inherent in it stem from the problems in the ISBD. In order to integrate the concept of ongoing publications into *AACR2,* we must also be willing to revise the structure of the ISBDs. Fortunately, this process has already begun!

When revision began on the ISBD for computer files, now to be called "electronic resources"—*ISBD(ER)*—the early drafts stated that the scope of the ISBD covered only monographic computer files. After protest from serialists, the scope was reconsidered and the resulting document now covers both serials and monographs. This same process needs to occur for all materials.

However, this is only one aspect of the problem. For if we decide that content should be the beginning point rather than carrier, the scope of *ISBD(ER)* would be pared down to only those items that are nontextual.

Another basic problem is the *ISBD(G)*, the basis for *AACR2* chapter 1, which we have stated is too book-based. We recognize that this is not an easy issue. All of the needs and ramifications must be carefully examined. But at the very least, the types of changes that have integrated seriality into the *ISBD(ER)* chapter should be continued.

We understand that *ISBD(S)* is scheduled to be revised and hope that the ideas expressed at this conference will be taken under consideration.

Conclusion

We see now that seriality is not a class or format, but a fundamental dimension of the work. This ongoing dimension must be reflected in the cataloging code through a shift in emphasis from the detail of one item "frozen in time" to the identification of the publication or work as a whole. The approach of the FRBR study, conceptualizing the catalog record as a table of attributes and values, lays the groundwork for such an alternative method of bibliographic control.

New forms of library materials, new types of catalogs, and new user expectations do not change our ultimate goals of providing access, facilitating control, and sharing the workload in a cost-effective manner. The imprecision of today's automated Internet search engines and the proliferation of web sites that merely point among themselves remind us of the real strengths of our cataloging infrastructure. Our commitment to standards, the compatibility of our records, and our achievements with cooperation are the keys to our success. Authority control and standardized formatting assure effective data retrieval, minimize redundancy, and facilitate portability and exchange of bibliographic information. The specifics of terminology and cataloging conventions are merely the tools we use to achieve our goals.

We appreciate the opportunity afforded by this conference to work with our colleagues to design new means to achieve those goals, reshaping the cataloging rules to meet new challenges while remaining faithful to the spirit and intent of our profession.

Summary of Recommendations

RECOMMENDATION 1: Adopt a three-dimensional approach to the cataloging rules.

RECOMMENDATION 2: Incorporate the concept of the "ongoing publication" into the cataloging code.

RECOMMENDATION 3: Adopt Model B as a short-term solution. Work towards the adoption of Model C as a longer-term approach.

RECOMMENDATION 4: Retain description based on the earliest issue for publications issued successively; for publications issued in a single updating part, base the description on the latest iteration.

RECOMMENDATION 5: For ongoing publications, replace the concept of "chief source" with that of "source of title." Allow greater flexibility for the selection of title within the parameters of the prescribed sources. Define new terminology for sources within online publications.

RECOMMENDATION 6: Adopt an approach that allows for multiple cataloging conventions for handling title changes in the rules. Following the principle that the method for cataloging should be appropriate to the form of issuance, apply successive entry to changes of entry for successively issued publications and a latest entry approach to changes of entry for updating publications.

RECOMMENDATION 7: Modify the rules for title changes to reduce the number of meaningless title changes.

RECOMMENDATION 8: For ongoing publications, create rules that focus on *identification* rather than *transcription.* Consider new displays and arrangements of data that might result from and facilitate such a focus and that would keep similar information together in the record.

RECOMMENDATION 9: Create a conceptual chapter that would be the first chapter in a new or revised code.

RECOMMENDATION 10: Explore ways in which to arrange rules to facilitate a three-dimensional approach.

Short-Term Implementation Plan

While we would like to see all of the recommendations acted upon, we recognize that some are more critical and/or easily achievable than others. A number of the recommendations would require changes not only to *AACR,* but also to the MARC formats, utilities, and local systems. Recognizing the difficult task that awaits the Joint Steering Committee following the conference, we have developed a short-term implementation plan that could precede the development of a new code or a major revision of the existing code. The recommendations below are those that we feel are most critical for the successful cataloging of serial publications.

1. Redefine serial to be "a publication in any medium intended to continue indefinitely." [Model B].
2. Produce a new chapter for single-part updating publications, some of which will be serials and others monographs.

   Begin with the Hallam work and develop additional rules as needed for databases and other types of electronic publications. This should be done as soon as possible.
3. Define new sources of information and develop new concepts that apply to remotely accessible publications.
4. Reexamine the definition of title change in 21.2A with a view to reducing the number of serial records.

   Begin by comparing the current rule with the ISSN definition of a title change to see where improvements can be made. Further suggestions made by the CONSER AACR Review Task Force included not considering as a title change the addition, deletion, or change in:

- a word denoting frequency or type of publication, the name of the issuing body appearing at the beginning of the title,
- or the name of the recipient of a report.

5. Add a rule to chapter 21 to cover changes of entry for single-part updating publications.

Notes

1. We are using the term "publication" in a broad sense to refer to any catalogable item.

2. IFLA Study Group on the Functional Requirements for Bibliographic Records, *Functional Requirements for Bibliographic Records: Draft Report for World-Wide Review* (Frankfurt am Main: Deutsche Bibliothek, 1996).

3. A collection of logically interrelated data stored together in one or more computerized fields, usually created and managed by a database management system. A database usually has a single chief source with updated contents searchable by author, title, and subject.

4. We are using this to refer to the online phenomenon of a collecting device for publications, information, multimedia, and links to other sites. An example would be the Library of Congress web site.

5. Tom Delsey, "Standards for Descriptive Cataloging: Two Perspectives on the Past Twenty Years," in *The Conceptual Foundations of Descriptive Cataloging,* ed. Elaine Svenonius (San Diego: Academic Press, 1989), 59.

6. Some of these are numbered monographic series.

7. Adele Hallam, *Cataloging Rules for the Description of Looseleaf Publications,* 2nd ed. (Washington, D.C.: Office of Descriptive Cataloging, Library of Congress, 1989), 2.

8. A recent development is that, rather than submitting individual issues for copyright, publishers such as MIT Press are submitting articles.

9. Ann Okerson, *Directory of Electronic Journals, Newsletters, and Academic Discussion Lists,* 3rd ed. (Washington, D.C.: Association of Research Libraries, 1993), i-ii.

10. Erik Jul, "Revisiting Seriality and Periodicity," *Serials Review* 22, no. 1 (spring 1996): 71.

11. Gregory Wool, "Bibliographical Metadata; or, We Need a Client-Server Cataloging Code!" (paper presented at the conference "Finding Common Ground: Creating the Library of the Future without Diminishing the Library of the Past," Cambridge, Mass., March 1996).

12. Barbara B. Tillett, "Future Cataloging Rules and Cataloging Records," in *Origins, Content, and Future of AACR2 Revised,* ed. Richard P. Smiraglia (Chicago: American Library Association, 1992), 112.

13. For a detailed history of the multiple versions controversy see: Crystal Graham, "Microform Reproductions and Multiple Versions: U.S. Cataloging Policy and Proposed Changes," *Serials Librarian* 22, no. 1/2 (1993): 213-34.

14. Walt Crawford and Michael Gorman, *Future Libraries: Dreams, Madness, and Reality* (Chicago: American Library Association, 1995), 66.

15. Ed Jones, "Serials in the Realm of the Remotely-Accessible: An Exploration," *Serials Review* 22, no. 1 (spring 1996): 77.

16. A third category is that of the collection which doesn't directly relate to the discussion and therefore has been omitted.

17. While preparing this paper, serious consideration was given to suggesting that a new third category of single-part updating works be created. However, while such works do require special rules, there is little value to defining them separately in MARC. Thus, we prefer to think of them as a subset of serial or monograph.

18. Draft standard Z39.71, supplied by co-chair Martha Hruska.

19. The National Library of Canada has not followed *AACR2* on this aspect of recording the description but has continued the pre-*AACR2* practice, as shown by the preferred designation.

20. The types of uniform titles we are referring to were not created under *AACR* rules, so this was not a problem.

21. This would be analogous to the multiple 643 fields for publication information in series authority records.

22. *Anglo-American Cataloging Rules,* prepared by the American Library Association, the Library of Congress, the Library Association, and the Canadian Library Association, North American Text (Chicago: American Library Association, 1967), 189.

Acknowledgments

The authors wish to thank a number of people who contributed their thoughts, ideas, and experience. We first want to recognize the contributions of the CONSER AACR Review Task Force, which began meeting several years ago to review the changes we might like to see made. Once the invitation to participate in the International Conference was extended to Hirons and Graham, task force members met to contribute ideas for both the written paper and oral presentation and many of their ideas are reflected in this paper. Task force members are: Sara Shatford Layne (UCLA), chair, Jo Lynne Byrd (formerly MIT), Karen Hsu (NYPL), Kristin Lindlan (University of Washington), Judy Knop (American Theological Library Association), Judy Kuhagen (LC), Jeffrey Myers-Hayer (LC), and John Riemer (University of Georgia). Thanks also to Maureen Landry and Les Hawkins at LC for participating in the discussions and sharing their expertise.

We particularly want to thank two very special contributors who generously shared their thoughts and ideas through written contributions and numerous impromptu discussions. Regina Reynolds (LC) was instrumental in developing the model for ongoing publications and the concepts behind it. She also shared her perspective on ISSN and how the changes proposed in the paper would impact that standard. Ed Jones, former CONSER cataloger at Harvard and more recently a professor at Rosary College, helped clarify some of the concepts regarding the nature of serial publications and contributed to the discussion on successive and latest entry. We are greatly indebted to the contributions of both Regina and Ed, to the Task Force, and to the many serial catalogers who have shared their thoughts and ideas with us.

DISCUSSION

The Hirons/Graham paper received general approval not only from conference participants but also from the conference discussion list participants.

Terminology was the first topic discussed at the end of Hirons' presentation: the contradictory nature of the two words found in the term "uniform title," the problems in applying FRBR terminology to serials, and the need for *AACR2R* terms to be clearly defined either in the text or by references in the text.

In reply to a question about the use of a uniform work heading to encompass two different editions or versions of a work, one of which is, and one of which is not, a serial, the authors stated that it would cause difficulties in properly expressing holdings in our present systems.

The authors noted the duplication of effort caused by the use of both a key title and a uniform title. The use of the authoritative form for a corporate body when needed to qualify a uniform title not only distinguishes but also identifies, and provides more consistency in a shared database. On the other hand, a key title does not function as well because of its association with the ISSN and the policy of the assignment of a new ISSN when a title changes.

One participant was concerned that the authors' recommendation to move away from the variable to the constant and from transcription to identification would create problems for scholars who cite exactly from the page or screen that they see. In particular, the changing nature of title information in Internet resources appears an insoluble problem at the moment. Another participant stated that transcription is the original evidence we use to make decisions about responsibility, editions, etc., and it would be a shame to lose that evidence. The authors assured the audience that they do not oppose transcription, that they want to preserve title changes. However, there are many places where flexibility is needed to allow more judgment.

In response to a question the authors affirmed that they are only advocating latest entry cataloguing for cumulative serials as opposed to sequential serials irrespective of medium. Approval was expressed for the distinction made between cumulative serials and sequential serials; *AACR2* could easily accommodate this idea.

Hirons mentioned a recent web problem: the unbundling of articles, i.e., articles mounted on the web before an issue of a journal has been assembled. A database of such articles would now be catalogued as monographs because it is not issued in successive parts. Rules should be developed so that periodical articles would be catalogued as serials, regardless of the form in which they are issued.

8 ◆ Access Points for Works

RONALD HAGLER

Terminology and a Little History

The working title assigned to me for this paper incorporated the traditional terms "main entry" and "corporate entry." "Entry" and "main entry" persist in librarians' jargon, embedded as they are in the English-language cataloguing codes of this century including *AACR2R*. The core meaning of "entry" has always been "a single bibliographic description of a catalogued item" (my own jargon-freed version). The multiple-entry unit-record card file, a knowledge of which is assumed in the terminology of the cataloguing codes of the twentieth century, could contain more than one such description per item. Each of them, being self-sufficient, must contain an indication of its own particular file location or, in the terminology of the codes, a "heading."

Each of the several records for the same item in a unit-record manual catalogue is identical except that a heading is brought as needed into filing position. Increasingly, even processing information once kept only in a cataloguing or acquisitions department appeared in the public record since its routine reproduction on unit cards was easier than its selected suppression. Other catalogue formats became increasingly rare through the century because of the inefficiency of making the various records for the same item different from one another in fullness and/or arrangement of data.

In any manual catalogue, to locate a record is automatically to see all of it. No additional term being needed to distinguish the whole record from the indication of its file location, the meaning of "entry" merged with that of "heading," making them synonymous in much cataloguers' and reference librarians' shorthand. "Look for the entry *Harvard Studies in Economics*" means both "examine the description of this item" and "search for it under H." The locational meaning of "entry" took on a specialized aspect when subsumed into the context of "main" entry and applied to the item being catalogued rather than only to its catalogue description. Thus the following phraseology, unsanctioned by any cataloguing code, is still common: "The entry for this book is Smith, John" or "The entry is the title, *Five Romantic Plays*."

214

A logical record, the complete set of data related to one catalogued item, is the enlarged and automated successor to the full manual unit record whose creation is the purpose of the cataloguing codes. With its MARC content designators, local holdings, locations, and even its linkage to acquisitions and circulation data, etc., it is certainly an entry—but who ever causes it to be displayed as such except a cataloguer in the process of creating or revising it? What the end-user sees is only a selection of its data elements assembled from many different files. Its ephemeral display on a monitor screen thus differs according to the stage of the retrieval process or the direction of any programmer, now often including the searcher who is given the opportunity to customize the interface. What can "entry" mean in the context of an OPAC?

OPAC technology also divorced the act of searching from that of displaying data. In recognition of this, the term "access point" appeared in *AACR2* twenty years ago to emphasize that not only the elements once called "headings" but also other data elements, codes, and single words not traditionally regulated by the codes could be search keys. Invoking one of these (or now more than one in Boolean combination) begins the process of assembling, from among various files, elements of particular logical records selected and assembled for display as tailored to the particular request. At an OPAC, neither searching nor viewing is as tied to the application of a cataloguing code as they are in every manual system.

The term "main entry" raises yet more complex issues, the focus of most of this paper. A century separates the OPAC from Charles Jewett's proposal to distribute copies of cards from a central production agency as a means of reducing local cataloguing costs. During this time, the term acquired layers of meaning beyond the linguistically obvious. When much of the significance of this term for the manual catalogue was rendered irrelevant in the OPAC, the core of practical significance it retains is now too often misunderstood or has been thrown out with the bathwater.

"Corporate entry," the other term I was originally asked to address in this paper, is not used in a cataloguing code and never conveyed any meaning except by allusion in the context of the terms introduced above. This term is shorthand for a principle of authorship gradually developed and elaborated from 1852 (Jewett originated it, too) to the 1970s, then changed radically by *AACR2* into a pragmatic response to a limited problem. It can be no surprise that in its continued use, this term is now even more misunderstood than the others.

When the original JSC wrote *AACR2* in 1974-77, its members knew and considered many consequences of automation. Yet in those years, the practical end of that automation in the vast majority of libraries was only to make more efficient the production of familiar unit cards to file into their existing manual catalogues. We are constantly reminded that there are still many libraries in which this is what automation means in 1998. However familiar cataloguers were with the information-retrieval capabilities of a database management system (DBMS) by the mid-1970s, the interactive catalogue was still a relative novelty to end-users. For better or for worse, the authors of both *AACR2* and *AACR2R* a decade later chose not to cut users of the manual catalogue entirely adrift. JSC's preparation for the foreseeable stages of automation was a clearer focus on defining the separate elements of the *content* of an ideal bibliographic record than on the features an OPAC was bound to change, namely the display of these elements to a user and the then nontraditional potential search keys and techniques.

JSC empathized with cataloguing department administrators but did not bow to their main concern, the cost of any change which would involve revised input of existing records. It sympathized with cataloguers who, even if they welcomed changes in practice and cheerfully learned some new vocabulary, saw no pressing need to abandon all the jargon born in the manual context. Could old terms not be understood in a new context? However, transferring the above terms of the manual catalogue into the context of the OPAC inevitably changed their meanings and confused the issues to which they were once applied. I now think it would have been better had *AACR2* (or at least the 1988 revision) abandoned these troublesome terms in favour of a slate of different ones as needed in the automated context to which the code was increasingly addressed. The best I can do is to avoid these terms in my following discussion, except for the section directly concerning "main entry."

The Document versus the Work

Others at this conference are attempting to define *work* and *document* in this evolving era of digitization. Whatever it has meant, the physical document has been the raison d'être for the bibliographic record throughout cataloguing history. Whether or not it should be so in the future, identifying and describing a document still takes precedence over identifying any work(s) it contains whenever pragmatic considerations (many of them based on the practicalities of the manual catalogue) preclude a consistent and clear separation of the two entities. The limited authorization in 1.1G to create more than one work-based description for a document has fallen into disfavour, but we remain ambiguous in describing the document/ work relationship.

AACR2, divided into two parts, distinguishes the document from the work more explicitly than any previous cataloguing code. Descriptive elements for the bibliographic record are transcribed according to part I from the "natural language" either of the document itself or of the cataloguer, permitting their objective comparison with a copy of the document or with any other description of it. Conversely, the retrievable (access) elements formulated according to part II are intended to identify a work, not necessarily any document embodying it (see 20.1). They are made subject to vocabulary control precisely to separate them from the natural language of the document as necessary to accomplish their purpose.

Every controlled-vocabulary access point has a basis in natural language. Its form has been standardized so that the records for various manifestations of a work can be found together at a predictable file location in a search of the "browse" type (the only type available in the manual catalogue, where random-access "finding" is not possible). In the manual catalogue since Cutter (to whom strict vocabulary control can be traced), very few document-related natural-language data elements were made accessible. In view of limited searching potential, retrieving manifestations of a work was given priority over finding an individual document. As discussed in more detail below, access at an OPAC mingles natural-language and controlled-vocabulary searching. The transparency of this to the average end-user is but another reason for much current confusion regarding document and work.

Titling straddles the venues of work and document, a fact underlying much of the perceived problem which occasioned JSC's request for this paper. A natural-language title (title proper) can be counted upon to identify *only* the document bearing it. That this is just as valid a catalogue function as identifying a work does not mean the two should be confused as representing the same function. The reliability of a title proper *also* to identify a work is the contentious issue. This is not a hair-splitting distinction, yet alas, even librarians sometimes fail to realize its implications. When nonlibrarian programmers and systems designers are not adequately informed of the reason for the distinction, they naturally respond that the distinction is irrelevant because all forms of titling can be made accessible on the same basis. To the cataloguer, however, distinguishing between the natural-language title of a document (a "title proper") and the controlled-vocabulary title of a work (a "uniform title") is the very basis of bibliographic control over the work, as distinguished from that over the *document;* but it is only the basis: more is needed.

Consistently for centuries in cataloguing and all other formal methods of citation or reference in Western civilization, a title of any kind (proper or uniform) is not used in isolation to identify a work. A person is identified by his or her surname *followed by* given names and perhaps dates and other elements in separate subfields. A corporate body is identified by its name and perhaps one or more other elements such as the name of a higher body. The type of corporate body defined as a "conference" is *always* identified using a number of separately subfielded data elements. It should not be a surprise that it may take two data elements to identify a *work:* a juxtaposition of a titling element (a uniform title, not necessarily a title proper) *and* the name of its author (or one of them) if one is available. Furthermore, the latter of these two elements is traditionally considered the more important and takes precedence in any filing/searching sequence. Problems of multiple or unidentifiable authorship, association with a corporate body, and/or of multiple titling complicate this simple principle and gave rise to complex cataloguing rules. Should this have caused the whole principled structure to collapse, as it seems to have in practice?

Document versus Work in the Context of "Main entry"

I use "entry" and "heading" as *AACR2* does in this section, an analysis of *AACR2* practice unabashedly intended to defend that practice. Vocabulary-controlled work-identification is related, but *not* identical, to applying an access point according to *AACR2* chapter 21 to a main entry. *Every* "entry under the heading for . . . ," whether "main" or "added," provides access to a work. The "main" entry relates specifically to a document. It identifies the work which according to chapter 21 either constitutes that particular document as a whole or is the most prominent work within the document. An "added" entry may identify (1) a different work within or related to the document or (2) the same work as the "main entry," but in an alternative manner.

To illustrate the latter case, Smith and Jones wrote *College Chemistry.* Provided the published filing rules are observed, "Smith . . . College Chemistry" is the file location of the main entry heading and "Jones . . . College Chemistry" is the file location of the added entry. The former is called "main" because it guarantees standardization in identifying *both* the document *and* the work (or primary work) it embodies in a single-entry listing and to facilitate linking document-records.

The prescribed heading for either the main or an added entry names only one person or body (if any), not two or more, as is permissible in a citation according to *The Chicago Manual of Style,* Turabian, etc. The name of only *one* person or body is linked for filing (consistently with the theory and under current filing rules) with a title (if relevant, a uniform title) to identify that work and collocate its various manifestations when browsing a file. Work-identification as such is not the issue in 0.5, only document-identification. The rule itself implies the distinction between these in prescribing the need for the former but the optionality of a traditional aspect of the latter.

The work identified in a document's main entry heading is not necessarily the *only* work contained in, or related to, that document. An anthology, collection, edited compilation, conference proceedings, serial, or similar document (in ISBD terms, a "host item") contains more than one work, each of them a "component part" (or, to emphasize its nature as a separate piece of writing, a "component work"). The host item as a whole may be treated as a work in its own right but access points relevant to it, such as its compiler's name or collective title, may have little obvious connection with any of its component works. The Paris Principles and *AACR2* logically conclude that this kind of work, not being by one person or group, is primarily identified not by an author but by a title (or uniform title) alone.

That *Elizabethan Plays* edited by Matthew Crooks contains Ben Jonson's *Volpone* is not self-evident from any data elements pertinent to the document as a whole. Under such circumstances, cataloguing codes, including *AACR,* provide more than one technique for describing and/or providing access to component works. Techniques to provide access only are treated in *AACR2* chapter 21 (notably at 21.7), where the record for a host item sometimes must, sometimes may, be displayed at the access point(s) for some or all of its component works. This is what is meant by "added entry [record for the host item] [to be displayed] under the heading for [the component work]." The universal work-identifier is prescribed for this purpose. It is described both in the terminology "name-title" (when a name is available) and in the general rule for these access points, 21.30G, where the fact that the title is to be a uniform title if relevant is emphasized.

Techniques to provide a description specific to the component work are gathered into *AACR2* chapter 13. These are (1) brief mention in a contents note within the full description of the host item, (2) a separate full "analytical entry" for the component work, within which the host item is briefly mentioned, and (3) a multilevel description, containing a full description of both host and part. Products of the A&I services are routinely based on work-identification of component works rather than on document-identification of host items; each service uses its own descriptive format. In all these cases, however, when an access point is provided for the component part, it consists of the same two elements traditional for any work-identification: a personal or corporate name as relevant plus a title. In *AACR* practice, both are vocabulary-controlled. In A&I practice, the personal/corporate name is sometimes vocabulary-controlled; the title almost never.

No matter how "work," "expression," and "manifestation" are ultimately defined for cataloguing purposes, the cataloguing codes of this century interrelate these for retrieval using "added-entry" name-title headings for expressions and manifestations which are distinct enough from that in the catalogued document to warrant different work-identifications (cf. 21.10-18 *passim* and 21.28; 21.30G is always relevant in determining the form of the required heading).

Subject headings have not been the direct concern of Anglo-American cataloguing codes since Cutter's. However, all these codes have been accepted as the determinants of the form of controlled-vocabulary subject headings for persons, corporate bodies, places, and works. The greatest impact, albeit indirect, of 21.30G is to govern the form of a subject heading for a work.

AACR and the Limitations of the Independent Manual File

Each record (entry) in a manual file is an indivisible combination of an access point with at least some descriptive elements. Economic, space, and portability limitations, particularly of large, internationally significant manual bibliographic files, often precluded multiple access points per document. When a document could be represented in only one file location, not only that location but also the internal filing arrangement of the data elements had to be predictable and meaningful, the latter almost invariably meaning work-related. Contrary to the assumption of many, the ill-named "main entry heading" (a term not common in the codes themselves and used in *AACR2R* only in 13.4 and 13.5) is not in principle a single data element, the name of an author, but the *two*-element work-identifier discussed above: an author's name (provided there is one available) in controlled-vocabulary form, along with a title, also in controlled-vocabulary form (that is, a uniform title where relevant).

Catalogue filing rules, although published separately from the codes after Cutter's, remain linked with them. Both ensure that the work-identifying combination is kept together in subfiling under any additional access point, whether "added" or "subject." *AACR2R* still bears vestiges of its origin in the era not only of the manual but of the dictionary catalogue in taking these filing considerations for granted. *AACR2* did not significantly breach either technical or economic limitations of a manual catalogue. Whenever the issue is access rather than description, it concentrates on access to the *work* and thus remains largely silent on access to the many natural-language descriptive elements, whether singly or in combination, whose inclusion in the record it prescribes (for example, date of publication or distribution, physical format, status as a government publication). The date of a work (not of a document), surely one of its significant identifying elements, appears in *AACR* only in a possible note and as a rare, if potential, part of a uniform title in a late subfiling position. This datum, descriptive of the work rather than of the document, is intended to be sought generally in reference sources rather than in the catalogue.

Consistent work-identification is the basis of chapters 21, 25, and 26 of *AACR2*. It was a cop-out that application of chapter 25 is "optional." The rules can only accomplish consistent work-identification and expression/manifestation-relating if the options are adopted. The option exists because in manual catalogues in many smaller libraries, it made more sense to apply uniform titles selectively rather than across the board, where many would seem redundant and potentially confusing. Now that, at an OPAC, record content is separated from its display, and as we move toward a world of multiple catalogues searched via the Internet using the potential for transparent merging with the Z39.50 protocol, optionality is recognized as less and less desirable.

The Code and the OPAC: Deconstructing the Bibliographic Record

Programmers are now largely freed from practical limitation in programming cost or processing time as they seek innovative ways to manipulate and display the data in a bibliographic file. Reference librarians and end-users now have greater influence than a cataloguing code in defining what characteristics are put into effect in these processes (the latter by their ability to customize output at many OPACs). The commercialization of competing processing systems ensures that search commands and display style are now far from uniform among them. Many desirable retrieval features impossible in any manual system are commonplace at an OPAC. However, no searcher "sees" the contents of an interactive catalogue in the way anyone could instantly grasp much of the scope and content of a manual one. The flexibility offered by a single system and the differences among various systems the same user might encounter can be confusing. It takes more training, and advance planning of each search, to successfully use an OPAC than a manual catalogue. Is the more casual user too often turning away unsatisfied?

As at a manual catalogue, the searcher at an OPAC can access any traditional code-required access point in phrase-indexed mode (as a whole access point locatable in a browse at its first word). Unlike at the manual catalogue, the OPAC searcher can also find a single word or code from *within* a phrase-indexed access point controlled by *AACR* or from natural language ("free text") in the descriptive portion of the record. An OPAC *permits* ad hoc Boolean collocation of an author's name and a uniform title (the work-identifying "main entry"), but that begs the question of why it does not provide that collocation routinely as a single easily searchable element, as was the case in the manual catalogue envisaged by all the cataloguing codes and filing rules of this century.

The need for easy work identification has not suddenly vanished. There would be no issue if every end-user automatically considered the difference between a work and a publication or document, but this is not a distinction of which most nonlibrarians are conscious. The code's rules for an "entry" prescribe units of bibliographic data as they should be displayed to the searcher. A record "hangs together" best when presented this way, whether on a card or on a monitor screen. Considerable latitude is provided in 1.0D as to what data elements comprise an acceptable entry but, like intelligible filing, that rule is often ignored in current interface software. Perhaps it is a hankering for the individualism of the past, no longer tolerated in cooperative record creation, which makes librarians so prone to opt for idiosyncratic variation in their OPAC record displays, even beyond the dictates of the vendor!

The balance between controlled-vocabulary and natural-language searching done in practice at an OPAC is not as skewed in favour of the latter as one might think. The MARC format regulates the form of far more controlled-vocabulary search keys than does *AACR,* including the codes prescribed in dozens of 0XX (and some other) fields, actually or potentially used for direct searching or for limiting a search on other keys. These coded data elements now form an integral part of a bibliographic record. Whether *AACR* should regulate them, or at least acknowledge their existence in some detail, must be explored by JSC with other interested groups.

File Sequence and Work Identification

Those who program for OPAC retrieval have paid much attention to the function in which the OPAC is clearly superior: finding needles in haystacks. They have not devoted much attention to matching the manual catalogue's success in the browse-and-compare function, a necessary one when sequencing multiple hits in response to a work-related request. An OPAC that does not follow the rules of filing as well as data display should admit defeat in a major objective of the catalogue.

The searcher who wants whatever Ludwig van Beethoven had a hand in composing retrieves it easily at the access point for the person. However, the sequence in which the hits are displayed at an OPAC depends on its interface. It is not necessarily one which collocates all versions of the same composition. Anyone wanting to choose from among all the available scores of the composer's final symphony—or to find any work to which it is related or any work which discusses it as a subject—should not have to browse through every record retrieved under the composer's surname.

If the OPAC interface does not sequence a hit-list so that records relating to a single work appear as a group (which is all too common), the wise searcher uses Boolean operators to match *Beethoven* in a name index with some word(s) in a title index, certainly in this case including *Symphony* and perhaps *D minor.* Furthermore, the searcher must be aware that the title wording to be input must be that of recognized work-identification in the musical context, and not necessarily that of scores' title pages with their potentially different languages and word order. Inputting *choral* would not achieve the desired result, even though the symphony is often known as Beethoven's Choral Symphony. In effect, this reconstructs, but ad hoc and with little help from the interface program, the "main-entry" combination of author-title work-identification which is automatic in every Western cataloguing code from that of Bodley's first librarian to *AACR2R*—and in every filing rule associated with them. That the computer can "find" any character string is therefore not the issue. Keyword and Boolean search capabilities do not supplant sequential browsing as efficient means of locating works and revealing relationships among their manifestations. Rigorous authority control, a cataloguing code's unique contribution to bibliographic organization, should not be sacrificed at the very point it is most needed: the end-user search.

It took fifteen years after *AACR1* and MARC to devise filing rules for catalogues which could, on the whole, be computer-programmable. During that period, codes were revised to help accommodate the change from human filer to stupid computer. Still, another fifteen years later, OPAC interfaces for the "browse" function are still being programmed without implementing filing rules compatible with cataloguing codes, particularly with respect to the work-identifier combination of elements. No wonder commercial searching systems are reluctant to publicize their filing subroutines!

The MARC Format Confuses the Issue

Any title proper, alternative title, parallel title, etc., is primarily an element of *document* description/retrieval, not of *work* identification/retrieval. A uniform title is designed *only* as an element of work-identification, but was used for centuries only as an ad hoc file-organization device for exceptional and problematic material. This is the historical reason for its application remaining officially "optional." Just when *AACR1* made "uniform" work titling a universal principle in the identification of a work as such, MARC content designation was being devised so that the Library of Congress unit-card format, even its typographic style, could be reproduced. The uniform title as a universal cataloguing principle was not incorporated into MARC tagging, which therefore shows it as a work-based access point (tag 130) only when no author's name is also present. When an author's name is also present, the uniform title is assigned a tag in the 240s along with the document-titling tags. This has prompted OPAC designers and searchers to make it searchable not as a necessary adjunct to the author's name in name-title access to a work via a name (author) index, but rather as just another titling in a title index, where there is not much point in searching for it independently. This is not a fault of the cataloguing code, which makes it clear that the "title" in a name-title access point is *always* a uniform title where one is relevant. It is the fault of the MARC format and cataloguers' inability to override the corner-cutting and misunderstanding of those who set the patterns for OPAC file indexing and display.

The MARC content designation of subject and "added-entry" access points for works is also confusing. These bear tags 600 through 630 and 700 through 730. Fields 630 and 730 contain a uniform title only, with the title element in subfield *a*. However, if there exists a name associated with the work, one of the other tags in these ranges is used and subfield *a* contains that name while the uniform title for the work is assigned to subfield *t* (title)—and possibly others. That both the name and the uniform title are contained in the same field at least ensures that both elements are recognized as necessary to work-identification. This is, however, inconsistent with the treatment of these two work-identifier elements when, as described in the previous paragraph, they appear in two separate tags. Alas, the opportunity to include this rectification of the MARC format in the package of major revisions of the early 1990s was ignored.

The Incomplete Name Authority File Also Confuses the Issue

That for many years catalogue automation only meant more efficient card production for existing manual files provided no incentive to rationalize the relationship between an authority file and a bibliographic file. End-users were encouraged to consult the manual subject authority file (generally not the local one, but the printed *Library of Congress Subject Headings (LCSH)* from which locally used headings are de facto extracts). A name authority file typically existed only in the cataloguing department for file maintenance, primarily to control the use of cross-references. It was, therefore, common for it to contain records only for the small proportion of names requiring such a reference. Names of works used as name-title access points for "added" access were also routinely included, for no better reason than that they came from a "tracing" (7XX or 8XX field). As each library changed from a merely automated to a fully interactive catalogue, the authority file suddenly became the file through which *every* authority-controlled name had to be accessed. All had to be transferred formally into that file whether or not they required any cross-references.

Personal and corporate names were easily transferred from 1XX and 7XX tags of catalogue records to the new name-authority file; place names were often left only in the subject-authority system regardless of their other uses. Alas, the names of works as such (in the name-title form, remember) were left in limbo. The few which already existed in the manual authority file became part of the automated one by default rather than design. The existing reasons for adding new ones (cross-references, the need to support an added-entry access point) continued to be respected; but as a group, works were not added to the authority database. The automated name authority file, which the end-user must now use and typically sees on the OPAC monitor screen as the first result of a "browse" for a name, appears as a confusing mixture of many person/corporate-body identifications along with a meagre few work-identifications. What is the end-user to make of the fact that a "name" browse elicits many work-identifiers consisting of a uniform title alone, such as Bible, . . . but only a scattered few as author-plus-title? It is left to the bibliographic file to show the existence of any work through the coordination of author and title. However, while this combination is inseparable wherever it appears in the manual catalogue, the output display at an OPAC cannot be guaranteed to show these two elements in their necessary conjunction.

A clear work-identification is essential in a subject search. The user looking for something about Shakespeare's *Hamlet* (the work) is not looking for something about Shakespeare (the person), so when a local subject authority file was automated (in many cases constructed from scratch from *LCSH),* it *had* to distinguish them even if the automated name authority file in the same system does not. Works form but a small part of a typical subject authority file, so including them routinely was never challenged even though they are not found in the published *LCSH.* Proposals to merge name and subject authority files are always under discussion because any name access point can also serve to identify the subject of a document. Perhaps the merger will finally force the issue of including the name of *every* work in the authority file and end the totally inconsistent and therefore confusing way in which the work is now related to the whole authority structure.

What Complications Are Introduced by a Corporate Body as "Author"?

The theoretical answer is "none." The practical problem, if one exists, is historical. Any of the reasons analyzed above may make it desirable to attach the name of a corporate entity rather than that of a person to a title proper or to a uniform title. However, different-language or different-version manifestations do not bulk large among the problems presented by corporate publications. What is much more of a problem is something *not* common among anonymous works or those of personal authorship: the high incidence of nondistinguishing titling. When is *Annual Report* in itself an adequate identification of a work?

The concern with personal authorship evident throughout Western cataloguing history led to the construction of an increasingly shaky theory of authorship by corporate bodies. Initiated by Jewett, this developed through *AACR1* by which time it was spinning out of control as the identity of the corporate body intruded ever more pervasively into the process of report writing in its name by individuals whether in its employ or on contract. *AACR2* abandoned most of the theory, retaining its useful core in 21.1B2 because some works *do* express the corporate nature of a body as much as others express the personal nature of an author. Otherwise, *AACR2* is pragmatic, not theoretical, in sometimes identifying a work by using a corporate name plus a title. The limits to this practice in 21.1B2 have been modified since they were established in the 1978 text but it would not hurt to review them again to clarify that nondistinguishing titling is the second reason for including a corporate name as the first element of a work-identifier.

Considering a serial publication as a work provides the best test of this reasoning. Although serials provide plenty of examples of documents whose titling is deliberately designed to be unique, they also provide the best examples of documents whose titling seems designed precisely to deflect work-identification *away* from title wording and *toward* the name of a corporate issuing or sponsoring body. Finally, serials provide the best examples of the document whose titling combines corporate naming with other title words or symbols ambiguously (again, perhaps deliberately).

Those who wrote *AACR1* in the mid-1960s tried to reconcile the still evolving theory of corporate authorship with a pragmatic need to identify a serial in terms an end-user could relate to citations to the same serial appearing elsewhere. That this was impossible was finally acknowledged ten years later by people who worked on both *AACR2* and *ISBD(S)*. They also ensured that the long-standing practice of writing different rules for serials than for monographs did not survive the integrating trend on which *AACR2* is based.

ISBD(S) establishes a "key-title" as the appropriate work-identifier for a serial. This access device requires the precoordination of two data elements only when the title alone does not provide unique identification; the other element is often, but not necessarily, a corporate name. The fact that a key-title appends the other element to the title, rather than vice-versa, is an insignificant difference in the context of automated retrievability of separate elements, but is very significant in a search of a "browse" sequence. Neither element within a key-title is vocabulary-controlled. This does not mean that a key-title differs totally from work-identifiers as described above. The mandate of those who wrote *ISBD(S)* precluded consideration of vocabulary control, but links in an authority file equate controlled-vocabulary with natural-language forms.

That any two-element key-title as a whole is a standardized, or kind of uniform, title is acknowledged in *AACR2*-based cataloguing in two ways. The key-title is a required element in area 8 of the description and as such is a potential access point. The extensions to rule 25.5 now commonly adopted to create a uniform-title "main" access point for a serial with a nonunique title proper prescribe the key-title sequence (the title comes first), although adopting vocabulary control for the other element. Thus key-title and *AACR2*-based identifiers of serials are at least related in both theory and practice if not, alas, identical twins.

How Much of a Problem, and to Whom, Is Work Identification?

In the majority of cases a work has one author, or one whose predominance can be objectively ascertained, or none who can be practicably identified; and its only documentary manifestation bears one title proper. This is doubtless the major reason why the sometimes complex implications of work-identification treated in this paper are widely ignored and the need for work-identification treated as esoterically exceptional rather than routine. The uniform-title and/or name-title techniques analyzed in this paper were originally applied centuries ago in single topical fields where work-identification has been a prevalent problem: anonymous works of ancient and mediaeval times, primary legal materials, music. No example in *AACR2R*'s chapter on uniform titles is from a current scientific area, for example.

A formalized technique of work-identification is also more important in a database in which a searcher is likely to encounter documents containing the same work in different-language versions. Again, the supremacy of English in current science/technology writing worldwide minimizes the need for a technique designed to collocate different-language manifestations of the same work. Current social-science material, on the other hand, is quite national in character; the language may not be English, but translation is far from routine. Among the A&I services, distinguishing document-identification from work-identification is not a priority. In fact, their major concern is subject-concept-identification, largely outside the scope of a cataloguing code.

For all these reasons, those most keen on developing state-of-the-art search techniques, whether in a library or in an A&I service, tend to focus attention on what they consider more pressing file-structure and concept-retrieval problems. Work-identification may be of greatest concern to those whose needs have been addressed only more recently in the development of automated information retrieval: humanitarians, historians, critics of literature, philosophy, and music. Should this diminish its importance in the creation of bibliographic databases and the programming of search/display techniques?

File Maintenance and Cost Considerations

In the 1960s, Seymour Lubetzky examined the various ad hoc methods of file organization then used to collocate the records for different manifestations of a work in manual catalogues. "Filing titles" ("corner-marks" in Library of Congress terminology) were a method applied at the filing, not the cataloguing stage. "Conventional titles" were a grab-bag of cataloguers' constructs and therefore gradually brought under the purview of cataloguing codes. The "main-entry" combination of author plus title elements was so deeply embedded in all of Western cataloguing history that it was not questioned as the basis for all other methods of file organization.

Out of all these, Lubetzky formulated the general principle which found its way into *AACR1,* that a controlled-vocabulary title is applicable to *every* case of work-identification. He called it a "uniform title." Why its application has remained "optional" in theory but is getting less optional in practice is discussed above, but the economic dimension of those decisions remains to be explored. Practices evolving during the late stages of the manual catalogue were strongly influenced by (1) the cost of repetitiously rekeying (typing) individual records and (2) a not unrelated desire to display only what the average student or faculty user of an academic-library catalogue needs and can comprehend readily. Redundancy was so shunned that from 1949 through to the implementation of ISBD, Library of Congress practice even sanctioned (nay, required) tampering with titles proper! For example, the first word of the three-word title *Shakespeare's Complete Works* was omitted from the title transcription because it was contained in another part of the record (not even a descriptive part, but the author-access point). In the case of serials, the consequences were disastrous: *Journal of the American Statistical Association* lost its last five words, becoming merely *Journal* following a corporate-name access point!

Redundancy has become a nonissue in the digital record as storage and processing costs continue to fall. Indicator bytes are filled more with blanks than with significant codes; statements are made in words in one field and essentially repeated in code in another; the publication date appears in two separate fields (so why does the work-date appear nowhere?). The MARC format is being added to constantly in order to provide for data elements nobody thought significant for a manual record, some of them of use to but few specialist searchers. Meanwhile, the customizable user interface eliminates any problem of displaying potentially confusing or redundant data elements to a searcher who does not need to deal with them. The recommendations which follow would mean extending the redundancy inherent in automated bibliographic control at, I think, not excessive expense in terms of its benefits.

AACR, once considered to establish a high (and therefore expensive) level of input requirement, now seems a very modest input standard, even including all its "optional" features. MARBI and like committees are filling the gaps left by JSC's tradition-bound view of what data elements might ever be desirable, making it less certain what constitutes a "standard" catalogue record and which body or bodies officially control its definition. Individual library and consortium policies determine what data are actually input, whether as text or as code. The commercial software producer has become a virtually equal partner with the above-mentioned groups in determining what search-and-display potential is actualized.

Theory versus Practice

The lack of a glossary definition of what constitutes a separate "work" for purposes of work-identification, or even of what is an "item" for cataloguing purposes (a series? a monograph within the series? a single topical issue of a serial?), has not prevented codes of the past three centuries from collocating evidences of a given work or from supporting a judgement of whether an item does or does not warrant a separate bibliographic record. They do so through their individual rules, not through definitions, because bibliographic presentation is of seemingly infinite variety. To apply the code to a particular work or item displaying any bibliographic complexity requires ad hoc professional judgement based on experience of this variety. Dare I hazard a guess that problem-causing complexity is limited to 5 percent or fewer of the items processed in an academic library and 1 percent in a public library?

Almost every cataloguing code up to Cutter's was written for implementation in one institution, even if adopted more widely. Lubetzky's aborted attempt of the 1950s and early 1960s explored the limit of theorizing. The preeminence of the products of the Library of Congress makes us think we are economically dependent on outguessing what it would do faced with any given bibliographic problem. We expect, for example, LCRIs of increasing complexity to define when LC will create separate records when two items differ in this or that minor (or not so minor) detail. There can be no end to this expectation other than that LC do all the cataloguing for everyone.

Still, the Anglo-American codes of the twentieth century have been written in the context of cooperation rather than of copying. Today's mode of distributive cataloguing in which many contribute to a single database requires the flexibility built into *AACR2,* and perhaps more than is already there, for variant but equally "correct" cataloguing of the same item in different situations. I do not consider it a violation of theory to take account of specialist points of view when prescribing the form of work-identifiers for different classes of works; for example, ballets, performances, serials. Perhaps even the "cardinal principle" of 0.24 is too rigid a specification for those who find it pragmatically useful to base a catalogue record on the work, listing its many documentary manifestations within a single record. But in choosing any of the options provided, two consequences must be considered: (1) the options chosen may complicate the programming of the OPAC interface and (2) any departure from more commonly accepted norms limits the availability of acceptable records to download from external sources and the assurance with which those elsewhere can search the database.

Recommendations: The Document *and* the Work

The term "main entry" should have been abandoned long ago if only because of the animus and misunderstanding its antiquated aura has attracted in the age of the OPAC. However, the concept, theory, and practice it was intended to describe remain sound and should not have been thrown out with the bathwater. The consequence has been the removal of work-identification as a subliminal effect of all file browsing, leaving it to a more difficult stage of a search process: the ad hoc Boolean coordination of elements of a creator's name and titling. As a work can appear in more and more documentary forms, physical and electronic, work-identification is a more fundamental requirement in information retrieval now than ever before, perhaps now more necessary than document-identification.

It is for others at this conference to redefine "work" and suggest how to define the inter-work relationships of the expression and the manifestation. To whatever entities result from this redefinition, I recommend that JSC:

1. change *AACR* terminology to distinguish the work more clearly from the document and introduce the term *work access point* to express the concept which is the focus of this paper. (This and the next recommendation are the easy ones for JSC.)

2. rephrase *AACR2R* taking the OPAC, and not the manual file, as the expected locus of bibliographic searching; options in favour of those maintaining manual files may be desirable, but these should be the exception, not the rule, rather than vice-versa.

3. rephrase *AACR2R* in the context of separate bibliographic and authority files. (This and the next recommendation are the radical ones for the rewriting of *AACR2*.)

4. identify a work as such *only* on an authority record using existing rules for precoordinating the name of an author or predominating author (if one is available) with a title proper (a uniform title wherever relevant), and including the relevant equivalence, hierarchic, and associative links useful for phrase-searching and word-searching (it may or may not be useful for existing name-authority files to be maintained separately from the proposed work-authority files).

5. state that adherence to the code requires an agency to provide access to every work appearing within each catalogued document. (Administrators will ignore this recommendation as outside JSC competence but at least the very low standard of compliance now phrased within the code—generally the "rule-of-three" and for monographs only—should be raised; it may have to be "optional," but don't make it so easy to shirk the responsibility.)

6. urge a return of work-identification, a principle in all of Western cataloguing history, to the design of OPAC interfaces in accordance with the intent of the code. (This recommendation may be dismissed as irrelevant to the topic of this conference because it is addressed primarily not to JSC but to OPAC designers and programmers.)

This should all nicely fall into place with the proposal now circulating for a kind of ISBN for works!

Conclusion

Having recommended specifically, I now generalize. The code is analogous to a political manifesto, not to a statutory edict. It is written based on what the market will accept. Pragmatism, not theory and only partially principle, is the operative word in code writing. I doubt that any amount of theorizing will result in a satisfactory definition of either "work" or "document," for example, but that does not mean it is impossible to define them pragmatically. Details of filing rules (but within the limits of accepted principle!) have long varied from library to library. The rebellion which reached members of the U.S. Senate in late 1972 over the implementation of ISBD, and the almost nonimplementation of *AACR2* in 1978 and 1979, also demonstrate that code writing is not for the idealist. Still, ISBD and *AACR2* did win out (after a fashion) in the end.

Does JSC really lack the clout to dictate to the establishment of commercial OPAC-software vendors on the issues of filing and display of data elements? Cataloguing judgements are complex because bibliographic retrieval is complex, not because cataloguers are obscurantist or because a lay user should only be allowed to have what he or she can find unassisted in the OPAC. The lowest common denominator cannot be allowed to become what is easily programmable. How can someone without the requisite education and/or experience be expected to make cataloguing judgements, including the judgement of whether or not an existing record located for downloading adequately matches the situation in hand (that is, both the item itself and the catalogue to which its record will be added)? Those who expect such a person to design, or have veto power in the designing of, an OPAC interface are unworthy administrators. Computer applications improve retrieval capability; their success at cost-cutting in any area involving operations other than purely clerical ones remains to be proven. Must we give greater weight to the latter?

DISCUSSION

In the absence of Ronald Hagler, Lynne Lighthall presented the summary of his paper and answered questions.

One participant spoke as an administrator: he would welcome a much greater level of detail in bibliographic records in terms of tables of contents, etc. However, because such added detail is costly, he would not want to make it a requirement for all libraries to catalogue to that level of detail. Lighthall believed that Hagler would agree with this statement.

Lighthall reported that Hagler was surprised by the reaction to the term "main entry" on the conference electronic discussion listserve. He wondered why the term causes such confusion or excites such animus. People should not blame *AACR2;* rule 0.5 permits libraries to use the option of alternative heading entries. The majority of libraries are following Library of Congress practice.

Beyond MARC[1]

MICK RIDLEY

My Perspective (or Prejudices)

I'm not a librarian but a database specialist, doing research in a Computing Department in a team including librarians with a British (sometimes European) view of the world. This research has been funded by the British Library R&D Department (now Research and Innovation Centre), Document Supply Centre, and the European Union-Telematics for Libraries programme.

This means that I am a receiver or user of MARC records rather than a creator (or modifier or enhancer). And my comments about MARC should be seen in that light, and hence I will tend to talk about MARC records as I've seen them, which is often not the same as how they should have been if they had been catalogued in the way you (or I) would do it (or the way the standards suggest).

What we have been doing (or trying to do) in a number of recent projects is to compare MARC records, find which are for the same items, find which are the best. More recently we have been trying to extract the maximum information from the records to produce more useful online catalogues. The difficulties of doing this have motivated the observations that follow and led me to believe that we need a new kind of catalogue record.

Questions

The principal questions that I am addressing are:

- Is MARC simply an embodiment of *AACR?*
- Do we need a transfer standard for catalogue records?
- What is a good structure/format for catalogue records?

- Is the same structure/format needed for transfer, database storage, and presentation to users?

And on the way I would also like to ask a few others that I don't know the answers to.

Standards Are a Good Thing But. . .

MARC has been amazingly useful at enabling the exchange of information (records), and it provided a starting point for extensive automation but, and it's a very big but, its very success and all-pervasiveness have meant that it has influenced, for ill in my opinion, the storage and organization of catalogue information. My particular concern is that there is a strong tendency to store either MARC records or unitary records based on them that contain all the information about an item. The card catalogue moved to inside the computer. There is of course a body of work that has been questioning this approach; Michael Heaney's "Object-Oriented Cataloging" [2] seems to sum up many of the issues. MARC wasn't meant to do that; it is (explicitly declared to be, in the case of UKMARC) "a communications format . . . for the exchange of records between systems." [3]

It is also explicitly a bibliographic record standard "defined for or extended to books, serials, cartographic materials, music, and audio-visual materials." [4]

There has also been a proliferation of MARCs (this sometimes seems to be almost a national pride issue, although that is unfair since some at least have tackled character and language issues). This may be less noticeable in North America, but in a networked world not only do we need standards but international ones, i.e., ones that stretch as far as the networks. We can convert between MARCs, but it can be a pain to do it, and some differences can result in a loss of information, e.g., systems that only have one 500 tag for notes can collapse information from many tags into this but can't *automatically* restore the original.

I think we need to consider "How do you have good standards?" And more specifically, from my point of view, "How do you have good standards for automated systems?" From attempting to work with existing MARC records it seems to me that there are problems in *AACR2,* and hence MARC, over things that are optional, or allow scope for (mis)interpretation. Such things are anathema to automated systems.

The status of uniform title as optional is one (disastrous to me) example. Its absence from most records makes trying to cluster records for the same item together very difficult.

An example where decisions require consulting external sources was found in work I did on Greek material for Project Helen, where Cavafy may or may not be the most common transliterated form of the Greek poet's name, depending on what sources you consult. Rule 22.31 states "choose the form corresponding to the language of most of the works," which seems to have led the British Library to use Kavaphes and the Library of Congress to use Cavafy. Presumably in both cases a correct choice was made, but the different decisions reflect the different existing holdings of those libraries. [5]

Physical format is one area (which I discuss in more detail below) where a greater degree of clarity is needed about what we are cataloguing and why it is needed. Here there seems to be little distinction between medium and equipment needed to use the item. And in practice this opens the door for misinterpretation.

It would also be sensible to avoid default assumptions, such as no language means the English language and no format means a book. This may be OK in a localised environment but is storing up trouble for the networked world where querying an overseas picture library is little harder than querying a local branch library.

To produce records that can be easily used in automated systems we also need to avoid two things:

1. the ever-increasing list that starts as (a) to (e) with nice clean distinctions but grows towards (z) with very fuzzy edges to each group;
2. the black hole of *other* into which is put all sorts of material with all sorts of explanatory notes.

Having made a stand against the *other* category and bottomless pit that is *Notes,* I'm very unwilling to ban them since I know there are occasions when they are supremely useful and that there really are some things that don't fit into any other category. But in practice they are often abused, that is, used when the information should clearly be provided elsewhere. Anyone who has sought out information on large-print editions will have suffered this. There are clearly notes that fulfill a useful function, but are these best gathered together at the (conceptual) end of the MARC record? Language information may have appeared in 008, 041, and 546, but as a pragmatic consideration is it more likely that better, more consistent records will be created if all language-related material is together? It is, of course, possible to display fields in any order one chooses but I feel that it would be beneficial to associate notes with the area they annotate. This would also have the benefit of letting us collapse edition information (including edition notes) if the subdivisions were not wanted, rather than the present situation where all notes (on edition, physical format, language, etc.) are collapsed together. It is also worth noting that some notes may refer to a work, such as summary notes, others to a particular manifestation, such as a publication note, and still others, such as a note that a book includes the author's annotations, may refer to the individual copy.

We need categories that are taxonomic, that is, cover the full range of possibilities, yet still allow for future growth. (I think here it's worth mentioning an aspect of Barbara Tillett's work[6] that hasn't been commented on as much as some. That is, her work on relationships wasn't just a list of relationships, but was an attempt at a taxonomy, a complete categorisation.) Returning to physical format, we want to specify the medium at one level into a comprehensive set of categories, e.g., text, sound, image. (I leave it to others to decide the details of such fundamentals such as whether moving images are a base category or a subset of image.) We need to allow for material that is multimedia (or some other *new* medium) not by the ad hoc creation of new criteria but being able to repeat the medium category.

It seems to me also that one solution here is to allow for a more hierarchical structure of information in records. This will also permit users to disregard a level of detail they do not want. This would allow us to categorise that software was on a disk at one level and at another whether it was $3\frac{1}{2}$ inches, $5\frac{1}{4}$ inches, or CD, and at yet another file formatting or machine level information.

This would mean that it would be possible to use such records to group software together for OPAC displays and, for example, separate out software on CD-ROM from text on CD-ROM. At present, pertinent information in this area may be scattered through the MARC record in coded form in 008 material designation and 037 and in more textual form in 300 and 531, 542, or other note field in UKMARC.

Things That Surprise Me about Cataloguing and Libraries

I'm still amazed by the amount of discussion about main entry and access points. Even though relational databases may not be the ideal for bibliographic uses, they do teach us that we should be able to query *anything* and that sorting and displaying criteria can be controlled by users. Indexes are just a device for making queries go faster, and are hidden from just about everyone.[7]

Isn't it reasonable to be able to query a catalogue to find out how many large-print books (or books in French or CDs) it has? If I've found a good introduction in one of the volumes of Marx's writings published by Penguin, shouldn't I be able to find what other Penguin editions of Marx are available? This, I know, raises issues of authority control over publisher information and what sort of series information is useful.

What Things (Objects) Are These Catalogue Records Of?

I think that in plans for the future we need to avoid the primacy of print. Books aren't going to disappear, but they will change (are changing). They have to live alongside a variety of other media including networked resources that may have some very different behaviours from print (and materials like CDs, videos, and even software on disc). Here I'm thinking of issues such as the notion of edition for information that is being continually updated. In saying this I don't want to fall for the "books are dead, long live the Internet" hype, but I do want to recognize that even a lot of printed material, such as serials, have in general been poorly served by the OPAC and cataloguing rules at present. We need a model that represents the book and its web site and software, the work that starts online and then becomes a book (e.g., Krol's *The Whole Internet User's Guide and Catalog* or many Java texts). The model must fairly represent the journal that has online and print versions (e.g., *Journal of Artificial Intelligence Research* which starts online and then has a printed version later, and the situation we have at Bradford—certainly not uniquely—where we have some journals in the library, but we also have versions available on the web, and for some of the journals also available on the web we don't have printed versions).

I feel that looking at the Internet as a *new* medium is a useful technique for questioning old assumptions and seeing if the old ideas still fit. I also think that it represents a major challenge for cataloguing.

Having said that, I'd like to look in more detail at a more traditional area, that of physical form, since we have been investigating how this is used at present in a current research project. We have been looking at it as part of our work on BOPAC2[8] where we are attempting to offer different ways of sorting and displaying large retrievals. One feature that we wanted to offer, and was suggested by users, was the ability to choose only books or videos, etc. (Here I should add that we are working on data retrieved via Z39.50 where we haven't been able to specify that restriction in the search.) Looking at this area, in an attempt to do something with the MARC records the search retrieves, has opened up more questions and not given us any answers yet. What exactly is the physical format information telling us? And here I would emphasize that I'm referring to the information we get on MARC records delivered as the result of a search: *AACR2* as is has been implemented rather than the ethos or true spirit of *AACR2*. Format seems to be a mixture of two things, the content, i.e., pictures, sound recordings, moving pictures, and the technology needed to use the item, i.e., whether it is a microfiche or microform, a videorecording, or a movie film. There are two issues at play here and neither is being well served. If I want the motion picture of *Wuthering Heights,* I may care about whether it is on film or video, but probably at a different level from the distinction between text versions and "recordings of a dramatisation" of it. Similarly I might like to group text, microfiche, and microfilm together as different formats of the text, in which case issues of normal text and large-print information, which is often found elsewhere in the catalogue record, may be relevant. The situation gets worse when we move on to something like a CD-ROM. Its physical form may be a CD-ROM, so we need a CD player, but what are the content/software/hardware issues? What is the CD-ROM really? It may be simple text that is held on this medium or a set of pictures. If it is text, is this held in one of a number of different formats that might be used, such as HTML, Postscript, PDF, or images of pages? If it is the latter, it could be in the same file format, e.g., j-peg files, as a CD of photographic images. It would then need similar software to the CD of photos but we might wish to categorise it with other texts rather than with the photo CD. Or the CD may use a proprietary format only easily intelligible to specialised software. What machines does the CD run on? And if we can answer these questions for CD-ROM, can we answer them if it's a DVD or other disc format that the future may bring?

What we need to catalogue is the intellectual content (the work), the forms (manifestations) in which it is found, and the links and relationships between works and manifestations. And we need to do this with a clear distinction between these different functions.

And Who Will Create Records for Them?

If a lot of information is being created (avoiding the question of what's worth cataloguing), how much can be done automatically? Is this the lesson of the Internet search engine? Is the counterpart that the producers of information rather than national bodies do more? If so, how much do we trust them? This assumes (not unreasonably, I think) that most material is in electronic form, but it also suggests that something like a serial should have all its parts accessible.

I know there are numerous efforts to provide access to serial contents via abstracts and contents listings, both printed and online. But these are apart from the *normal* catalogue and often involve re-keying or scanning activities. It should surely be possible to create records from the electronic copy that provide us with information on an article in a journal that can be put into a catalogue. This should allow us to access that article in the same way that we would expect to find *Bleak House* within Dickens' *Collected Works* in a catalogue.

Here I would like to differ to some extent with Pat Oddy, who in her book *Future Libraries, Future Catalogues*[9] suggested that there would only be a limited number of electronic texts. I believe that there are a number of issues here and it is important to recognise that increasingly texts exist in electronic forms, either originated by their authors or by publishers. This is not to say that this is automatically the primary means of transfer and presentation for those texts. They do, nonetheless, exist as electronic texts, and we may wish to consider how these are likely to be used, archived, and accessed over a long period of time. Do we see a long-term future for microfiche theses and reports? Will there be an electronic life after death for out-of-print books?

And How Do You Get the Records and How Much Do They Tell You?

In a networked world you can access things you couldn't in the past, or at least get them more easily, and there are a number of protocols like http which are of necessity very open. That is, you can see the source of web pages. There are similar issues of access, for instance with Z39.50,[10] which commonly works by transfer of MARC records. Will people come up with another (lower in content than MARC) standard for this exchange, or charge as you would if the MARC record were being supplied to build a catalogue? If you don't allow access to your MARC records, what structure do you provide in the records that is still useful?

It is possible to imagine a simple structured record that tagged author, title, publication, physical description, ISBN, subject, and note fields, each of these tags being an aggregation or selection from a number of MARC records. The result would be similar to the detail shown in a full record on most OPACs. Exactly how much detail should be shown (or would be acceptable to suppliers) is not clear. Wool[11] surveys current practice in this area.

It's not clear what financial models work in a networked world; we can see publishers (information sources or providers) coming up with a variety of different models and testing the water to see what works for them.

If libraries have a policy of access rather than holding, how do they demonstrate that in their OPAC? How do you differentiate between things you have, things you have online here, things that you know are online elsewhere, and things that are elsewhere but can be brought to you (ILL and document delivery and eventually electronic delivery)?

What We Should Be Aiming For

I think we need a work-based system, with a three-level structure:

- The Work
- The Manifestation
- The Copy

This sort of structure has previously been suggested, e.g., Heaney[12] and the Multiple Versions Forum[13] and was the basis of the work we did on BOPAC1.[14] This can then be used for the differing needs of database storage, record exchange, and OPAC display.

Database Storage

This three-level structure suggests a demarcation between parts of the catalogue record.

With this structure everything has a uniform title, the title of the work. Within a database many items can in fact be lists, so there is no limit to how many variant versions you might have, no issue over where an author comes in a list, no problem over repeating information, since it doesn't need physical repeating. It just exists as a link to the original. The record never exists as a whole; it is always the sum of a number of parts that can be accessed in any way and put together by the links between parts of the *record*. Some information may also be part of more than one work or manifestation. A work that is Dickens' *Collected Novels,* for example, may be seen as containing both the work *Bleak House* and a particular manifestation of that work. All the information pertaining to this version of *Bleak House* may be the same as would be held for an individual volume of the same edition, and hence the *Bleak House* information within the *Collected Novels* may only be links to existing work and manifestation information. The *Collected Novels* would have its own copy or holdings information, of course. Just as a "Collected Works" contains a number of works, an edited collection or issue of a serial may contain a number of articles (or works). A work-level record should exist for each of these articles in the same way that it would for *Bleak House* within the *Collected Novels*. The records for the collection and the individual article would of course link to the same manifestation. Separation out and standardisation of some of these features would also make links to related works simpler. A critical work would then be linked to the *work* it was about and a translation to both the *work* and possibly the particular *manifestation* it was based upon if, for example, it was known to be a translation of a second edition.

Record Exchange

A record for transfer can always be constructed by putting together the work and manifestation parts to make a self-contained record. If the receiver already knows the work, he or she discards that bit and links the manifestation part to his or her existing work record. If not, he or she can save the work part, save the manifestation part separately, and create the copy part of the record. Work records would of course have to be able to contain other work records nested within them.

OPAC Display

A different looking complete record is assembled for OPAC display; in particular following Bradford OPAC1 it may not be a set of complete work/manifestation/copy records but a tree of work < manifestations < copies. This notion shouldn't be unfamiliar, since current OPACs at least do it with regard to copies of a particular version; they just don't, or can't, follow the logic through. And there is no reason why these things can't be configured for personal preference, over things such as prioritising books in a local branch, choosing which other distant resource to search, etc.

Authority

I feel we need to avoid the term "authority file" because it suggests the wrong thing. (Just as some other terms need to be renamed to break the link with card catalogues and printed bibliographies.) What we need is not a separate stand-alone list, which often seems hard to use or link into other systems, e.g., the UK names authority file has many very brief records that are little more than a personal name. What you really want is to be able to query the work part of a large (your national library's) database, which should hopefully be available online. At the OPAC you don't want to be told to "see also"; you want the system to do that for you (and possibly explain what it has done).

How Do We Get Where We Want to Be from Where We Are Now?

Can the transition be made? A new system seems like a big shock, but how many systems are the same as they were (say) ten years ago? How many libraries have changed systems entirely, or changed the hardware, the operating system, etc. (without complete collapse of the system)?

What we did in Bradford OPAC1 showed that we can create the new structures from existing MARC records; there may be problems, but it is a start. Some records can be grouped together and the work information separated out automatically. Other records, because of existing cataloging anomalies, need individual attention. And once you have a system like this, you can see how it is easier to add new records, how they relate to other records, and how anomalies show up more easily. From a system like Bradford OPAC1 you could still produce old-style MARC records for export, so users of old systems are not cut off; they could migrate at some (not fixed) time.

Standards

The old standards have been library ones. There is a need to embrace wider standards, particularly in the areas where records are marked up (or structured or tagged). We need to look at SGML, and in the area of character sets we need to look at Unicode.[15] There is a lot of general (i.e., not tied to single application areas) software widely available to process these. It would be a good thing if library systems were less of a specialist market; the use of common standards will help this. As I said earlier we need to be looking at international standards that cover all areas that networks might do. To this end, although we must acknowledge the AA of *AACR*, we will, I hope, want to look as widely as possible.

Mark-Up, SGML, HTML, and XML

I have nothing in particular against the actual file format of MARC, but if a widely used structure can give us the same results and allow us to use more general-purpose software, then I think we need to consider it very seriously. Since the popularity of the web has made HTML (which is a SGML application) common, SGML would seem to be the mark-up of choice. There may well also be benefits in this approach; because publishers have been significant users of SGML, much material that we want to catalogue may already be in this form. At a more personal level, word processing and text formatting packages are offering HTML or SGML as output formats. We need to be aware of other developments, such as XML, Extensible Markup Language[16] (sometimes called SGML-Lite), which are providing generalised tools that may be useful to libraries.

One feature in MARC's favour has been the use of numeric tags, which has helped to free it from a bias in favour of English unlike HTML whose tags have their origins in English terms. Do we need to come up with a compromise that makes the tagging structure more easily readable by the nonspecialist? I think probably not, since it should always be possible to create records from data that is tagged and structured in some other way. For example, we should be able to parse the TITLE tag of an HTML document to create a 245 (or whatever it is to be). On the other hand, there may be a strong case for renaming (and renumbering) to emphasise a break from old traditions. And similarly we can always turn numeric tags into the display terms or styles that we need. Here there is, perhaps, a lesson to be learnt from web browsers and the notion that, for example, a heading or block quote can be shown in a number of different ways. The stylistic choices may be the browser's, the author's, or the reader's.

Character Sets and Unicode

I hope I can interest people in the issues of character sets, since they are very important, although I do recognise that they may not seem interesting at first. I would like to give some background on this area, and I hope those who are familiar with it will bear with me while I attempt to evangelise on the issue to others. I will also try to avoid too much technicality.

The problem with most character sets in use on computers is their limited size. They are restricted to 128 or 256 different characters, since they are based on each character being stored in one byte in the computer's storage. Not all of this range is available for printed characters, since some positions are used for control codes, such as end-of-file, and other positions are used for tab and new-line. This sort of range may be OK for modern English, but it is insufficient for many uses, for example, most bibliographic situations. Single-byte character sets can also be used for other alphabets such as Greek, but a file that uses a Greek character may well appear to be rubbish if read by someone expecting the Roman alphabet. Even among English speakers, transferring files from Windows to Macintosh can produce odd results for characters outside the A-Z range. Most MARC formats have a character set that is satisfactory for the language of its country of origin but can cause problems if you want anything a little out of the ordinary. Even the use of the cedilla or tilde in Spanish may be problematic, let alone whole different alphabets such as Cyrillic.

One solution to this problem has been the use of escape sequences to notify software that the character set was going to change and that the position that was an accented O is now a capital sigma. This technique has had limited use but seems likely to be superseded by the use of multibyte character sets. Here we allow more than one byte per character and hence increase the range of characters that we can represent. This means that one character set (Unicode) will let us represent all the different languages and alphabets of the world.

One effect of using Unicode will be to permit the storage of records in their correct script and, if transliterated versions are needed, these can be produced automatically, on demand, by software. This will end one situation where the computerized catalogue has often been a step back from the card catalogue. Up to now many computer systems would only allow the storage and display of the transliterated record; the original script would not have been present at all. At least the card catalogue could have had a transcription of the real original text as well as a transliterated version.

The library community has a good record of involvement in the development of Unicode. And some good work has already been done in using Unicode for MARC records in projects such as the European Union–funded CHASE project.[17] Having addressed the topic from an introductory point of view, I would also like to make a few comments at the more complex end of the topic. For those who already know something of this area, you may have wondered why I have emphasised Unicode rather than ISO10646. The reason is that I would like to stress again the benefits of being able to use standard commercial (nonlibrary specific) products where possible. And here the developments are for Unicode rather than ISO10646, although I do recognise that bibliographic use may well need the greater resources of ISO10646 for such things as records of documents in nonliving languages, etc. Unicode is significant because it is the underlying character set for Java, which I believe will be very important, and Unicode (rather than ISO10646) support is being built into new computer operating systems such as Plan 9 and Windows NT.

This isn't to say that there are not still a lot of issues over Unicode, as anyone familiar with the debates over Korean and Han unification will know, but I feel it is coming.

If Unicode and more complex records seem to be a problem, remember that it is software that is increasingly expensive, not hardware, especially storage. How big is a catalogue record, how big are your Word documents, how big are the pages that you download from the web, especially those that include images? There is no need for you to store your records using the Unicode character set. You merely need to be able to translate to and from it; what you do internally is your own business. However, MARC is *only* the transfer medium.

I accept that at the moment there is a gap between these two ideas and one of the big problems of HTML has been the poor character set support, but change is on the way both in terms of character set support in standards and commercial support[18] (e.g., Netscape's Marc Andreessen's web article on future support for Unicode[19]).

Conclusion

Returning to my initial questions: I don't believe that MARC is *simply* an embodiment of *AACR*. A transfer medium for catalogue records should be that, a transfer medium, and therefore may have a different structure to the records we store and display. The same set of cataloguing rules may apply but to different structures, structures that are suited for particular purposes and with rules for conversion between these different forms.

Notes

1. This text is substantially that posted to the conference web site with some typographic errors corrected. A few changes as a result of comment on the preconference listserve or in light of developments are added as other footnotes. My presentation followed the format of the paper here with one major exception, which was that I included a demonstration of BOPAC2. When I first wrote this paper in early 1997, work on BOPAC2 was still at an early stage and so only some reference was made to it here. BOPAC2 was operational by the time the preconference discussion started and was mentioned on the listserve, particularly with reference to main entry. I therefore demonstrated some aspects of the system as a way of highlighting what was possible with MARC records. I said that depending on your point of view BOPAC2 showed how good or bad current records were. I do not feel that this is the place to reproduce that presentation, since the system is still under development and its appearance is not the same as at the time of the conference. It is also now publicly available on the World Wide Web for those who wish to see it.
2. Michael Heaney, "Object-Oriented Cataloging," *Information Technology and Libraries* 14, no. 3 (September 1995): 135-53.
3. *UKMARC Manual,* 3rd ed. Part 1 (London: British Library Board, 1989), pt. 1: 1.
4. Ibid.
5. Evelyn Cornell, Amelia Hatjievgeniadu, and Michael J. Ridley, "Searching for Non Roman Script Terms," in *Electronic Library and Visual Information Research: ELVIRA 2,* ed. Mel Collier and Kathryn Arnold (London: Aslib, 1995), and E. Cornell, *Project Helen Name Preliminary Report 2.1* (Bradford, Ore.: University of Bradford, Dept. of Computing, 1994).
6. Barbara Tillett, "A Taxonomy of Bibliographic Relationships," *Library Resources & Technical Services* 35, no. 2 (April 1991): 150-58.

7. This paragraph raised a number of points of discussion on the preconference listserve. One point was whether my criticism of relational databases was at odds with Tom Delsey's E-R and O-O analysis of *AACR2*. I did not feel that it was and was only attempting to point out the *semantic gap* between such analysis and what can be implemented easily with a relational system. The fit between analysis and implementation in an object database system is a better one. Another point was whether indexes should be visible. My use of index is perhaps a database one rather than a library one. I would agree with points raised on the list that *browsable lists of headings,* whether authors, subjects, or whatever, are useful aids but these in my opinion should not be direct access to index files but *constructed* to help users, as such a list might be created using soundex or other algorithms, rather than a simple alphabetic list from an index file. I was also trying to stress that in many current systems there is a simple equation that says *that which is indexed is queryable and nothing else is.* Therefore, cataloguing decisions mean that some information gets indexed and is queryable while other information is not.

8. BOPAC2, http://www.comp.brad.ac.uk/research/database/bopac2.html.

9. Pat Oddy, *Future Libraries, Future Catalogues* (London: Library Association Publishing, 1996).

10. Z39.50, http://lcweb.loc.gov/z3950/agency/.

11. Gregory Wool, "The Many Faces of a Catalog Record: A Snapshot of Bibliographic Display Practices for Monographs in Online Catalogs," *Information Technology and Libraries* 15, no. 3 (September 1996): 173-95.

12. Heaney, "Object-Oriented Cataloging."

13. *Multiple Versions Forum Report: Report from a Meeting Held December 6-8, 1989, Airlie, Virginia* (Washington, D.C.: Network Development and MARC Standards Office, Library of Congress, 1990).

14. F. H. Ayres, L. P. S. Nielsen, and M. J. Ridley, "Bibliographic Management: A New Approach Using the Manifestations Concept and the Bradford OPAC," *Cataloging & Classification Quarterly* 22, no. 1 (1996): 3-28, and F. H. Ayres, L. P. S. Nielsen, and M. J. Ridley, "Design and Display Issues for a Manifestation Based Catalogue at Bradford," *Program* 31, no. 2 (April 1997): 95-113.

15. Unicode: http://www.stonehand.com/Unicode.html.

16. XML: http://www.ucc.ie/xml/.

17. Martin Fisk and Anthony Brickell, "PROLIB/COBRA-CHASE 10169, Character Set Standardisation: Migration Strategies to Unicode for National Bibliographic Databases: Final Report" (unpublished).

18. The drafts for the specification of HTML 4.0 (available from W3C) state that the document character set is ISO10646 or Unicode.

19. Marc Andreessen, "The *World Wide* Web," http://www.netscape.com:80/comprod/columns/techvision/international.html.

Acknowledgments

I'd like to thank Fred Ayres and Lars Nielsen, the other members of our team at Bradford.

DISCUSSION

The first question involved the problem of an OPAC search for an item by joint authors, e.g., Masters and Johnson, a search that will not find the item. The participant believed that this was not a good reason for eliminating main entry, because main entry works well for the vast majority of items. To eliminate it would undermine the structure of the catalogue. Ridley agreed that there is a problem and that a solution should be sought. However, he stated that perhaps the term "main entry" should be eliminated, not the structure of the catalogue record.

Another participant agreed with Ridley about the folly of prescribing displays. In the beginning ISBD was developed as a display format to enable people to use bibliographic records in languages not understood locally and is certainly useful for national bibliographies. In a general library a line-by-line tagged display is probably better.

One participant noted that the array was pre-established in a card catalogue and asked what the potentials and the limitations are in carrying out that function in a multidatabase environment relying on protocols such as Z39.50. Ridley stated that Z39.50 can return data in various formats, and it is relatively simple to put data into complex structures. Many things are possible, but how many are useful? What are the future demands? If you have it right structurally, other applications ought to be easier to develop at not a great cost. It could mean heavier costing at first with a long-term payback. Another participant said that there is already a mechanism for arrangements in filing rules.

In reply to a question about what problems were caused by *AACR2* rather than MARC, Ridley said that, for example, many things are listed in notes that should be elsewhere in the record. Notes are free text and making links with free text is difficult. He was not certain that the problem lay with *AACR2*'s principles but rather with its application.

Interest was expressed in Ridley's statement about SGML facilitating technology. It was hoped that it would be possible to maintain the current structure of *AACR2* and MARC and use them with SGML to get any display wanted. Ridley agreed that SGML had a lot of potential because it is a unifying technology.

Uniform titles are just as useful in a brief entry catalogue as in a catalogue with fuller records because of the need to collocate various editions and versions. Problems arise in shared cataloguing when some libraries use uniform titles and some do not. One participant suggested that uniform titles should be made less optional than they are now. Ridley would like to have mandatory uniform titles.

One participant stated that catalogues either have a controlled vocabulary, which is expensive, or cheaper data with an expensive computer. In the latter case, a lot of time and money is spent getting far inferior results in essentially dealing with keyword searching. No matter how fancy the apparatus or the engines, the searcher will get unsatisfactory results. Anyone who uses a browser on the web knows the disastrous results of keyword searches. The reason why library cataloguing is unique in this area is the concept of rigourously controlled vocabularies and of spending money at the beginning of the process to the benefit of thousands of users later.

Conference Discussion Group Reports

10

AACR Principles Group

JSC Charge
- List *AACR2R* principles
- Would the use of modeling techniques be appropriate?
- List priorities for action
- Recommend agencies, committees, or groups that may provide background, research, or other data

Report   The group felt that the present explicit principles are satisfactory, with the caveat that there is a need to change some terminology, e.g., "media" to "forms of expression," "libraries" to "any agency that wants to form a catalogue." JSC should consider reinstating useful statements of principle from *AACR1* that were dropped from *AACR2*. The group recommended as a first priority a statement about a succession of steps. First, a statement about the functions of the catalogue should be made. From the statement of these functions the principles on which a catalogue is based should be derived. From these principles the cataloguing rules should then be developed.

    Build into the statement of principles an assertion that one of the functions of a catalogue is to bring together in a useful way whatever objects will be necessary for a particular search. Essential to the retrieval process is an intelligent collocation of works and the relations of works in a useful way so as to prevent a search response of a thousand records. Any such collocation or relation should link objects/records appropriately in terms of *Functional Requirements for Bibliographic Records,* linking works to works where appropriate and works to manifestations where appropriate. The rules should bring together, or facilitate the bringing together, those elements that belong together. To this end, entity relationships or object-oriented modeling techniques should be used as a background. The group did not recommend or try to identify any specific implementation of such techniques.

The rules should help cataloguers and inform others who will use the rules for applications of some kind. There should be a statement that library catalogues are one component of a larger virtual catalogue and that these catalogues have to function in a wider world.

The group believed that rule 0.24 is not an *AACR2* principle, but rather a method of procedure. They agreed with Tom Delsey that rule 0.24 is tied to the present *AACR2R* arrangement of chapters. This arrangement needs to be revisited if *AACR* is revised.

The group did not have time to develop suggestions about agencies, committees, or groups that might provide background, research, or other data.

Introduction Group

(Other than Principles)

JSC Charge
- What is the purpose of *AACR2R?* Should it be related to other guidelines, e.g., MARC, specialized guidelines?
- Should there be guidelines for OPAC display?
- Should there be a layperson's introduction?
- List priorities for action
- Recommend agencies, committees, or groups that may provide background, research, or other data

Report
The group that discussed the content of the introduction of any revision of *AACR2* indicated four priorities. The first one should be a statement about why we catalogue, followed by the second priority, a description of what the catalogue does. The third priority would highlight the role *AACR2* plays in creating a catalogue. And the fourth priority was for clear, concise wording with no jargon that is difficult to understand. These priorities could be considered the layperson's introduction recommended several times in the preconference electronic discussion. However, the group did not discuss "teachability" because the general feeling in the group was that this was more about a person being a good interpreter to those being taught than the simplification of rules.

Reference should be made to the fact that *AACR2R* is ISBD-based, that MARC is the principal carrier, and that there may be other methods involved in carrying cataloguing information. The introduction should not include a specific list of possible carriers that might become out of date during the effective life of a particular edition of a cataloguing code.

One section of the introduction should deal briefly with the importance of catalogue display and how display affects the usability of the catalogue. If the display is poor, the richness of the catalogue may be completely lost. Filing rules should be mentioned in concert with the discussion about display, but no specific filing rules should be prescribed. It is important to state that the way records are displayed and the way they are filed are both affected by how they are catalogued.

The group recommended that the specific introductions to parts 1 (0.21-0.29) and 2 (20.1-20.4) be examined to see if they still function as they were originally intended to do, if they should be expanded, or if some of the beginning introduction's content (0.1-0.14) should be transferred to either of the specific introductions.

Specialized cataloguing guides, such as those for archives, law, music, and nonbook materials, are necessary because *AACR2R* is not intended to explain every cataloguing problem.

At the end of the introduction describe the revision process so that people will know how they can send suggestions and complaints about the rules.

The historical information about the *AACR*'s development is important, but it should be moved to an appendix so that when the book or computer file is opened, the introduction immediately tells the reader about the content.

The group had no suggestions about agencies, committees, or groups that might provide background, research, or other data.

At the end of the report one person in the audience disagreed about mentioning MARC in the introduction because the future may well bring other means of exchange.

Case-Based Rules Group

JSC Charge
- Should *AACR2R* be all things to all people?
- What is the best way to accommodate the needs of special collections?
- List priorities for action
- Recommend agencies, committees, or groups that may provide background, research, or other data

Report   The group had three recommendations, the first two based on Gorman and Oddy's paper.

RECOMMENDATION 1: Precisely define case-based rules. Analyze special case-based rules in part 2 in light of the review of the principles of *AACR2R* with a view to isolating and eliminating special case-based rules.

RECOMMENDATION 2: Synthesize the rules for special materials so that general libraries would not have to obtain specialist manuals. *AACR2* should contain mandatory minimum elements for these materials. State that specialist manuals certified by JSC should be consulted for materials requiring elaborations.

RECOMMENDATION 3: Review related existing standards and establish ongoing relationships with relevant bodies that produce cataloguing codes based on *AACR2,* e.g., Canadian Council of Archives and law and music library associations.

At the end of the report a member of the audience asked how JSC would certify specialist manuals. The group's representative replied that the group did not produce a clear prescription, but agreed that some kind of relationship was needed between JSC and related organizations. Michael Gorman, one of the editors of *AACR2* and *AACR2R,* remarked that JSC's charge was not to certify every page of a manual, but rather to identify and certify bodies that are trustworthy to carry out that function. This was done in the past with the cartographic materials manual. He further recommended that JSC work with CONSER to make the CONSER manual a manual for cataloguing serials. The group's representative agreed and restated the group's recommendation: the people or group charged with writing a manual would be writing in the spirit of *AACR2.* For example, a specialist group in Canada would take their work to the Canadian Committee on Cataloguing, which would tell the specialist group whether it would meet with JSC's approval. If approved, the national committee would forward the manual to JSC.

Terminology Group

JSC Charge

- List the terms that need reworking
- List the terms that need redefinition
- List priorities for action
- Recommend agencies, committees, or groups that may provide background, research, or other data

Report

Terminology must be clear, concise, and jargon-free.

The glossary works well, but it must be edited and updated as an integral part of the process of working on *AACR2,* and not amended as an afterthought.

JSC should ensure that common-usage definitions, such as those found in *Webster's Dictionary* or the *Oxford English Dictionary,* be given for any words *AACR2* uses. If there are any deviations from the common-use definitions, those usages should be explained, e.g., "common usage is . . . , in *AACR2* it is. . . ."

The group strayed off the topic of terminology to recommend a chapter on authority control.

It is important not to confuse translation and internationalization. A survey should be conducted into who is using the code, who wants to use the code, and for what purpose the code is used in order to inform the discussion and decision about the scope of internationalization. For example, the Asian market may only want to use *AACR2* for its Western-language materials rather than applying it to its own language materials.

A member of the audience asked the group to put in a plea for a multilanguage dictionary of cataloguing terms.

In response to questions from the audience, group members mentioned "publication" and how it applied to computer files, "uniform title," and "work" as words that need precise definitions.

At the end of all the group reports audience members identified the following additional terms that need either reworking, added to the glossary, or added to the glossary if the words will be found in a revision of the code:

> authority record
>
> class
>
> computer file
>
> designation and other area 3 terms for serials
>
> edition, including simultaneously issued editions in all formats
>
> item
>
> object
>
> record
>
> unpublished materials
>
> view, e.g., in managing numerical and data files
>
> terminology found in *Fundamental Requirements for Bibliographic Records*

Seriality (Ongoingness) Group

JSC Charge
- Address all recommendations
- List priorities for action
- Recommend agencies, committees, or groups that may provide background, research, or other data

Report   As requested, the group discussed all the recommendations.

RECOMMENDATION 1: *Adopt a three-dimensional approach to the cataloging rules.* The group discussed how this could be done without a major *AACR2* revision and suggested that ongoingness be treated in the *AACR2R* introduction by describing a monograph and a serial.

RECOMMENDATION 2: *Incorporate the concept of the "ongoing publication" into the cataloging code.* The group offered the following definition of a serial: serials can be either sequential, i.e., issued in successive parts, or cumulative, as with databases and bibliographic entities that are updated, such as loose-leaf services. The group then discussed loose-leaf services, which are ongoing, and loose-leaf publications, which come out in editions. They felt that loose-leaf publications could fall to the left of the line in Model B in the monograph category; Model B appears to work rather well here.

RECOMMENDATION 3: *Adopt Model B as a short-term solution. Work towards the adoption of Model C as a longer-term approach.* The group decided that Model B is appropriate at this time because getting rid of "serials" is problematic. We may want to think about Model C in special instances and specific cases. However, publications with successive issues coming out in web-site-type formats may be more practically treated as cumulating serials. We need to work with the ISSN centres to solve some of the serials problems.

RECOMMENDATION 4: *Retain description based on the earliest issue for publications issued successively; for publications issued in a single updating part, base the description on the latest iteration.* The group agreed with this recommendation, but did not talk about a way to give the latest publication information in the record. This is important information for many constituencies.

RECOMMENDATION 5: *For ongoing publications, replace the concept of "chief source" with that of "source of title." Allow greater flexibility for the selection of title within the parameters of the prescribed sources. Define new terminology for sources within online publications.* The group expressed some caution about too much flexibility. They also discussed whether all electronic serials should be considered cumulative. Even though these publications may have successive issues, the fact that they are coming out in the web-site-type of format means that it may be more practical to treat them as we would cumulating serials.

RECOMMENDATION 6: *Adopt an approach that allows for multiple cataloging conventions for handling title changes in the rules. Following the principle that the method for cataloging should be appropriate to the form of issuance, apply successive entry to changes of entry for successively issued publications and a latest entry approach to changes of entry for updating publications.* The group recommended that we work with the ISSN centres to develop appropriate rules for updating ongoing serials.

RECOMMENDATION 7: *Modify the rules for title changes to reduce the number of meaningless title changes.* These rules should be harmonized as much as possible with the ISDS guidelines so that our records are compatible. While this harmonization is fairly close at present, we should work with ISDS for further improvement.

RECOMMENDATION 8: *For ongoing publications, create rules that focus on identification rather than transcription. Consider new displays and arrangements of data that might result from and facilitate such a focus and that would keep similar information together in the record.* The group agreed that the title should be transcribed. Prescribe only the order of elements for the designation, not how they are recorded within that order. The hot topic was the statement of responsibility and whether it should be recorded for serials. This was not done in *AACR1* and earlier rules. A statement of responsibility is at the same time both identifying and confusing, because over time the body named in the statement of responsibility may change. The group decided to leave the rules as they are now.

The group did not discuss recommendations 9 and 10 because they had already dealt with these issues.

The first of the recommendations in the short-term implementation plan in the Hirons/ Graham paper was to create a separate chapter for single-part, updating works. The group preferred putting monograph works into *AACR2R* chapter 1 and serial works into chapter 12, as a way of incorporating this suggestion into the existing structure.

Further issues were discussed. The rules in chapter 25 are optional; the group would like an exception made for serials and their translations. JSC should look at the relationship between uniform titles and key titles in order to resolve conflicts.

The following were identified as possible agencies, committees, or groups that may provide background, research, or other data: ISSN International Center and the national centres; the ISBD(S) committee; the American Library Association Committee to Study Serials Cataloging and similar committees in other countries; CONSER Operations Committee; the British PCC; and the American Association of Law Libraries and other associations of law libraries because of the impact on legal materials. National MARC communities are not as important, but there could be some impact on MARC citation developers because some work is being done on linking citations from abstracts and indexes to master records for serials.

Unfortunately, the question period was lost because the tape ended at this point and the words at the beginning of the next tape were meaningless.

Main Entry Work Authority Records Group

JSC Charge
- Should a multitiered record structure be implemented?
- If so, how should it be implemented?
- List priorities for action
- Recommend agencies, committees, or groups that may provide background, research, or other data

Report
The group decided to concentrate on the work authority aspect, rather than the main entry aspect.

The group agreed that work authority records are a good idea because they would increase the usability of the catalogue for our users; increase the efficiency of searching in the catalogue; increase the cost-effectiveness of the cataloguing process itself; and aid designers in designing systems by articulating the actual design and structure of a catalogue.

The following assumptions were the basis for setting the group's priorities: (1) the term "work" as defined in *Functional Requirements for Bibliographic Records;* (2) we already have a camel and do not want to create a llama; (3) the process should be timely; and (4) solutions should be systems dependent. The group did not want a quantum shift, preferring a gradual shift to make use of what we already have as much as possible, e.g., existing rules, bibliographic and authority records, and the structures already in place. They recognized that there is a difference between the work authority records and records for expressions we now have, but declined to undertake the task of defining them.

The group reaffirmed the usefulness of uniform titles for collocation and identification in fulfilling the second objective of the catalogue. Their first priority was to recommend that the Committee of Principals develop a method of using conceptual modeling, as described by Tom Delsey, to sort out the existing practice in describing uniform titles and in creating uniform titles, and specifically to work toward defining what should be included in the authority record for a work, what are the attributes of a work, how they are now defined in *AACR2R,* and any problems that might exist. The Committee of Principals should hire a consultant to do the initial modeling and form a control group to work with, and test out the recommendations of, the consultant.

The second priority concerned changes to *AACR2R* and has two parts. First, chapter 26 should include a statement about the value of the authority structure and their multipurposes. Authorities and cross-reference structures are useful as linking devices. They facilitate collocation in the catalogue and the actual workings of the catalogue and cataloguers. In addition, the group recommended an explanation about the purpose of *AACR2R*'s part 2 and suggested that its purpose is to create a controlled vocabulary which allows collocation and access to entries in the catalogue. A catalogue has a controlled, syndetic structure.

The third priority involved identifying a process for extracting elements from existing bibliographic records to create work records and looking at the feasibility of automatic generation of authority records. This should be done in consultation with systems developers and vendors, researchers in this area, and MARBI.

The fourth priority asked JSC to publicize a vision for the future and communicate this to library administrators, cataloguers, colleagues, systems developers, and vendors. The group recognized that with the legacy of the existing bibliographic and authority records, radical change cannot be recommended. JSC should articulate where cataloguing rules are going, why changes are being made, and that studies are being undertaken. The vision might state that the objective is to maximize the usefulness of the catalogue's syndetic structure to improve the usefulness of the catalogue. It is a step in the right direction toward radical change if we are in a position to manipulate data in such a way as to create some of the structures suggested by Rahmatollah Fattahi and others.

In the question period that followed, Tom Delsey, a member of the IFLA Study Group on the Functional Requirements for Bibliographic Records, commented on the study group's assumption about the definition of "work." Those responsible for the content of *Functional Requirements for Bibliographic Records* tried to point out in the document that the boundaries for "work" were defined simply for the purposes of illustrating the model; there are valid reasons for seeing those boundaries differently. Despite what some commentators thought, the "work" definition was not reflecting *AACR2R* specifically. There is still work to be done in terms of defining boundaries that are appropriate to *AACR2R.* The Main Entry Work Authority Records Group's representative replied that the group did not endorse the FRBR definition; there was not enough time to deal with it.

An audience member asked, in regard to the third priority, whether this recommendation was also made with a view toward the routine extraction of such authority records from bibliographic records as the cataloguer is creating a bibliographic record. The group's representative replied that there was some discussion about whether this work would be precoordinated or postcoordinated, whether a cataloguer would create the authority record in the process of cataloguing, or whether in some cases a record could be generated automatically after the fact. Could we articulate when one or the other would be needed? Would some changes to the rules facilitate one or the other?

Two administrators asked whether a work authority record would mean more work for cataloguers, and one remarked that authority records can be sucked out with the existing technology. Administrators need to know the percentage of cases where cataloguer intervention is necessary and sufficiently small so that the benefit to the user would be offset by whatever additional cost there might be. The group's representative responded that the group had talked about the issue of the optionality of uniform titles and the impact this would have on people who do not normally do this work. They believed that the impact of this issue should be part of the report of the study group mentioned in the first priority. The report should include when it can be done, when it cannot be done, how to facilitate the doing in more cases, whether it is worth doing and, if so, why.

Content versus Carrier Group

JSC Charge
- Should the content rather than the carrier be the basis of the catalogue record?
- If so, how should it be implemented?
- Give some consideration to the microform and multiple versions issues
- List priorities for action
- Recommend agencies, committees, or groups that may provide background, research, or other data

Report
The group suggested that *AACR2R* should stress primacy of content over physical format and that the physical form of an item is not always the class of material to which an item belongs. JSC should consider changing rule 0.24 by removing "physical" and "in the first stance" in the first sentence. This sentence would, therefore, read: "It is a cardinal principle of the use of part I that the description of an item should be based on the class of materials to which this item belongs." The last sentence of that paragraph should be changed to include: "in the case of reproductions the original or the previous form of issue may be used as the starting point. . . ." This change would require a definition of "reproduction" not currently found in *AACR2R*. There also needs to be a discussion about what to do when an item exhibits characteristics of more than one class, e.g., cartographic materials in a digitized format, the establishment of a precedent of format, and the issue of general material designations for these items.

The group recommended a rule that indicates no research is required if some particular information is not available on the item being catalogued.

The group mentioned the issue of simultaneous publications and decided they could be handled in separate rules, e.g., a rule or a reference indicating that a reference should be made for simultaneous editions and what form that reference should take. This proposal would, in essence, make the Library of Congress rule interpretation for microforms the basis for the rule about microforms. However, the current practice results sometimes in descriptions that are hybrids, e.g., a general material designation in the title statement of a description that was for the original. This should be revisited. In addition, the definition of "computer file" in the glossary needs to be reconsidered.

The group gave a high priority to these changes because (1) many users have already adopted them as a practical solution and will continue not to follow the present rules in *AACR2R* in this regard; (2) the MARBI proposal to change the coding of digitized materials to treat only data files and numeric files as computer files and to treat other materials according to their original type, as reproductions or other physical classes, has been approved. This decision rests properly in the cataloguing community, not in the MARC format community. If we do not make the change in 0.24, something needs to be done about this change to the MARC format. The group thought that some of these changes may be more easily implemented if the rules were restructured in the manner suggested by Tom Delsey, i.e., based on ISBD areas. While this would provide flexibility for the inclusion of new materials, it is not a requirement for implementation.

The problems involved in the cataloguing of multiversions, microforms, and reproductions would all be addressed by redefining the cardinal principle in rule 0.24.

During the question period a member of the audience suggested that many problems might be solved by revising chapter 9 and adding "electronic" as appropriate to any general material designation. One person stated that a commentator on the conference's listserve indicated that this was being done by some agencies with the general material designations for cartographic materials. Another person noted that there was a CC:DA proposal to change the general material designation for computer file to that recommended in *ISBD(ER)*. The group representative replied that the group believed that the general material designations should be studied.

An audience member responded to the group's proposed change in the wording of rule 0.24 by saying that it was not so much a matter of the word "physical" as a matter of re-examining what is meant by "class" and why items are classed one way or another. The group's representative replied that a review of a definition of "class" had been implied in their recommendations.

Internationalization of *AACR2R* Group

JSC Charge
- How far should *AACR2R* be internationalized?
- What parts should be internationalized?
- List priorities for action
- Recommend agencies, committees, or groups that may provide background, research, or other data

Report   The group decided that *AACR2R* should be internationalized because (1) the globalization of information and the increasing amount of records exchange with those outside the Anglo-American community necessitate compatible exchange formats; (2) of increasing user access to international information through web sites, etc.; (3) of cost savings through copy cataloguing.

The "how" of internationalization should be a cautious, evolutionary process which aims at true integration, not simply an add-on approach. As a first step, JSC and the Committee of Principals should invite interested countries to set up mechanisms for dialogue and a means by which proposals for change can be sent to JSC. After a few years, internationalization should be revisited to see how successful it has been, whether it can be extended in some way, and whether the structures that govern the code should be reviewed to allow a wider international dimension. The group stressed that the management structure should be manageable. At this second stage, the code should be renamed because "Anglo-American" would no longer be appropriate.

The group recommended that JSC be aware of the international dimension of rules when making revisions. The removal of many case-based rules would make internationalization easier to implement because, for example, it would be a major stumbling block if *AACR2R* had to formulate rules for the legal systems of many countries. We need a core code that would define entities to be encoded, particularly for authorities. Unicode will allow us to handle the problems of language and character sets. We should link in with other international standards, e.g., MARC, ISBD, and the new IFLA initiative on the form and structure of corporate headings.

The group listed the following priorities:

1. that JSC set up closed user group sites/lists to enable dialogue between JSC and those countries that have national committees with national interfaces;
2. that JSC investigate ways in which revisions can be internationalized;
3. that JSC conduct a survey to discover the countries outside the Anglo-American community that are using *AACR2R,* the countries that are using *AACR2R* as the basis for their own codes, and the countries that are interested in using *AACR2R;*
4. that JSC develop three tiers of membership in an evolutionary manner. The three tiers would be in this order: full members, i.e., current members; affiliated members, i.e., countries using the code as it stands; and interested parties, countries that have a code based on *AACR2R.*

The agencies, committees, or groups that may provide background, research, or other data are the IFLA Section on Cataloguing, the IFLA Office for UBCIM, national cataloguing committees, supranational bodies, e.g., the Consortium of European Research Libraries, LIBER (Ligue de bibliothèques européennes de recherche), the International Standards Association and especially ISO T46, and those associated with research projects, e.g., REUSE, the harmonization of Russian cataloguing with *AACR2R,* COBRA (Computerized Bibliographic Record Action) led by the British Library, and ONE (OPACs Networked in Europe).

One audience member stated that Unicode does not belong in *AACR2R,* but rather in a MARC manual. The group's representative answered that the group did not intend Unicode to be part of *AACR2R.* It was recommended to facilitate the tools we need, such as the greater internationalization of authority files.

Review Process Group

JSC Charge
- How should JSC interface with other review processes?
- Are there alternate ways in which this process can be done?
- Should this process be evolutionary or gradual, but not glacial?
- List priorities for action
- Recommend agencies, committees, or groups that may provide background, research, or other data

Report
The group made the following recommendations in no particular order of priority.

- National committees supporting JSC representatives should find a way to come to most decisions without having to meet face-to-face.
- Define a clear relationship between the secretariat and the publisher. The Committee of Principals should review its relationship with the publishers to ensure timely responses.
- Publicize the review process better by using a web site to explain the process of submitting proposals and ideas.
- If there is a substantial revision of *AACR2,* an editor should be appointed and a clear definition developed about what groups may feed into the revision. This should all be done on an eighteen-month fast track.

Participants' Response to the Groups' Recommendations

Conference participants were asked to vote on the three most important priorities on a group rather than an individual priority basis. The recommendations of the Principles Group and the Seriality (Ongoingness) Group received an equal number of votes as the first priority, followed by those of the Content versus Carrier Group as the third priority.

JSC Actions Following the Conference

J SC met for three days after the end of the conference and established a plan to be implemented in conjunction with the Committee of Principals for AACR. The following items for immediate action were approved during the JSC meeting.

Items for Immediate Action by JSC

- Pursue the recommendation that a data modeling technique be used to provide a logical analysis of the principles and structures that underlie *AACR*.
- Create a list of the principles of *AACR2*.
- Formalize the recommendations on seriality endorsed during the conference and introduce them into the rule revision process.
- Solicit a proposal to revise rule 0.24 to advance the discussion on the primacy of intellectual content over physical format.
- Maintain an *AACR* web site.
- Publicize and reaffirm, on the *AACR* web site, JSC policies, procedures, and activities, as well as the current processes for submitting rule revision proposals emanating from within or without *AACR* author countries.
- Develop a mission statement for JSC.
- Determine if there are any existing surveys on the extent of use of *AACR2* outside the Anglo-American community and, if no such survey exists, conduct such a survey.

Although action is being taken on all of these recommendations, as of this writing (May 1998) two major projects have been initiated. The first deals with the recommendation to undertake a logical analysis of the principles and structures upon which *AACR2* is based. Although past studies have been mentioned in several conference papers, a brief review of these studies is given here as a background to the JSC undertaking. Several of those who have advocated a reexamination of conventional data structures have endeavoured to illustrate and test the value of reconceptualizing the bibliographic record by sketching out (and in a few cases, developing in considerable detail) conceptual models for the restructuring of bibliographic records and databases. Not long after the publication of the second edition of *AACR,* Michael Gorman posited a new schema for the logical restructuring of bibliographic data into a number of linked packages of information for use in what he envisioned as the developed catalogue. More recently, that same notion has been further developed by Michael Heaney, who has deconstructed the MARC record using the techniques applied in object-oriented analysis, and by Rebecca Green, who has used an entity-relationship analysis technique for the same purpose. Building on work done by Barbara Tillett on the representation of relationships in bibliographic databases, Gregory Leazer and Richard Smiraglia have developed a conceptual schema for modeling derivative relationships within bibliographic families of works. And in what is in some respects the most comprehensive undertaking of this kind to date, the IFLA Study Group on Functional Requirements for Bibliographic Records has used the entity-relationship analysis technique to develop a model designed to serve as a framework for relating bibliographic data to user needs. Tom Delsey recommended a logical analysis in his paper, noting that such an analysis would provide a framework for evaluating the end product of the cataloguing code against the criteria of accuracy, flexibility, user-friendliness, compatibility, and efficiency.

With the approval of the Committee of Principals, JSC asked Delsey to proceed with the development of a formalized schema to reflect the logical structure underlying *AACR2.* The objective is to use the schema as a tool to assist in the reexamination of the fundamental principles underlying the code and in setting directions for its future development. In the meantime, JSC is developing a list of the principles on which it believes the code is based. Eventually, that list will help to inform the discussion when the Delsey study reveals the true logical structure underlying the data in the record. A comprehensive analysis of the logic of the code will be essential in order to satisfy ourselves that its theoretical underpinnings are sound, that it is capable of accommodating change, that it can continue to be responsive to user needs, that it can interface effectively with other systems for bibliographic control, and that it is cost effective.

The second major thrust that JSC has undertaken since the conference deals with issues related to seriality. Crystal Graham and Jean Hirons recommended that the concept of "serial" be redefined by removing the requirement for numbering and successive parts. While the definition of serial used in *AACR2* ("a publication in any medium issued in successive parts bearing numeric or chronological designations and intended to be continued indefinitely") is consistent with other internationally accepted definitions, including those in *The ALA Glossary of Library and Information Science,* the *ISBD(S),* ISDS, and ISO 5127, Graham and Hirons felt that it needed to be modified to accommodate ongoing publications that did not strictly meet the current definition. In their subsequent consultations, however, they have discovered that a more encompassing approach would be superior, and they are now investigating alternatives which would embrace the concept of ongoing entity as the overarching concept under which other categories of entities such as "serial," "loose-leaf," and "database" will fall. Although participants at the conference agreed that Model B was the best approach for the near term, work subsequent to the conference suggests that the disadvantages of redefining "serial" may outweigh the advantages and that a better approach is to more clearly define the "ongoing" concept expressed in Model C. Intensive consultation will take place during 1998 with a view to making formal recommendations to JSC by late 1999. While this has the appearance of being somewhat slow, it does ensure that a wide consultation can take place before change is made and also ensures the possibility of coordination with the international community including CONSER, ISDS, and IFLA.

The International Conference on the Principles and Future Development of AACR has helped JSC to develop a plan of action which will test the applicability of *AACR* in the current and future environments and balance the need for a sound and workable cataloguing code with the cost of cataloguing and the cost of change. Projects are under way to investigate potential approaches. Before deciding on any change to the cataloguing code, JSC will give careful consideration to the implications of such change, particularly on the costs of cataloguing. As is its ongoing policy, wide consultation will be undertaken and further use will be made of the JSC web site.

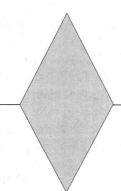

Authors and Conference Participants

Authors **Tom Delsey** is currently Director General, Corporate Policy and Communications, at the National Library of Canada. He has a fairly long history with cataloguing standards, dating back to 1979 when he was first appointed to the Canadian Committee on Cataloguing. That same year was his first as the National Library of Canada's representative on ABACUS (the Association of Bibliographic Agencies of Australia, Britain, Canada, and the United States). He has also been active within IFLA as chair of the Standing Committee of the Section on Cataloguing, as chair of the Working Group on an International Authority System, and as a member of the Standing Committee of the IFLA Section on Serial Publications. For the last several years Delsey has been a consultant to the IFLA Study Group on the Functional Requirements for Bibliographic Records. Tom Delsey has published a number of papers on bibliographic standards, authority control, and serials.

Since receiving his M.L.S. from the University of Teheran in 1979, **Rahmatollah Fattahi** has worked in the cataloguing department of a number of academic libraries in Iran. As the head of the Technical Services Division, Ferdowsi University Central Library, he was in charge of a shared cataloguing system from 1981 to 1991. He has published books and articles mainly on descriptive cataloguing, including the translation of *AACR2R* into Persian. His major interest is in designing and developing a new structure for the bibliographic record. He has developed a "Prototype Catalogue of Super Records" based on the concept of a multilevel record structure. In 1996 Fattahi did his Ph.D. research on the relevance of cataloguing principles to the online environment. He is now assistant professor at the Department of Library and Information Studies, Ferdowsi University of Mashhad, Iran.

Michael Gorman is Dean of Library Services at the Henry Madden Library, California State University, Fresno. From 1977 to 1988 he worked at the University of Illinois, Urbana, library as successively, Director of Technical Services, Director of General Services,

257

and Acting University Librarian. From 1966 to 1977 he was successively, Head of Cataloguing at the *British National Bibliography,* a member of The British Library Planning Secretariat, and Head of the Office of Bibliographic Standards in The British Library. He has taught at library schools in his native Britain and in the United States—most recently as Visiting Professor at the University of California, Berkeley, School of Library and Information Science (summer sessions). He was the first editor of the *Anglo-American Cataloguing Rules, Second Edition* (1978) and of the revision of that work (1988). He is the author of *The Concise AACR* (1989); editor of, and contributor to, *Technical Services Today and Tomorrow* (1990); and editor of *Convergence* (proceedings of the second National LITA Conference), and *Californien,* both published in 1991. *Future Libraries: Dreams, Madness, and Reality,* co-written with Walt Crawford, was honoured with the 1997 Blackwell's Scholarship Award. His most recent book, published by ALA in 1997, is titled *Our Singular Strengths: Meditations for Librarians.* Gorman is the author of more than 100 articles in professional and scholarly journals. He has contributed chapters to a number of books and is the author or editor of other books and monographs. He has given numerous presentations at international, national, and state conferences. Michael Gorman is a fellow of the [British] Library Association, the 1979 recipient of the Margaret Mann Citation, and the 1992 recipient of the Melvil Dewey Medal.

Crystal Graham is Head, Digital Information and Serials Cataloging at the University of California, San Diego. She began her professional career as the Associate CONSER Project Director at Cornell University. She also worked as serials cataloger at New York University and as Latin American studies monographs cataloger at UCSD before assuming her current position.

Graham has written widely on serials cataloging, multiple versions, and microform cataloging and is the author of the Association of Research Libraries' *Guidelines for Bibliographic Records for Preservation Microform Masters.* She served as the representative to the ALA Committee on Cataloging: Description and Access for both the ALCTS Serials Section and the ALCTS Reproduction of Library Materials Section. She also served on the faculty of the ALCTS Institute, "Serials Cataloging in the Age of Format Integration," and is the author of "What's Wrong with AACR2: A Serials Perspective," published in *The Future of the Descriptive Cataloging Rules: Papers from the ALCTS Preconference, AACR2000.* Crystal Graham is the 1998 recipient of the Bowker/Ulrich's Serials Librarian Award.

Ronald Hagler is professor at the School of Library, Archival and Information Studies, The University of British Columbia. He was one of the original faculty of the School at its inception in 1961. His teaching areas include publishing, the history and sociology of communication, historical bibliography, and archival description and indexing; but the primary focus of his teaching and other professional work has always been bibliographic control in libraries. He was involved with the development of the *Anglo-American Cataloguing Rules* from 1964 through to the publication of *AACR2R* in 1988, serving at times on the Canadian national committee and the Joint Steering Committee for Revision of AACR. He was also involved in the preparation of the two editions of the concise version and the two editions of the French translation. He wrote *Where's That Rule?,* a guide to implementing the change from *AACR1* to *AACR2,* and three editions of *The Bibliographic Record and Information Technology* (the first with colleague Peter Simmons). He is engaged in practical bibliographic work in two catalogues of books in the Arkley Collection of Historical Children's Literature at The University of British Columbia Library. Ronald Hagler received the Margaret Mann Citation in 1990.

Jean Hirons is the CONSER (Cooperative Online Serials Program) Coordinator at the Library of Congress. She began her professional career as the Head of Cataloging at Southeastern Massachusetts University (now University of Massachusetts–Dartmouth). She subsequently worked as a cataloger at Catholic University and spent over six years at the U.S. Government Printing Office, where she supervised serials cataloging. In 1983 she came to the Library of Congress as the Head of the CONSER Minimal Level Cataloging Section and also served as assistant to the CONSER Coordinator. She assumed responsibility for CONSER in 1993, following the resignation of Linda Bartley, and was officially named Coordinator in 1997. Her major accomplishments are the *CONSER Editing Guide* and *CONSER Cataloging Manual,* which have become the standard tools for serials cataloging. Hirons served on the faculty for two ALCTS serials cataloging institutes, has given numerous workshops and training sessions, and has written a number of articles dealing with serials cataloging and CONSER. She is the editor of *CONSERline,* the online newsletter of the CONSER Program. In 1986 Jean Hirons received the Bowker/Ulrich's Serials Librarianship Award.

Lynne Howarth completed her Ph.D. in library and information science and was appointed to the Faculty of Information Studies, University of Toronto, in 1990, becoming Dean in 1996. She has taught at McGill University (Montreal), Ryerson Polytechnic University (Toronto), and in the library techniques diploma program at three colleges of applied arts and science in Ontario. Current teaching and research are focused on the creation and application of bibliographic tools and standards, the organization and management of knowledge-based systems, and modelling technical services operations in libraries. As part of a nationally funded collaboration with Joan Cherry, she is co-investigating the design of more effective bibliographic record content and displays in online and web-based catalogues. She has published several articles on the management of technical services, on the application and use of bibliographic standards, and on the content and quality of bibliographic records.

Ralph W. Manning, the conference chair, is Heritage Officer (National and International Programs) at the National Library of Canada. He holds a B.A. from the University of Toronto, an M.A. from Carleton University, and an M.L.S. from the University of Western Ontario. Manning is active in the Canadian and international cataloguing community. From 1984 to 1995 he was in charge of the National Library of Canada's Office of Library Standards, where he was responsible for cataloguing policy as well as international standardization activities. He has been a member of the Canadian Committee on Cataloguing since 1984 and its Chair since 1987. A member since 1987, he has been the Chairman of the Joint Steering Committee for Revision of AACR since 1996. He was a member of the Canadian Committee on MARC from 1984 to 1995 and was its chair from 1984 to 1988. Manning is also a member of the IFLA Professional Board. One of his key activities at the present time is the coordination of national and international activities in the area of preservation of library materials. Ralph Manning is a recipient of the Commemorative Medal for the 125th Anniversary of the Confederation of Canada.

For most of her career **Pat Oddy** has worked at The British Library in various capacities, beginning in 1974 as a cataloguer responsible for the descriptive cataloguing of legal deposit materials for *The British National Bibliography* and culminating in 1994 in her present position as Head of Cataloguing. Since 1972 she has been active in the Library Association's Cataloguing and Indexing Group and was the group's representative to the

Standing Committee on Official Publications from 1982 to 1985. She was a member of the Library Association/British Library Committee on AACR2 from 1986 to 1997, and was The British Library's representative to JSC from 1990 to 1996, serving as JSC chair from 1991 to 1996. Oddy was a member of the Executive Council of the Program for Cooperative Cataloging from 1994 to 1995. She is the author of *Future Libraries, Future Catalogues,* of articles published in professional journals, and of papers delivered at professional meetings. She is a fellow of the Library Association.

Mick Ridley is a Senior Computer Officer at the Department of Computing, University of Bradford, with special responsibilities for databases. He recently co-authored *Object Databases: An Introduction.* He has been involved with research into bibliographic databases for the last ten years. This work on a number of projects, such as DOCMATCHII (an investigation of linking citations to online full texts of biomedical journal articles), QUALCAT (a British Library–funded project on bibliographic database duplication and quality control), and Project Helen (a European Union–funded project concerned with Greek-language issues in bibliographic records), has been concerned with issues of matching between databases, duplicate detection, character sets, and MARC formats. Recently he has led the BOPAC projects which have investigated issues of display for large and complex OPAC retrievals. Between receiving a degree in chemical engineering from Leeds University and a master's degree in computing from Bradford University, Mick Ridley worked in the book trade, first in book selling and then in publishing.

Sherry L. Vellucci is currently Associate Professor in the Division of Library and Information Science at St. John's University, New York, where she teaches courses in bibliographic control, information technology, academic libraries, and special libraries. Prior to her 1992 appointment to the St. John's faculty, she held positions as a cataloger at Princeton University, Head of the Performance Collection at Westminster Choir College (Princeton, N.J.), and Director of the Library and Media Center at Westminster Choir College. She holds a doctorate in Library Science from Columbia University, a master's degree in library science from Drexel University, and a bachelor's degree in music from Rutgers University. She has served on the board of the Music Library Association (U.S.) as Treasurer and Member-at-Large, and is currently the editor of the *MLA Technical Reports Series.* She is also active in the International Association of Music Libraries, Archives, and Documentation Centres (IAML), currently serving as Vice-Chair of the IAML Cataloging Commission and Member-at-Large of the IAML-US Branch. Sherry Vellucci recently received the Music Library Association's Special Achievement Award in recognition of her path-breaking research in the area of bibliographic relationships in music catalogs and their implication for system design in future catalogs. She serves on the editorial board of the journal *Cataloging & Classification Quarterly* and is the author of numerous publications, her most recent being *Bibliographic Relationships in Music Catalogs,* issued by Scarecrow Press.

Jean Weihs, the conference director and editor of this book, has taught cataloguing to students in faculties of library and information science, library technician programs, and school library programs. While most of her professional life has involved the teaching and practice of cataloguing, she has also been a reference librarian and a bibliographer and has worked in academic, public, school, and special libraries. *Nonbook Materials: The Organization of Integrated Collections* (co-authored with Shirley Lewis and Janet Macdonald) was one of the primary sources for the development of rules for nonbook materials in *AACR2*. In addition to the four editions of this work, she has been the author or co-author of seven other books, most recently *Special Libraries: A Cataloging Guide* and the second edition of *Standard Cataloging for School and Special Libraries* (both co-authored with Sheila Intner), and more than 100 articles, papers, and book reviews published in professional journals or as parts of books. She has served on over forty-five committees and task forces of professional organizations, notably as Canadian Library Association representative to the Canadian Committee on Cataloguing (1978-1986), its chair and representative to JSC (1981-1986), and JSC chair (1984-1989). Jean Weihs is the recipient of nine awards including the Margaret Mann Citation, the Queen's Jubilee Medal, and the Canadian Association of College and University Libraries Blackwell Award for Distinguished Academic Librarian.

Since 1983 **Martha M. Yee** has been Cataloging Supervisor, UCLA Film and Television Archive; from 1980 to 1983 she was Assistant Head, Catalog-Bindery Division, UCLA Biomedical Library. She received a B.A. degree in Chinese languages and literature from Pomona College, and M.L.S. and Ph.D. degrees, both specializing in cataloging, from UCLA. The topic of her Ph.D. dissertation was "Moving Image Works and Manifestations." She is the author and co-author of many articles, papers, and reviews published in professional journals and as chapters in books. Her latest work (co-authored with Sara Shatford Layne) is *Improving Online Public Access Catalogs*. Yee has been actively involved for many years in many professional organizations and has served on more than forty committees, boards, and task forces of these organizations.

Participants

Candy Bogar, Manager, Development Librarian, Data Research Associates, Inc.

Jennifer Bowen, Associate Head, Technical Services for Cataloging and Automation, Sibley Music Library, Eastman School of Music, University of Rochester

Sue M. Brown, Director, Professional Services, The Library Association, and The Library Association representative to the Joint Steering Committee for Revision of AACR

Rodney Brunt, Senior Lecturer, School of Information Management, Leeds Metropolitan University

John D. Byrum, Jr., Chief, Regional and Cooperative Cataloging Division, Library of Congress

Michael Carpenter, Associate Professor, School of Library and Information Science, Louisiana State University

Dale Chatwin, Assistant Director, Library Services, Australian Bureau of Statistics Library

Helena S. Coetzee, Senior Lecturer in Library Science, University of Pretoria, South Africa, Chairman, SAILIS Subcommittee for Bibliographic Standards

Joe Cox, Co-manager, Faculty of Information Studies Library, University of Toronto

Gordon Dunsire, Head of Information Strategy and IT Development, Napier University Library, Scotland

Stuart Ede, Director, Acquisitions Processing and Cataloguing, The British Library, and The British Library representative to the Committee of Principals

Nick Eden, Acting Head of Record Creation, Acquisitions Processing and Cataloguing, The British Library (representing Sally Strutt, The British Library representative to the Joint Steering Committee for Revision of AACR)

John Espley, Principal Librarian, VTLS Inc.

Robert B. Ewald, Senior Cataloging Policy Specialist, Cataloguing Policy and Support Office, Library of Congress

Jan Fullerton, Assistant Director-General, Collections and Reader Services, National Library of Australia

Ed Glazier, Senior Analyst, Development Division, Research Libraries Group

Eugenie Greig, retired, formerly Associate Librarian (Cataloguing), Macquarie University Library, Sydney; observer at the International Conference on Cataloguing Principles, Paris, 1961

Kent M. Haworth, University Archivist and Head, Special Collections, York University, Canada

Michael Heaney, Head, Foreign Language Cataloguing, Bodleian Library, Oxford University

Sten Hedberg, Assistant Director, Head of Swedish Department, Uppsala University Library, and representative, National Swedish Standing Committee on Cataloguing and Indexing

Steven L. Hensen, Director, Planning and Project Development, Special Collections Library, Duke University

Elise Hermann, Library Advisory Officer, Biblioteksstyrelsen (Danish National Library Authority)

Ann Huthwaite, Bibliographic Services Manager, Queensland University of Technology Library and the Australian Committee on Cataloguing representative to the Joint Steering Committee for Revision of AACR

Laurel Jizba, Head Cataloger and Assistant Professor, Branford Price Millar Library, Portland State University

Natalia Kasparova, Chief, Department of Catalogization and Alphabetical Catalogues, Russian State Library

Maureen Killeen, Bibliographic Specialist, A-G Canada Ltd.

Irina L. Klim, Director, Information Resource Center, United States Information Service, St. Petersburg, Russia

Sara Shatford Layne, Head, Cataloging Division, Science and Engineering Library, University of California, Los Angeles

Lynne Lighthall, Associate Professor, School of Library, Archival and Information Studies, The University of British Columbia (representing Ronald Hagler)

Jan Maslen, Associate Librarian (Technical Services), La Trobe University, Australia

Ann Matheson, Keeper, Department of Printed Books, National Library of Scotland

Sally H. McCallum, Chief, Network Development and MARC Standards Office, Library of Congress

Janet Mitchell, Managing Director, OCLC Europe

Karen Muller, Executive Director, Association for Library Collections and Technical Services/Library Administration and Management Association and alternate American Library Association representative to the Committee of Principals

Monika Münnich, Head, Descriptive Cataloguing Department, Universitätsbibliothek Heidelberg, Germany

Ingrid Parent, Director General, Acquisitions and Bibliographic Services, National Library of Canada

Glenn Patton, Manager, Product Planning and Implementation Department, OCLC Inc.

Lenore Rapkin, Cataloguing Librarian, McGill University Law Library

Paule Rolland-Thomas, Professeur titulaire honoraire, École de bibliotechéconomie et des sciences de l'information, Université de Montréal

Brian E. C. Schottlaender, Associate University Librarian, University of California, Los Angeles and American Library Association representative to the Joint Steering Committee for Revision of AACR

Marianne Scott, National Librarian, National Library of Canada, and National Library of Canada representative to the Committee of Principals

Ross Shimmon, Chief Executive, The Library Association, and The Library Association representative to the Committee of Principals

Margaret Stewart, Chief, Standards and Support, National Library of Canada, and Secretary to the Joint Steering Committee for Revision of AACR

Elaine Svenonius, Professor Emeritus, Graduate School of Education and Information Studies, University of California, Los Angeles

Joan Swanekamp, Chief Catalog Librarian and Head of Cataloging, Yale University

Winston Tabb, Associate Director for Collection Services, Library of Congress, and Library of Congress representative to the Committee of Principals

Chris Taylor, Manager, Information Access and Delivery Service, University of Queensland Library

Hugh Taylor, Head of Cataloguing, Cambridge University Library

Barbara B. Tillett, Chief, Cataloguing Policy and Support Office, Library of Congress, and Library of Congress representative to the Joint Steering Committee for Revision of AACR

Irina Tsvetkova, Deputy Director, The National Library of Russia

Verna Urbanski, Head, Copy Cataloguing Section, Thomas G. Carpenter Library, University of North Florida

Andrew Wells, Director, Technical Services, National Library of Australia

Terry Willan, Business Development Analyst, BLCMP Library Services Limited, U.K.

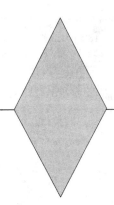

Topical Index

continued

Name Index

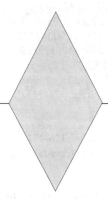